An
Early
Encounter
with
Tomorrow

An Early Encounter with Tomorrow

Europeans, Chicago's Loop, and the World's Columbian Exposition

Arnold Lewis

University of Illinois Press

Urbana and Chicago

Publication of this book was supported by grants
from the Graham Foundation for Advanced Studies
in the Fine Arts and from the Henry Luce III Fund
for Distinguished Scholarship administered by
The College of Wooster.

First paperback edition, 2001
© 1997 by the Board of Trustees of the
University of Illinois

∞ This book is printed on acid-free paper.

Library of Congress Cataloging-in-Publication Data

Lewis, Arnold.
An early encounter with tomorrow : Europeans,
Chicago's Loop, and the World's Columbian
Exposition / Arnold Lewis.
p. cm.
Includes bibliographical references and index.
ISBN 0-252-02305-6 (cloth : alk. paper)
ISBN 0-252-06965-x (pbk. : alk. paper)
1. Eclecticism in architecture—Illinois—Chicago.
2. Architecture and society—Illinois—Chicago—
History—19th century. 3. Chicago (Ill.)—Buildings,
structures, etc. I. Title.
NA735.C4L49   1997
720'.9773'11—dc20   96-25325
                                                CIP

1 2 3 4 5 C P 5 4 3 2 1

For

Martha

David

Paul

and

Beth

Contents

Illustrations

Preface

THIS BOOK is divided into two parts. The first focuses on the rise of Chicago's reputation internationally in the last four decades of the nineteenth century, specifically on the reactions of European visitors who thought Chicagoans had engaged the present more aggressively than did they by welcoming new ideas and procedures and by developing processes in which speed and efficiency were valued. In the judgment of foreign visitors, this mentality had produced marvelous and appalling consequences for the city's center. In the second part I have organized this criticism according to specific themes: foreign attention to American commercial architecture and the implications of tall office buildings for European architectural debates in the early 1890s, capitalism's effect on the rhythm of the Loop, the nature of the diametrically different though complimentary residential neighborhoods, and European assessments of the plan and architecture of the World's Columbian Exposition.

My interpretation of the collision between thoughtful Europeans and Chicago's startling Loop in the early 1890s rests primarily on published material. An immense number of books and newspaper and journal articles, the overwhelming majority from Great Britain, France, and Germany, verified the lively, close attention foreign observers paid to urban transformations in the United States in these years, particularly in Chicago. These reactions were written by professionals—educators, novelists, essayists, reporters, social scientists, architects, engineers, business people—as well as by lay observers fortunate to have the means and the desire to explore the United States at a time of dramatic economic, social, and technological change. Though I have drawn from the accounts and insights of both the trained and the untrained, I have tried to identify, when possible, the background of each commentator. In the biographical appendix that follows the main text in this volume, I have provided brief sketches about the primary observers and their activities.

In writing this book I have generalized about the respective national reactions of the British, French, and Germans, believing that individuals who share cultural experiences and traditions tend to share presuppositions, but I have also tried to name individuals who did not conform to a prevailing national perception. The British, French, and Germans wrote more and better commentary about Chicago in these years than did observers living elsewhere in Europe. Though these three nations dominated regional European thought, I have also included judgments of Chicago that appeared in Belgium, Switzerland, and Austria, countries where French and German opinion was often restated.

I marvel at those magical institutions called libraries, holding in awe those who through history have thought it important to allow strangers from distant cities or lands to walk in from the street and to ask to see titles collected and cared for by people they had never met. As I visited libraries in the United States and abroad, I was treated again and again with respect, as if I were actually doing a favor to the institution on which I now depended. My first thank you then goes to those nameless, but still remembered, faces behind reference desks who made access to long-sought volumes possible and who often wanted to know if what I had found was as valuable as I had hoped it would be. Among librarians in Europe, I am particularly grateful to those who assisted me at the Royal Institute of British Architects Library and the British Museum in London; at the Bibliothèque Nationale and the Bibliothèque Ste-Geneviève in Paris; at the Institut für Kunstgeschichte in Bonn; and, in Munich, at the Zentralinstitut für Kunstgeschichte, the Staatsbibliothek, the Deutsches Museum, and the Architektur Sammlung of the Technische Hochschule. The public libraries in American cities, specifically, in Cleveland, New York, and Boston, were important for their collections of books on the United States written by foreign travelers. I also depended heavily on university libraries in the United States: Columbia, Wisconsin, Cornell, UCLA, Ohio State, Pennsylvania, and Penn State. With its promise of one-stop shopping, the Library of Congress guaranteed an economical use of time for short-term visits. In Chicago I found gracious assistance and encouragement at the Chicago Historical Society, the Newberry Library, the Chicago Public Library, and the Burnham Library of the Art Institute of Chicago. The latter was the source of the photographs for figures 40, 66, and 67. Finally, I thank the librarians of the College of Wooster for their sustained contributions despite their intimate knowledge of my measured pace.

In my bibliography of books and articles published after 1914, I have acknowledged those twentieth-century authors who have shaped my understanding of cultural change in Western Europe and the United States in the late nineteenth century. This shaping was continuous, each new article or book incorporated as a result of a subtle, sometimes not so subtle, adjustment to previous understanding. A few authors, however, not only enriched my sense of context but also showed me how I might lift the account and interpretation of context to the level of readable argument. To these individuals, I am particularly grateful. Sigfried Giedion alerted me to European fascination with American simplicity and practicality. Andrew Lees demonstrated with verve the varieties and complexities of urban perception. Donald Olsen found words and deeds to present cities as artistic creations. Rainer Hanns Tolzmann enabled me to understand that the Loop represented a new congruency, a compound in which art lost its "high estate" yet remained essential. Stephen Kern's focus on the importance of shifting temporal and spatial thought in the late nineteenth century encouraged me to argue that new perceptions of time and space were basic to the Loop's shape and character. Finally, I owe much to Bessie Louise Pierce for reassuring me that Chicago had long been regarded as an international experiment station on the route to modernism.

In bringing this study to publication, I wrote two different books, the first shaped independently and the second radically transformed by the insights and recommendations of others. I thank early readers Wim de Wit and David Van Zanten, who know the history of Chicago so well, for their sound advice and insights. I am indebted to Richard Martin at the University of Illinois Press for finding several excellent, unnamed readers whose perceptive suggestions made the job of later changes easier and more enjoyable than I initially expected, and to my editor, Carol Bolton Betts, for her sound guidance and reassuring competence. I have also been pleased that a number of friends were willing to read what I had written about Chicago, among them Rudolph Janu, Robert Kliment, Naomi Miller, Mark Klemens, Heather Fitz Gibbon, Clara Patton, and Mary Beth Raycraft. Their comments and corrections have affected the final version.

Though the translations from the German and French are ultimately mine, I am grateful for the assistance I received from Jane Hancock, Judithe Jacob, Laura Bachhuber, David and Betty Wilkin, Miriam Stewart, Katie Maier, and Sara Patton. Dan Younger, Kearston Schmidt, and, especially, Rod Williams deserve much credit for their efforts to reproduce as clearly as possible images that appeared in nineteenth-century newspapers and journals. I counted heavily on Rudy Janu's photographic advice. I thank a number of friends and professional colleagues who in large and small ways were important at decisive moments along the way, among them Keith Morgan, Barbara Reed, Linda Phipps, Eric Rosenberg, David Stewart, Joan Weinstein, George Galster, Shelly Grunder, Craig Zabel, Susan Munschower, Duncan Berry, Joanna Hitchcock, Roger Conover, Leland Roth, Robert Bruegmann, and Joseph Siry.

My research has been supported over the years in numerous ways by the College of Wooster, particularly through its generous leave program. When specific funds were needed to complete or subsidize a project, my requests for additional funds were never denied. I have also been the fortunate recipient of two awards from Wooster's Henry Luce III Fund for Distinguished Scholarship, established by a grant from the Henry Luce Foundation. Without these awards, this book would not yet be completed. I am grateful to the Graham Foundation for Advanced Studies in the Fine Arts for its generous support of the publication of this volume.

Finally, I thank my family, Martha, David, Paul, and Beth. The depth of their loyalty and the value of their wise, often sobering criticism cannot be conveyed in a few words. I alone know how much their standards, intelligence, good judgment, perceptive insights, and constant encouragement permeate this book.

An
Early
Encounter
with
Tomorrow

Introduction

IN THE LAST HALF of the nineteenth century Chicago enjoyed the most advantageous location of all cities in the industrializing world. It prospered because the diversified riches (grain, agricultural commodities, livestock, coal, iron, timber) of the upper Mississippi basin required a regional receiving, processing, and distribution point. Located between the Great Lakes and a tributary of the Mississippi River ten miles to the west, it was a harbor from which boats departed for the Gulf of Mexico and from which ships had sailed to Great Britain since the late 1850s. The expansion of a rail network across the United States necessitated a major terminal at the southern tip of Lake Michigan because lines could not lay tracks to serve northern states and territories until they were west of this point. By 1870 the city, only forty years old, had become the world's busiest railroad junction.

Chicago was able to attract enough new citizens to meet the increasing demands of its resource-rich region. The rate of increase of its population in the nineteenth century was extraordinary, putting it in a separate category of urban development. In this period in which European cities emerged as political, social, commercial, and cultural centerpieces of regions and even nations, urban populations increased at unprecedented rates. Between 1850 and 1890 the population of London jumped from 2.3 million to 4.2 million people, Paris from 1.1 to 2.3 million, and Berlin from 387,200 to 1.5 million. These figures meant that London almost doubled (1.8 times), Paris more than doubled (2.3), and Berlin more than quadrupled (4.2) their populations. Significant population growth also characterized American cities in this forty-year period; New York's population rose 4.1 times, from 660,800 to 2.7 million. Despite these impressive statistics on both sides of the Atlantic, those of Chicago in the same period were incomparable. Its population increased 36.7 times, numbering approximately 1,100,000 people by 1890. Chicago's development from a frontier village numbering only "six or seven American families" in 1827 to the world's sixth-largest city in 1893 is proof that something unique happened there in these years. Paradoxically, the city was both product and preview. Giuseppe Giacosa, an Italian playwright and librettist, declared in 1893 that anyone who ignored Chicago did not understand the nineteenth century for that city had become its "ultimate expression."[1] On the other hand, as an urban phenomenon without a mitigating past, it was the one metropolis in the Western world that seemed to have more to do with the century to come than with its own.

Chicagoans were not responsible for the fortunate location of their city nor for the fact that its extraordinary growth coincided with westward expansion and the nation's economic boom after the Civil War. They could take credit, however, for the style in which they responded to the opportunities and responsibilities thrust upon them. In theory, they might have resisted evolving, mounting demands; in practice, they did not. They bragged that Chicago was capable of dispatching new or seemingly insurmountable challenges and even delighted in demonstrating how these could be answered quicker and more efficiently than was thought possible. Alert to function, cost, and the time required to complete a project, Chicagoans seemed to comprehend the meaning of the phrase "time is money." They were not unaware that their views and practices sometimes disregarded assumptions Europeans often took for granted—for example, that humans should control their destinies, that public civility was a given, and that art deserved a privileged position—but in the late nineteenth century there were essential material needs that required immediate attention. The speed and efficiency of processes became their primary concern; they would compensate for the demise or temporary suspension of niceties in the bright, slower years ahead.

To realize objectives quickly, Chicagoans engaged the present. In this respect they acted like Americans in other parts of the United States, though their means were sometimes more decisive and experimental. Engaging the present meant living in the here and now, not in the past. Without regrets they discarded outmoded attitudes and procedures in favor of those more effective in addressing shifting contemporary demands. Living in the present also meant forging ahead, even risking accident and death, before theories had been thoroughly tested. Chicago's present was so transitory that its citizens had little time to dote on their victories. In an age of "quick transformations," as the French economist Paul de Rousiers called the early 1890s,[2] it was wiser to assume impermanence than permanence. The nurturing of progress by the citizens of Chicago took precedence over their concerns for stability or preservation. Living in the present also meant developing faster and faster means to increase volume, making processes more efficient through simplified systems and lighter materials, through standardization and the subdivision of labor. These practices could be seen in the meat-processing systems at the Union Stock Yards and in balloon framing and skeleton construction in the building industry.

Chicago was a paradoxical American city, for it was both a representative and an exceptional example of urban development in the United States in the late nineteenth century. It was representative in the sense that similar commercial-industrial expansion could be observed in other midwestern cities. It was exceptional because its transformation was expressed so concisely in space and time. Spatially, the heart of Chicago, the Loop, was named in the 1880s when cable cars and horse cars looped around the business district before commencing their return runs to residential neighborhoods. In 1897 the Union Loop was opened, an integrated series of elevated tracks constructed along Wabash Avenue and

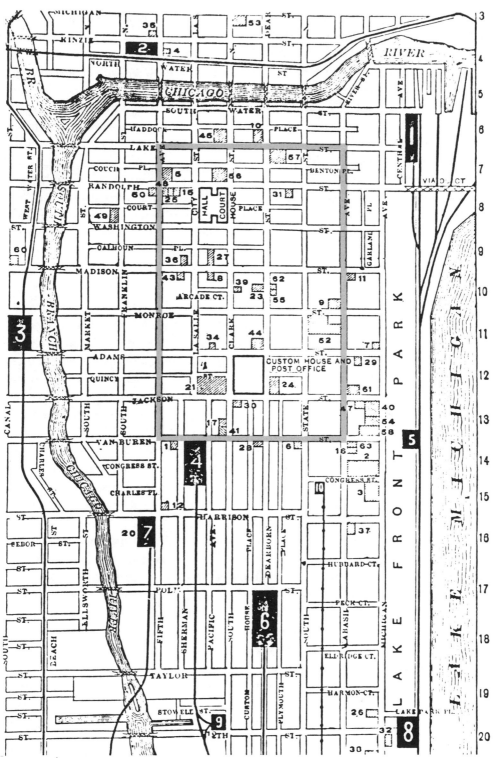

Figure 1. Map of central Chicago indicating location of hotels and depots (Rand McNally, *Views of Chicago*, 1898).

Lake, Wells (Fifth Avenue), and Van Buren Streets (fig. 1). Temporally, the distinctive form of this kilometer-square zone seemed to Europeans and to Americans living in eastern cities to have been formed in a relatively brief period of time during the late nineteenth century. To Americans living in Boston, New York, or Philadelphia, the Loop, with its tall buildings, aggressive traffic, and huge crowds, was not unexpected. Their city centers also were undergoing similar kinds of physical and cultural change. To observers from Britain, France, and Germany, however, accustomed to a more authoritative past and a present less impermanent, speed-oriented, and all-consuming, the eager engagement of Chicagoans with the moment seemed qualitatively different.

None of the surprising elements of the integrated Loop was more valuable to inquisitive Europeans than its new multistoried office buildings. Products of the city's commercial-industrial intensity, these "temples of labor" offered irrefutable proof of forces transforming modern life. They also contained the control rooms from which the city's economic development was planned, as well as the work stations of thousands who made Chicago's street crowds so memorable. With their astounding heights, extensive facades, and the dark canyons they produced at street level, these early skyscrapers transformed the appearance and mood of American business districts. However, for British, French, and German critics in the early 1890s the ultimate value of the multistory commercial building, which became the international symbol of city, was its role in clarifying the "purposefulness" of the Loop. Of all the lessons the materialistic schoolroom of Chicago offered to attentive Europeans, the decision of its leaders to devote the center of their city to the pursuit of profits, and their efficiency in integrating all essential elements in the Loop to realize this objective, were the most profound. In this revelation, the functioning office building was central.

Europeans brought to the city a perspective dissimilar to that of Americans living along the East Coast. Their reactions differed because their presuppositions shaped by their experiences were different. In his elegant study of London, Paris, and Vienna, *The City as a Work of Art*, Donald Olsen explained, "The actual resident, his perceptions dulled by familiarity, will have less to tell us than the foreign critic or visiting tourist. The latter will be on the alert for whatever makes the foreign city different from his own, the distinctive tone that gives it its special character, and he can make comparisons that would not occur to the person for whom the city is the background for daily life."[3] Walking into the Loop around 1890 was for hundreds of British, French, and German visitors an early encounter with tomorrow, an encounter analogous to entering a time warp. The Loop, an evolving consequence of accelerating pressures and innovative means to cope with them, was inhospitable to many of their preconceptions. At first, it made no more sense to foreign observers than their own first expressions of shock made to Chicagoans, who, having lived with the daily changes of their city, considered its continuous transformations normal and necessary. Regardless of their inclinations toward change or the status quo, regardless of the extent to which they proclaimed Chicago a modern schoolroom or an urban failure, their encounters, particularly their initial ones, were seldom painless. The Loop had brought the future to the present, but it was not the kind of future European observers had mused about.

In his thoughtful essay entitled "Contemporary Art and the Plight of its Public," Leo Steinberg reminded us that the confrontation with the new often leaves us with a "sense of loss, of sudden exile, of something willfully denied—sometimes a feeling that one's accumulated culture or experience is hopelessly devalued, leaving one exposed to spiritual destitution." We are not always ready, he argued, to sacrifice those assumptions and practices that others in the name of progress have discarded.[4] For foreign visitors, endorsing Chicago, the shock city of the day, was tantamount to forsaking the values they cherished. On the other hand, repudiating Chicago left them vulnerable to charges of being reactionaries. Europeans struggled with this dilemma; Americans did not.

The Loop was also sobering for foreign visitors because it was an advanced manifestation of social and economic changes they were facing in their own cities. The future was always coming to the present in bits and pieces, usually in forms so veiled or unorthodox one wondered how they could possibly alter the familiar patterns of life. But in the center of Chicago a piece of tomorrow in the form of a functioning, interdependent business system had materialized, enabling curious observers to study a demonstration of an urban future instead of having to imagine one.

Chicago's central district stimulated some Europeans and troubled others. It implied that city centers of the coming twentieth century, at least in the United States, would be business zones of unprecedented integration and efficiency, where the need for quicker speeds would radically alter horizontal and vertical movement and systematize office procedures, and where new inventions could make work more pleasant. Yet the Loop's real vision of the future was also disquieting for it implied the demise or transformation of elements central to European understandings of a modern city. Chicago had discounted history, ignored traditions, demoted and reconstituted art, endorsed a district unsympathetic to privilege and short on civility, a zone where one moved smartly at one's own risk because cable car drivers had schedules to meet and workers who laid franchise conduits were too booked to fill their excavations properly. Furthermore, Chicago's progress had produced dark skies, muddy and littered streets, soot that penetrated windows, and a river on which birds could walk on thick water.

The lively and abundant body of European criticism could not have been written in these years by Americans. Responding to Chicago from different experiences and expectations, American critics did not think of their contact with the Loop as an encounter between a reassuring past and a disquieting future, but Europeans did. For a brief period in the early 1890s, the Loop fascinated foreign observers, its daily reality often outdistancing their speculations about tomorrow. Chicagoans had yielded without organized objection to the transforming forces of the late nineteenth century, producing a central zone characterized by a form and style dissimilar to the business districts of London, Paris, or Berlin where new pressures had been partially deflected by stronger social, economic, and artistic resistance.

Notes

1. Quoted in Bessie Louise Pierce, *As Others See Chicago: Impressions of Visitors, 1673–1933* (Chicago: University of Chicago Press, 1933), 276. The remark was taken from Giuseppe Giacosa, "Chicago and Her Italian Colony," *Nuova Antologia 128* (March 1893): 16–28, translated by L. B. Davis.

2. Paul de Rousiers, *American Life,* trans. A. J. Herbertson (Paris: Firmin-Didot, 1892), 436.

3. Donald Olsen, *The City as a Work of Art* (New Haven: Yale University Press, 1986), 6.

4. Leo Steinberg, "Contemporary Art and the Plight of Its Public," *Harper's,* March 1962, 31–39.

Part One

Chicago:
Laboratory
of
the
Future

Prophetic

1

Encounters

with

Modernity

Heroic Growth and Optimism

AMONG THE amazing metropolises of the nineteenth century, Chicago was the only one in the Western world in the 1890s that did not exist at the century's beginning. When Fort Dearborn was built at the mouth of the Chicago River in 1803 to establish a military presence on land formerly controlled by native Americans, London had a population of nearly 1,000,000, Paris had 550,000 citizens, and Berlin had 175,000. By 1830 the fledgling trading community of Chicago numbered about fifty settlers. By 1893 Chicago had become an internationally known metropolis with a population of more than a million, its area (182.9 square miles) larger than any other city in the world. This extraordinary growth in population and area in less than seven decades was a principal cause of European fascination with Chicago in the late nineteenth century. Its quantitative development raised questions challenging traditional assumptions of many foreign observers about history's role in influencing the pace and direction of the present, the importance one should grant the present, the vulnerability of permanence, the rate by which change occurred, and the power of forces transforming contemporary urban life.

European visitors to the United States, primarily British, began to include Chicago in their travel accounts in the middle of the century. They tended to depict the town as a raw but lively place attempting to meet the demands of new settlers in the upper Midwest. Early commentaries were usually anecdotal, often condescending, commending Chicago's vigor but noting its social instability and lack of cultural opportunities. Tourists sometimes mentioned its potential importance though few prior to 1865 cited hard evidence to support their predictions. In accounts of the last half of the 1860s, however, the image of Chicago as a boisterous frontier town was being replaced by that of a major regional center. "Chicago has grown to be the largest market in the world for corn, timber, and pork; the three great exports of the United States," reported Sir Morton Peto, a member of the British Parliament from Bristol and author of a study of American population, agriculture, and economics.[1] His use of numerical proof was early evidence of the tendency of many of Chicago's foreign critics to reinforce their surprise at the city's visual impact with facts and figures. The evolving image of Chicago in the last half of the century was shaped increasingly by a slow shift from visitors' personal experience to statistical evidence and from reports of generalists to those written by specialists and professionals.

Among the characteristics of life in Chicago most fascinating to European visitors in the years around 1870, two attracted considerable attention: the quickness with which projects were completed there and the apparent readiness of its citizens to take on seemingly impossible tasks without fear of failure or regret. The label "lightning city," which referred to its unprecedented rate of growth and to the speed and efficiency of its procedures, became perhaps its most popular international tag in these decades, suggesting visitors' familiarity with the value Chicagoans placed on the use of time. They observed that saving time in Chicago was important, and that it was done in various ways: through simplifications, shortcuts, standardization, dependence on the machine, or refinements in systems of production.[2] The city's perceived concern about time was not considered unique; for decades Europeans had observed like attitudes in other parts of the United States. However, some visitors thought Chicago's attempts appeared to produce more concentrated, dramatic, and memorable results. In this, and many other respects, foreign observers did not consider Chicago distinctive because its priorities and attitudes differed basically from those observed in other American cities, but because it seemed to crystallize and clarify priorities and attitudes visitors had noted elsewhere. Between 1870 and the early 1890s no American city was cited more frequently by Europeans as the most remarkable yet representative city of the United States.

Referring to Chicago as "something of a wonder," *Chamber's Journal* in 1861 may have been the first foreign journal to cite another noteworthy tendency of its citizens—not to ponder an action one day and carry it out the next, but to go ahead and do it.[3] In the years around 1870 visitors found the best proof of their generalizations about the absence of procrastination in the massive effort to raise the central district to insure better drainage[4] and in the attempt to improve the quality of drinking water by reversing the direction of flow of the Chicago River. Beginning in 1856 downtown roadways and sidewalks were elevated four to ten feet and existing buildings either jacked up and reset on higher ground or moved to other locations. Some Europeans first knew Chicago as the city that lifted itself out of its mud. Always discussed in positive terms abroad, this feat symbolized breadth of conception, decisiveness, and the propensity to look beyond customary or prudent limits. Intrigued with this operation, visitors often embellished it, recalling large buildings rising on jacks[5] while business continued inside, and houses, sometimes three chained together, being pulled to suburban lots with their chimneys smoking. Chicago's capacity for domesticating the absurd appealed to foreign tourists eager to collect tales underscoring the exotic nature of their travels in the New World.

Yet there were sacrifices many visitors, understandably, were not as willing as Chicagoans to endure. They were often less sympathetic to the consequences of progress once they had experienced them personally. Expecting cities to be orderly, settled, and attractive, they complained throughout the late nineteenth century about the disordered and unfinished state of central Chicago. If culture flowed from settlement, Chicago's perpetual change could be counterproductive. Visitors were not always as tolerant as natives about temporary sidewalks at different levels, inconvenient piles of building materials, and the danger not only to pedestrians but also to patrons assured by profit-motivated hotel managers that their ascending bodies in no way were endangered. Getting on with it heroically was one thing; living with the disruption caused by the compulsion to be contemporary was another. Chicago's engagement with the present might be admirable, but there were costs in human terms some Europeans were unwilling to pay.

The attempt to reverse the direction of the Chicago River was praised abroad without reservation and was considered more remarkable than raising the level of downtown streets. The feat was achieved by dredging more deeply the existing Illinois-Michigan Canal, enabling the waters of Lake Michigan to flow southwestward through the city and eventually into the Mississippi River system and the Gulf of Mexico. Europeans mused that Chicagoans had made their river "run uphill." The scheme worked effectively for only a brief time after completion in 1871 because additional drainage in the southwestern part of the city silted the new cut and slowed the water's flow. Nonetheless, the achievement was well publicized at home and abroad. This celebrated, but flawed, operation became primary evidence around 1870 for those visitors who believed that anything was possible in Chicago.

The period following the devastating fire of 8–10 October 1871, which began on Chicago's southwest side, consumed the business district, and then continued northward to Lincoln Park, was probably the first and the last time in the nineteenth century that British, French, and German observers expressed an emotional attachment to the city. In less sentimental moments before and after, Chicago was usually viewed abroad as disconcerting, amazing, or instructive, but rarely as inspirational. Europeans, however, were moved by the pluck, determination, and optimism of the citizens of a city destroyed by fire. Stirred by tales of postfire regeneration—for example, the quick relocation of the central post office to insure mail delivery by the next day[6]—individuals and groups abroad responded with empathy and donations.[7] The city's cockiness, boorishness, incessant "dollar spinning," and other perceived negative traits were momentarily forgotten as Europeans praised the spontaneous effort of Chicagoans to lift their city out of its ashes, as earlier they had lifted it out of its mud. In the early 1870s Chicago became the Western world's heroic phoenix, an international symbol of hope and revitalization. Travelers who visited the city in the wake of the fire were exhilarated by its communal spirit and inspired by its lesson of confident renewal, some admitting its example had prompted fresh personal resolutions.[8]

Visitors were often intrigued by the community's optimism after the fire, in part because it seemed irresponsible, almost irreverent, given the high death toll, the numbers made homeless, and the extent of the destruction. Had such a catastrophe occurred in Britain, France, or Germany, the weight of cultural loss might not have permitted such a buoyant rebound. By contrast, Chicagoans seemed surprisingly unsentimental about their disaster. In fact, the *Chicago Tribune* on 30 March 1873 emphasized the advantages of eliminating old mistakes, contending that "Chicago was set forward ten years by the fire." As individuals whose ties with history were much longer and firmer, many Europeans found these positive reactions to the calamity curious. On the one hand, they granted, Chicagoans were wise not to cry over spilt milk; on the other, they seemed too casual about the loss of cultural and physical reminders of yesterday. However, it was not until about 1890 that foreign critics in numbers searched deeper for the implications of Chicago's light attachment to its past.

Foreign observers also noted that Chicagoans took strange pride in the fire, treating it not as an event of horror but as a civic trial through which they had successfully passed. In all his conversations in the city, Friedrich Bodenstedt, a German poet, editor, and fiction and travel writer, claimed he had never heard anyone who had experienced the fire complain about it. To the contrary, "they retold the story as if they were triumphant warriors in a victorious battle."[9] Foreign travelers, even before the fire, had noted a difference between their own responses to adversity and those of the people they met in Chicago. David Macrae, a Scottish minister and author who visited the United States not long after the Civil War, recalled one incident:

> Sitting in a friend's office in Chicago, a young man called in quest of a situation. My friend had no place to give him, but he said, after a moment's reflection, "I don't think there is any one in the field yet who sells boots and shoes for commission. You might try that." "But I don't know anything about that business." "Well, learn. You know the difference between shoes and boots. Start with that. If you are worth anything you will soon pick up the rest." The youth went off at once to see about it; and is probably by this time a newspaper editor or a captain of one of the lake steamers.[10]

In Britain, Macrae reflected, each individual was supposed to be suited for a particular profession or job, but not in Chicago where life was more fluid and opportunities, or at least optimism about opportunities, abounded. Europeans who commented on the rebuilding of the city often mentioned the ability of its citizens to overcome setbacks, to adapt to unexpected circumstances, to convince themselves of better days ahead. They took defeats lightly because they believed the present was an inevitable improvement on the past and, likewise, the future an inevitable improvement on the present. Experience had not prepared most visitors for the mentality that prevailed in Chicago in the 1870s, a mentality they had encountered in other parts of the country. By contrast, they tended to have greater respect for the wisdom of the past, were more hesitant about spontaneous engagement with the present, and believed personal futures were more determined by tradition and rank and less by the unexpected opportunities of a transient scene.

Simple postfire sympathy declined during the last half of the 1870s to be replaced with uneasy admiration. Observers tended to interpret Chicago as an increasingly important city primarily because they began to sense the implications of its accelerating population, its keystone role in the development of the Middle West, its mounting volume of industry and trade. This realization changed the relationship between critic and city. Though the shift was subtle and by no means uniform, foreign observers became more inquisitive, reflected longer about the meaning of the city, and voiced comparative judgments, calling it, for example, the "chief artificial wonder of the New World," the "most remarkable city of the Union," the "most wonderful place" seen on the trip. Though Europeans usually judged Chicago in relation to American cities, a few widened the pool to include the metropolises of the Old World. For them Chicago became "one of the finest commercial cities in the world," the "most wonderful city of modern times," the "most remarkable manifestation of modern civilization extant."[11] Those who took Chicago more seriously sometimes revealed an uneasiness not as evident earlier when travelers had generalized from firmer and loftier heights. However, the disconcerting aspects of Chicago—its materialism, crassness, hectic pace, transience, its casual regard for tradition and elites—still seemed far removed and inapplicable to European urban developments at the end of the decade.

The criticism about Chicago published abroad before 1880 was not very sophisticated. It was written mainly by generalists—educated, wealthy travelers, who, for the most part, were curious about America after the Civil War or who wanted to see interior areas of the country before further settlement. Their stays were often short despite their common conclusion that Chicago was one of the highlights of an American tour. They did what tourists on limited schedules in the twentieth century do; they used their eyes, noting observable evidence for which their experiences at home had not prepared them. They described what they saw and reached quick conclusions about the possible meanings of what they had seen. They were better at describing than analyzing, and they were more fascinated with results than causes, though these tendencies did not mean their accounts were dull or uninformative.[12] British travelers significantly outnumbered the German and the French. Though they represented the advantaged in all three countries and could have reacted more conservatively to American democracy, they were also adventurers, individuals with the gumption and curiosity to make the long journey.

Laboratory of the Future

In 1882 Friedrich Bodenstedt sensed Chicago's compatibility with its age even before the age had been clearly identified. He argued that detailed descriptions of any given moment of Chicago's contemporary condition were not worth the effort because the city changed so quickly. Facts and figures implied measurement, but the city's flux defied measurement. This was true of the United States in general, he wrote, but especially so of Chicago.[13] He was the first, though not the last, European to mention the problem of trying to write with authority about a city whose norm seemed to be accelerating transformation. Foreign criticism assumed that a perceptive observer ought to be able to study a subject and produce a report that would be valid for a period of time. Bodenstedt rejected this assumption. Even if such a report about Chicago were accurate when completed, he reasoned, it would be invalidated quickly, raising questions about its initial purpose and extended value. By calling attention to the rapidity of change and the normality of perpetual transformation in Chicago, Bodenstedt identified the central theme of the city's modernity. Chicago was not the first remarkable city of this urbanizing century, but it was the only one that seemed to have more to do with the century to come than with the one in which it existed. Among these wonder cities—Manchester, London, Paris, Vienna, Berlin—Chicago was the first of the age of electricity, an age in which change came with unprecedented speed.

The European opinion that Chicago was an up-to-date city was not new in the early 1880s. However, in these years, and continuing with increasing frequency into the first half of the 1890s, scores of British, French, and German observers considered it the Western world's urban laboratory of commercial and technological experimentation. These claims were not confirmed yet in the textbooks of the day, but they appeared in travel accounts, articles—particularly those published in technical and architectural journals—and often in lectures given by returning visitors. Furthermore, most of those who reached this conclusion about Chicago also argued that if one wished to observe the purest and most contemporary demonstrations of the fruits of American democracy, capitalism, and science, Chicago, more than Boston, New York, Philadelphia, or, St. Louis, was the city to visit. By comparison, Europeans thought Boston was too English to be a real Yankee metropolis, Philadelphia too old fashioned, and St. Louis, though centrally located, not yet influential enough to serve as a model. Only New York rivaled Chicago as the prototypical American city of the modern day. It owned a stronger and longer cultural heritage, had a much bigger population, and processed a greater volume of trade. And, in the judgments of some, it could challenge Chicago at the level of its most exasperating qualities. One visitor exclaimed, "Ah: The first sensation of New York, how intense, bizarre and bewildering!—Everything boasts of excess and American bad taste."[14] Yet those who contended Chicago around 1890 was the most American of cities discovered there a focus, an intensity, a purposefulness they had not sensed to the same degree in New York. "In New York business is the big word, in Chicago, it is the God, the first and last reason of every action and thought," wrote a French traveler, Georges Sauvin.[15] These visitors also sensed Chicago's ability to absorb the farfetched, or as the Berlin author and editor Paul Lindau put it, to regard as normal that which would have been considered exceptional elsewhere.[16]

According to foreign critics of the late 1880s and early 1890s, the ability of Chicagoans to focus on the heart of the contemporary matter could be seen in the effective way they utilized their abundant advantages inherited from nature. Blessed by a lake and river that connected their city with both the Atlantic and the Gulf of Mexico, by a system of inland seas that made inevitable the appearance of a major railroad exchange at its southwestern corner, and by rich timber, mineral, and agricultural resources within quick shipping distances, Chicago, in the view of one foreign journal, occupied the most propitious site in all the world for a developing city in the last half of the nineteenth century. Numerous visitors observed that Chicagoans had exploited these natural advantages brilliantly. Their purposefulness was also aided by their youthfulness. James Bryce, a respected British authority on American institutions, claimed that Chicago still reflected frontier habits—instinctive reactions conditioned by necessity—that were no longer as influential among coastal populations.[17] Furthermore, without a past, Chicago was more driven by the contemporary pulse. Europeans also thought they could observe in the city a purer state of present-day urban, industrial-commercial development than they could in New York with its longer history, closer ties to Europe, and rising aristocracy of wealth. Citing artistic evidence, Jacques Hermant, a Parisian architect who visited America in 1893, argued that at that time New York was concerned about good taste but Chicago was still building itself day by day. He believed that Chicago would eventually succumb to the temptation to be refined, but that at that moment it remained an unadulterated commercial city.[18] Finally, Chicago's central district, the Loop, became for Europeans the ultimate revelation of the city's unique ability to focus its priorities and to process them efficiently. Chicago's business center was concentrated, its desirable addresses packed into an area about the size of a square kilometer; New York's extended over three miles. Foreign visitors sensed a different urban atmosphere the moment they walked into this space. Its concentration intensified the impact of its buildings, traffic, and crowds, verifying and clarifying the transforming forces of modern life many of them had been slow to acknowledge. The Loop of the early 1890s has provided historians with a unique opportunity to examine the provocative but also disquieting encounter between Old World presuppositions and New World realities.

How well did Western Europeans know Chicago in the early 1890s? This question is difficult to answer. No reliable measurement exists. Some observers regarded the city as a barometer of change. On the other hand, there were many educated people in France and the German-speaking countries before 1890 who paid little attention to the Windy City. Until that time the British were more likely to direct attention to Chicago by calling it "the city of the age," "the concentrated essence of Americanism," or the municipality in the forefront of "absolute newness." Similar expansive statements, particularly in technical and architectural journals, increased on the Continent after 1890.[19] However, some observers, who claimed Chicago would have to be seen to be believed,[20] experienced the truth of this insight when they encountered skeptical audiences at home.

There were other signs around 1890 that Chicago's international reputation was rising. More social scientists abroad cited statistics about its growth and volume of trade.[21] The tone of foreign commentary about the city was also changing, sometimes revealing longstanding expectation. "CHICAGO. That is a well-known name, and here is the well-known city that owns it," was the opening sentence of J. J. Aubertin's chapter on the city in *A Fight with Distances* (1888).[22] Satire, another indicator of recognition, also increased and was expressed with greater familiarity. "Here is a bit of Yankee newspaper criticism: We see that a bizarre building in Chicago is to be decorated with 'life-size griffins in terra-cotta.' That is like Chicago. In no other city in the world would an architect profess to know what is 'life size' for 'an imaginary creature which never lived at all.' We like that— 'an imaginary creature which never lived at all.' It's almost as clever as the 'life-size' griffin."[23] Although its weight is impossible to measure, the diverse evidence of European fascination with Chicago in the late 1880s and early 1890s increased steadily, especially on the Continent, until 1894, when it began to decline.

In 1892 the French economist Paul de Rousiers, one of the more perceptive Europeans to comment extensively on Chicago, remarked that "America has ceased to be an object of curiosity in becoming an object of dread."[24] For Europeans the United States had been the most closely watched economic, political, and social experiment of the nineteenth century. An offshoot of Europe, its ancestral seeds had been cultivated in relative isolation in an atmosphere sympathetic to industry, technology, and democratic institutions. Paul Bourget, the respected French novelist whose eloquent comments on Chicago and the exposition have been quoted by American historians more frequently than those of any other foreign writer, acknowledged Europe's curiosity about the impact of new ideologies and methodologies on the American people. We know the history and nobility of the world we understand, he wrote, but know little about the new forms being created over there and their implications for the future. Would democracy honor art and thought above the utilitarian level? Would science destroy mystery and poetry? Concern about answers to these questions, plus the fact that the Americans did not seem to worry much about them, were reasons, he claimed, "this country is so intensely interesting to us."[25] Earlier in the century, when the United States seemed more remote and its developments inapplicable to European patterns, commentators paid less attention to questions such as Bourget's, but by 1890 the United States was more competitive and seemed geographically closer. Shifts in the relative percentages of world industrial output among Britain, Germany, and the United States between 1870 and the period 1896–1900 confirm this competition: 32 percent to 20 percent for Britain, 13 percent to 17 percent for Germany, and 23 percent to 30 percent for the United States,[26] whose industries were infiltrating European markets with attractive products that were cheap, light, and effective. In the late 1880s French soldiers carried in their knapsacks tinned meat packed in Chicago.

Rousiers was thinking beyond economic competition with the United States when he claimed in 1892 that "Europe begins to feel uneasy, and the Old World nations are asking if, after all, they must seek for new models among these barbarians."[27] The majority of the foreign critics who wrote about Chicago in these years probably would have considered his doleful prediction a bit premature. In the early 1890s they believed themselves freer than he implied to treat Chicago's modern ways as distant lessons that could be modified or rejected rather than as inevitable future models for Western Europe. On the other hand, they would have understood what he meant by barbarians though they seldom referred to Chicagoans as such in print.

When visitors passed judgment on the city's cultural life, their assessments were surprisingly similar. They considered its citizens geniuses of production but adolescents in the realms of art and ideas. Impressive victories in the material world could not mask Chicagoans' primary flaw. They were *gemein*—in Goethe's phrase, "was uns alle bändigt, das Gemeine" (that which holds us all in bondage, the common/ignoble). As guests usually treated with kindness and generosity by citizens, visitors were reluctant to be critical, but privately most of them considered the city an intellectual and artistic hell. A few, such as A. G. Stephens, Rudyard Kipling, and Oscar Wilde, were blunt. "Life without industry is barren, and industry without art is barbarian," Wilde instructed his Chicago audience in February 1882.[28] In one shouting match, Stephens told a local booster that there were higher things in life than being "a hustling horde of pig-killers."[29] Startled by "the masses" in the Loop, visitors occasionally depicted Chicagoans as people with limited imaginations or desire to learn. Friedrich Dernburg, who published his reports on the Columbian Exposition in the *Berliner Tageblatt,* regretted the event had not been held in Berlin where people really could have appreciated it.[30] British travelers were more likely than those from the Continent to make an issue of culture; writers from technical fields seldom did.

Those who wrote exasperated responses to Chicago's cultural scene did so for a number of reasons. They wanted to be helpful, to warn its citizens to desist from parochial bragging about quantitative achievements and technological wonders that only embarrassed the refined. They made the effort to set Chicagoans straight because they assumed their definition of culture was valid for other societies, even new ones in new regions of development. The authoritative air of some writers' rebukes suggest absolute faith in their positions. Yet a few protested too much, revealing not just impatience but uneasiness. Perhaps more was at stake than just their dislike of grime, greed, and pedestrian thinking. Rudyard Kipling's passages on Chicago in *American Notes* (1891) have been cited often as an indictment of the city, yet his attack could also be interpreted as a passionate defense of a way of life that was eroding.[31] He defended class and privilege against the masses, referring to the local citizens as "savages." His poem, "I know thy cunning and thy greed, Thy hard high lust and willful deed, And all thy glory loves to tell of specious gifts material," was a deposition in favor of high-mindedness. His concern for the preservation of manners and propriety was revealed in his comments on the Palmer House—a huge marbled hall "crammed with people talking about money and spitting about everywhere. Other barbarians charged in and out of this inferno with letters and telegrams in their hands, and yet others shouted at each other." Fundamental to his anger was the fact that artistic and behavioral conventions, still protected by and for the upper classes in Britain, lost their subsidy in Chicago, and particularly in the Loop, where all significant components (social, artistic, economic, technological) were integrated in a new kind of compound.

The Loop also represented a critique of the notion, manifested more clearly on the Continent, particularly in the capital cities of Paris, Vienna, and Berlin, that central-core districts belonged to the upper classes. Compared to the most celebrated example of the day, the boulevards of Paris, the Loop harbored more diversified weekday populations: laborers, managers, secretaries, clerks, shoppers. Some were native born, some were immigrants, some were refined, and some were coarse. Several visitors thought the crowds on Chicago's downtown streets, consequences of the concentration of the highest buildings in the world, were the largest they had seen in any American city.

European curiosity about the conduct of the Loop's throngs reflected the growing apprehension in Western Europe about the masses, a concern soon to be articulated in Gustave Le Bon's famous study *The Crowd,* published in France in 1895. Le Bon claimed the present day was a crucial period for Western civilization because the masses were destroying traditional religious, political, and social systems. The revolution in science and industry had created new conditions, opening the door to changes in communal values and practices. Uncertain of the outcome of this developing threat, he expressed the anxiety of the privileged in Europe in the mid-1890s.

> To-day the claims of the masses are becoming more and more sharply defined, and amount to nothing less than a determination to utterly destroy society as it now exists, with a view to making it hark back to that primitive communism which was the normal condition of all human groups before the dawn of civilization. Limitations of the hours of labour, the nationalization of mines, railways, factories, and the soil, the equal distribution of all products, the elimination of all the upper classes for the benefit of the popular classes, etc., such are these claims.[32]

Visitors were discomforted by Chicago's crowds. Though people in the Loop were not necessarily rude, they had little time or inclination for polite exchange.

Despite the Haymarket Riot of May 1886 and Chicago's publicized reputation as the capital of anarchism in the United States, foreign visitors in the early 1890s concluded there was a fundamental difference between the thousands of Americans in the Loop and "the masses" of Europe. Critics were relieved to discover these quick-moving throngs were not politically destabilizing. Individuals among them seemed disinclined to dismantle the democratic, free enterprise system because they were too busy using it to improve personal conditions. This was confirmed by their public behavior, a behavior superbly adapted to the purposeful setting of central Chicago. In fact, the sense of alienation to which some Europeans referred stemmed, in part, from their inability to mesh as instinctively with this environment as did local citizens.

According to Georges Sauvin, who wrote one of the most thoughtful commentaries on the Loop, its sidewalk populations were not classless, despite being composed of individuals who came from backgrounds without name or tradition, unlike systems in Europe, more entrenched in France and Germany than in Britain, in which origins were different, names counted, and tradition affected rank. Class structure was unavoidable, he concluded; the richest, at the top, were the most respected. Though the banker did not mix with the tram conductor nor the industrialist with the porter, Chicagoans separated themselves into different groups influenced by work rather than ancestry. Before his arrival, he feared that the rise of ordinary people in a democratic, egalitarian society would come at the expense of the "superior classes." "Chicago proves, on the contrary, that the general level will rise without restricting those with natural talents; all these people want to know how to read and make money except the great writers, the true scholars, the artists and the thinkers."[33] In short, the British, French, and Germans who studied people in the Loop were put off by their absorption with business—an uncivil way to treat strangers in their midst—but were reassured by their pursuit of work as their primary means of self-improvement.

Despite their fascination with Chicago and their conviction that its experiments and systems were internationally significant, Europeans did not find the Loop a lovable place. It was impersonal not humane, ugly not beautiful, unkempt not orderly, crass rather than noble, intimidating instead of being reassuring. Visitors missed spatial variation, mixed use, oases for rest and quiet, a slower pace, an atmosphere of civility, buildings sensitive to human scale confirming the importance of art, monuments verifying an estimable past, ornament that delighted even if it obscured. Chicago's progressive ways, which attracted visitors in the first place, were also disquieting, forcing them to question assumptions that seemed reasonable and benevolent at home. Though they arrived with confidence in their ability to determine what was reasonable, a capacity developed consciously and unconsciously from experiences in Britain and on the Continent, the Loop confounded many of them. To dismiss its reality was, of course, foolish, but how could earnest observers take it seriously when it disregarded so many norms on which their presuppositions rested? Their inability to incorporate the Loop in their understanding of the present, even in their visions of the future, forced some to take extreme positions. Unable to account reasonably for this zone, a few demonized it.[34] The French editor and author Octave Uzanne called Chicago "that Gordian city, so excessive, so satanic."[35] William Archer, a London drama critic, likened it to the "fuliginous city of Dis, piled up by superhuman and apparently sinister powers."[36] For these critics common sense in Chicago had lost out to senselessness, and senselessness was out of control. The point of these quotations is not to argue that the Loop was shaped by fiendish forces,[37] but to demonstrate that some foreign observers, their imaginations and systems of belief unable to cope with its reality, found justification in the uncanny. The remarks also reveal the power of the center of the city to challenge the belief that the difference between reasonableness and the unreasonableness was obvious "to every right-thinking man."

In the early 1890s significant numbers of lay travelers, intellectuals, and professionals in Western Europe acknowledged Chicago as a new kind of city expressive of a contemporary turn in Western culture, a city of the present, not the past, a city of constant transformation, where the latest technological innovations were welcomed to facilitate the course of laissez-faire capitalism. These Europeans were both intrigued and appalled by its actions and results. While Chicago offered a peculiar window on the future, it also closed many doors to the past. Foreign critics struggled to comprehend its meaning, sometimes grateful for its ability to frame contemporary trends and sometimes annoyed by its disregard of assumptions and practices legitimized by the past. The city was significant as a contemporary indicator because its leaders had rejected the hope that culture in the late nineteenth century could be protected from erosion by positivistic forces, assuming instead an inevitable integration of economic, social, technological, and artistic factors. Unlike Kipling's Britain in which an established core attempted to preserve the primacy of art and etiquette outside of, or even above, the dynamic spheres of science and aggressive capitalism, the Loop demonstrated a novel congruency of public behavior, architecture, profits, and contemporary techniques. In the Loop, art and good manners did not function as veneers, hiding or denying the transforming powers of change, but as integral, though altered, elements of a comprehensive unit.

In the twentieth century we have recognized the contribution of the Loop's commercial architecture to modernism but have underestimated or forgotten that Chicago in these years was the Western world's most advanced metropolitan laboratory. We have often celebrated the Loop's remarkable buildings, sometimes in aesthetic isolation, without realizing what foreign critics discovered, that this architecture was a byproduct of new attitudes, demands, and means. Contemporary Europeans regarded the architects of the early skyscrapers as anonymous realists who dealt with changing conditions. We have focused on personalities, celebrating individual roles while slighting the importance of the social and economic context in which they worked. It was Chicago's sudden power and purposeful integration that made it such a focal point in these years. Twentieth-century historians have underestimated its importance in late nineteenth-century discussions about the course of Western culture. Its weight and value as a barometer of transition at the beginning of the modern period were substantially greater than that of any novel, the entire oeuvre of an avant-garde artist, or any successful scientific or technical experiment of the day. It was not an event of a summer like a great international exhibition, but an evolving organism of a million people. It grew from necessity, not pretext, and its legendary existence was not fiction but fact. Unobligated to the past, it was free to concentrate on the ideas and methodologies of the present. Realizing that the useful duration of each new approach and form was limited, Chicagoans showed profound understanding of nineteenth-century transience by holding lightly to every feat about which they bragged profusely. Chicago, particularly its instructive Loop, offered Europeans a crystallization, unstaged and fluid, of new and prophetic urban acts and consequences.

Notes

1. Morton S. Peto, *The Resources and Prospects of America* (London and New York: Alexander Strahan, 1866), 93.

2. For example, Macrae, who toured the United States in 1867–68, realized the importance of time when he studied the transfer of grain from a ship in the Chicago River to one of the many elevators along its north and south branches. To unload the ship a device similar to British river-dredging equipment was lowered into its hold. Buckets, "small and touched with Chicago lightning," dug at the grain repeatedly, carrying it up to a scale-hopper at the top of the storage shed. The hopper opened when a predetermined weight was reached, discharging the measured wheat into lower-level bins for storage or into freight cars waiting within the building. Macrae recognized that the final results depended on a fresh analysis of the problem and the systematic utilization of simple mechanical means to maximize production. David Macrae, *The Americans at Home,* vol. 2 (Edinburgh: Edmonson and Douglas, 1870), 195.

3. "A City Elevated," *Chamber's Journal* 35 (26 January 1861): 49. To my knowledge, this was the first time in a European publication that the word "wonder" was used as an adjective for Chicago.

4. At a level only a few feet above the water of Lake Michigan, streets of the central district did not drain well. Threatened by yearly outbreaks of cholera and typhoid and aware of the ineffectiveness of existing sewers, the city council passed legislation in March 1855 to raise the level of both the streets and the sidewalks. Work began in 1856 and continued into the 1870s. Underneath the new street level and above the level of the water table in spring, engineers created an integrated system of brick sewers that emptied into the Chicago River. See Frank J. Piehl's clear article, "Chicago's Early Fight to 'Save Our Lake,'" *Chicago History* 5 (Winter 1976–77): 224–25.

5. According to Newman Hall, "One special 'block' was pointed out to me. There were about a dozen very large hotels and warehouses, six or seven stories high, and solidly built of stone. The walls at the bottom having been cut from the foundation, 10,000 jacks were placed below. One man was stationed to every six, and at an appointed signal every man gave his six screws half a turn." Hall, *From Liverpool to St. Louis* (London: Routledge, 1870), 144. The *Deutsche Bauzeitung* in 1868 (p. 480) carried an article entitled "Chicago und seine Häuserhebung."

6. C. B. Berry, *The Other Side* (London: Griffith and Farron, 1880), 112.

7. Bessie Louise Pierce reported that Thomas Hughes, author of *Tom Brown at Rugby*, with the assistance of Browning, Tennyson, Darwin, and Kingsley donated eight thousand books to the Chicago Public Library, organized in 1872. Pierce, *As Others See Chicago* (Chicago: University of Chicago Press, 1933), 211–12.

8. The prose of the American author Grace Greenwood was more animated than that of most travelers from across the Atlantic; nevertheless, she spoke for many of them when she wrote, "You catch the contagion of activity and enterprise, and have wild dreams of beginning life again, and settling—no, circulating, *whirling*—in Chicago." Greenwood, *New Life in New Lands* (New York: J. B. Ford, 1873), 15. A British traveler, Ephraim Turland, stated, "Anyway, while in Chicago I feel disposed to turn my face towards the rising sun and a future day." Turland, *Notes of a Visit to America* (Manchester: Johnson and Rawson, 1877), 73. Ebenezer Howard, author of *Garden Cities of Tomorrow*, claimed that the years he worked in Chicago in the late 1870s increased his optimism and idealism and encouraged him to pay more attention to his imagination. See Dugald MacFadyen, *Sir Ebenezer Howard and the Town Planning Movement* (Manchester: Manchester University Press, 1933), 10–11.

9. Friedrich M. Bodenstedt, *Vom Atlantischen zum Stillen Ocean* (Leipzig: F. A. Brockhaus, 1882), 264.

10. Macrae, vol. 1, 21.

11. For authors who argued that Chicago had become a city of national or international significance, see Ernst Frignet and Edmund Garrey, *États-Unis d'Amérique* (Paris: Jouaust, 1871), 88; A. G. Gérard, *Itinéraire de Québec à Chicago* (Montreal: C. O. Beauchemin and Valois, 1868), 88; Leopold Kist, *Amerikanisches* (Mainz: Franz Kirchheim, 1871), 644; Charles E. Lewis, *Two Lectures on a Short Visit to America* (London: privately printed, 1876), 51; J. B. Loudon, *A Tour through Canada and the United States of America* (Coventry: Curtis and Beamish, 1879), 66; Ém. Malézieux, *Souvenirs d'une mission aux États-Unis d'Amérique* (Paris: Dunod, 1874), 80; William Robertson and F. W. Robertson, *Our American Tour* (Edinburgh: Privately printed, 1871), 54–58; Louis de Turenne, *Quatorze mois dans l'Amérique du Nord*, vol. 1 (Paris: A. Quantin, 1879), 34–35; John Watson, *Souvenir of a Tour in the United States and Canada* (Glasgow: Privately printed, 1872), 47; see also Berry, 114, and Hall, 138.

12. Among the longer or more thoughtful general accounts of Chicago before 1880 were those written by Frignet and Garrey, Gerard, Kist, Lewis, Macrae, and Turenne; see also John Leng, *America in 1876* (Dundee: Dundee Advertiser Office, 1877). Henryk Sienkiewicz, who was not a Western European, saw Chicago on his trip to the United States between 1876 and 1878. The win-

ner of the 1905 Nobel Prize for literature, he thought the city came closest to a fantastic description of twentieth-century cities he had read. See Charles Morley, ed., *Portrait of America: Letters of Henryk Sienkiewicz* (New York: Columbia University Press, 1959), 48. The only extended discussions of Chicago to appear in foreign architectural journals during the decade were A.W.L., "Chicago and Its Architecture," *Building News* 34 (8 March 1878): 233–34, and F., "Architekten-Verein zu Berlin," *Deutsche Bauzeitung* 12 (13 April 1878): 150–52, the latter a presentation to a large audience at the Verein by one of its members, Herr Bartels.

13. Bodenstedt, 270.

14. Octave Uzanne, *Vingt jours dans le nouveau monde* (Paris: May and Motteroz, 1893), 17.

15. G. Sauvin, *Autour de Chicago* (Paris: Plon, 1893), 98.

16. Paul Lindau, *Altes und Neues aus der neuen Welt* (Berlin: Carl Duncker, 1893), 373.

17. James Bryce, *Social Institutions of the United States* (New York: Chautauqua Press, 1891), 207, 248.

18. Jacques Hermant, "L'art à l'exposition de Chicago," *Gazette des beaux-arts* 73 (September 1893): 242. His article was continued in the November and December issues of the journal.

19. The Marquis de Chasseloup-Laubat reported in 1893 that nothing was more instructive or fascinating in the United States than Chicago. Chasseloup-Laubat, *Voyage en Amérique et principalement à Chicago* (Paris: Société des ingénieurs civils de France, 1893), 16. An Austrian who identified himself only as J. S—r in writing "Die 'hohen Häuser' in Amerika" (*Wiener Bauindustrie-Zeitung* 10 [22 June 1893]: 447), claimed that when America was mentioned in conversations, everyone instinctively thought of Chicago.

20. Max O'Rell [Paul Blouët] and Jack Allyn, *Jonathan and His Continent,* trans. Madame Paul Blouët (New York: Cassell, 1889), 46.

21. In 1886 the British historian James Anthony Frounde called Chicago the "highest example in the present world of the tendency of modern men to cluster into towns." "A Briton's View of Us," *Chicago Tribune,* 20 February 1886, 12.

22. J. J. Aubertin, *A Fight with Distances* (London: Kegan Paul, 1888), 55.

23. Editorial, "[Yankee newspaper criticism]," *British Architect* 29 (20 January 1888): 42.

24. Paul de Rousiers, *American Life,* trans. A. J. Herbertson (Paris: Firmin-Didot, 1892), 10.

25. Paul Bourget, "A Farewell to the White City," *Cosmopolitan,* December 1893, 138–40.

26. Alfred D. Chandler Jr., "Fin de siècle: Industrial Transformation" in *Fin de siècle and Its Legacy,* ed. Mikulás Teich and Roy Porter (Cambridge: Cambridge University Press, 1990), 33.

27. Rousiers, 11.

28. Lloyd Lewis and Henry Justin Smith, *Oscar Wilde Discovers America* (New York: Harcourt Brace, 1936), 167.

29. A. G. Stephens, "A Queenslander's Travel Notes, 1894," in *A. G. Stephens: Selected Writings,* ed. Leon Cantrell (Sydney: Angus and Robertson, 1977), 408.

30. Friedrich Dernburg, *Aus der weissen Stadt* (Berlin: Julius Springer, 1893), 72.

31. Rudyard Kipling, *American Notes* (Philadelphia: Henry Altemus, c. 1899), 107–8.

32. Gustave Le Bon, *The Crowd: A Study of the Popular Mind* (New York: Macmillan, 1896), xvii.

33. Sauvin, 100.

34. Perhaps the first European to call Chicago a frightening place was L. de Cotton. He recalled, "The moment of the arrival was painful; I felt an instinctive need to glance behind, and something cold pressed my heart. Oh! What an awful city! But, after all, 'Go ahead, never mind!' the American motto says." Cotton, "A Frenchman's Visit to Chicago in 1886," trans. George J. Joyaux, *Journal of the Illinois Historical Society* 47, no. 1 (Spring 1954): 48.

35. Uzanne, 171.

36. William Archer, *America To-Day* (New York: Charles Scribner's Sons, 1899), 103.

37. Most critics attributed the achievements and failures of the city to creativity, greed, or sloppy management. H. G. Wells did not blame evil gods when he declared "undisciplined" Chicago the nineteenth century's classical example of avaricious industrialism. Wells, *The Future in America* (Leipzig: Bernhard Tauchnitz, 1907), 66–70.

Disquieting

2 # Manifestations

of

Urbanism

IN THE EARLY 1890s most observers in Britain, France, and Germany thought Chicago's potential unlimited but worried about the inability of leaders to resolve numerous environmental problems before continuing their headlong plunge into the future. After all, the Europeans reasoned, before a city contemplated functioning in new ways, its first responsibility was to function well. They lectured Chicagoans relentlessly, trying to convince them of the foolishness of plans for expansion, quicker speeds, or taller buildings when their existing record, amazing in many respects, was sadly flawed. A visit to Chicago was not just a visual experience for Europeans; they heard it, smelled it, and felt it, especially in the vicinity of the Loop. Even the dirtiest of British and Continental cities, they contended, did not threaten Chicago's reputation as a filthy and poorly managed municipality.[1] Visitors empathized with Chicagoans, wondering how they could tolerate such smoky skies, dirty and dangerous streets, and a stinking and visibly polluted river. Was no one in charge? Was no one able to discipline capitalism for the good of the whole community? Chicago was certainly not the only large city in the United States suffering from sanitary inadequacies. Europeans concentrated on Chicago because of its pioneering reputation, its inability to resolve housekeeping crises while dispatching with ease other equally formidable challenges, and because the Loop concentrated and magnified the negative consequences of unhindered speculation.

Chicago's citizens were proud of the way in which they had created a world city from nothing in so brief a period of time. They realized they had to put up with conditions that were often frustrating, dangerous, nerve-racking, or unhealthy, but they also knew they had overcome obstacles and deficiencies in the past and would do so again in the future. For the present, however, their principal desire was to sustain Chicago's momentum. The *Inland Architect and News Record* (popularly known as the *Inland Architect*) of Chicago endorsed this course in June 1888. Predicting good economic winds in the years immediately ahead, it claimed that the nation and the city were "in a better condition than ever to enter upon the race of progress and development which the genius of the people has made possible and inevitable."[2] The journal in 1888 reflected local conviction that little could or should prevent Chicago from experiencing a material future more impressive than its past.

In fact, Chicagoans themselves were quite aware of the environmental problems in the heart of their city. They complained constantly about the smells, sludge, and health threats of the Chicago River, the smoke, smog, and soot that discolored and polluted their air, the filth of their downtown streets, and the inconveniences caused by constant construction that angered pedestrians and sometimes endangered their lives. Though not new, these problems were exacerbated during the 1880s as more commercial activity was packed into the same number of blocks. No building had been built higher than eight floors in the 1870s, but in 1882 the Montauk Building by Burnham and Root reached ten stories and in 1885 the Mallers Building by J. J. Flanders, twelve stories (fig. 2). By 1894 there were more than twenty commercial buildings at least twelve stories high in this zone. As congestion increased, individuals and groups called for a reexamination of existing priorities, trying to address these problems before they became worse. Their efforts were bolstered by the decision of Congress in February 1890 to name Chicago the nation's host city for an international exposition commemorating the four-hundredth anniversary of the discovery of the New World by Columbus, an event initially intended to be held in 1892 but dedicated 12 October 1892 and opened on 1 May 1893, as the World's Columbian Exposition. Realizing their city would be on national and international display, citizens rededicated efforts to improve appearances and the quality of life throughout the city, especially in the central district. However, restraining aggressive capitalism to improve the community's welfare threatened the momentum of free enterprise, which had shaped Chicago's distinctive image. During the years of preparation for the exposition, the city struggled to address seemingly incompatible concerns—how to maintain its place in "the race of progress" and how to create an environment beneficial for human beings.

The Condition of the River

The Chicago River, defining the northern and western edges of the business district, was the coronary artery of the city. Approximately a mile west of Lake Michigan, at Wolf Point (fig. 3), the north and south branches joined to form the main channel, the three streams providing a protected harbor forty-one miles long that was lined with granaries, lumber yards, and manufacturing plants. Overused as shipping channels and polluted by industrial sludge, the branches were further contaminated by the city's sewage, 85 percent of which in 1893 emptied directly into them. Concerned about excessive traffic and contamination, some city leaders recommended a lakefront harbor that would diminish or phase out inland wharves. However, this alternative was not acceptable to the business community because $200,000,000 worth of material was transported yearly on the river in the early 1890s. Although the Chicago Tribune constantly howled about "our

Figure 2. Mallers Building, Chicago, 1884–85, J. J. Flanders (*L'architecture américaine*, 1886).

filthy river," its editors believed the needs of manufacturers and shippers took precedence—"anything that interferes with the free movement of this mighty flood of produce . . . increases the difficulty and expense of handling," and thus plays into the hands of Chicago's competitors, they declared in June 1891.[3]

The "deep-cut" canal of 1871 did not clean the river as effectively as expected, though it did reverse the flow of the main channel. Instead of the river flowing into Lake Michigan, the water of the lake flowed westward into the river and then through the South Branch to the rivers of the upper Mississippi basin. In 1883 the pumping works at Bridgeport on the South Branch, closed for more than a decade because they were considered unnecessary, were reopened. Pumping 35,000 to 40,000 cubic feet per minute, they increased the flow of the river, thus reducing the pollution of its water. Under earlier and normal conditions this system worked, but as the city's population grew, the volume of sewage increased, reaching approximately 45,000,000 to 50,000,000 gallons daily in 1885. Furthermore, the level of the lake, always lower in December than in July, varied from year to year. When torrential rains hit the area, as they did in August 1885 and February 1887, the pumps and the modest declivity of the canal were unable to handle the runoff. Waters from the Des Plaines River overflowed into the Ogden Ditch, which paralleled the canal, and backed up into the Chicago River. Under these conditions, its current slowed and sometimes reversed.

When the river was sluggish, it was offensive; when it reversed directions, it became

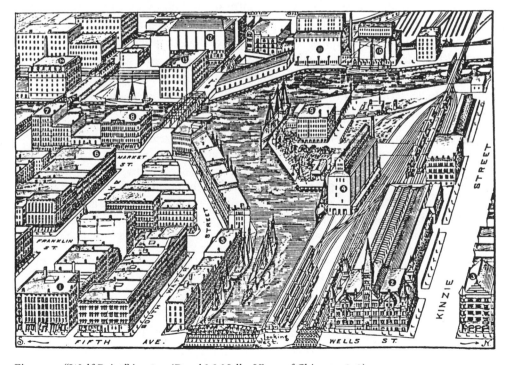

Figure 3. "Wolf Point" in 1893 (Rand McNally, *Views of Chicago,* 1898).

Figure 4. The odor of the Chicago River—"Letting the stench through a bridge" (*Chicago Tribune*, 7 July 1889).

dangerous. The smell of the stream, especially in summer, ranged from unpleasant to nauseating, depending on one's distance from the water. Reporters fabricated stories about opening swing bridges to let the stench, not the river traffic, pass through (fig. 4), or the advisability of attaching to tug prows an "odor cutter," a paddlewheel with scoops, to enable boats to move faster through the dense air. The effluvium was so concentrated, they mused, that when dried and cut into blocks it was better than concrete for foundations. Tug captains had stronger reasons to curse than to laugh. In certain locations they could not draw water because it fouled their engines. Because gas companies on the South Branch dumped so much refuse into the river, sections of it became potentially combustible. Descriptions of the deterioration of the river in 1889 obscure the distinction between fact and fiction.

> Still farther on, after turning into the South Fork, this putrid scum lies out in the river itself in great floating masses. The bloated carcasses of dead animals are lying on the surface everywhere. A dozen at a time may be seen—and smelled—as the stagnant mass is stirred up. Sparrows are walking about on the surface with the chippering unconcern of a waterfowl. This villainous mass of indescribable filth gathers in places so thick that it not alone will bear up a light winged searcher for food, but sleek, long-tailed rats scurry around without the slightest heed that they are walking on a river.[4]

City leaders might have continued to tolerate such conditions on the sluggish river, but deaths, resulting from the contamination of Lake Michigan's water when the river reversed directions, compelled them to act.

Flooding in August 1885 forced the river to back up into the lake, polluting not only immediate coastal waters but also extending to the crib two miles out in the lake where fresh drinking water was supposed to enter the tunnel. Two years later rains turned the river into a "mill-race," producing a defined stream of sewage at least a mile long in the lake, which then spread to envelop the crib. Sampling the water at the intake, the crib supervisor defined its quality as "pretty bad." Reacting to such incidents, the *Tribune's* cartoonists offered a biologist's view of the lake's bacterial content (fig. 5). Spurred by high typhoid rates in 1881, 1885, and 1886, the Illinois legislature passed the Sanitary District Enabling Act in 1889, which authorized the construction of the Chicago Sanitary and Ship Canal. The "Big Ditch," at least 20 feet deep and from 110 to 201 feet wide, paralleled the former canal.[5] Opened in January 1900, it finally turned the Chicago River, which then flowed into it as a relatively clean, one-directional stream.

This mammoth project came too late to prevent the severe typhoid outbreaks in 1890 and 1891 when, respectively, 1,008 and 1,997 people died in the city. The death rate for typhoid alone in 1891 reached 16.64 per 10,000—more than 7 percent of all deaths in Chicago that year. Comparative figures convey the seriousness of the epidemic. This rate was eight times greater than Berlin's in 1889. In May 1891 there were more deaths from this disease in the city than in any twelve-month period between 1888 and 1891 in New York City. Despite a significant drop in typhoid-related deaths in 1893, in part due to a new crib four miles from shore, reports identifying Chicago with typhoid circulated in Europe prior to the exposition. The *Lancet* of London sent a water tester to ascertain if it was wise for British citizens to visit the Columbian Exposition in 1893. Chicago's officials were embarrassed, but the report, published on 9 April 1893, proved to be helpful. "In respect to colour, total solid matter, hardness, chlorine and oxygen required to oxidize organic matter, Lake Michigan water is seen to be superior to the choicest of London's supply."[6] A pipeline was also constructed to bring pure water from springs at

Figure 5. Lake Michigan water (*Chicago Tribune*, 16 August 1885).

Waukesha, Wisconsin, to the exposition grounds. However, there was little anyone could do about the smell of the river, described as "stinking" in July of 1893 when thousands of visitors from other cities and countries were in town to see the exposition.

The "Curse of Chicago"

During these years Chicagoans were more concerned about the air of their city than they were about odors or disease traceable to the river. The smoke-laden atmosphere above the city was not considered to be life threatening, but its intrusiveness and persistence earned it the title of "the curse of Chicago." Depending on the right wind and one's location on the downtown streets, the smells of the river could be temporarily forgotten. Smoke was more pervasive. There were occasions when the smoke was less annoying—when air currents blew the black clouds eastward over the lake, or in the summer when the boilers of office buildings could be turned down. Even at that time of year, those in the central area still had to cope with fallout from tugs on the river and locomotives that pulled up to the edge of the commercial district. Thus, throughout the year, but especially from October until April, the skies over Chicago carried dark reminders of choices made below.

Though the sun might be shining elsewhere in Illinois, according to newspaper accounts, Chicago could be dark, not just at eight in the morning, but also at noon. On still days in winter, street lights might be on all day. Offices that normally depended on natural light might be illuminated by gas jets and electric lights throughout the working hours. Visibility at street level was sometimes limited to a few blocks. Furthermore, the tall buildings caused drafts that brought down dirty air, described as "simply choking," which was so saturated with soot and moisture that it soiled clothes as well as building surfaces.

Because most European visitors to Chicago had not seen anything comparable in the centers of their own cities, they often resorted to "poetic" images to describe the smoke that blanketed its commercial district. Calling Chicago "a true Hell in winter," Ernst von Hesse-Wartegg, a Viennese-born, prolific travel writer, likened the sight of huge buildings enveloped by smoke and fog to subterranean landscapes, suggestive of "the elephant caves of Ceylon," or to "thickly populated catacombs excavated by Titans."[7] William Archer, from Britain, discussed the air of Chicago as if it were one of the keys to understanding the city. Claiming that in the realm of smoke, New York was to Chicago as Mont Blanc was to Vesuvius, he wrote:

> The smoke of Chicago has a peculiar and aggressive individuality, due, I imagine, to the natural clearness of the atmosphere. It does not seem, like London smoke, to permeate and blend with the air. It does not overhang the streets in a uniform canopy, but sweeps across and about them in gusts and swirls, now dropping and now lifting again its grimy curtain. You will often see the vista of a gorge-like street so choked with a seeming thundercloud that you feel sure a storm is just about to burst upon the city, until you look up at the zenith and find it smiling serene. Again and

again a sudden swirl of smoke across the street . . . has led me to prick up my ears for a cry of "Fire!" But Chicago is not so easily alarmed. It is accustomed to having its airs from heaven blurred by these blasts from hell. I know few spectacles more curious than that which awaits you when you have shot up in the express elevator to the top of the Auditorium tower—on the one hand, the blue and laughing lake, on the other, the city belching volumes of smoke from its thousand throats, as though a vaster Sheffield or Wolverhampton had been transported by magic to the shores of the Mediterranean Sea. What a wonderful city Chicago will be when the commandment is honestly enforced which declares, "Thou shalt consume thine own smoke."[8]

Industrialization and urbanization had changed the color of the skies over nineteenth-century cities in both the United States and Europe.[9] But in Chicago, a place where impressions were seldom vague or delicate, smoke rose to legendary levels, inspiring tourists to imaginative similes to communicate its reality.

People who lived with the smoke problem daily in the heart of the city were fed up. Real estate agents were particularly frustrated. They told stories of clients, on the verge of renting new office space, who leaned on a desk and discovered their hands were black. The agent's reply, "the rooms haven't been dusted for fifteen or twenty minutes. That's all," often scuttled the deal. Some office managers reported they had moved several times until they had found a location that was relatively clean. Firms located in taller buildings could be worse off than those in six- or seven-story structures if winds blew smoke from lower stacks against higher adjacent walls. Even when windows were closed, soot entered the interiors.

In order to marshal support for its war on smoke, the *Tribune* interviewed a number of architectural firms in August 1888.[10] All complained about the negative effects of smoke on both drawings and buildings. At the office of Treat and Foltz, Mr. Treat demonstrated the seriousness of the problem by rubbing his clean hand over a drawing he had been studying. Other designers concurred, showing the reporter smudged plans and sketches, as well as dirty shirt cuffs. Those interviewed also claimed the dirty air influenced their designs. Because bright surfaces suffered in Chicago, they hesitated to introduce warm colors. Somber colors were the only sensible ones to use, and even these became darker in time. New buildings looked old within a few years. Streaks appeared in channels where water flowed regularly. Some thought the grime that obscured texture and details encouraged designers to be more straightforward. They also cited the corrosion of stone, metal, and painted surfaces by creosotelike particles in the air. Copper was the most resistant of the metals, but it was not totally immune.

Archer's reference to the commandment about consuming one's own smoke was a comment on the city's antismoke ordinance, adopted in May 1881 after years of lobbying by the Citizens Association. Impressed with this action, the *British Architect* in September 1884 praised the "wise fathers" who ruled Chicago. They had required owners of buildings to reduce the amount of smoke that spewed from their stacks or pay a fine each time they were convicted of disobeying the law. However, enforcement of the ordinance was often lax or sporadic, and citations prosecuted in court did not always lead to convictions. Smoke inspectors based their charges on visual evidence, which could be easily challenged. With thousands of stacks contributing to the problem, defendants could claim they were being singled out while neighboring polluters were being ignored.

At the root of this controversy was the unwillingness of owners to spend much money to improve conditions in the business district. They were not insensitive to the issue, and many probably supported the spirit of the ordinance, but in the 1880s and the early 1890s they were not yet ready to take radical steps to correct the problem. The cause of the pollution was bituminous coal, the "coal of the West," more accessible and approximately half as expensive as anthracite or hard coal, which produced less pollution. In the business district alone there were more than two thousand boilers connected to more than twelve hundred chimneys. These consumed almost a million tons of bituminous coal yearly, one-eighth of the total consumption of the entire city around 1890. Estimates in 1891 indicated that annual costs for fuel would rise from eighteen million to twenty million dollars if the city shifted to anthracite, a step business leaders admitted they were unwilling to take.

Their preferred solution was to install high-heat furnaces or to try to limit air pollution by attaching smoke consumers to less efficient boilers. The latter was a step that tended to produce modest, sometimes uneven, results. There were many attachments to chose from, most costing under $700, but few, if any, that offered consistently satisfying results. The Home Insurance Company Building, possessing the "model boiler plant in the city," was sometimes termed a serious polluter and sometimes cited as proof that smoke could be controlled. There were too many variables to produce consistency. The attachments varied in design and performance, and all furnaces required careful handling. Some owners, defending the system they had installed, blamed their stokers for not keeping the temperatures in the furnaces high enough.

Despite the law and the halfhearted efforts of owners to comply, the skies over the heart of Chicago became heavier as the decade of the 1880s passed. Convinced that this was the most disregarded of all ordinances, Joseph Medill, editor of the *Tribune*, began in the last half of 1888 to name buildings that were conspicuous offenders and to publish illustrations of their smoky contributions to the city's atmosphere. Based on photographs taken by his reporters, these cuts usually showed the top floors of identified buildings, the stacks that emitted the smoke, and the darkened skies above. Among the first commercial structures cited were the Home Insurance Company, Counselman, Royal Insurance, Mallers, Board of Trade, and Phoenix office buildings, as well as the Palmer House and the Auditorium. The newspaper continued for several years to name the principal "smokers," often identifying the newest and tallest business buildings as the worst polluters of the central district, as it did when it singled out the Masonic Temple of 1891–92 by Burnham and Root (fig. 6). Crusaders in this campaign for clean air repeatedly cited the Edison Electric Company with its ten boilers as the ultimate smokemaker in the Loop area. Not coincidentally, this centrally located company, "which shares with Popocatépetl the distinction of being the largest active volcano,"[11] made more money the darker the sky became.

Figure 6. "Masonic Temple and some of its neighbors" (*Chicago Tribune*, 3 January 1892).

With the help of other newspapers, Medill persisted, though he irritated many in the business community and bored others by publicizing the issue relentlessly. With some impatience the *Inland Architect* in September 1888 referred to a piece in the *Tribune* as "perhaps the thousandth time" the paper had focused on the smoke nuisance. Nevertheless, the campaign was partially effective. The smoke inspector of the city became more active, claiming in 1890 to have prosecuted 485 offenders, 299 of whom paid the fifty-dollar fine. With the penalty so low, a company could ignore the law fourteen times before it became more cost-efficient to install an average-priced smoke consumer. Despite indications that the city government was taking the ordinance more seriously, conditions in the downtown area continued to deteriorate, in part because pollution from tugs and locomotives had become worse. On 23 December 1891, representatives of fifteen prominent clubs and civic organizations met at the Union League Club—whose furnace had previously been awarded a pictorial onion—to discuss the problem. Six weeks later the Society for the Prevention of Smoke opened its office.

The creation of the society was an indication of the changing outlook of Chicago's business leaders, spurred by the coming exposition. It signaled a stronger awareness of their social responsibilities and new thinking about the broader purposes of their city. Not surprisingly, this watchdog group was formed in the years just before the exposition when outside attention was drawn to Chicago. In this period, newspaper editorials often asked "what will visitors think of us if they see . . ." and then listed specific problems or deficiencies the city had to address. The exposition, a product of the "go-ahead" mentality of the city, was also a catalyst for its improvement.

The society represented a shift of municipal stewardship from the elected to the powerful. The organization was created because local government had not been able to enforce its ordinances and because Medill's efforts lacked compulsion. The society learned quickly and used power effectively. When it realized that educational programs were ineffective, it concluded that those who disobeyed the law would stop only when compelled to do so. With a staff of investigators and lawyers who brought suits in the name of the city but represented the society in court, it claimed impressive results by the end of its first year—"between 300 and 325 smoke nuisances . . . have been removed; the locomotive smoke nuisance within two miles of the business center has been reduced 75 per cent; the tug nuisance has been reduced between 90 and 95 per cent."[12] Though this report was inflated, the group had demonstrated tactical savvy in reacting to the smoke nuisance. However, the causes of the problem were too deep to correct overnight. *Moran's Dictionary of Chicago* in 1910 admitted that despite repeated efforts "the fact remains that the city is still afflicted in a very large degree with dusky incubus."

The Futile Fight against Filth

In the early 1890s Chicago was also known, and repeatedly reprimanded, for the amount of garbage, litter, mud, and dirt that accumulated on its streets and alleys. Shortly after Congress named Chicago as the host for the coming Columbian Exposition, municipal officials and citizens groups discussed steps that should be taken to prepare the city for the event. The objective of most of the improvement societies was a cleaner and more attractive environment. They called for enforcement of ordinances, citizen action to beautify and embellish the city, reduction of street encroachments, and closer cooperation between citizens and elected officials to give Chicago a more scrubbed appearance. These groups may have concentrated on litter and dirt rather than on smoke, because smoke, though pervasive, was ephemeral, while litter and dirt could be located, picked up, and deposited out of sight.

The debris that collected in the downtown came from litter dropped by pedestrians and transport, from careless bill-posters, and from janitors who violated city regulations by throwing trash and sweepings into streets and alleys. The streets of the First Ward, the business district, yielded approximately ninety tons of refuse daily in 1891. The managers of the Auditorium angered smoke fighters by trying to help trash collectors. Each day they burned in their basement furnaces one and a half carloads of waste collected from the offices and the hotel in the building. In suburban areas the trash placed along the curb was often scattered by wind or animals because residents complied irresponsibly with the vague ordinance specifying a "suitable and sufficient receptacle." For the center of the city the ordinance was more specific but often unenforced. An unidentified office building on Dearborn Street in 1892 placed the ashes from its furnaces in dozens of open five-gallon containers. After breezes had redistributed a portion of the ash over neighboring streets on several occasions, street cleaners finally took the cans as well. When trash was picked up, it was usually taken to suburban pits to decompose. Despite constant talk about increasing the number of municipal incinerators and placing them around the city, Chicago at the time of the exposition burned only a fraction of the thousand-plus tons of garbage and debris it collected daily.

Paved streets in the downtown section became dirty when contractors hauled dirt from building sites in wagons that were overloaded or loosely fitted with boards. There were also numerous horses in this densely packed area, some of them hitched for long periods of time. When heavy rains came and the sewer system was unable to drain the center effectively, despite earlier efforts to improve drainage, the water mixed with the dirt and filth to create deplorable conditions. "The sight of so much mud and so many different kinds of mud is enough to make some men contemplate suicide," wailed the *Tribune* for 12 December 1890. Because some of the alleys in the business area were not paved, the conditions there were worse. In winter, frozen mud could also be dangerous. The principal winter problem was caused by the plows of grip-car companies that cleared their tracks but pushed piles of snow to either side in violation of laws requiring them to remove what they had plowed. During the winter of 1893–94 angry citizens retaliated by blocking the tracks with mounds of snow that had been pushed aside. Although not responsible for clearing snow from suburban streets, the sanitation department was often criticized for its slow and inefficient removal efforts in the business district where it was responsible.

Proponents of a cleaner city also cited the relationship between accumulated filth and disease. Dr. Oscar C. De Wolf, appointed city health commissioner by Mayor Carter H. Harrison in 1883, worried about excessive saturation of the ground when the snow melted, fearing that the combination of dampness, decay, and sewer leaks encouraged the microorganism that caused cholera. Arguing a correlation between slushy streets and the number of people with colds or influenza, he also warned Chicagoans to be careful during periodic winter thaws. Despite the typhoid scares of 1890 and 1891 and the assumption that disease increased with urban filth, Chicago's death rate in 1892 was actually lower than that of New York, Boston, Baltimore, or Philadelphia, and during the January–April period of 1893 its rate of 19.18 per thousand per annum compared favorably to 26+ for Paris and 19.53 for London.[13] Observers abroad predicted higher buildings would lead to higher death rates among the poor.[14] In Chicago, however, there were countering factors, among them, the sparse population of the Loop from evening to morning, the city's high percentage of single-family homes, and a low population density.

The campaign to control filth differed from that of the Society for the Prevention of Smoke in some revealing ways. The society was male, club-based, and powerful. The attack on dirt was led by the Municipal Order League, composed of liberal women with less access to Chicago's wealth and influence. The society was formed quietly in surroundings of leather and walnut. The league held a public meeting on 27 March 1892, in the Central Music Hall, attended primarily by middle-class women. "It is safe to say there was not a Worth gown or a Virot bonnet in the hall," reported the *Tribune*. The businessmen's fight against smoke was largely pragmatic; the program against dirt was both pragmatic and moral, moral in its inclusiveness and shared responsibility. The league used the crisis to put young boys to work in Young Citizens' Street Cleaning Brigades. The women also formed kitchen committees to pass out literature about garbage handling to neighbors and agreed to print instructions in various languages for distribution in tenements. These women believed that, in addition to assessments, the stewardship of all was needed to keep Chicago clean. As housekeepers of the city, they promised to give officials no peace until they eradicated filth.

Unfortunately, the women were less successful in the halls of power than the men. Eight months later President Ada Sweet announced her organization had decided visits to the health commissioner and other officials were futile. The league had done what it could. It was now up to all the people to apply pressure. A few months earlier Mayor Hempstead Washburne had also asked the people to act, but for a different reason. Chicago's inability to cope with its waste was not caused by inefficiency or mismanagement, he claimed, but by insufficient funds to hire enough scavenger teams to service the more than seven thousand miles of streets and alleys in the city. If the people wanted a cleaner city, they would have to pay for it.

As the following statement from a *Tribune* editorial in March 1892 demonstrates, advocates of a cleaner city used the coming Columbian Exposition to goad citizens to action.

> When the health officials and others interested in sanitary matters from London, Paris, Berlin, and other great metropolitan cities look upon our ill-conditioned streets and alleys, view our careless and indifferent scavenger service, smell our disease-breeding garbage boxes, see our city's offal at our front doors, they will very seriously question the assertion that we have health boards or health departments whose object is or should be the city's cleanliness.[15]

Reformers did not need the exposition to convince the people of the problem, but they brandished it as a weapon in their campaign for immediate action. With time running short, reformers used their leverage more aggressively. On 30 November 1892, the *Tribune* carried an editorial stating that if visitors to the coming spring's exposition arrived today, "Chicago would be denounced as the dirtiest city on the face of the globe." Its prediction came true. Speaking at Hull-House the following March, New York's candid and courageous housing critic and photographer, Jacob Riis, was blunt. "You ought to begin housecleaning, so to speak, and get your alleys and streets in better condition; never in our worst season have we had so much filth in New York City."[16] When the exposition opened, the condition of the central streets had been improved but was still poor. Visitors from abroad sometimes noted the marked contrast between clean, attractive fairgrounds and the dirty streets of the functioning city.

Obstructions in the Streets

In his exposé of moral degeneration and public corruption in the city, *If Christ Came to Chicago!,* William Thomas Stead, the British editor of the *Review of Reviews,* claimed in 1894 that "the first impression which a stranger receives on arriving in Chicago is that of dirt, the danger and the inconvenience of the streets."[17] By inconvenience he meant holes in the road surfaces, objects and stored materials that often cluttered the sidewalks, challenging the agility of pedestrians, and the temporary walkways that slowed the movement of crowds (fig. 7). Crossing thoroughfares was also inconvenient because companies that laid pipes or wires underneath the surface often left holes unfilled for periods of time or replaced the road blocks unevenly. Crammed with mechanical and horse-pulled vehicles that moved at different speeds, downtown streets became danger zones in which pedestrians were challenged by debris, holes, and impatient drivers.

Despite these problems, the quality of the road surfaces in the Loop was much better than it was in other parts of the city, where not even half of the roadways were paved. Many finished roads in the suburbs were not good because the system employed was cheaper and less durable, resulting in some legendary cavities that cabmen knew from experience. There were five basic systems of paving—granite block, cedar block, macadam, asphalt block, and sheet asphalt. Cedar block was the most common suburban type. Cedar logs were cut into six-inch sections, packed tightly together on a sand bed, and filled in with gravel and coal tar. This surface, which lasted about seven years, was good for horses and moderate loads but could not withstand heavy weights. Sheet as-

Figure 7. Temporary crossing, State and Washington Streets (*Chicago Tribune,* 18 December 1892).

phalt, the bicyclist's choice, became popular for residential streets around 1890. This compound, though cheaper, was too fragile for the business district, where granite block was required by ordinance in the 1880s.

Granite block was the most expensive road material used in Chicago, costing about four times as much as cedar and 50 percent more than asphalt. Though stronger and more durable, this surface could become slippery when wet, causing serious problems for horses. Because it was laid in blocks on packed limestone and sand, it could also become uneven. Granite laid at the base of the skyscraper canyons was the noisiest of all systems, according to office workers who sometimes closed windows to concentrate. At the time of the exposition more than 1,000 miles of streets had been improved, including most of those in the business district, and 4,252 miles of sidewalks had been constructed, mainly of wood except for those in the center of the city, which were usually of flagstone.[18]

On the sidewalks pedestrians encountered two types of physical obstructions—goods for sale or waiting to be carried into stores and contractors' equipment and materials. Merchants were permitted to use the outer four feet of a sidewalk to store materials temporarily, but they could leave them legally for only two hours. This regulation was ignored daily along South Water Street and Wabash Avenue in the wholesale district. Even in retail sections, such as the west side of State Street north of Randolph, the sidewalk looked like an isthmus in a sea of crates, chests, boxes, and materials on display. Aggressive street vendors, mentioned by a number of Europeans, added to the congestion.

The construction of new buildings and the renovation of old ones often blocked the movement of crowds. City officials, recognizing that the building of enormous structures required ground to store supplies and machinery, had been generous in allowing contractors to use public space. Builders were permitted to fence off the sidewalk in front of a site and could extend this barrier eight feet into the street, if necessary. However, they were prohibited from cutting stone and mixing mortar on the street and also could not leave rubbish there. At their own expense, contractors were expected to construct a lighted "substantial sidewalk" of wood around any barricade that reached the street. Contractors usually took advantage of the privilege of extending work space but did not always provide pedestrians with a well-protected walkway, as the *Tribune*'s editorial drawing of the construction of the Hartford Building in 1892 pointed out (fig. 8). Although contractors in eastern cities of the United States were pressured to store materials closer to or inside the building once its lower floors were up, firms in Chicago tended to maintain their fences, some of them erected beyond the eight-foot limit. Newspaper reporters took photographs to show the disparity between the congestion of citizens on the outside of a fence and the relatively open areas used by workers on the inside. Citizens accused builders of retaining their fences as long as possible in order to profit from surfaces rented to advertising companies. Signmen required a permit from the city but paid the contractors for the space they used. More serious than increased congestion was the possibility of injury, particularly when curving tracks swung the end of cable cars close to the stream of people walking in the street. On the other hand, some contractors began to realize it was unfair as well as poor business to disregard public complaints. After

Figure 8. Fenced area in front of the Hartford Building—"How not to do it" (*Chicago Tribune*, 11 December 1892).

Figure 9. Protected sidewalk in front of Columbus Memorial Building —"How to do it" (*Chicago Tribune*, 11 December 1892).

the George A. Fuller Company in 1892 built a high shed over the unimpeded sidewalk around the construction site of the Columbus Memorial Building at State and Washington Streets, the *Tribune* praised Fuller for considering the convenience and safety of the public (fig. 9). Furthermore, by hoisting heavy items through the skeleton of the structure and by storing equipment and materials inside the perimeter, the company exhibited a kind of entrepreneurial concern for public interest that had not been characteristic of the past but was becoming increasingly important. European observers were not usually aware of the subtle shifts taking place in the fight over public space between private capital and groups advocating greater safety and convenience for citizens.[19]

Firms that held franchises—the cable car companies in addition to those offering telephone, telegraph, electric, gas, centralized heat, and water services—also increased the danger and inconvenience to citizens in downtown streets by their irresponsible performance. They were required to get permission from the city council to dig up road surfaces in order to lay pipes, cables, and conduits or to build tunnels. The council usually granted permission because these companies rewarded aldermen for their support. Concentrating on their own objectives, franchises acted without much concern for coordinated planning, thus creating a condition William Dean Howells assailed in *A Traveler from Altruria*: "you see the sewers that rolled their loathsome tides under the streets, amidst a tangle of gas pipes, steam pipes, water pipes, telegraph wires, electric lighting wires, electric motor wires and grip-cables; all without a plan, but make-shifts, expedients, devices, to repair and evade the fundamental mistake of having any such cities at all."[20] Competition compounded the problem. In May 1888 there were three different telephone companies and two electric companies trying to get permission to excavate. Repairs and heavier demand meant old trenches often had to be reopened. Excavation work was so constant and the necessary replacement efforts so sloppy that franchises undermined the efforts of those trying to get the streets ready for the exposition. Less than a month before the opening of the fair, a telephone company holding rights in the central district received permission to dig in twenty-five places. On the eve of the exposition, Dearborn, La Salle, and Lake Streets, though paved, were not in good condition; a local reporter referred to the east side of Dearborn as a "corduroy road." Despite their obligation to leave road surfaces as they found them, companies that excavated in the streets sometimes failed to fill the cavities, as the *Tribune*'s sketch of State Street between Madison and Monroe in July 1892 indicated (fig. 10). Often franchises replaced granite blocks without the patience or skill with which they had been originally laid, causing depressions or mounds as the newly packed base settled.

Though astounded by the Loop's evidence of change and expansion during the boom years of the late 1880s and early 1890s, Europeans criticized Chicagoans for tolerating conditions they claimed would not have been tolerated in the major cities in Britain or on the Continent. Chicagoans responded to these attacks by acknowledging that their city's center must become a much cleaner, safer, and more attractive environment than it presently was. However, they were less disturbed about these problems than were their foreign guests. They had lived with some of them for decades. Furthermore, most citizens were convinced they could be corrected or significantly improved in time. During

Figure 10. Holes in State Street between Madison and Monroe Streets (*Chicago Tribune*, 29 July 1892).

the early 1890s, despite the exposition's brightening international spotlight, Chicago's leaders were not yet ready to take drastic action that might slow the momentum of heroic capitalism. For example, owners of commercial buildings remained unwilling to forgo soft coal, while hoping they could find less costly means to curtail the pollution for which they were partially responsible. Reform groups grew in number, diversity, and strength, pressuring the city council to pass stricter laws and codes, and entrepreneurs to become more sensitive to communal needs, but their efforts did not produce satisfying results in these years. Though the campaign to beautify the city before the exposition was not without some successes, its victories were random and often too temporary to affect fundamental causes.

Virtually every European who visited Chicago wondered why such a progressive city could not also be an attractive city. No traveler in these years described the Loop as beautiful or pleasant. Many called it the dirtiest, smokiest, and smelliest city center they had ever seen, their consistent conclusions transcending national and professional backgrounds. Nonprofessional observers tended to dwell longer on its failures, warning colleagues at home to resist Chicago's example at all cost. But even architects and engineers, though impressed by the efficiency of new office buildings, could not understand why authorities did not attack urban cleanliness with the same degree of purposefulness. Litter on the streets or smoke in the sky were natural themes for travelers to address for their discovery required no research. An understanding of causes was not necessary when one's senses immediately confirmed that Chicago's urban priorities were skewed. Though Chicago's bolt into the future encouraged some to question the slower development of their own cities, its unsanitary, messy ways were clearly unacceptable; the majority of visitors concluded that the New World still had much to learn from the Old.

The Example of Paris

Europeans who faulted Chicago did so with conviction because they had experienced and observed on the other side of the Atlantic cleaner, more attractive, and better-run city centers—urban cores that served and affirmed the citizens who used them. British travelers compared Chicago with familiar British cities, and French and German observers likewise used cities and towns in their own countries as norms when judging the quality of life in the Loop. Frequently, they cited their respective capitals—London, Paris, and Berlin—because many of them lived close to these cultural centers or were associated with publications or institutions located there. Though we could compare Chicago with a composite of contemporary cities in Britain, France, and Germany, this would be more contrived than looking briefly at the one city considered in these years to be the most livable in the Western world, the one that gave hope to metropolitan authorities in Europe and the United States. During the last half of the century Paris rose to a place of honor and admiration unchallenged by any contemporary municipality. Critics from other countries agreed that it was unrivaled for its unique blend of beauty, charm, culture, vitality, and order.

Unlike the Loop, where no one seemed to be in charge, the heart of Paris conveyed the impression of municipal control. Based on an imperial model, its centralized form of government was dominated by the prefect of police, who exercised wide-ranging authority over many aspects of communal life, including supervision of utility franchises. Occasionally a foreign observer, uneasy over unaccountable power, expressed concern about the potential for abuse in this office and the plethora of rules it issued, but such criticism was drowned out by the steady chorus of praise for the city's superb management. Crime was low. Vehicular accidents appalled authorities, who took strong action to minimize them. Street workers were required to reset loose paving stones immediately, to repair cracks in asphalt as soon as they appeared, and to surround open manholes with protective railings. Approximately 3,600 people swept the streets of Paris daily, and 5,000 garbage carts were used to remove the trash that had been collected. When this phase of the cleaning process was completed, all of the streets were then flushed and reswept. In addition to providing well-managed basic services, the municipal government of Paris was also sensitive to the importance of public comfort. It had spent huge sums of money to eliminate confusion, unpredictability, and unreasonable conditions. Pedestrians could wait for omnibuses at numerous heated, covered stations where they obtained tickets guaranteeing them a place on the vehicle. Streets served them with huge compressed-air clocks, kiosks, pissoirs, and hot-water towers. Parisian officials also acted as though one of their responsibilities was to delight people, because they took the time and spent the money to create objects and conditions appealing to the senses. There were more than seventy monumental fountains scattered throughout the city. The banks of the Seine became popular promenades. The steam-driven boats that ferried 15,064,000 passengers across the Seine in 1888 were forbidden to use piercing whistles. On either side of the wide, smooth boulevards were generous sidewalks planted with trees that

made the scale of the street seem more intimate. Ornament on the buildings of the boulevards proclaimed the importance of history and creativity, as well as visual pleasure.
Foreign tourists did not object to Victor Hugo's unconcealed and justified pride when
he stated that the "human race has a right to Paris."[21]

Paris was also reassuring because it advanced deliberately. City officials did not rush
into action, which might be wasteful or imprudent. Aware of the latest technology employed in other cities, they often persisted with traditional approaches while planning
methodically to incorporate new ones. Despite the installation elsewhere of electric street
lighting, Paris continued for several years with gas, using the interim to lay a network of
electric cables under the sidewalks. Resisting rapid transit in its central district much
longer than in some major cities, authorities eventually opened the electric-powered
Metropolitan underground in 1898. Wise planning and tough bargaining resulted in
strong municipal control over utility companies, which in turn produced good service
but had to pay heavily for the privilege.

In the late 1880s and early 1890s when Chicago seemed to visitors to change daily,
Paris had already proven by its extensive rebuilding program directed by Baron Georges
Eugène Haussmann that modern cities could accommodate change without necessarily
disparaging the past. Chicagoans acted as though their brief past interfered with their
participation in the present, or was not relevant to it, while Parisians behaved as though
the present was a continuing expression of history. Chicago left the impression its program was extemporaneous, vulnerable to the winds of progress, while Paris seemed to
be a city moving consciously forward, adjusting to the new but doing so with respect
for order and beauty.

Although the majority of visitors to Chicago did not remain long enough in the city
to conduct reliable research on the causes of its disordered state, thus accounting in part
for the descriptive rather than analytic nature of their assessments, they had opinions and
shared them with their readers. The void created by the absence of a plan for the city and
by the leadership's narrow interpretation of its civic responsibilities was filled, they believed,
by greed. Chicagoans put up with physical inadequacies, they reasoned, because the time
was ripe for "dollar hunting." There was a relationship between Chicago's demonstration
of progress and its poor housekeeping. Continued development was more important than
consolidation. Profits today, stability and aesthetics tomorrow, seemed to be the prevailing attitude. Observers were surprised at the lack of opposition to making the dollar sign
the prime symbol of the city's core district because they had always assumed municipali-
ties were culturally richer organisms that should express nobler aspirations or encourage
activity counterbalancing business. The city council did not appear to inhibit developers
or franchises, and individual aldermen accepted bribes when existing rules interfered with
the necessities of capitalism, convincing a number of observers that no one, indeed, was
in charge of this perplexing city. Furthermore, the work force seemed to accept the com-
mercialization of the Loop as inevitable, tolerating inconveniences for the convenience of
speculation. Few visitors looked beyond monetary gain for reasons to explain why Chicagoans put up with their disordered city. They tended to overlook, for example, the new work

opportunities and greater financial security gained by the thousands employed in expanding bureaus and stores. Nor did they explain that those who worked in the Loop might have been able to endure its unpleasant aspects because they could leave it for more pleasant neighborhoods at the end of the day.

Yet foreign critics were ultimately more concerned about the implications of Chicago's center for their own cities than they were about the welfare of its daily population. Would an age of "quick transformations," a phrase coined in 1892 by Paul de Rousiers, lead to unfinished and disordered cities in Europe? Few thought this was unavoidable. The majority believed their own cities could survive the threat of modern change if they could accommodate new ideas to old patterns through sound planning, steps they had not observed in Chicago.

The relentless editorials in the *Tribune* and the efforts of reform groups indicated that the citizens of Chicago probably agreed with Europeans who criticized the appearance and physical condition of their city, but these same citizens also would have been much less troubled because they viewed these faults, assumed to be temporary, as unavoidable costs of a decisive moment in modern history, one so exhilarating and important that its flaws, as proof of its reality, did not justify stopping the experiment. Given enough time, contended Elia W. Peattie, a Chicago native, even a detractor could discover in today's grime the promise of tomorrow.

> If he comes from some well-regulated, cultivated, and placid town of the eastern part of this country, or from England or Germany, he feels shaken out of poise and peace by a tremendous discord. He sees a city ankle-deep in dirt, swathed in smoke, wild with noise, and frantic with the stress of life. He sees confusion rampant, and the fret and fume of the town rise and brood above it like hideous Afrits.
>
> But as time goes on . . . he experiences a change of sentiment. He ceases to be shocked, and becomes interested. It occurs to him that if commerce is ever epic, it is so here. He feels the beat of the city like the vibration of mighty drums, and the thing he thought a discord he discovers to be the rhythm of great movements. The drab sky, the dirty streets, the dusky air, the dark-clothed figures of the people, are all in harmony, and it seems dramatically fitting that a city in the throes of its toil should wear its working clothes. It is grimy with its labor, and breathless and noisy forging its Balmung with mighty shouts.[22]

Condemning the Loop for its physical and environmental weaknesses was an easy and regular exercise for European critics. After all, who could object to the notion that contemporary cities in Europe and the United States should be livable urban centers or to the conclusion that Chicago's failures in this respect were obvious? Some foreign observers acknowledged the reasonableness of both of these conclusions and, at the same time, could understand the excitement and hope in Peattie's ultimate affirmation of her flawed but dynamic city. These were the critics for whom their encounter with Chicago was most valuable because it widened their perspective, enabling them to respect a past that provided a stabilizing rudder and a present that didn't allow time to look backward, to sense both the consequences of "discord" and the "rhythm of great movements."

Notes

1. George Warrington Steevens, a journalist for London's *Daily Mail,* called Chicago the "most squalid" place he had ever seen. Octave Uzanne claimed the city was already beyond the ability of the Latin mentality to cope with it. Ferdinand Wohltmann, a professor at the University of Breslau, was thankful there was no such city in Germany. George Warrington Steevens, *The Land of the Dollar* (New York: Dodd, Mead, 1898), 144; Octave Uzanne, *Vingt jours dans le nouveau monde* (Paris: May and Motteroz, 1893), 171; and Ferdinand Wohltmann, *Landwirtschaftliche Reisestudien über Chicago und Nord-Amerika* (Breslau: Schlett'sche Buchhandlung, 1894), 15.

2. "Building Outlook," *Inland Architect and News Record* 11 (June 1888): 80.

3. "Our Choked-Up River," *Chicago Tribune,* 18 June 1891, 4.

4. "Chicago's Deadly River," *Chicago Tribune,* 7 July 1889, 9.

5. Louis P. Cain, "The Creation of Chicago's Sanitary District and Construction of the Sanitary and Ship Canal," *Chicago History* 8 (Summer 1979): 98–110.

6. E. Fletcher Ingals, "Chicago's Sanitary Condition," *Forum* 15 (July 1893): 589.

7. Ernst von Hesse-Wartegg, *Chicago: Eine Weltstadt im amerikanischen Westen* (Stuttgart: Union Deutsche Verlagsgesellschaft, 1893), 19.

8. William Archer, *America To-Day* (New York: Charles Scribner's Sons, 1899), 106–8.

9. A painting by William Wylde in 1851 depicts Manchester as a town surrounded by stacks and covered with a dull yellow veil. A two-page color reproduction of this painting is included in Mark Girouard, *Cities and People* (New Haven: Yale University Press, 1985), 260–61.

10. "A City's Smoke and Soot," *Chicago Tribune,* 18 August 1888, 3.

11. "Dark as a Dungeon," *Chicago Tribune,* 1 December 1892, 3.

12. "Year's Smoke War," *Chicago Tribune,* 17 December 1892, 1.

13. Ingals, 592.

14. "Bricks and Mortar," *Builder's Journal* 4 (16 December 1896): 299.

15. Statement by Andrew Young in "They Merit Censure," *Chicago Tribune,* 16 March 1892, 12.

16. "Our Filthy Thoroughfares," *Chicago Tribune,* 21 March 1893, 4.

17. William T. Stead, *If Christ Came to Chicago!* (Chicago: Laird and Lee, 1894), 187.

18. Bessie Louise Pierce, *A History of Chicago,* vol. 3 (New York: Knopf, 1957), 313.

19. See the informative article by Perry Duis, "Whose City? Public and Private Places in Nineteenth-Century Chicago," *Chicago History* 12 (Spring, Summer 1983): 2–27 and 2–23.

20. William Dean Howells, *A Traveler from Altruria* (New York: Harper and Brothers, 1894), 283.

21. Quoted in Norma Evenson, "Paris, 1890–1940," in *Metropolis 1890–1940,* ed. Anthony Sutcliffe (Chicago: University of Chicago Press, 1984), 259.

22. Elia W. Peattie, "The Artistic Side of Chicago," *Atlantic Monthly,* December 1899, 828.

The Urban

3

Transformation
of Time
and Tempo

Domesticating Change through Humor

THE RATE OF CHANGE in Chicago made some observers uneasy. Difficult to believe, it was, nevertheless true; Chicago's exceptional growth in a short period of time was a fact that could be proven. But proving it was not reassuring; the city's continuing explosion exceeded the abilities of visitors to comprehend. At that juncture, several European observers called on satire and humor as their initial response to the problem—with more reasoned responses to follow.

In their confrontation with new expressions of changing realities, authorities since the 1850s have often resorted to humor as a means of dealing with them. The discomforted have utilized humor in a variety of ways; many of these were employed by Europeans writing about Chicago. Humor bridged the gap between what they believed to be reasonable and what they discovered in the Loop. Visitors used humor when they were unsure of themselves, turning the mocking of a subject into a form of control. Jokes also became the nervous laughter of those who caught unwanted visions of their own urban futures in the reality of Chicago. Humor was used as a psychological respite by inserting it as a humanizing touch in an account skeptical readers might dismiss as farfetched. It provided a shield that gave some protection from potentially hostile readers. If one could laugh about an amazing or threatening development, one could present that information without necessarily endorsing it or appearing to take it too seriously. Concluding that Chicago was itself a realistic tall tale that could not be pared down to accommodate European comprehension, some relied on Bunyanesque yarns to make their points. According to Leopold Gmelin, a professor of architecture at the Kunstgewerbeschule in Munich, St. Peter replied to God's question about an unannounced newcomer to heaven by explaining he was a chimney sweep working on a Chicago skyscraper.[1]

Critics even relied on humor to prove they were not joking. The fun poked by Europeans at Chicago was not very subtle. It relied on hyperbole, puns, and juxtapositions, but seldom on irony or complex constructions.

Visitors joked about the aspects of the city they considered most startling. Their inclination to be humorous increased when the distance between their expectations and the realities they found increased. The theme provoking the most humorous comments about Chicago was time, a category that included their reactions to the city's history, to the speed of its human and mechanical movements, and to the rapidity of its transformation. This was the same gap between presuppositions and reality that had prompted visitors twenty years earlier to dub Chicago the "lightning city."

Presuppositions affect the thrust and nature of humor. This can be demonstrated by comparing American jokes about Chicago with those published abroad. Individuals who had lived in Boston, New York, or even Cincinnati were not shocked by the speed of Chicago or its transient nature. All major cities in the United States were developing rapidly, their accomplishments of only yesterday made obsolete by larger and more impressive contemporary triumphs. Proud of economic and cultural achievements in their own communities, citizens of prospering cities in the East and Midwest became increasingly parochial as they tooted their municipal horns while minimizing or disparaging the accomplishments of rival cities. This competition was exacerbated by metropolitan newspapers more concerned with civic promotion and sales than with fairness or accuracy, a tendency acknowledged by the editor of Chicago's *Tribune*. "The remarkable and unvarying prosperity of Chicago creates a hostility in other communities which finds expression in constant misrepresentations calculated to impair the confidence of the country in the future of this city."[2] The flaws of Chicago satirized by other Americans, primarily in city dailies rather than in the more responsible popular journals, were its moral and cultural failures, such as the amount of alcohol its citizens consumed, its high divorce rate, or its citizens' reputed lack of intelligence. While Europeans were most startled by the city's expression of aspects of time, Americans ridiculed its politics, crime, and boondock ways.[3] Humor about the city published abroad was usually benevolent; humor published at home was not.

Panmure Gordon, an English traveler who called Chicago the city of "perpetual haste," claimed there were no old people there because they had not had time to grow old.[4] Exaggerations like this were often employed to make the point that Chicagoans seemed to be always in motion.[5] Constant motion was consistent with the metabolism of the city. According to a British tourist, Sara Jane Lippincott, Chicago "grows on Independence days and Sabbath days and all days. It grows o'night."[6] Europeans tended to cite two reasons for citizen restlessness. Chicagoans were depicted as doers, not thinkers. Furthermore, they were people who had no time to waste in their drive for monetary and material success. This was a city in which a moment of stillness became an uncanny event.[7]

Shocked by the swiftness of processes in the city, a few visitors implied that Chicago had altered in a qualitative way the nature of procedures. Europeans tended to think of a process as a phenomenon containing discrete sequences, each of which had to be resolved before the next one could begin. In Chicago, by contrast, steps seemed to be jammed together or overlaid, creating an impression of simultaneity rather than sequentiality. Referring to Hotel Lamont, one of the instantaneous hotels near the grounds of the Columbian Exposition, the British artist Frederick Villiers wrote, "It was gutted by fire whilst I was there. At the time the firemen were carrying charcoal out of the rear, the upholsterers were carrying in carpets at the front."[8] In Chicago, actions anticipating a useful future mingled with and pressured actions disposing of a no-longer pertinent past. Most foreign observers preferred order to pell-mell dispatch. The latter approach might save time, but it produced functional results only for the short run, not thorough or long-lasting artistic results.

The theme that Europeans joked about more than any other, particularly in the early 1890s, was the city's transient state. Marie T. Blanc, one of many to comment on this, created a dialogue in her book *The Condition of Woman in the United States:* "When were you in Chicago?" "Last week." "Oh, well! Then you know nothing about it. The city has been entirely changed since then."[9] Blanc and many others were fascinated by the persistent inclination of Chicagoans to act in the present even if it meant repudiating recent triumphs. Observers often remarked that judgments about Chicago based on evidence gathered yesterday were invalid, a point Friedrich Bodenstedt had made in 1882. Statistics about the city were obsolete before they could be published.[10]

Writers joked about two speeds of transience in Chicago, one for the city's sense of time, the other tied to temporal norms in Europe. To grasp the rate of Chicago's swiftness, visitors claimed they had to jack up their imaginations, but even when they cheated, they still missed the mark. There were a number of variations on the tale about the growth of the city putting liars out of business. Some of these may have been inspired by the *Tribune*'s yarn (12 July 1892) about the realtor who died knowing he had lied extravagantly to prospective clients about the potential returns on property, only to be cleared in heaven because his wild promises fell short of performance. Several writers suggested it might be wiser to think about Chicago in irresponsible rather than responsible ways. Speak loosely about it if you want to get closer to the truth, advised the German travel authority Ernst von Hesse-Wartegg, while Max O'Rell, a popular French writer, warned that what appears to be a joke today may become a reality there next week.[11] Human responses also required assistance to cope with the new scale of the Loop. Two people were needed to view its tall buildings, claimed an English visitor, the first to look halfway up and the second to complete the task.[12] Even stretched imaginations could not contain the new reality. The inability of fiction to keep up with fact was uncanny, leaving visitors, even some American visitors, with the feeling they had lost control. Writing in the *New York World*, Arthur Brisbane observed that Chicago could not be properly described because traditional language had been invented before the city was created.[13]

Humor revealed the uneasiness of Europeans trying to make sense of Chicago and explain it to audiences at home. Defined by European humor, at least, Chicago's modernism was a consequence of the city's contemporary understanding and uses of time.

"Time Is Money"

One of the principal ways the city expressed its concept of time was through the importance it attached to speed and efficiency in its daily operation. Foreign observers noted throughout the United States a quicker pace than they were accustomed to in their own countries. This was to be expected for a population viewed as young, adventurous, and confident. However, around 1890 Europeans increasingly attributed Yankee hurry primarily to the desire of citizens to take immediate advantage of the country's riches and opportunities to improve their lives and those of their families. Paul de Rousiers, author of the most systematic foreign analysis of the economic growth of the Midwest and West in the early 1890s, contended the American "works hard and ever tries his fortune; so that American life, in a measure, is all consecrated to business. *Business!* that is the word which the lips of the Yankee or the colonist pronounce the oftenest, and one reads such preoccupation on their faces. In meeting one another, the greeting is 'How's business?' It is the first subject they think of speaking about."[14] Unlike many cultivated individuals in Britain and on the Continent, Americans made no bones about their enthusiasm for business and its importance in their lives.[15]

Foreign observers often worried about its apparent centrality, particularly in Chicago, wondering if their relentless pursuit of wealth would not exhaust citizens, leaving them little time or inclination for enjoyment or self-improvement. The French architect Jacques Hermant, a delegate to the Columbian Exposition, was derisive on this point, categorizing the city as a place "where the respect of art is completely unknown, where the people (who are prevented by a narrow religious upbringing from showing their delight and openly enjoying their pleasures) think that laughing and getting angry is a waste of precious time, where everyone's sole goal in life is to earn a lot of money, and when they have earned a lot to use it to earn still more."[16] Regardless of their views about the acquisition of wealth, visitors by the early 1890s realized the close connection between making money and saving time. In developing better means to increase the volume of production per hour or per day, time was becoming commodified. By 1890 "time is money" was a phrase foreign writers sometimes used to account for the rapid movement, as if in cadence to an invisible metronome, of thousands on the streets of the Loop.

Some Europeans studied the actions of Chicagoans during the business day. They noticed behavior in public they were less likely to observe in London, Paris, or Berlin, for example, the conduct of business people at the noon meal. To visitors accustomed to a protracted period of midday dining and conversation in favorite European cafés, the hasty lunch in the Loop seemed nerve-racking and uncivilized. Notes on office doors reading, "Away for lunch; back in five minutes," meant profits took precedence over taste buds at this time of day. Since lunch breaks were too short and distances too great to permit a proper noon meal at home, clerks and bosses frequented restaurants promising fast service. Signs like "Quick Lunch" and "Chops in a Minute" attracted larger numbers than did advertisements promising a fine cuisine in a slow-paced setting. One visitor reported, "In the Opera Restaurant at Chicago—a place much frequented by merchants—I had the curiosity to time five or six gentlemen at their dinners, and found the average number of minutes taken by each to be three and three-quarters. All of them had two courses—one of them had three. There were no seats; the customers swarmed in front of a long metal counter like a public-house bar."[17] Eating rapidly in order to return to work was less difficult for Europeans to understand than their realization that these business people were not embarrassed to show their impatience in public.

Observers were also intrigued by the impact of "saving time" on business rituals. On the Continent and in Britain the pursuit of a contract was an art form, requiring time, patience, good manners, and nurtured trust. Before signing on the dotted line, the parties might meet over wine several times in order to become better acquainted. The noon hour, treated as a necessary but short interruption by most business people in Chicago, provided their counterparts abroad with opportunities for unhurried but purposeful conversation. The American deal usually lacked this kind of deliberate cultivation. Knowing the personality of the individual with whom one was dealing was less important in Chicago than securing the contract without further delay. In Europe, however, more so in France and Britain than in Germany, there was still hope that good manners not only could survive in the world of modern transactions but also could influence it positively in the process.

In their addresses to the *Société centrale des architectes français* on 10 May 1894, Adolphe Bocage, a Parisian architect who represented the society at the Columbian Exposition, and Jacques Hermant commented on the nature of the Chicago-style contract. Bocage described a typical encounter: "Now a visitor arrives; the boss greets him by pushing his hat back, and quickly, before the visitor has thought to take off his coat and sit down, a business deal is concluded. A handshake, 'All right,' are all that is needed for the contract. No trifling rules of politeness, nothing which is not strictly business." One businessman, according to Bocage, hung a sign behind his chair that said, "I have read all the newspapers this morning; I have a barometer and thermometer at home; let's talk business, and not waste time."[18] Hermant observed, "A yes is a yes, a no is a no, a word is a word, and often in three minutes, without any signature, a business deal is concluded, one which we would discuss for months."[19] Though both men may have exaggerated the rituals they had observed, no visitor ever claimed the Loop's business people were more patient or formal than those on the other side of the Atlantic. French and English observers admired the trust and confidence implied by the handshake, which temporarily supplanted a signed document, but most of them still considered this substitution too tentative and informal for their tastes. Businessmen in the modern world, they believed, were still better off executing contracts without depreciating the importance of the individuals involved or forgetting the long-term advantages of proper negotiation.

Streamlining Slaughter and Construction

Chicagoans, who moved smartly on the street, in the workplace, and even at lunch, extended the art of saving time beyond personal acts to innovative methods of production and faster technology. Their most celebrated demonstration of saving time occurred not in office buildings but at the Union Stock Yards. By 1890 the systematization and mechanization of the packing industry in Chicago was well known in Europe and ranked at the top of the "must-see" lists of foreign visitors to the city. The majority of those who mustered the courage to take the tour expressed two basic reactions. The first was unmitigated revulsion at the sights, sounds, and smells; the second, a cloud-parting realization that they had witnessed principles central to the extraordinary increase of American production. During 1892 the number of hogs slaughtered at the yards was 4,778,290, an average of more than 15,000 per day, assuming a six-day week. To process such quantities, the result of a "stupendousness" of conception, in the words of Paul Bourget,[20] the speed of the operation was crucial.

According to Paul de Rousiers, the process depended on several conscious decisions. Productivity subsumed art and previous practices. In order to handle the demand, the authorities at the yards had not worried about decorum. The scenes in the various slaughterhouse departments were aesthetically offensive but the process was quite efficient. Chicagoans were not ashamed of this systematic killing of animals; to the contrary, they bragged about the numbers of hogs dispatched, and the managers on the site were proud to show the stages of the process to visitors. Instead of complicated machinery, this system depended on relatively simple equipment that performed discrete tasks that were integrated with specific acts by workmen who seemed to be mechanically inspired. The pig was chained by the hind leg and lifted through a hole in the ceiling to a higher level where it was hooked on a continuous slanting rod. Moved by gravity or pushed by hand, the animal was stopped at specific stations where men repeatedly performed the same restricted action—stabbing the throat, dipping the carcass in boiling water, activating the scraper, removing the head, dissecting the prime parts—a system instructively illustrated in Albert Tissandier's *Six mois aux États-Unis* (figs. 11, 12, 13). Because this division of labor required repetition, each worker elevated his simple, quick act to the level of high art. These workers did not know much about a hog and could not dress it as would a European apprentice, but they also did not have to train long to perform a job that many of them would hold only until a better one was available. Their narrow skills were necessary in order to keep up with men at other stations who had already fulfilled their responsibilities and sent the hog on its way. The speed of the whole operation determined the minimum speed of each worker.

Chicago's builders depended on many of these same principles in erecting houses based on the balloon frame system, which in the United States had superseded heavy beam mortise-and-tenon joint construction. The new system relied on lighter joists and studs held together by nails (fig. 14). Historians believe it was introduced in Chicago in the first half of the 1830s.[21] The frame house, quickly and easily assembled, caught the attention of several European critics during the late 1880s and early 1890s. Julius Lessing, the director of the Kunstgewerbemuseum in Berlin, observed, "There is hardly anything more remarkable for us than to see an American house being built."[22] Some carts loaded with boards and sacks of nails arrive, and work is ready to commence, he ex-

Figure 11. Hanging hogs at the Union Stock Yards (Tissandier, *Six mois aux États-Unis*, 1886).

Figure 12. Boiling hogs at the Union Stock Yards (Tissandier, *Six mois aux États-Unis*, 1886).

Figure 13. Machinery for scraping the hide of hogs at the Union Stock Yards (Tissandier, *Six mois aux États-Unis*, 1886).

plained. The boards are sorted at the site, and the required pieces are cut to length without much concern for waste. With astounding skill and a supply of nails held in aprons or in their mouths, carpenters erect the basic frame of a house in a few hours. Boards of two, three, or four thicknesses nailed together serve as beams or as door and window jambs. After the inside and the outside of the frame have been covered with boards, the house is finished, he reported. Critics who, like Lessing, were attracted by the process of erecting a frame house, usually mentioned the lightness of the materials used and the flexibility of turning them into stronger supports. However, these features were not as significant to them as the quickness with which the framework could be completed. Lessing even exaggerated the speed of construction in order to impress upon German readers the importance Americans assigned to the time required for building.[23]

Rapid building could be advantageous, but it could also be interpreted as an unwise trend in American architecture. Balloon framing disregarded traditional lap-joints and groove-and-tongue joints, as well as mortise-and-tenon work with heavier timbers. For those who believed the quality of a product was related to the time required to produce it, nailing light boards together in a moment was a shortcut encouraging merely expedient architecture. Furthermore, this system seemed suspect because builders did not need a long apprenticeship in order to nail joists to studs. Houses built quickly without a conspicuous sense of craft and solidity also raised fears among Europeans that wooden houses in the United States were too insubstantial to last long. Some observers, mistakenly assuming these structures were meant to last only for the lifetime of the family commissioning them, interpreted the preference for wood and quick construction as another example of American planned obsolescence.

Though impressive as models of rapid construction, these houses did not fulfill European expectations about tradition, craftsmanship, and durability. A few visitors

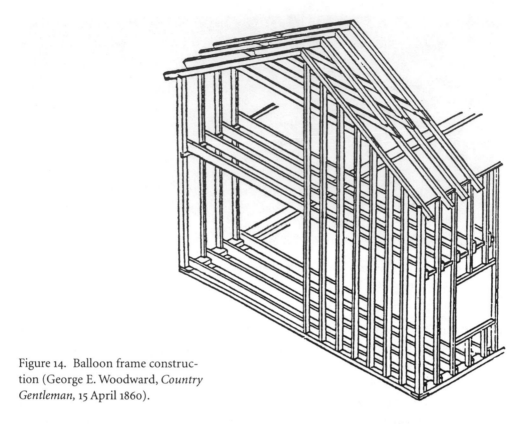

Figure 14. Balloon frame construction (George E. Woodward, *Country
Gentleman,* 15 April 1860).

predicted the Americans would set aside their expedient ways when the nation was more
settled; others realized how entrenched the new system of framing had become. Karl
Hinckeldeyn, who was probably the most respected German authority on American
architecture during the 1880s, explained that builders who emigrated from Europe had
little impact. They had tried to introduce properly joined roof trusses but native contractors rejected such troublesome innovations because they exceeded commercially
required joint strengths and took too much time.[24] Architectural professionals abroad
acknowledged that American methods of framing expressed priorities most of them did
not share. Instead of thoroughness, complexity, artisanship, and protracted effort, balloon framing, like the approach of the meat packers, was an adequate, simple system that
could be executed quickly by abundant, cheap, unskilled labor. At the stockyard and in
balloon framing, Chicagoans valued speed and developed the technical, material, and
methodological means to increase production. Though dissimilar operations, hog packing and wood framing produced greater volume in shorter periods of time.

Critics discovered in Chicago numerous operations based on principles similar to
those used in meat packing and balloon framing, for example, the transfer of grain from
ships in the river to elevators along its banks or the building of roads for the exposition.
"In Chicago they re-make roads by the mile at a time. On the swamp which has marked
the bed of the road, a succession of hurrying wagons shoot tons of stone chippings which

are leveled by an army of laborers, just in time for the load of circular cedar blocks, which are couped, placed, packed, and spread with pitch and gravel, and the road opened for traffic in an incredibly short space of time."[25] These systems, which aimed at a maximum volume of production through faster processes, tended to substitute larger numbers of unskilled workers, discrete but simple steps performed rapidly, and lighter equipment and materials for traditional hand work, unified operations, and complicated machinery. In the 1830s Tocqueville, aware of these tendencies, explained that financial success in the United States depended on the discovery of some better, shorter, and more ingenious method of production plus a larger output of goods of slightly lower quality. In the early 1890s foreign visitors and Chicagoans often viewed this approach from different perspectives; the Europeans expressed concern about the possible decline of quality, while the local citizens bragged about the increase in volume. These reactions reflected differing presuppositions, the first assuming that private values could still influence the world of business, and the other accepting the mechanization of public life.

Systematizing Procedures

In studying American architecture in the last decades of the nineteenth century, foreign critics discovered that firms accelerated production, not only through innovative construction procedures but also through their priorities and organization. For more than two decades before the Columbian Exposition, professionals abroad had lectured American designers on the inadvisability of haste in the creative process. From their standpoint, impatient architects, too sure of their abilities, mistakenly interpreted the quantity of their work as a sign of their brilliance.[26] Throughout the 1880s *The Architect* and the *British Architect* in London continued to advise designers in the United States to stop looking for shortcuts to fine art, in part because their sins were already washing up on European shores, threatening to undermine time-tested procedures.[27] Not all critics objected to American shortcuts, but those who did usually opposed them on grounds that saving time ultimately cheapened the process and the product. In the early 1890s some foreign observers disapproved of architects who began construction on commercial buildings before all the drawings were finished or who took photographs of completed projects instead of taking the time to produce a proper artistic record of them.[28]

The organization of the modern architectural office in the United States was viewed abroad as an outgrowth of the emphasis on increased production and efficiency. Larger firms around 1890 adopted the departmental layout, dividing and subdividing space according to their staffing and production systems. Commenting on an office he had seen in New York, H. W. Lockwood, a British architect, told the members of the Sheffield Society of Architects and Surveyors in northeastern England that such spatial organization facilitated the "speed demanded from everybody in the States," but to the detriment of artistic quality.[29] Much attention was paid on both sides of the Atlantic to the new offices of the large firm of Burnham and Root in the Rookery Building in Chicago. A description, sometimes illustrated, appeared first in the *Inland Architect* and then in the

Engineering and Building Record and the *American Architect* in January 1890, followed a few months later by articles in *La semaine des constructeurs* and *Le moniteur des architectes* in Paris.[30] Instead of a large universal room, Burnham and Root's layout was compartmentalized—separate spaces set aside not only for the principals and key personnel such as chief engineer, superintendent, librarian, and bookkeeper, but also for draftsmen who worked together although in a number of semi-enclosed bays (fig. 15). Additional rooms served the basic needs of the staff, from a vault to safeguard drawings to a gymnasium to keep employees fit and alert. This approach to the organization of an architectural office impressed professionals abroad because it was determined by the needs of both personnel and process. After the firm's needs had been analyzed and separated into distinct though related functions, these functions were then expressed spatially in an integrated, efficient plan. Personnel who often interacted with each other were located in adjacent or nearby spaces. Reminiscent of workers at the slaughterhouse, each person was assigned a station ideally located to facilitate his or her particular contribution.

The layout confirmed a new reality: contemporary designing on a large scale was no longer treated as an individual art but as a collective process. Pressured by an abundance of commissions, some from clients who wanted their projects completed in the shortest possible time, the firm of Burnham and Root apparently looked for changes that would speed up or make more efficient aspects of its operation. Its chief engineer introduced an early form of photocopying, an enormous hectographic device capable of re-

Figure 15. Drafting room of the firm of Burnham and Root, Chicago (*Inland Architect,* September 1888).

producing multiple copies of drawings. With the use of aniline pigments, he was able to duplicate as many copies as needed in colors close to the original. This process saved time and money and increased accuracy by eliminating error-prone "tracing boys." Though architects abroad praised the concern of principals about office efficiency, some wondered if such changes might alter "architecture" as they knew it. Jacques Hermant worried that the profession in Chicago had been smitten by the priorities of business, reducing artists "to mere artisans, who sell their merchandise, who set up offices of forty or more draftsmen, and, whenever Lake Michigan becomes too inclement, can set off to breathe the warm air of the Mexican Gulf, while their 'plan-factory' brings them in their millions" of francs.[31] Foreign architects, respectful of the response of Chicago's firms to the requirements of business, nevertheless hoped they could update the grand tradition without becoming servants of speculation.

The main reason Chicagoans did not share their guests' concern is that they did not think anything had gone wrong. To the contrary, they thought of themselves as heroes and heroines who, more than New Yorkers and far more than the British, French, or Germans, really understood the nature of modern times. They believed they had not abused old means but created new ones, means that were indigenous rather than alien to the late decades of the century. They had devised an art of speed that could produce useful products for the benefit of many. Conscious of what they were doing, those who shaped Chicago were ever ready to read global significance into their acts. Referring to the completion of four exterior floors of Burnham and Root's Ashland Block in thirteen days, the *Tribune,* under the heading "Knows no Parallel," declared it a milestone in the history of rapid constructive skill, a peg "on which would hang a vaster deal of comment and sober speculation by the greatest builders of the world than any similar event ever known."[32] Future generations, the editors predicted, would treat it as "a daring piece of fiction" in an age of exaggerations.

Chicagoans did not apologize for their quicker processes; they were proud of them and wanted to share them with the unconverted. When the manager of a boot factory in the city learned C. B. Berry was an English tourist, he offered to measure his feet on the spot and present him with a new pair of shoes in seventeen minutes.[33] Foreign travelers who went to Chicago remarked how frequently they were encouraged to observe its versions of speed, as if this were one of the qualities by which the city should be remembered or judged. They were told repeatedly how many pigs could be killed in a minute at the stockyard, how quickly the express elevators of the Masonic Temple reached the top floor, how fast the cable cars could move once out of the crowded downtown streets.

The naive pride of individual citizens could be excused, but not the flagrant boosterism of municipal authorities who viewed the saving of time as a local discovery worthy of ad-agency promotion. City officials eager to show their respect for time and their ability to devise means for economizing it often subjected visiting dignitaries to demonstrations of the city's alarm systems, which could be activated from call boxes located on the sidewalks of downtown and suburban streets. In the early 1890s there were approximately two thousand fire alarm boxes in Chicago. When the handle of one was pulled, it set off an alarm at that box, notifying policemen in the neighborhood, as well as a dispatcher in the nearest firehouse. Timing a response at one of the firehouses, Ernst von Hesse-Wartegg claimed it took three minutes for sleeping men to awaken and depart the premises on horse-pulled fire engines, hose wagons, and ladder trucks.[34] The fire department, consisting of more than one thousand firemen and five hundred horses, responded to an average of twelve calls a day in 1891. When a policeman heard a street alarm go off, he rushed to the nearest patrol box. He would open the box and turn the pointer to a specific word on a dial—"Accident," "Fire," "Thief," "Murder"—and then would push the button. This alerted the officer on duty at the police station nearest to the box, who determined the size of the squad a particular call merited. Prepared to go into action at any time, the patrol system in 1890 numbered thirty-five horse-drawn wagons, each manned by two to eight officers. Patrol boxes also contained telephones permitting two-way communication between the street and the district station.

Claiming these systems originated in Chicago, city officials, especially Carter H. Harrison, who was elected mayor consecutively for two-year terms between 1879 and 1887 and again in 1893, loved to show visiting dignitaries how well they worked. Halting an official tour temporarily, Harrison would ask an honored guest to activate one of the alarm boxes and then urge the VIP to note how much time elapsed before the requested wagon arrived. In October 1890 then-mayor De Witt C. Cregier put on a similar display of prompt response for a large delegation of British and German iron and steel experts then touring the United States.[35] These demonstrations are revealing. Harrison and Cregier had selected speed and efficiency as a highlight of a brief official tour for important international guests. If either mayor had visited London or Paris, would his hosts have chosen demonstrations of accelerated processes as a distinguishing feature of their cities?

Profits and the Speed of Construction

About 1890 European technical and architectural journals noted the speed with which the multistory office buildings of the Loop could be erected or improved. Before this date, foreign observers had regarded height as the distinctive innovation of this new architecture, but increasingly they underscored the importance of rapid construction. In the last half of the 1880s, there was not enough office space in the Loop to handle the rising speculative demand.[36] Unwilling to expand a commercial district roughly five-eighths of a square mile, the business community and the city council accepted the logic of increasing the number of floors per building. The value of central property soared. According to one estimate each of the 155 acres of land within the Loop in 1893 was worth $2,600,000 even before the value of its architecture was calculated; or, to demonstrate the increase another way, the same land was 1,200 percent more valuable than it had been at the time of the 1871 fire.[37] During May of 1892 seven major office buildings opened in the Loop—the Woman's Temple, Masonic Temple, Unity, Ashland, Title and Trust, Venetian, and the Monadnock Block, in addition to the fourteen-story Great Northern Hotel. Chicago's continued boom seemed assured. In his official report for 1892, J. Hayes Sadler, British consul in the city, identified the United States and Chicago as the most prosperous country and city in the world.[38]

To reflect the boom, each property in this district was reevaluated as if it held a sixteen-story building. Since few of the properties actually contained sixteen-story structures, the yield on land supporting older and smaller buildings dropped drastically. Owners faced limited choices: to improve existing buildings or to tear down less-profitable structures and erect modern, taller ones.[39] Removing a property from the market at this moment meant losses, but the current high rents and a seemingly insatiable demand for space in the Loop promised future gains that could more than compensate. Whether investors decided to remodel or to start from scratch, speed was imperative. There were several options for those who decided to improve their "old vaults." They could leave the exterior of the building basically unchanged but redecorate the offices and modernize the interior by installing the latest electrical fixtures and faster elevators. They could also increase the height of an existing structure. In 1889 two floors were added to the Real Estate Board Building at the corner of Dearborn and Randolph Streets. Below a new galvanized-iron skylight, contractors created a spacious central light shaft which illuminated all of the stairs and corridors from which the offices opened. Some opted for more drastic reconstructions that resulted in virtually new buildings. Instead of removing the five-story Chamber of Commerce Building at the southeast corner of La Salle and Washington Streets in order to put up a block of thirteen floors, its owners decided to lift the old structure (90 by 180 feet) on jacks, dig up the original foundations, and replace them with new ones. The interior walls and the roof of the old building were removed and the metal cage rose through the old shell. Iron columns were placed behind the original exterior piers of stone and the piers were recut to express cleaner lines and permit larger windows. Only the stonework at the entrances reminded pedestrians of the former building (fig. 16).

These "repairs," especially the more conservative transformations, often turned out to be costly because improved office space did not necessarily satisfy the desire of firms for addresses in one of the latest tall buildings. In the strong market of the first two years of the nineties, a number of owners and leasees decided to remove old buildings entirely. Replacing them with new ones was a more effective way of capitalizing on soaring rents. The new Ashland Block by Burnham and Root supplanted an office building of the same name, built after the fire at a cost of $200,000, that was fully occupied at the time of its demolition. Another example was the Hawley Building at the corner of Madison and Dearborn, considered one of the finest office buildings of the city when completed in 1872. But tastes also had changed, and the black walnut finish of its first two floors had been painted yellow to brighten its appearance. Despite continuing to function at full capacity, the Hawley was ordered demolished in May 1892 to make way for the fourteen-story Hartford Building, which contained more offices at considerably higher rents. Europeans quipped about Chicago as the only city in the world where solid, attractive office buildings of relatively recent vintage, some taller and better equipped than comparable structures in European capitals, could be considered "old." But to Loop investors, destroying functional architecture could be profitable. Their margin of gain

Figure 16. Chamber of Commerce Building, Chicago, 1888–89, Baumann and Huehl (*Industrial Chicago*, 1891).

was directly affected by the length of time it required architects and contractors to complete replacement buildings.

The contemporary skyscraper framed by a skeleton of steel became the most visible and popular proof abroad for those who believed that in Chicago time had indeed become money. The misconception in Europe that these huge buildings would require many years to complete faded during the early 1890s when foreign critics discovered the crucial role of the skeleton system in this architecture and also the reasons why entrepreneurs encouraged its use. International publicity about the record time for finishing the exterior walls of four floors of the Ashland Block was a major factor in informing architects abroad about the temporal advantages of this kind of construction. On January 17, 1892, the *Chicago Tribune* published two illustrations of work in progress on the Ashland Block, one from a photograph taken on 5 December 1891 and the other from a photograph taken on 18 December 1891 (figs. 17, 18). During this thirteen-day period, the outer walls of four floors were attached to the steel frame by bricklayers and terra-cotta setters. Daily, pedestrians lined the sidewalks below to watch the steam-driven cranes

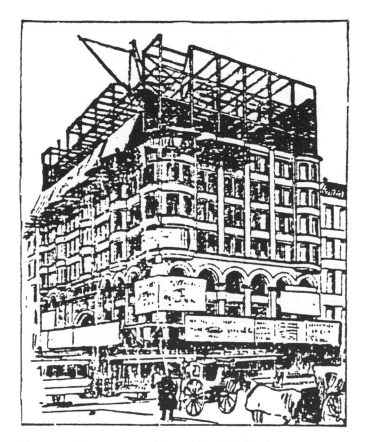

Figure 17. Construction of the Ashland Block, Chicago, 1891–92, Burnham and Root, based on a photograph taken 5 December 1891 (*Chicago Tribune*, 17 January 1892).

Figure 18. Construction of the Ashland Block, Chicago,
1891–92, Burnham and Root, based on a photograph taken
18 December 1891 (*Chicago Tribune,* 17 January 1892).

hoisting the steel girders and dropping them gently into place or workmen installing
terra-cotta slabs with the ease of children playing with blocks.

The British consul in Chicago, J. Hayes Sadler, may have been one of these sidewalk
spectators, for he included the information from the *Tribune* in one of his reports to
London in 1892.[40] He explained that four exterior levels of the building, measuring 140
feet by 80 feet at base, had been completed at a rate of one floor every 3¼ days. This news
reached architectural circles in Europe through various channels. The *American Architect,* a journal that normally arrived in London, Paris, and Berlin about six weeks after
publication in the United States and was read by journal editors in those cities, paraphrased Sadler in its 10 September 1892 issue. Wider circles of the profession in Germany heard about the feat through the *Centralblatt der Bauverwaltung,* which had learned
about Sadler's report from a summary published in the *Architect* of London.[41] The
Zeitschrift des oesterreichischen Ingenieur- und Architekten-Vereines in Vienna referred to
Sadler's information on 6 October 1893. A French visitor, Georges Sauvin, mentioned the
feat in his *Autour de Chicago,* also published in 1893.[42] In the official German government
report on the Colombian Exposition, Franz Jaffe, a delegate to the fair, explained that

the entire exterior of the Ashland Block had been completed in approximately two months.[43] By the end of 1892 the phrase "Chicago construction" was not unknown abroad. In the year prior to the exposition, foreign critics began to emphasize the "unbelievable rapidity" of this new process and the "incredibly short time" in which a steel-framed building's exterior could be finished. During the exposition, May through October of 1893, visiting professionals and lay people could watch a number of projects in progress, the best-timed probably the New York Life Insurance Building, on which excavation began on July 14, the foundations started August 3, and the steel frame completed September 29 (fig. 19). Gustav Benfey, who discussed the Fisher Building by Burnham and Company in late 1895 for the *Baugewerks-Zeitung,* verified the speed of its construction through dated illustrations (fig. 20).[44]

Although the skeleton system was considered the primary reason why the contractors and architects could complete structures of twelve to sixteen stories within a two-year period, a fraction of the time that would have been required for buildings of similar cubic footage in Europe, it was not the only time-saving step European visitors discovered. In his influential report, Sadler also stressed the size of the work force on the Ashland Block, which consisted during the day of approximately sixty iron and steel workers, one hundred brick masons, and thirty-five terra-cotta setters. The *Tribune* had reported that the masons, supported by an army of hod carriers, worked so near to each other it was necessary for all of them to stand. In order to complete the building as soon as possible, contractors on the Ashland Block also hired approximately fifty men to work during the night. To induce nonskilled laborers to work odd shifts and on holidays, they increased the normal pay of 22 cents an hour to 33 cents at night and 44 cents on holidays. The smaller night crew, covering the hollow-tile flooring with concrete, bricking in the steel and wrought-iron frame, or setting the terra-cotta slabs, worked with the aid of electric lights and gasoline lamps scattered through the skeleton. In winter, laborers were protected from Chicago's cutting winds by means of a heavy canvas stretched from the base of the floor being walled to the skeleton girders of the floor above, and by salamander stoves that also helped to dry the salted mortar. (Night laborers as well as workers protected by canvas windbreaks are shown in figure 21.) The authors of *Industrial Chicago* reported in 1891 that there was "now little difference between summer and winter, or day and night, work."[45]

Time was also saved by not waiting for one process to stop before starting another. "They do not wait, as we do, for the mortar to set in the lower walls in order to continue building them," reported Adolphe Bocage.[46] Furthermore, new commercial buildings continued to sink into Chicago's soft subsoil for months after their opening. There were hundreds of time-saving steps, some major, some not, some that seemed penny wise and pound foolish yet were ostensibly efficient and within the limits of safety. When builders and designers in Chicago decided to get on with their big buildings, there was little they thought a European professional could teach them.

Despite angry charges that haste cheapened architecture, there were professionals in Britain, France, and Germany who commended the architects of Chicago for their procedures, not because they wanted to emulate these steps but because they considered them

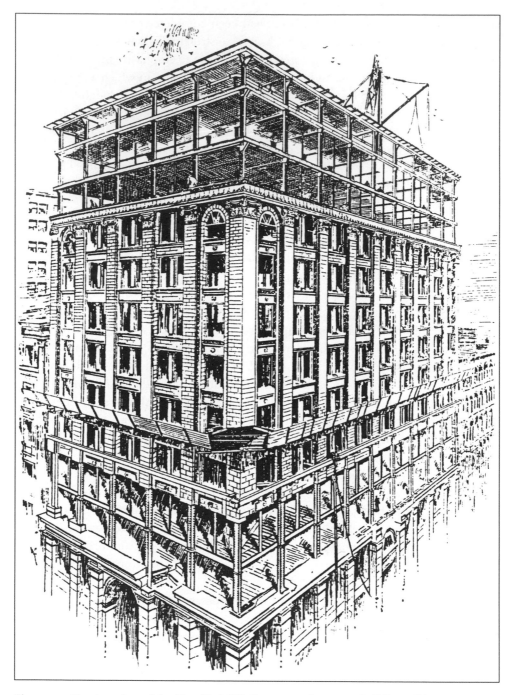

Figure 19. Construction of the New York Life Insurance Company Building, Chicago, 1893–94, Jenney and Mundie (*American Architect*, 10 February 1894).

arbeitet wurde, aus Deutschland stammt, da unpartheiische Unterfuchungen nachwiefen, daß der deutsche Zement der zuverläßigfte aller derartigen Fabrikate ist. In dem beigefügten Grundriß zeigt die äußere doppelte Linie das um das Haus gehende Trottoir an, das hier in Amerika den Eigenthümern des betreffenden anliegenden Haufes gehört, deshalb meistens unterbaut und zu Kellerräumen verwendet wird. Die Kreuze geben die Stellen der Säulenfüße (Fig. 4) über dem Konkret an, die elliptifche Linie am oberen Theil des Grundplans bezeichnet das Fundament des Schornfteins. — Nachdem fich der Beton in den Käften gründlich gefetzt, wurden Stahlträger, 30 cm hoch, eng zufammen daraufgelegt und wieder mit Beton ausgefüttert, der ebenfo gemifcht wurde, wie vorher befchrieben, nur daß die Steine ftatt 4 cm nur 1 cm groß waren. Quer über diefe Lage wurden wieder 50 cm hohe Stahlfchienen 5 m lang gelegt, die mit kräftigen Verfteifungen verfehen waren. Ungefähr 100 t Stahl find für die Platten und Träger, auf denen die Säulenfüße ruhen, verwendet. Damit war die eigentliche Fundirungsarbeit, die nach ihrem Entftehungsort, als

Sig. 6. Aufnahme vom 12. November 1895. Der höchfte Punkt erreicht!

Sig. 7. Aufnahme am 12. Dezember 1895.

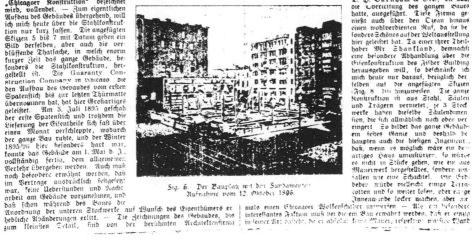

Sig. 5. Der Bauplatz mit den Südamerice. Aufnahme vom 12. Oktober 1895.

„Chicagoer Konftruktion" bezeichnet wird, vollendet. — Zum eigentlichen Aufbau des Gebäudes übergehend, will ich mich heute über die Stahlkonftruktion nur kurz faffen. Die angefügten Skizzen 5 bis 7 mit Datum geben ein Bild derfelben, aber auch die verblüffende Thatfache, in welch enorm kurzer Zeit das ganze Gebäude, befonders die Stahlkonftruktion, hergeftellt ift. Die Guaranty Construction Company in Chicago, die den Aufbau des Gebäudes vom erften Spatenftich bis zur letzten Thürmatte übernommen hat, hat hier Großartiges geleiftet. Am 3. Juli 1895 gefchah der erfte Spatenftich und trotzdem die Lieferung der Eifentheile fich faft über einen Monat verfchleppte, wodurch der ganze Bau ruhte, und der Winter 1895/96 hier befonders hart war, konnte das Gebäude am 1. Mai d. J. vollftändig fertig, dem allgemeinen Verkehr übergeben werden. Auch muß noch befonders erwähnt werden, daß im Vertrage ausdrücklich feftgefetzt war, keine Ueberftunden und Nacht arbeit am Gebäude vorzunehmen, und daß fchon während des Baues die Anordnung der unteren Stockwerke auf Wunfch des Eigenthümers erhebliche Abänderungen erlitt. — Die Zeichnungen des Gebäudes, bis zum kleinften Detail, find von der berühmten Architektenfirma

D. H. Burnham & Cie., die auch die Oberleitung des ganzen Baues hatte, ausgeführt. Diefe Firma genießt auch über den Ozean hinaus einen wohlverdienten Ruf, da fie befonders Schönes auf der Weltausftellung hier geleiftet hat. Da einer ihrer Theilhaber Mr. Shankland, demnächft eine befondere Abhandlung über die Eifenkonftruktion des Fifher Building herausgeben will, fo befchränke ich mich heute nur darauf, bezüglich derfelben auf die angefügten Skizzen (Fig. 8 bis 10) hinzuweifen. Die ganze Konftruktion ift aus Stahl, Säulen und Trägern vernietet, je 3 Stockwerke haben diefelbe Säulendimenfion, die fich allmählich nach oben verringert. So bildet das ganze Gebäude ein feftes Ganze und deshalb behaupten auch die hiefigen Ingenieure, daß, wenn es möglich wäre ein derartiges Haus umzuftürzen, fo würde es nicht in Stücke gehen, wie ein aus Mauerwerk hergeftelltes, fondern unfallen wie eine Schachtel. Ein Erdbeben würde vielleicht einige Terracotten und fo weiter lofen, oder einige Innenwände locker machen, aber nie male einen Chicagoer Wolkenkratzer umwerfen. — Als ein befonders intereffantes Faktum muß bei diefem Bau erwähnt werden, daß er einzig in feiner Art dafteht, da er abfolut keine Mauer, refpektive mafsive Wand

ON THE EIGHTH FLOOR

AN EIGHT-STORY BALCONY

Figure 21. Working at night on the Ashland Block, Chicago, 1891–92, Burnham and Root (*Chicago Tribune*, 6 December 1891).

creative responses to conditions over which firms in the city had little, if any, control. However, this did not mean that European architects suddenly advocated quicker building procedures at home. Most professionals in Britain, at least, did not call for faster methods in the early 1890s, and many remained skeptical of them for the remainder of the decade. Speeding up a job was not a new concept to British architects.[47] However, they were less willing to sacrifice or threaten priorities that seemed more important, priorities rooted in their definition of architecture. They were less prepared to relinquish their control over design, to restrain their skills of expression to satisfy unimaginative budgets of entrepreneurs, to forgo their right to hide prosaic internal content behind street facades ennobled by historic ornament, to make a fetish of function, to welcome technology and respect its impact on design, to design repetitiously for the sake of Mammon, to cheapen old methods of construction by fads that robbed structure of dignity and strength, to work by the clock rather than by the ideal. They were more inclined to view themselves as artists, rather than as processors of somebody else's common agenda. Viewed in isolation, Chicago's acts of quickness were impressive, often astounding, some even useful and worthy of extended European reflection, but they came with a price in the early 1890s that many visitors, lay tourists as well as architects, thought was too high to pay.

Speed and Accidents

Most European observers of the Loop realized business could be conducted efficiently within its circumscribed space because transportation to the suburbs or to other cities was located a brief walk from most office buildings, and that numerous railroad stations, which surrounded this district, enabled business people from out of town to contact clients shortly after their arrival. According to Paul de Rousiers, the ideal office could never be located close enough to the center of this bustling arena in which attitudes and technology had simplified and quickened transactions. To illustrate this point, he quoted a businessman who claimed the number of firms within a building and the concentration of many commercial buildings in a small area enabled him to attend to numerous deals per hour, and, if a lawyer were needed, to get legal help without going outside. The whole system, argued Rousiers, depended on these "blessed business buildings."[48] The logical extension of this reasoning was the creation of an enormous complex, housing all of the companies scrambling for an address in central Chicago. The Loop came close to this futuristic concept.

Though ingeniously planned to facilitate transactions, almost every foreign critic judged the Loop to be a flawed city center. Despite its efficiency, most visitors shook their heads, convinced by experience that contemporary city centers should be more than zones catering to money changers. Great cities, they believed, should also memorialize the past, provide for recreation, leisure, and even residence, speak to the eye through art, and nourish the mind and spirit through institutions of culture. Their experience in the Loop provoked many, the French in particular, to express appreciation for their own cities. With the exception of the Gare Saint-Lazare, explained Rousiers, the major railroad terminals of Paris had been built away from the center. "We will not permit a sacrifice of elegance to quicken communication, because Paris, above all, is an elegant city. Chicago has no such pretensions."[49] It didn't matter to Chicagoans if huge stations spoiled the beauty of their city, he continued, because "the risk of losing a little time in it" was the more important issue. In any case, he added, the quality of Chicago's center meant little to the powerful who, at the end of the day, could escape to their residential sanctuaries in the suburbs.

Europeans concluded that the demands for faster procedures and services had made the Loop a more dangerous area. They cited a number of reasons for this intolerable development. First, they believed capitalism's pressure for newer, bigger buildings would increase injuries in the Loop. Though they had difficulty finding published statistics about accidents in the building industry, they assumed a close connection between haste and construction deaths. They reasoned that accidents were inevitable when laborers worked twenty-four hours a day in summer and winter to complete in two years structures much higher than the tallest office buildings in Berlin or Paris. Furthermore, the sight of workers balancing on a thin skeleton of steel reinforced this conclusion (fig. 22). The foreign press abroad often played up news of construction disasters in the city, in part to justify its opposition to high buildings. Visitors also cited the danger of loose ends, Chicago's failures to finish projects before beginning new ones. Reporting on the Columbian Exposition for the *Zeitschrift des oesterreichischen Ingenieur- und Architekten-Vereines,* Otto H. Mueller claimed he faced "life-threatening or terrifying situations almost every day," for example, when he took shelter from the rain in an unmarked opening, not realizing he was standing at the base of an elevator shaft.[50]

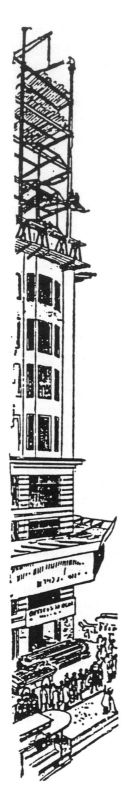

Figure 22. Dangers faced by workers on the skeleton of the Hartford Building, Chicago, 1892–93, Henry Ives Cobb (*Chicago Tribune*, 27 November 1892).

Secondly, they pointed to the pace and size of sidewalk crowds caused by so many large public buildings, office blocks, retail stores, and wholesale companies in a constricted space. Battalions of pedestrians served and visited these cheek-by-jowl buildings. Impatient office workers, delivery men, clerks, secretaries, and shoppers at crossings increased the possibilities of mishaps.[51] Ernst von Hesse-Wartegg described one experience he had while walking on a crowded sidewalk within a block of the Chicago River. Suddenly people around him began to run as if ordered to attack. He ran, knowing he might be trampled if he didn't. When he heard a shrill noise, he finally realized a ship was approaching, and the swing bridge would be turning shortly. Everyone was running. Then the pavement under his feet broke in two. He saw the surface of the dirty water below at the same time an iron grating behind him cut him off from the rest of the crowd. His immediate neighbors jumped, one falling into the water, shortly to be rescued by a nearby boat. He jumped, clinging to the end of the bridge as it swung into the middle of the stream.[52]

Most of the daytime population of the business district rode grip- or horse cars whose lines passed through the heart of the city. Cable cars were faster than horse-drawn vehicles, attaining speeds of five to six miles an hour in congested areas and up to twelve in the suburbs.[53] Human error and mechanical failure were the principal causes of their collisions. Accidents often occurred when one or both vehicles were turning a corner or when a delivery man attempted to cross the tracks before the grip car passed. Drivers could not always count on the ability of their teams to pull loads quickly enough on surfaces torn up by excavation or made slippery from rain or snow. Another type of crash was caused by the malfunction of the clamping or braking mechanism (fig. 23). When the brakes failed on a car going through the La Salle Street Tunnel on 1 May 1888, it smashed into a laundry wagon sandwiched between it and a stationary cable car ahead (fig. 24). Reformers cited these frequent accidents and breakdowns as further evidence of the abuse of franchises by business people more concerned about profits than reliable, safe service.[54] Prefiguring twentieth-century street congestion, the Loop was probably the world's most dangerous urban zone in the early 1890s, its challenges to walker and driver caught in a painting by Childe Hassam (fig. 25) depicting the activity at the corner of State and Madison Streets. Human, animal, and mechanical speeds competed with impatience for open space in its restricted area.

Chicagoans discovered early one of the disadvantages of modern technological systems: breakdowns could lead to traffic tie-ups of unmitigated proportions. Hypothetically, if three coal wagons spilled their contents on the tracks at three crucial intersections (La Salle opposite the mouth of the tunnel, State and Madison, and Wabash and Madison), service on almost all the cable and horse lines in the central district would be disrupted. If a private cab lost a wheel, however, it could be removed from the street, or if a horse-car was disabled, it too could be withdrawn from the tracks. But one grip car unable to disengage from its system could cause extensive damage by plowing ahead until the weight it was pushing broke the clamp. In October 1893 this occurred at the corner of Wells and Washington, the malfunctioning car collecting nine other trains, twenty-

Figure 23. Interior of cable car with cross section of gripping mechanism
(Tissandier, *Six mois aux États-Unis*, 1886).

Figure 24. Collision in the La Salle Street Tunnel (*Chicago Tribune*, 2 May 1887).

Figure 25. Cars, cabs, and pedestrians at the corner of State and Madison Streets, painted by Childe Hassam (*Scribner's Magazine*, May 1892).

seven cars in all, before it stopped (fig. 26). Chicago's transportation system was quick, but it also confirmed the vulnerability of centralized operations to discrete breakdowns or malfunctions.

The most shocking accident statistics involved locomotives at unguarded crossings at grade. Though these injuries and deaths occurred outside of the Loop, they were nevertheless tolerated by companies within it. By 1893 there were 1,375 miles of track crossing streets at 2,000 points within the city limits, the vast majority still unprotected. This was a longstanding problem caused by the railroads' disregard of a city ordinance prohibiting speeds in excess of ten miles an hour within city limits, and also the failure of the city council and the companies to cooperate in erecting gates or stationing flagmen to guard the crossings. Madame Léon Grandin, a Parisian who lived in Chicago from July 1892 until May 1893, explained: "From time to time the train crossed streets where carriages, promenaders, circling children, all scattered and without fear of the train, nothing protecting them but their own prudence; the train tracks as open as those of the tramways, no barrier, no guard, only a bell on the front of the locomotive warned pedestrians to take care."[55] Railroad companies not only disregarded this speed limit, they announced their guilt ahead of time by publishing schedules requiring faster speeds. In 1887 an investigative reporter pointed out that most lines forced their engineers to travel at least twice as fast as the ordinance permitted in order to maintain schedules. Certain trains on the Pittsburgh, Fort Wayne, and Chicago line were scheduled to average thirty-five miles an hour between stops within the city. Because railroad officials believed their companies were the key to Chicago's remarkable development, they disregarded public criticism despite the bloodshed. When sued by individuals, they paid witnesses to testify falsely or appealed cases from court to court until plaintiffs could no longer

Figure 26. Multi-car collision at the corner of Wells and Washington Streets (*Chicago Tribune*, 20 October 1893).

afford the costs. William T. Stead wrote the bluntest condemnation of railroad arrogance: "For years past the city has protested, but protested in vain. The railroads ride rough-shod over the convenience, the rights and the lives of the citizens. Sisera with his 900 chariots never tyrannized more ruthlessly over the Hebrews than the railroads with their fire chariots of steel have lorded it over the city of Chicago."[56] The yearly number of injuries caused by the railroads exceeded one thousand as early as the mid-1880s. According to Stead, there were 1,699 people killed by trains within city limits between 1889 and 1893: 257 (1889), 294 (1890), 323 (1891), 394 (1892) and 431 (1893).

Appalled, numerous Europeans called for an immediate end to this slaughter. When nothing was done about it in the years leading up to the exposition, they tended to agree with A. G. Stephens: "it is cheaper to kill people than to elevate the railways, and human life in Chicago is nothing compared with money."[57] That higher profits might be worth the sacrifice of lives was the ultimate horror of Chicago's modernity, yet perceptive critics, knowing that "speed of execution is a necessary prerequisite in America,"[58] realized one of the realities of the prophetic metropolis was the tightening connection between good returns on investments and the devaluation of life. Others had noticed the collective indifference of Chicagoans to accidents and injuries. If a wagon lost a wheel or a horse was run over, hardly anyone paid attention, reported Hesse-Wartegg in 1893.[59] Citizens hit by cable cars were moved to the side of the tracks to enable the traffic to continue.[60] The intricate cogs of the city must turn; let the user beware. Regardless of how we identify the causes—progress, economic expansion, or the "go-ahead" mentality—they speeded up Chicago's daily life, which, in turn, increased the likelihood of accidents and deaths on the job and in the streets. In this respect Chicago was again the Western world's most dramatic clarifier of unintended consequences of progress. Because Europeans came from industrializing nations that were also experiencing a quickening of life that affected public safety, they studied the city, not to repeat its mistakes but to avoid them, confident their own leaders could control modernization without the human sacrifices Chicago tolerated.

Chicago's Neurasthenia

Europeans worried about the effects of the faster pace of urban life on the nervous system. Almost every outsider remarked about the hectic atmosphere of the Loop area. In search of an appropriate patron saint for Chicago, William T. Stead suggested St. Vitus. Could the citizens maintain their daily pace indefinitely without showing its effects? Though European visitors doubted that they could, they lacked the data, expertise, and even the language to discuss this possibility in a competent manner. The language used by Europeans to account for the hyperkinetic atmosphere of the Loop explains, in part, their difficulties in grasping its modernity. For example, Hesse-Wartegg likened the movements of its crowds to "an infantry attack." His choice of this image might have been meaningful in conveying the magnitude of a given characteristic of Chicago—for example, its speed, confusion, cacophony, odors, or heights—but inclusive metaphors were inadequate to cope with a new phenomenon the Loop revealed. This ground zone was unique because its movements, intensity, and compactness subjected people within it to the overlays, intersections, collisions, and juxtapositions of an infinite number of magnified stimuli. The literary or military analogies of Europeans were too sluggish and too unified to catch the episodic, staccato simultaneity of the Loop's life. In the early 1890s the American writer Charles King came the closest to expressing its accumulative discords when he offered a verbal equivalent for the early evening activity at the corner of State and Madison Streets:

> Collisions, shocks, wild plunges for hats that go skimming among the trampling feet; crash in the street, locking wheels, cracking whips, plunging horses, declamatory policemen, blaspheming drivers, slang, billingsgate, uproar, clatter, ear-piercing screams. . . . Clang lang, lang. "Who you shovin?" Clang lang. Bang, bang, bang. Yells. Shouts. Furious clangor of gongs. Rush, uproar. Hi! hi there! Look out! LOOK OUT! Bang. Bang. Clang. OUT OF THE WAY! Rush-scurry.[61]

King found means to cobble a partial word-picture of what several European authors sensed and what Futurist painters would try to put on canvas around 1910—the simultaneity of unexpected, interpenetrating urban fragments and jolts. His avalanche of volatile interruptions exposed the comparative orderliness and linearity of Hesse-Wartegg's phrase, "infantry attack." The Loop's revelation of the competitive vibrations of the modern city, vibrations that would not be well expressed in art or literature for another twenty years, intrigued Europeans in the early 1890s, but their earnest descriptive language and unified narratives were incapable of expressing the Loop's multiplicities and disjunctions.

During the last decades of the century researchers on both sides of the Atlantic realized urban life was exerting a toll on the human nervous system. In 1881 George M. Beard published *American Nervousness: Its Causes and Consequences,* in which he discussed, among other issues, the connection between clocks and punctuality and the decline of casualness, the quicker communication that enabled citizens to read all the troubles of the world in the morning newspaper, and the intensification of noise caused by advanced machines and faster transportation. "Modern nervousness is the cry of the system struggling with its environment," he warned.[62] In 1892 in France, Max Nordau combined evidence of mounting stress as a factor in the higher death rates in Europe with figures showing a constant rise in the increase of crime, mental illness, and suicide to argue in *Degeneration,* "We stand now in the midst of a severe mental epidemic; of a sort of black death of degeneration and hysteria, and it is natural that we should ask anxiously on all sides: 'What is to come next?'"[63]

Chicago would have been an excellent city in which to have conducted research on developments that made Nordau's question pertinent in 1892. Europeans knew about its skyscrapers by this date, and they also knew about the city's high rate of suicide, murder, and divorce, as well as its citizens' reputation for consuming alcohol. Yet visiting social scientists did not investigate carefully in the early 1890s the possible effects of the city's double-time pace on its inhabitants. William Stead, who may have spent more months in residence and examined social and political problems in greater detail than any foreign critic before 1894, focused on moral decay and municipal corruption rather than on neurological overload. This does not mean critics ignored signs of frayed nerves. Many expressed concern about the stability of citizens who seemed so driven, and a few amateur psychologists generalized about what was happening to Chicagoans under this kind of pressure. The most alarming claims were made by A. G. Stephens: "Everything is done at the highest possible pressure of nerve and muscle. The result is that at forty the hustler is a worn-out man, broken in health and spirits, with a 'pile' from which he vainly seeks happiness. During a fortnight at Chicago I counted seven suicides of business men, some well to-do, others losers through speculation, all driven out of life by depression consequent on nerve exhaustion. The pace is literally killing."[64] Stephens also cited an active drug culture that he attributed to the city's preoccupation with "hustling." Despite such allegations, the majority of foreign observers concluded that Chicagoans appeared to adjust to quickening speeds without noticeable signs of mental or emotional deterioration.

Notes

1. Leopold Gmelin, "Architektonisches aus Nordamerika," *Deutsche Bauzeitung* 28 (20 October 1894): 520.

2. "Lies about Chicago," *Chicago Tribune,* 12 May 1885, 4.

3. New York papers, particularly the *Sun,* treated Chicago savagely, especially between 1889 and 1891, the years that included the selection of the city as the country's host city for the coming international exposition. The quality of this satire was poor.

4. H. Panmure Gordon, *The Land of the Almighty Dollar* (London: Frederick Warne, 1892), 182–83.

5. Mocking locals sitting on rocking chairs in hotel lobbies, one visitor remarked that Chicagoans were so addicted to motion that they moved even when sitting. Learning that an early cemetery was to be closed and the bodies relocated, another observed that even the dead had to "move on" in Chicago.

6. This is one of many quotes from foreign visitors in the useful and richly illustrated survey by Harold M. Mayer and Richard C. Wade, *Chicago: Growth of a Metropolis* (Chicago: University of Chicago Press, 1969), 35.

7. At a social gathering John Kerr Campbell, a British traveler, saw a man he thought he knew but wasn't sure. "We thus stood fully two minutes staring at each other in perfect silence, and two minutes is a long time in Chicago." John Kerr Campbell, *Through the United States of America and Canada* (London: S. W. Partridge, 1886), 212.

8. Frederick Villiers, "An Artist's View of Chicago and the World's Fair," *Journal of the Society of Arts* 42 (8 December 1893): 51.

9. Marie T. Blanc [Th. Bentzon], *The Condition of Woman in the United States* (Boston: Roberts Brothers, 1895), 56.

10. "The Iron and Steel Institute in America," *Engineering* 50 (31 October 1890): 507.

11. Ernst von Hesse-Wartegg, *Chicago: Eine Weltstadt im amerikanischen Westen* (Stuttgart: Union Deutsche Verlagsgesellschaft, 1893), 4; and Max O'Rell [Paul Blouët] and Jack Allyn, *Jonathan and His Continent,* trans. Madame Paul Blouët (New York: Caselle, 1889), 46–47.

12. John Kendall, *American Memories* (Nottingham: E. Burrows, 1896), 182.

13. Arthur Brisbane, "Praise for Chicago," *Chicago Tribune*, 12 July 1892, 9.

14. Paul de Rousiers, *American Life*, trans. A. J. Herbertson (Paris: Firmin-Didot, 1892), 13.

15. In *America and the Americans from a French Point of View* ([New York: Charles Scribner's Sons, 1897], 90–91), the anonymous author contended that the privileged in class-conscious Britain affected an air of being idle; it was bad form to "talk shop" or to imply that one ever worked at all. Snobbery required inquiries such as, "How are you amusing yourself?" By contrast, Americans addressed each other by asking, "What are you doing?" implying that not to be doing something was an unnatural state. Americans felt more acceptable, he argued, when they were busy up to their ears. They talked constantly about how busy they were, complaining about the lack of time but failing to take necessary steps to address the conditions they cited. Admitting that one "had no time" was, in effect, an admission of success.

16. Jacques Hermant, "L'art à l'exposition de Chicago," *Gazette des beaux-arts* 73 (September 1893): 243. See also "The United States Exhibition of 1892," *Engineering* 49 (7 March 1890): 305. Chicagoans also acknowledged that making money was important to them. In his novel *With the Procession* (1895), inspired by the city, one of Henry B. Fuller's characters declares, "This town of ours . . . is the only great city in the world in which all its citizens have come for the one common, avowed object of making money. There you have its geniuses, its growth, its end and object; and there are but few of us who are not attending to that object very strictly." Henry Blake Fuller, *With the Procession* (New York: Harper and Brothers, 1895; reprint Chicago: University of Chicago Press, 1965), 203.

17. David Macrae, *The Americans at Home,* vol. 1 (Edinburgh: Edmonson and Douglas, 1870), 17.

18. Adolphe Bocage, "L'architecture aux États-Unis et à l'exposition universelle de Chicago," *L'architecture* 7 (13 October 1894): 335.

19. Jacques Hermant, "L'architecture aux États-Unis et à l'exposition universelle de Chicago," *L'architecture* 7 (20 October 1894): 343.

20. Paul Bourget, *Outre-Mer* (New York: Charles Scribner's Sons, 1895), 127.

21. See Paul E. Sprague, "The Origin of Balloon Framing," *Journal of the Society of Architectural Historians* 40 (December 1981): 311–19.

22. Julius Lessing, quoted from *National Zeitung*, no. 465, 1893, in Leopold Gmelin, "Architektonisches aus Nordamerika," *Deutsche Bauzeitung* 28 (3 October 1894): 487.

23. To explain why Americans wanted instantaneous domestic architecture, foreign critics usually cited the general impatience of the people, the dearth of housing for an expanding population, the desire of parents not to have married children living with them, and the desire of the young couple to have their own castle where they could raise a family without interference from neighbors. European observers were more interested in the architectural implications of free-standing houses than why couples in the United States demanded them and wanted to move into them as soon as possible. The best foreign discussion during the 1880s of the relationship between American life and domestic design is Emil Deckert, "Das amerikanische Haus," *Gegenwart* 32 (30 July 1887): 67–69.

24. K. Hinckeldeyn, "Hochbau-Constructionen und innerer Ausbau in den Vereinigten Staaten, *Centralblatt der Bauverwaltung* 7 (19 March 1887): 116.

25. F. Herbert Stead, "An Englishman's Impressions at the Fair," *Review of Reviews* 8 (July 1893): 33.

26. In the second edition of his popular *History of the Modern Styles of Architecture,* James Fergusson wrote in exasperation, "The perfection of art in an American's eyes would be attained

by the invention of a self-acting machine, which should produce plans . . . at so much per foot . . . and save all further trouble and thought." Fergusson, *History of the Modern Styles of Architecture* (London: John Murray, 1873), 499. In 1891 Robert Kerr, author of *The English Gentleman's House* (1864) and professor of the arts of construction at King's College, London, from 1861 to 1890, edited the third edition of Fergusson's book. He apologized to the American profession for "the hasty opinions" Fergusson had expressed, but this did not necessarily mean architectural circles in Europe now disagreed with his original charge.

27. For example, the influence of American architectural rendering in which "broad spaces are left quite white in the drawing, and brilliant contrasts of black and white sought for," was detected at an Academy exhibition in London in 1889 by a disapproving critic who believed this method led to quick but seductive sketches. Chiel, "Letter from London," *American Architect* 26 (27 July 1889): 40.

28. See "Architectural Drawings at Chicago," *Builder* 65 (2 September 1893): 167–70; and Franz Jaffe, "Die Architektur-Ausstellung fremder Länder," in *Amtlicher Bericht über die Weltausstellung in Chicago 1893,* vol. 2 (Berlin: Reischdrucherei, 1894), 1145.

29. "Proceedings of Allied Societies: Sheffield: Monthly Meeting," *Royal Institute of British Architects, Journal,* 3d ser., 1 (1893–94): 90.

30. A., "L'organisation des bureaux d'architectes aux États-Unis," *La semaine des constructeurs,* 2d ser., 4 (8 March 1890): 436–38, and (15 March): 452; and "Un cabinet d'architecte à Chicago," *Le moniteur des architectes,* n.s., 4 (1890): 11. Information about the new offices of the firm had been published in the United States in *Inland Architect and News Record* (September 1888), *Engineering and Building Record* (11 January 1890), and *American Architect* (25 January 1890).

31. "The *Gazette des beaux-arts* and the World's Fair," *American Architect* 42 (14 October 1893): 20. The *American Architect* published excerpts from Hermant's three-part article in *Gazette des beaux-arts.*

32. "Knows No Parallel," *Chicago Tribune,* 17 January 1892, 27.

33. C. B. Berry, *The Other Side* (London: Griffith and Farron, 1880), 116.

34. Hesse-Wartegg, 63.

35. Mayor Cregier was eager to show off the city's miraculous technology, especially since members of the group had explained that when they expressed amazement over innovations they had seen in other American cities, they had been told repeatedly, "Oh, that's nothing. Wait until you get to Chicago." At a predetermined point on the tour, Cregier instructed Sir James Kitson, president of the British Iron and Steel Institute, to set the dial and call for a patrol wagon. Within a short time Engine Company 10 arrived; Kitson evidently had made an incorrect selection. Red faced, Cregier again showed Kitson how to call for a patrol wagon. In 2 minutes and 25 seconds the Central and Armory wagons arrived. Next an ambulance was called, arriving in 2 minutes and 45 seconds. A fire alarm was pulled, bringing Engine Company 21 in 2 minutes, followed by two other trucks a few seconds later.

36. Property values in the central district increased, though not steadily, between 1871 and the early 1890s. In the aftermath of the fire, it was necessary to replace not only the equivalent office space that had been needed before the conflagration, but also to meet the new demands of the years of rebuilding. If the panic of 1873 had not curtailed the postfire expansion, the city might have enjoyed a dramatic building boom during the 1870s. However, real estate values remained sluggish through the reminder of that decade. Despite some indications of resurgence, interrupted by the recession in 1883–84, the city's extraordinary building spree did not begin until the last half of the eighties.

37. "A City of Vast Enterprise," *New York Times,* 24 December 1893, 20.

38. "Progress of Chicago," *Chicago Tribune,* 23 August 1893, 4.

39. Homer Hoyt, *One Hundred Years of Land Values in Chicago* (Chicago: University of Chicago Press, 1933; reprint, New York: Arno Press, 1970), 152–53.

40. Based on information from *Exchange* reported in "Rapid Building in Chicago," *American Architect* 37 (10 September 1892): 172.

41. M., "Ueber die ausserordentlich rege Bauthätigkeit und einige bauliche Sonderheiten in Chicago," *Centralblatt der Bauverwaltung* 12 (17 September 1892): 412. Without naming the Ashland Block, the *Centralblatt* writer mentioned a seventeen-story building (43 by 25 meters) in which a single floor was completed in the astounding time of 3¼ days.

42. G. Sauvin, *Autour de Chicago* (Paris: Plon, 1893), 97.

43. Jaffe, 1145.

44. Gustav Benfey, "Bau eines Chicagoer Sky-skraper," *Baugewerks-Zeitung* 28 (7 November 1896): 1196.

45. *Industrial Chicago,* vol. 1 (Chicago: Goodspeed, 1891), 480.

46. Bocage, 336. Marie T. Blanc cited another example—stores selling everything from clothes to kitchen utensils on the eighth floor of a building, the ground floor of which was still unfinished and open to the weather. See Blanc, 63.

47. The British architect Charles Heathcote, an R.I.B.A. Fellow, urged colleagues to consider some advantages of building quickly. "If a proprietor wishes a very quickly erected building he must pay the necessitated additional outlay enabling the contractor to effect it at a reasonable profit. Herein comes the American greater keenness at once. We do not, or have not, fully risen to the fact in the great bulk of our contracts that if a proprietor saves £1,000 in interest on his land value by quickening construction, it is a very good business to spend £750 in order to obtain it. It is of course no new thing to us, but we have not as fully realised it as we should. An American proprietor not only does appreciate this, but he acts on it, and will spend more than the thousand pounds actually saved in interest because he makes money by having his works and premises as a going profit-making concern all the sooner." Heathcote, "Comparison of English and American Building Methods," *British Architect* 60 (11 December 1903), 422.

48. Rousiers, 241. Though he was referring to business in New York, his point is more descriptive of Chicago.

49. Ibid., 61.

50. Otto H. Mueller, "Skizzen von der Weltausstellung in Chicago," *Zeitschrift des oesterreichischen Ingenieur- und Architekten-Vereines* 45 (8 September 1893): 494.

51. Police officers guarded each downtown intersection, but they had too many responsibilities to insure the safe movement of people going to the cars or crossing from one side to the other. The *Tribune* for 16 October 1892 (p. 33) described a scene at the corner of La Salle and Randolph that was evidently common. "At this moment a woman leading a 10-year-old child made an attempt to cross the street. A West Side cable train was going north, and this she saw and dodged. But as the couple cleared this danger a North Side train emerged from the tunnel, and at the same time a heavy express wagon cut in from the east side of the street. The frightened woman loosened her hold of the child and ran for dear life. The little girl turned back and started to cross the West Side track, but was caught by the officer just in time and held between the tracks until the danger passed."

52. Hesse-Wartegg, 25.

53. Introduced in 1882, the cable car system eventually expanded to eighty miles of track. The cars moved when the gripman standing in the middle of the lead car engaged the moving cable located between the tracks underneath the road surface. Stationary engines in various parts of

the city supplied the power for the endless metal ropes. The system tended to impress visitors more than those who used it daily.

54. Between 1 May and 6 August 1888, there were 22 accidents on the North Side line, one of three companies serving the city. Of these, 4 involved collisions with wagons, 2 with private cabs, 2 with other trains, 4 incidents in which sudden stops injured passengers, and 10 incidents in which pedestrians were killed or injured. In the late summer of 1888 there were 56 suits pending against the South Side line, most of the plaintiffs requesting compensatory damages ranging from $5,000 to $15,000 for personal injury. Fewer people were hurt in cable-car–pedestrian accidents than in injuries to car passengers caused by sudden stops or in collisions between vehicles.

55. Mme. Léon Grandin, *Impressions d'une Parisienne à Chicago* (Paris: Ernest Flammarion, 1894), 58, anon. trans. attached to copy in Chicago Historical Society.

56. William T. Stead, *If Christ Came to Chicago!* (Chicago: Laird and Lee, 1894), 194.

57. A. G. Stephens, *A. G. Stephens: Selected Writings,* ed. Leon Cantrell (Sydney: Angus and Robertson, 1977), 409–10.

58. Bocage, 336.

59. Hesse-Wartegg, 25.

60. This indifference anticipated the indifferent twentieth-century city, caught by Robert Musil in *The Man without Qualities,* published in 1930 but set in 1913 Vienna. Musil describes the need of pedestrians to have the efficient ambulance attendants remove victims from their midst, thereby reassuring them that regularity had returned. See Musil, *The Man without Qualities,* vol. 1 (London: Secker and Warburg, 1953), 6.

61. Charles King, "The City of the World's Fair," *Cosmopolitan,* November 1891, 63.

62. George M. Beard, *American Nervousness* (New York: G. P. Putnam's Sons, 1881), 138.

63. Max Nordau, *Degeneration* (1895; New York: Howard Fertig, 1968), 537.

64. Stephens, 409.

Historicism

4 and

Innovation

Contrasting Attitudes about the Past

CHICAGOANS conceived of their past and their present unlike contemporaries did in Western Europe. I do not mean to imply that all Europeans understood "the past" and "the present" similarly; the meaning of the past to a French citizen would not be identical to that of a German. Furthermore, there were disagreements among intellectuals in Britain, France, and Germany about the influence the accumulated culture of yesterday could or should exert on present-day culture. However, the dissimilarities among these national viewpoints seemed less significant when Old World attitudes were compared with those of the New. Regardless of nationality or assumptions about history, visitors from the three European countries discovered how much they had in common when they studied the manifestations of contemporary American thinking about the past, present, and future.

Henri Bergson in France and William James in the United States may have argued that time was not a phenomenon that could be divided into segments, but most Europeans, even at the end of the century, continued to think of the past as an entity that came before the present. Though unsure of when the former ended and the latter began, and vague about the functional relationship between the two, they treated the past as a unit of accumulated wisdom from which the present could benefit. They viewed it metaphorically as a platform of support, as a rudder that gave direction in choppy modern seas, or as a treasure chest of wisdom, models, and insights gathered over centuries. It provided lessons about how to succeed and how not to succeed, and, depending on the degree to which one believed there was nothing new under the sun, these lessons could be revered or treated lightly. History offered standards against which to measure current cultural development. Artists and architects found in it models of quality that some believed could never be surpassed. Even if one concluded that the present had left the past behind, a gentleman or lady of the day was expected to be knowledgeable about yesterday in order to function in contemporary social and cultural circles. As for the present, it was thought to have emerged mysteriously out of the past, drawing on the resources of the former while focusing on challenges previous generations had not faced. Like its predecessor, the present was also an entity possessing undefined but sensed temporal boundaries. The future was yet another segment, one lying beyond present time, its starting point always advancing as the present aged.

During their stays in the United States, travelers from Britain, France, and Germany often developed a deeper understanding and appreciation of their own national pasts. The New World reminded them that their histories were centuries old, stretching back at least as far as Roman civilization. Their lands were spatial containers of human deposits in historic time—ancient roads, ruined abbeys, walled castles. People had lived on those lands for so long that even remote hamlets had stories to tell, and local residents publicized them through shrines, museums, or festive reenactments. A village short on contemporary significance might attract outsiders curious about its anecdotal niche in history. The European past, long and evolutionary, continued to touch British, French, and German lives in countless direct and indirect ways.

The United States, by contrast, lacked the visible patina of prolonged occupation. On long train rides between American cities foreign travelers searched the landscape for evidence of early settlement without much success. While native Americans had lived lightly on the land, leaving few marks behind, Americans of European descent had occupied the land for a relatively short period of time. When they had built, they tended to build for necessity, not for delight, and rarely in anticipation of the requirements of tomorrow. These Americans were also poor stewards of yesterday's accomplishments, often ignoring evidence of earlier settlement or destroying it to make room for new structures. Inspired by the 1876 celebration of a century of political independence, Americans began to take their past more seriously, but most Europeans still thought they neglected it, and a few suggested there was not yet enough national history to justify the effort. James Bryce referred to a "feeling that nothing historically interesting ever has happened here, perhaps ever will happen." Americans visiting Europe had the better prospect, he contended, for they departed a land of "happy monotony" to enter countries where "everything is redolent with the memories of the past."[1] The American past was not only shorter, it seemed less nurtured, was less attractive, and carried less authority.

The histories of Paris and London were lengthy, dramatic tales, but the "history of Chicago" struck foreign observers as an odd phrase. True, its rise to a major metropolis in slightly more than sixty years could be documented, but the city's past did not qualify as a supporting platform because it was not substantial enough. As a rudder, it was too extemporaneous to provide trustworthy guidance. As a storehouse, the city's history contained creative answers to questions no longer being asked. That so much could have sprung from so little in so short a time was another miraculous aspect of the city's growth. As early as the middle decades of the century, foreign writers recognized its rocketing rate of change by calling it "instant," an adjective implying split-second transformation rather than sequential development over time. By identifying rapid change as the unique quality of Chicago's history, critics unwittingly had found evidence to support contemporary revisionist arguments on both sides of the Atlantic that time was a flux.

The development of Chicago, then, did not fit prevailing European notions about the present as an entity distinct from the past. Though this layered conception of time seemed useful when discussing the histories of major cities in Europe and even those in the eastern part of the United States, it was not useful when applied to the Windy City. Chicago's present had rocketed away from a past that was too brief and ephemeral. This explosion frustrated critical efforts to interpret the city's development as a series of historical stages, forcing observers instead to think of it as a constantly expanding process analogous to a flowing river rather than to a linked chain. The notion that "time is a flux and not a sum of discrete units," according to Stephen Kern, is related to the argument of William James, first articulated in 1884, that human consciousness was like a stream, a "stream of thought," not a series of thoughts separated from one another.[2] Chicago's development was like an indivisible current, one that widened and quickened as the century progressed. At the moment when Paul de Rousiers announced he was living in an age of "quick transformations," thus stressing the increasing transience of stages in Western culture, psychologists and philosophers were defining time as a phenomenon of unbroken duration.

Chicago's lightning development was not only a demonstration of urban flux but also proof of the limited power of its past to steer its ever-changing present. As was true of most Americans in these years, Chicagoans did not hate their past. It was simply behind them, a beginning point useful in measuring the distance traveled and feats accomplished. Their attitudes toward their history and the history of their country suggested pride, but little guilt. In February 1888 the *Inland Architect and News Record* of Chicago reacted to the complaint of an unnamed "sentimentalist" who had charged that America was not worth living in because it contained no ruins. The journal's editor declared that Chicagoans had been too busy fulfilling their destiny to lose time worrying about their city's brief past. Chicagoans regarded their freedom from the influence of the past as a distinct advantage, but most Europeans were less sure. Despite new theories about the nature of time, the notion that a benevolent historical past provided direction, instruction, and stability to a searching present was still popular in Western Europe at the end of the century. Arriving with this assumption, the majority of visitors, though fascinated, were troubled by a city that did not have time to take seriously the wisdom of yesterday, or, more accurately, a city that didn't have much of a yesterday.

Some were concerned that Americans in general and Chicagoans in particular seemed to know so little about Western history and, consequently, could not take advantage of its riches. This reaction was expressed with conviction in the 1870s when cautious critics occasionally reminded cocky American innovators about the dangers of disregarding "eternal laws." References to historic laws and rules appeared less frequently in their criticism of the 1880s and 1890s, but a few Europeans continued to urge Americans to pay closer attention to previous centuries because they believed history contained valuable lessons, especially for a young nation. One of these lessons was about foolhardy rushing, of trying to accomplish in a short span of time what properly should be developed over an extended period. This advice rested on certain assumptions. The slowness of a process was intricately entwined with the quality of its result. Despite shifts in style and themes, some observers contended, there were principles and rules that remained valid from generation to generation. This claim was made more frequently by those in the arts than those in science and technology. Since some critics continued to believe that the United States, even in the late nineteenth century, was still a cultural extension of the Old World, they reasoned that approaches still useful in Europe would also be useful on the western side of the Atlantic.

Criticism and Praise of Antihistoricism

History taught that profound culture required a lengthy period of maturation.[3] According to this reasoning, Chicagoans deluded themselves if they thought a few decades of Herculean effort would put their city in a class with London or Paris. Yes, they could anchor a vast railroad network in no time, erect the tallest buildings in the world, and even create an unexpectedly beautiful exposition, but they could not improvise culture.[4] If they had studied history, they would realize the futility of trying to rush this process. Observers were also frustrated by the incuriosity of city authorities who acted as though there was nothing they could learn from others. Critics wondered how officials in charge of one of the worst-managed cities of the Western world could be so incurious about systems of municipal governance that were working in Europe. To disregard the experience of those abroad who had resolved similar problems, such as dirt and pollution, struck visitors as shortsighted. For Chicago's leaders to act as if no one could teach them anything seemed arrogant. This attitude was also foolish for without curiosity those in power acted in a vacuum. In the Chicago vacuum they overestimated their abilities, which sometimes led to unfortunate results.

Negative criticism of Chicago's treatment of history often came from individuals of station and privilege who acknowledged the inevitability of change but who were also concerned about its threat to their sense of an ordered world. Among Europeans, this group was composed mainly of popular authors and essayists, artists, and connoisseurs, in addition to large numbers of ordinary tourists. They tended to urge Chicagoans to slow down, to put their town in order, and to be more skeptical of new ideas. Their advice was predicated on their view of the past as a useful storehouse of wisdom and authority that could counterbalance the disruptive leaps and tugs of progress.[5] Unfortunately, from the viewpoint of this group of critics, impatient Chicagoans were too vulnerable to these impulses. Chicago "is a city full of splendid starts, a city of wonderful moments, but there is nothing that is finished, that produces coherence, no point that offers a full, a total satisfaction," contended Friedrich Dernburg, feuilleton editor for the *Berliner Tageblatt*.[6] These critics exhorted its citizens to put down an anchor as soon as possible, to begin afresh in a collective act of consolidation. If not, they would continue to prove that haste did make waste.

A number of foreign observers wondered if the forthcoming World's Columbian Exposition could provoke Chicagoans to reflect, to anticipate, to coordinate. Perhaps the classical designs of the major buildings of the exposition meant the city was now ready to look backward with appreciation and respect. Paul Bourget was one of several who thought the exposition, "finished to the minutest detail," might signal the emergence of a more mature Chicago. However, the hopes of these critics exceeded their understanding. Chicago had not changed its personality, it had only expressed its self-confidence, attending to business at the same time it was putting on a spectacular show intended to please American and international visitors. The stunning appearance and orderly atmosphere of the exposition grounds did not have a significant immediate impact on the decisions of the city council. The lessons of the exposition registered later, at the turn of the century, when reform groups gained wider communal support. When the exposition closed, citizens breathed a sigh of relief, pleased to be able to concentrate again on fulfilling Chicago's destiny. The great event for which many individuals had made heroic sacrifices of time and money was now history and, therefore, the responsibility of no person or organization.

Attempts to preserve some of the buildings and grounds of the White City for the enjoyment of later generations, thus commemorating a moment of Chicago's past, were neither deeply felt or well organized. William T. Stead understood this better than any other foreign observer. The London editor was one of many who encouraged officials to save the buildings of the Court of Honor, not for future use, but as an inspirational architectural complex. Told that this could be done for approximately $25,000 a year, the South Park commissioners, who had the responsibility for the buildings, initially agreed to maintain the exteriors of the enchanting core of the exposition. However, the commissioners did not supervise the site closely; vandals and the homeless took over. Fires burned several structures, convincing those in charge to remove all of them around the Central Basin. Stead's reaction was crisp. "But Chicago, great in executing enterprises which can be executed under stress and strain of a strong stimulus, is not equally great in preserving and maintaining that which she has created."[7] He rebuked the commissioners for being irresponsible about this "heirloom of the continent." Reflecting the inclination of some Europeans to overvalue the implications of the exposition, Stead regretted that Chicagoans had minimized an opportunity to commemorate a significant event in their city's history. Worried about American progress and its possible transforming effects of their own culture, a number of foreign observers wanted to interpret the exposition as a sign of the resurgence of Old World values in the United States or, at least, an indication Americans were becoming more moderate. Those who reached these conclusions misjudged the intentions of Chicagoans, for whom the exposition was not primarily a declaration of new priorities, but a onetime demonstration, a feat to be carried off with typical flair, confidence, and dispatch before the city returned to business as usual.

In the years around 1890, European commentators freely offered advice to Americans on the question of whether they should pay more attention to their past or whether they should continue to move aggressively toward the future. Between these two extremes were the centrists, a sizable group of critics who admired the Yankees' enthusiasm for progress but often rejected the forms it took. In short, they called for progress but wanted reassurance; they endorsed innovation but insisted on good manners. The editors of the *British Architect* expressed this position well in January 1889: "We, however, fully expect that modern American architecture will outlive these crudities and curiosities, with increased study of what constitutes true and dignified architectural design; and that when more rhythm and fitness, proportion, and dignity are added to its original and picturesque qualities, we shall find in American architecture something which will beat the records and earn a reputation for the nineteenth century architect."[8] Those who called for moderation often imagined a time when American impetuousness and European restraint would be combined into an ideal unit. At face value this advice seemed open minded and judicious, and was advocated by many observers abroad, several of them influential. However, this course was unrealistic; it assumed that in the process of merging, neither the inclination to experiment nor the desire to preserve would be fundamentally changed, that characteristic portions of each could be functionally combined without either being significantly diluted. Furthermore, Europeans who asked Americans to water their wine counted on a compound that would be closer to water than to wine. They were confident that in this imaginary merger the weight of reason and tradition would be able to discipline contemporary speculation and technology.

The strongest support for American antihistoricism came primarily from European businessmen, social scientists, engineers, and architects. The American manufacturing system and the tools it produced had attracted attention abroad, particularly in England, even before the Civil War.[9] Throughout the last half of the century observers abroad commended the cheapness and lightness of American machinery. These commentators were also impressed with the simplicity, logical patterns, and clean finish of the products of this machinery, and, especially by the "adaptability to the end in view" of these products.[10] Engineers in the United States were also recognized abroad for tackling new problems afresh and finding direct, efficient ways of resolving them. However, the foreign reaction to architects in the United States in the 1870s was less positive. While critics recognized their technical and functional strengths, they did not consider them equally strong as artists. American designers had created buildings impressive for their convenience and comfort, but, in the judgment of many professionals, they seemed unschooled in the tradition of architecture and appeared indiscreet or clumsy when attempting to adapt its styles to contemporary needs. Though this failure was usually excused as the result of youthful egotism, several foreign critics treated Yankee designers as aesthetic felons. Anton Poschacher, an Austrian architect representing his government at the Philadelphia Exhibition of 1876, had rebuked American builders who called themselves "architects" and who made their own rules "as if they had a right to do so."[11] However, his viewpoint was voiced with decreasing frequency during the last two decades of the century, particularly in Germany and France.

Between the Centennial Exhibition of 1876 and the Columbian Exposition of 1893, there was a marked shift in the attitude of European architects toward their counterparts in the United States. Their earlier references to "eternal laws" were replaced gradually by criticism that praised American designers for their independence from the Grand Tradition. This transformation, in which a weakness defined by earlier critics became a strength in the opinion of some of their successors, was by no means complete. There were professionals in France, Germany, and Britain—especially in the latter—who continued to think American work was unacceptable and potentially dangerous. Nevertheless, as attacks on the tyranny of the past mounted in Western Europe, American work was cited more frequently in foreign architectural journals. In 1886 César Daly, editor of the *Revue générale de l'architecture et des travaux publics,* commended the American architect for treating the past like "an orange which he squeezes and sucks dry before tossing the peel away."[12] Contending that European architects dishonored history by turning its principles into anachronistic rules, a number of continental critics praised American designers because they seemed to focus on the immediate problem rather than on etiquette or conventions. Overestimating the independence of American architects, critics abroad implied no idols diverted their clear vision. "After a sojourn in America we Europeans realized that country is free from the oppressive influence exerted upon modern European life by obsolete laws," wrote Leopold Gmelin.[13] The French architect Paul Sédille noted in domestic planning the absence of the "vain rules of symmetry which are foreign to the needs of daily life,"[14] and Paul Planat, founder of *La semaine des constructeurs* and editor of *La construction moderne,* envied creators free from the domination of "consecrated masterpieces."[15]

Other critics used stronger language, contending historicism was not simply an obstruction but an evil. It sapped creative spirit, misdirected energy, and eroded hope for designers searching for an architecture reflecting their time. Hans Schliepmann, a Berlin critic, novelist, and government building official, claimed in 1894 that their respective relationships to the past comprised the fundamental difference between present-day architecture in the United States and in Germany. "There is the future; here the sinking past! There is freshness; here is the school which drags around on slow-moving legs the dry rot of antiquity. We lack originality. To put it crudely, we 'grind' too much; we drum into our heads the proportions of the ancients and the rule books of former styles until we are no longer ourselves but a thin extract of an excessively old culture. We do not create anew any more; we copy."[16] Schliepmann reduced a complicated situation to an either-or state in which German designers could determine if they wanted to be architects—by which he meant creators who resolved contemporary problems through contemporary means, as he concluded Americans were doing—or if they wanted to copy the solutions of previous architects. The primary villain in his argument was the persistent authority of the past in German architecture of the present. By the early 1890s there were many architects and critics in Western Europe who would have agreed with him, and who also believed that the relative independence from history enjoyed by American designers was the "immediate cause" of their sudden international notoriety.

Similar criticism had been published earlier in France. Several architects and journalists there, frustrated by the power of tradition at home, treated American domestic architects as if they were impeccable independents who never looked backward or compromised their integrity. Though inaccurate, this exaggerated image was useful in their attempts to urge the French profession to claim similar freedom. Paul Planat's *Encyclopédie de l'architecture et de la construction* characterized the Yankee architect as a "seeker, original or bold," whose free spirit was untrammeled by outmoded conventions and systems.[17] Marcel Daly, a son of César Daly and assistant editor of *La semaine des constructeurs,* depicted architects in the United States as uncompromising individuals, functioning without societal restraint. "The American advances without turning his head. Not chained to the artistic ways of his ancestors, he does not search for rules in the past; he sees only an arsenal of forms from which he draws freely, thus creating the most unexpected and also the most bizarre effects, for his liberty often leads to license. The spontaneous genius of the American is repulsed by copying, even by adaptation."[18] These French writers did not approach American architecture as disinterested critics but as impatient nationalists concerned about the inability of their profession to develop an architecture appropriate for late nineteenth-century French life. Because they were frustrated, their remarks were frequently categorical and expansive. They overstated faults at home and virtues abroad because they thought French work was mired in tradition while American architecture, by contrast, seemed inspired and free.

European professionals who attacked historicism and called for architecture contemporary in theory and in practice found exemplary models in American work in the years around 1890. They cited the free-standing houses of residential neighborhoods and the tall office buildings of the major cities as the most instructive types. In their collective judgment, domestic and commercial work was not only freer from the influences of the past than were American buildings devoted to cultural, governmental, and religious purposes, they were also planned more effectively for modern use. The house was purposeful because it was so inviting, convenient, and comfortable for the family. The skyscraper was purposeful because it served the needs of modern business effectively. That Chicago's contribution to the new commercial architecture of the United States was central was an accepted fact among European professionals by 1892. More so than single-family domestic architecture, office buildings, particularly those of the Loop, were valued abroad because they revealed how an architecture freed from history could be created from contemporary requirements and means. For Europeans attempting to find ways in which the present could function without the heavy intrusion of the past, the functioning Loop, not just its new buildings, became an instructive model in the early 1890s.

Engaging the Present with Confidence

In these decades of intensifying economic and political competition among Western nations, attempts to gauge the relative strengths and weaknesses of each were common. Comparing national artistic tendencies, Professor Robert Kerr, a Scot, in 1885 called the

British a practical people; the French, as everyone knew, were blessed by their artistic sensitivity; the Germans struggled aesthetically because they lacked *esprit*; while Italy was constrained by the weight of artistic tradition. The Americans, Kerr asserted, were waiting in the wings, preparing to move to center stage when the senior countries of Europe faltered.[19] Though contemporaries may have disagreed with his conclusions, few would have questioned the validity and usefulness of typing nations. On the issue of relative national contemporaneity, the British, French, and Germans thought that Americans living in the late nineteenth century were more at home with the emerging age of electricity than were any other peoples. Some implied the last decades of the century had become an age of youth discriminatory to old Europe—an age that only the young in mind and spirit could understand and exploit.

Europeans believed Americans had not only adjusted well to modern times, they had also acted to shape modern times. Accordingly, their success was partly due to their acceptance of new conditions and pressures, and also to their innovations, which were beginning to be felt in international trade, manufacturing, technology, and architecture. By the early 1890s some foreign critics were implying the existence of one "present" expressive of Europe and another "present" expressive of the United States. The European present was easier to predict. On the eastern side of the Atlantic, "now" signified a period of culmination defined by the accumulated treasures and learning of the past. It seemed comparatively more structured and orderly, shaped by factors that had evolved over long periods of time. In the New World the here-and-now conveyed the impression to visitors of a moment that seemed more transient and even ephemeral. It was an American, William James, who claimed the present became the past as soon as one tried to think about it.[20] The present in America also seemed more tumultuous and breathless, and citizens there appeared to be more impatient with it than were their counterparts abroad. Shorter in duration, something like a flash, it functioned less as a summary than as a quick prologue. Alexis de Tocqueville had sensed this in the 1830s when he wrote that if democracies were inclined to shut out the past, they were also predisposed to treat the present as a gateway to the future.

This growing suspicion abroad of a qualitatively different present in the United States developed from watching the ways in which Americans took action. Based on hundreds of accounts in this literature, some thoughtful, some superficial, some inquisitive, and some quite biased, critics collectively identified at least four attitudes and approaches that seemed to characterize the distinctive style by which people in the United States dealt with their present. Those four were: openness to change, acting with confidence, acting quickly, and assuming that each improvement or advancement would soon be superseded.

In reference to "openness to change," the staff of the British journal *Engineering* repeatedly argued in the late decades of the century that "the love of change and innovation" was as characteristic of the United States as was "the spirit of conservation" in European countries.[21] The journal urged its readers to judge new approaches on the basis of reason rather than feelings. If Britain hoped to remain competitive, especially with the United States, it argued, sentimental attachments could no longer be justified. This effort by *Engineering* was repeated by technical journals on the Continent, more frequently in Germany than in France, and with more urgency around 1890. Discussions of how best to adapt to change were replacing those concerned with the inevitability of change. Chicago was often mentioned in these debates.[22]

Acting with confidence was a second reason why Europeans thought Americans were effective in dealing with contemporary challenges. The confidence of Americans was a quality Europeans could admire better than they could emulate because it was inspired by conditions peculiar to the United States. Unpropertied Europeans would never be able to experience the dreams the vast acres of still unclaimed land inspired in citizens of the United States. Americans' tentative link with history left them free to move easily across these promising spaces, enabling them to possess the soil instead of the soil possessing them. Encouraged by their present relationship with their plentiful land, they were confident this relationship would be even more rewarding tomorrow.[23] Good prospects for raising their standards of living had also affected their view of work. The American seemed to enjoy work and was interested in it; "he knows there are openings for his progress." Immigrants with the courage to leave their countries and the pluck to begin again in another part of the world vigorously pursued the provable notion that hard work could lead to new dignity. The rich were eligible for similar rewards because "to work" was not an embarrassing prospect. "The sentiment in England that a man who belongs to an idle, leisured class is, for that reason, to be envied, forms one of the great drawbacks to progress and efficiency" in Britain, the architect Charles Heathcote claimed in 1903.[24]

Poised on the threshold of a future that promised greater rewards than previous futures, Americans anticipated the unknown not with fear but with enthusiasm. Though Europeans did not analyze the sources of American confidence well, they often commented on its ubiquitous manifestations. In describing his impressions of Chicago, an anonymous French visitor recalled a scene for which other incidents on his tour had prepared him. At one of the clubs in the city a stranger instructed his waiter to take the orders of others in the room and, turning to them, said, "What'll ye have, gentlemen?" The Frenchman could not get over the openness and generosity of an individual to people he had never met. "This cheerful, all-embracing 'What'll ye have?' sounds in my ears now, when I am so many thousand miles away, and I smile involuntarily as I think of the happy-go-lucky, prosperous, and genial young heirs of a mighty nation's wealth, to all of whom I would gladly say, as so many of them have said to me: 'What'll ye have?'"[25] The opportunities available to Americans in the late nineteenth century—for better jobs, for self-improvement, and even for making fortunes—were central to the development of national confidence. Without the belief that tomorrow would be better than today, without the means to test that belief, and without the testimonies of thousands that it could come true, the record of the United States and of Chicago in these decades would have been different.

Though blessed with golden opportunities, Americans still had to do something to turn them into realities. In his "Psalm of Life," Henry Wadsworth Longfellow stressed action as the key to national fulfillment.

Not enjoyment and not sorrow,
    Is our destined end or way;
But to act, that each to-morrow
    Finds us farther than to-day.
Trust no Future, howe'er pleasant!
    Let the dead past bury its dead!
Act—act in the living present!
    Heart within, and God o'erhead.[26]

Europeans might have doubted that Longfellow's readers followed his advice to "Trust no Future," but they did agree about the readiness of Americans to "act in the living present," believing this tendency fundamental to America's international surge. By contrast, the English poet and critic Matthew Arnold wrote in 1888, "We fumble because we cannot make up our mind because we do not know what to be after."[27] Some critics contended that in Britain and on the Continent to "act" meant spending energy trying to avoid taking action by substituting prolonged deliberation, or halfhearted trials, or action taken so late the original problem had changed. For Americans, however, action seemed to be a natural state of being. They appeared to be constantly doing something, not thinking about doing something, one reason why foreign consensus considered them stronger in practice than in theory. To "act" in the United States conveyed to foreign observers the implication of physical activity, of making, shaping, developing, constructing, all leading toward conscious goals.

Around 1880 British professional journals started to use the word "go-ahead" to describe the proclivity of architects in the United States to get on with it. The term, implying energy as well as decisive action, was soon adopted in Germany but was less common in French criticism. Its advantages and disadvantages may have been discussed for the first time at a formal meeting in 1882 at the Royal Institute of British Architects (RIBA).[28] Among European architectural circles in the early 1890s, the early American skyscraper was considered the ultimate example of both the wisdom and the folly of the "go-ahead" mentality. It was praised by critics who believed conservative habits, once effective, now inhibited inevitable development and was condemned by those who believed in progress but not at the expense of urban order, decorum, and tradition. Though unable to agree on its value, critics abroad attributed its development to confident action taken by American business people, architects, and contractors.

Thirdly, when Americans acted, they acted with dispatch; in the words of an unidentified writer for the *Deutsche Bauzeitung* in 1884, "they proceed to the solution without prolonged deliberation."[29] Europeans thought they knew the reasons for this tendency. Quick action stemmed from the national belief that time was precious and that those who hesitated in a period of flux and opportunity would be left behind. Foreign observers also thought Americans were more inclined to test new ideas in practice, assuming the process of trial and error would lead to a solution, even if it were only a temporary and potentially dangerous one. Ewan Christian, in 1882 the vice-president and later president of the RIBA, observed, "In the matter of new inventions Americans never hesitated; they did not wait, as did people in this country, until the new inventions had been 'perfected.'"[30] Americans also proceeded quickly because they were confident they would succeed. If they failed, as they often did, they shrugged off the setback. Resulting injuries or deaths did not deter them. According to Paul de Rousiers, this mentality could be best observed in Chicago.[31]

However, many Europeans disapproved, believing that the pace of American progress proved that haste still made waste. Yes, time was precious but not that precious. To dash off in pursuit of some objective without first developing a systematic, tested plan was unwise on a number of scores. One could lose control if one proceeded without deliberate preparation. Chicago was a prime example. Several critics wondered whether its citizens controlled their city's momentum or whether its momentum now managed them. It was also unwise to move too quickly because impetuosity diminished the prospects of using the experience of history. Specific critics rejected the argument that yesterday's authority might inhibit tomorrow's discovery, countering that without knowing the past planners could not effectively anticipate the future. Others were uncomfortable with the quick application of new ideas because this required faith in means that had not been refined, let alone proven. They worried more than did the Americans about possible failures, deaths, or wasteful acts such as the depletion of the forests of Michigan and Wisconsin.

Traditionless Technology and Innovative Architecture

In the early 1890s most European architects and contractors would have agreed that large public buildings should be erected according to regulations, should be completed without rushing, and, if one had the choice, should be overbuilt rather than underbuilt. In the Loop, however, where "time was money," clients pressured architectural firms to finish office buildings as soon as possible. To meet this demand, these firms experimented. Experimentation sometimes forced designers and contractors to define new practices instead of complying with the regulations authorities had established. From a European point of view this may have seemed irresponsible; from the standpoint of those involved in transforming the Loop it was inevitable. In 1891 the structural engineer Dankmar Adler admitted he and his colleagues who refined skeleton construction were forced to circumvent municipal restrictions to complete their contracts successfully. "That we build better to-day than we did ten years ago is partly due to the easy-going, happy-go-lucky administration of the building inspection department of this city for many years. Had we had an extremely efficient administration of this department, there would be no tall buildings to-day, for all of them are in one respect or another violations of paragraphs in existing ordinances."[32] New needs required steps not anticipated by existing regulations, and these demands changed so rapidly in Chicago that codes could not be rewritten fast enough to keep abreast of practice. This was a good example of the process—or the momentum—controlling architect and builder.

Arguments in behalf of both authorized construction and extemporaneous construction were expressed well by F. T. Reade, a British architect, and by Henry Ericsson, a Chicago contractor who had emigrated from Sweden. In 1889 Reade, an associate member of the RIBA, advised his audience at the institute to be sure to have skilled workers from the iron manufacturer on site when using iron in architecture. "The builder may properly be allowed to hoist and deposit large girders on their bedstones," he argued, "but all junctions should be made by the iron contractor."[33] At the time Reade made his remarks, Ericsson was working on the Monon Railroad Building in Chicago. In his autobiography he wrote, "The builder's art was in a stage of transition, and one was left to meet new and trying problems by his wits and native resources right on the job."[34] He explained that the cast iron columns and wrought iron beams for the Monon Building had been set by sailors from Sweden and Norway, courageous, resourceful workers with no training in iron work. Pressured by necessity, Ericsson was occasionally forced to reject presuppositions, to forget his training, and to make snap judgments in the heat of the process. In doing so, he confirmed the subordination of at least one branch of American engineering and architecture to evolutionary forces. Reade, on the other hand, viewed architecture as an independent art to be practiced at a level above the expediencies of the moment. Standing in the Loop, Europeans could understand better why some decisions had to be made on the site, but this was not the kind of architecture they had been taught to respect. Nor was it the kind of architecture most of them anticipated in the future.

Americans tended to welcome the convenience, comfort, or efficiency resulting from a particular innovation, despite the disruptive effects it might have on familiar procedures or environments. By comparison, Europeans were inclined to be more cautious, showing appreciation for greater efficiency but also concern about its threat to old ways of doing things. A number of British critics reacted in this manner when confronted by the open plan of American single-family houses made possible by central heating. Instead of focusing on the advantages of this heating system—cleanliness, lighter maintenance, spatial integration—skeptics resisted on social grounds, wondering if open planning would signal the end of the male den with its hearth, slippers, pipe, and closed door. Sentimental attachment to old habits was defended with greater vigor in the 1880s than in the 1890s and by the British more frequently than either the Germans or the French, but even continental critics thought the Americans worried too little about technology's impact on social patterns.

Mechanical and electrical innovations in the Loop and in the city's single-family houses had affected the manner in which Chicagoans interacted. The telephone was a case in point.[35] In 1882 a British visitor, Walter Marshall, noted that "everybody" in Chicago communicated by telephone, for without one a person would be "very much behind the age."[36] His observation tells us more about the people he met than the number of phones because only 2,610 were in use that year. If at times the appearance of being up-to-date was greater than its reality, Chicagoans, nevertheless, seemed to have had few reservations about using the latest machines to complete tasks more rapidly. In 1891 Max O'Rell described in detail how the telephone had transformed home management in

Chicago, permitting the mistress of the house to talk directly with her butcher, baker, and grocer about their daily specials and to place her orders without leaving her home.[37] Instead of sending her servants to make decisions, she made them, exerting greater control through lighter effort.

Europeans understood the advantages of the telephone, but some were initially hesitant to substitute technology for direct human contact. This reluctance was also encouraged by their greater suspicion of gadgets, the intrusion of which caused less consternation in the American home or office. Even in the 1920s Richard Müller-Frienfels could write, "In Europe—at least, in intellectual circles—such terms as 'mechanical' or 'machine-made' are employed as terms of censure, which are opposed to 'organic' or 'artistic.'"[38] Foreign reaction to gadgets in Chicago was positive when speed was imperative, for example, in the call boxes on the streets, or when social conventions were not at stake as in the labor-saving devices visitors discovered in their hotel rooms.[39] However, when some visitors looked into commercial offices and saw employees so dependent on their call buttons, Dictaphones, typewriters, telephones—they wondered if business, an art of human interaction, was becoming too impersonal. The *Architect* of London expressed this concern in 1883. "At the same time, with all its boasted efficiency, it must be admitted that the telephone cannot submit a sample of goods, or sign a contract, or evade a quarrel by the charm of a smile, or shake hands and join in a slight reflection over the settlement of a difficulty."[40] The strangeness of the new did not last long anywhere in the Western world at the end of the century. The reservation of the *Architect* would have seemed old-fashioned ten years later. In 1898 there were 31,600 phones in use in France and on the eve of the First World War there were over 600,000 in Britain, but the quicker acceptance of the telephone in the United States affected later usage, for ten million phones were in service there before 1914.[41]

The typewriter was an invention, adopted quickly in Chicago during the 1880s, that transformed the staff, clerical procedures, and tempo within individual offices. These machines helped to accelerate the already fast pace of American business, increased the formality of commercial correspondence, affected record keeping, and introduced a new personality into the office atmosphere—the young female secretary, or "typewriter," as she was known in the last decades of the century (fig. 27). There were approximately 3,000 machines used commercially in Chicago in 1886, 2,500 of them operated by women. Most of the secretaries knew shorthand, took dictation, and were expected to type at least forty words per minute. European visitors who described the interior activity of America's tall commercial buildings occasionally cited the typewriter as further evidence of the mechanization of the office, but they rarely objected to its growing popularly. In a spirited exception, however, an anonymous French observer railed against innovative equipment in American offices. Believing machinery could never replace human skill, he argued that the quality of employees, not the technical superiority of their machines, determined the quality of their performance. Nothing, he claimed, could take the place of cultured business people who understood and used proper conventions in their work. Americans, who had "far more mechanical devices, and [made] more use of them, than any other peo-

Figure 27. Secretary in a Chicago office—
"Ready for action" (*Chicago Tribune*, 17
October 1886).

ple," mistakenly tried to compensate for their lack of culture by hiding behind their machines. "This, I think, is partly the secret of the American love of the type-writer, the telephone, and the telegraph. It not only saves time, as they think at least, but it also saves an exposure of their own ignorance." Employees using gadgets wasted far more time than they realized, he claimed, time that would have been better spent learning to spell and to write a proper sentence. Personal service could never be replaced by mechanical expedients. The erroneous assumption that the typewriter and telephone would eliminate the pen would only distract Americans from mastering the ceremonious forms of social interaction.[42]

Rapid acceptance of equipment for the purpose of increasing efficiency and convenience was resisted by some abroad because they thought such gadgets were inartistic, too impersonal, and too intrusive, or because these devices could threaten longstanding business conventions. As long as personalized procedures, as opposed to mechanized procedures, could be sustained, those proficient in this art could turn their skills into an act of power by claiming that special training and even background were necessary to perform properly. The mechanization of the American office represented a leveling process that threatened this supremacy. Thus, the resistance of some advantaged foreign observers to faster office processes was, in part, a defense of the traditional importance played by personality and ancestry in European trade.

On the other hand, European business people were quicker than European architects to deal with contemporary realities. Many of them also attempted to protect their discipline from the onslaught of new means and pressures, but effectiveness in the field of business, unlike in architecture, could be determined by a clearer and more rewarding bottom line. As American economic competition mounted, more business people in Britain, France, and Germany called for reviews of national practices and a closer study of the causes of America's well-publicized and easily measured success. The

Germans expressed a greater sense of urgency and were also more open to American business priorities and techniques than were the French or the British. This attitude was evident in German architectural journals in the late 1880s and early 1890s, especially the *Deutsche Bauzeitung*. "One is only in the position to economize if one always and immediately acquires the newest and the best technology available on the market. This difference is all important . . . between Germans and Americans; the latter acquire quickly all those technical achievements which promise savings in both human labor and capital, while the Germans always seem to wait in the hope something better may turn up."[43] Though Europeans continued to object to the hasty implementation of new approaches and means, they were less critical of this tendency in the United States in the early 1890s than earlier. What was once viewed as a vice of youth was becoming a virtue of necessity.

The fourth reason foreign critics thought Americans functioned effectively in modern life was their understanding that in a period of rapid changes a successful answer would last only for a limited duration—until a different question or a better answer was developed. A persistently fluid context made fixed answers impractical and sometimes harmful. Although some Europeans thought it might be efficient to let innovative Americans do the experimenting and then to appropriate their useful results, others believed this approach, clever in theory, to be unwise in practice because modern life was not marked by permanent solutions. By the time a new refinement had been copied or adapted, that improvement also would have become obsolete.

In general, American manufacturers had followed a different course from those in Europe. Foreign observers, aware that innovation was valued in the United States, explained that this meant products there were refined continuously. Comparing British and American goods in an ironmonger's store, Charles Heathcote concluded that American patterns often had been changed two or three times since the last alteration of similar British items.[44] Hermann Maier, who wrote about skeleton construction for the *Deutsche Bauzeitung,* observed, "We are amazed to find over there German inventions which in the shortest time have been more thoroughly developed than they have been with us, while, on the other hand, what we regard as innovations have been in use in America for decades and are already old."[45] Because manufacturers in the United States realized their goods would become obsolete when subsequent refinements became available, they tended to produce tools and equipment that were lighter and less durable if compared to similar equipment manufactured abroad. These lighter products were strong enough to meet reasonable requirements but were not overbuilt. Tocqueville had referred to an American tendency to "diminish the intrinsic quality" of a product without making it ineffective. The recent history of the hoe was a good example. In 1880 those manufactured in England, like the hoes made twenty-five years earlier in the United States, were heavy, utilizing gravity to help the farmer penetrate the ground. By contrast, American manufacturers believed an efficient hoe, especially one used for destroying weeds, required lightness and a sharp edge. Its effectiveness depended not on weight that tired the farmer but on easier and, thus, more frequent motions—in effect, the substitution of speed for ballast. Refined over the years, American hoes tended to be much lighter, had longer, thinner handles and thinner, polished blades. They did not last forever but were more convenient to use.

European manufacturers also tried to protect innovative products from prying competitors. In the United States the assumption that all gains would be temporary worked against professional secrecy and encouraged, in the judgment of foreign observers, greater cooperation among associates in a given field than was true in Britain, France, or Germany. If one expected a product to be superseded, then it was smarter to spend time learning recent developments in that field in order to be the first with a refinement than to devote energies to maintaining secrecy. Consequently, manufacturers in a given trade knew well the histories and strengths of their competitors. Representatives from rival firms were often invited on friendly inspections to see recent improvements in products and the manufacturing operation. Cooperation of this nature meant that new ideas circulated quickly. A fresh approach tried in one section of the country would soon appear in other regions. These differences between American and European approaches in industry were determined, in part, by differing attitudes toward the nature of the present. Since American manufacturers and American architects shared similar views of that present, it is not surprising that the latter also believed each innovation would last for only a limited period of time, designed and built lighter structures rather than overbuilt, and shared know-how and innovations with one another.

The concept of temporary solutions was central to the development of tall buildings in Chicago. Dankmar Adler confirmed this in a letter he wrote to the *Economist* of Chicago, which was republished in the *American Architect and Building News,* and *Inland Architect* and reprinted abroad, in excerpted form, in the 17 July 1891 issue of the *British Architect.* Discussing the evolution of foundations, he pointed out the value of various systems, each of which had been or would be superseded. Timber and concrete had been used for the Board of Trade and Pullman Buildings; rail and concrete supported the Rialto, Phoenix, and Rookery Buildings; the Auditorium rested on timber, concrete, rail, and I-beam supports; and the Tacoma Building had utilized concrete and I-beam foundations. Although these had all served their specific purposes and increased general knowledge, he explained, "none alone is competent to carry the taller buildings of tomorrow, and still less the tallest buildings necessary to fulfill the demands of the day after tomorrow."[46] In a longer version of this statement in the *American Architect and Building News,* Adler asserted that the process would go on indefinitely, enriched by new combinations of existing principles, practices successful in other fields, and, in time, methods that had never been tested because they were as yet unformed in imaginative minds.[47]

Adler not only confirmed the limited duration of each solution but also offered a remarkable insight into the process through which contemporary change was occurring. By referring to a continuous but unpredictable give-and-take propelled by ideas, some relevant and some not so relevant, some developed and some still in incubation, he echoed William James's revisionist explanation of the nature of modern flux. "The world increases, not all at once and in a block, not according to the mechanical and regulated evolution of Spencer, but by an infinitude of special independent acts, by numberless absolute beginnings and upspringings not to be foreseen, by bits and pieces, thanks to the contributions of its divers parts to each bit and piece."[48] Consciously or unconsciously American manufacturers, engineers, and architects sensed the implications of this modern insight and acted on them in the 1880s and early 1890s with greater confidence than did their counterparts abroad. They conceived of their present in less rigid, monolithic, formal, and predictable ways. They searched for its particular essence and pulse rather than assuming that these could be understood from proven vantage points, and they were more accepting of its ostensibly confusing but integrated multiplicities.

Chicago's architects and builders, like American hoe designers, also favored less ponderous construction. The system of balloon framing for houses depended on timber lighter in weight and quicker to assemble than the hewn frame with mortise-and tenon joints of high-craft work. Young couples in the United States praised this method for its low costs and for its speed, enabling them to move into their own homes more quickly than could young couples abroad. Though Europeans considered frame houses attractive, they were not reassured by them, dubbing them "tinderboxes," citing their fragility in the face of North America's violent weather, and questioning their advisability for families with social ambition. When foreign visitors first saw the slender skeletons of multistoried office buildings outlined against the sky, they expressed similar concern, partially because they had been taught to associate the appearance of solidity with durability. This respect for strength was reaffirmed by the London Building Act of 1894, which required exterior walls to be bearing walls. Commenting on Mr. Reade's paper at the RIBA in 1889 on the uses of iron in building, Robert Kerr insisted, "Don't build strong, but stronger than strong."[49] In contrast, Dankmar Adler, commenting on the Tacoma Building in Chicago completed the same year by Holabird and Roche, claimed its significant achievement was the extent to which its designers had been able to reduce the weight of its walls and still maintain a margin of safety.[50]

The relatively free exchange of information among firms and contractors is another example of how priorities of architects in the United States paralleled those of American manufacturers. According to Adler, the absence of professional secrecy was a major reason for the sudden rise and refinement of Chicago's tall buildings within a short span of years. "Each of us has learned from the others and each has taught the others what to do and what to avoid, and together and all consciously working toward the same end we shall evolve before many years a system of foundation construction equal even on our soil to the bearing of structures perhaps thirty or forty stories in height."[51] In his study of the new architecture of the Loop, Adolphe Bocage noted a practice that would have seemed strange in France. Chicago's architectural firms, he reported, often had offices in the same building, even on the same floor. Discovering several adjacent firms that were connected by doors enabling them to use the same draftsmen, he concluded "that architects in America are not afraid of competition."[52] Rivals cooperated with one another because of the fluid state of the industry during the 1880s and early 1890s, the complexity of a new architecture that sometimes required an office to call on experts employed elsewhere, and the promising outlook that convinced designers and contractors there would be plenty of work for all in the immediate years ahead.

In summary, among the major nations of the Western world in the last decades of the nineteenth century, the United States was considered the one most compatible with the present. European observers believed its citizens exploited their present by being open-minded about its systems and possibilities, experimenting with confidence, implementing new ideas rapidly, and assuming that successful solutions would soon be replaced by better ones. No city revealed the consequences of this contemporary outlook better than Chicago, and no part of the city better than its central business district. Preoccupied with the demands of the moment, Chicagoans had not preserved well the evidence of their city's development. In a period of slower change one might cherish victories, but Chicago's phenomenal rate of development in the last half of the century permitted little time for reflection. Its leaders moved forward, paying scant attention to canons, conventions, and customs from other times and other places. Failures in direct application became instructive, not causes of recrimination.

Despite evidence in Europe of innovative thought and practice, the Loop offered the more convincing proof around 1890 that new conceptions of time were affecting the centers of cities. European visitors had two basic reactions to this realization. One was a sense of a stretched imagination. Chicago's business district was provocative, offering functional alternatives to their visions, fears, and rumors of what tomorrow's cities might be like. Its existence illuminated the future and culminated the past.[53] To Chicagoans themselves, their city was a rational expression of the present; to Europeans, who had defined the present in different terms, Chicago's version of the present looked more like the future. This was the reason why the Loop was so valuable to foreign critics. There they could study a working future, observing its means and ends, noting its priorities and the relative importance of varied elements, and deciding what to appropriate and what to avoid.

A second common reaction of European visitors to this encounter was a sense of loss when they realized Chicago, America's progressive city, was much less orderly, graceful, humane, and attractive than they would have preferred. If Chicago was an indicator of the future, it was not a future they wanted. Initially, some tried to dismiss the city as a temporary aberration or viewed it as an unfortunate development from which Europe could remain immune. But the rhetoric of denial was futile. When the words cooled, Chicago remained. Denial was then replaced by resignation, and resignation was often accompanied by anxiety. Chicago's existence challenged Europeans' belief that the past could continue to act as a wise governor on the present and their hope that the present would continue to serve the interests of art and privilege as had been true in the past.

Historians in the twentieth century have treated Chicago of the 1880s and early 1890s as a progressive city but have not written extensively about its international significance in these years. The major exceptions have been European and American architectural historians who have documented the crucial role architects and builders of the Loop played in the development of modern architecture. Though American historians have been fascinated with the city, they have tended to study it in relationship to other American cities. Against this backdrop, Chicago has appeared more distinctive than revolutionary, in part because these authors have stressed the logic of its development, and, like its citizens of a century ago, have tended to view this development as inevitable. Though Europeans of the twentieth century have been more alert to Chicago's international significance in the 1890s than have American historians, they have not reported well what contemporaries realized—that Chicago in these years registered more quickly and dramatically basic transformations that were affecting urban culture on both sides of the Atlantic. However, the city's moment of revelation was brief. Its economy faltered in 1893–94. Furthermore, foreign observers shifted their attention in the later 1890s from its remarkable development, applying its positive and negative lessons to their own cities. Chicago was proof that notoriety in an age of change could be short lived. The origin of its lessons soon became obscured as they were absorbed and integrated with fresher lessons from other sources. Yet, the initial reactions of exhilaration and shock described by the hundreds of European visitors who saw the city, especially in the early 1890s, affected current debates about the direction of contemporary culture in Britain, France, and Germany.

Notes

1. James Bryce, *Social Institutions of the United States* (New York: Chautauqua Press, 1891), 237, 242.

2. William James, "On Some Omissions of Introspective Psychology," *Mind* (January 1884), cited in Stephen Kern, *The Culture of Time and Space 1880–1918* (Cambridge, Mass.: Harvard University Press, 1983), 24. In developing my argument that Chicago's views and uses of time were central to its development, Kern's book has been invaluable to me.

3. According to the French architect Camille-Marie Piton, who reviewed the Philadelphia Exposition in 1876 for *Revue générale de l'architecture et des travaux publics,* "One is not able to create an artist from one day to the next; all the more reason when the question concerns a whole people, whom it is impossible in a few years to raise to the level of the senior nations of the Old World, where art has taken centuries to attain its real development." C. Piton, "Lettres de Philadelphie," *Revue générale de l'architecture et des travaux publics,* 4th ser., 4 (1877): 170.

4. See Friedrich Dernburg, *Aus der weissen Stadt* (Berlin: Julius Springer, 1893), 72.

5. The opposite point of view was expressed well by Henryk Sienkiewicz in *Portrait of America: Letters of Henryk Sienkiewicz* (ed. and trans. Charles Morley [New York: Columbia University Press, 1959], 50). Chicago's oldest citizens could look back only to emptiness, to the "primeval forest, and the vast silence of the prairies," he argued. A Polish author and winner of the Nobel Prize for literature in 1905, Sienkiewicz had been in the United States between 1876 and 1878. His comments about Chicago in the 1870s were imaginative and intelligent.

6. Dernburg, 28. Paul Bourget also noted the city's lack of finish in his well-known essay, "A Farewell to the White City" (*Cosmopolitan,* December 1893, 134). He wrote, "Here a concrete sidewalk, carefully tended, there a battered one of wood; one moment a properly paved street, the next a sea of mud where the grip-car tracks glisten with metallic luster."

7. Quoted in Bessie Louise Pierce, *As Others See Chicago* (Chicago: University of Chicago Press, 1933), 359.

8. "American Architecture," *British Architect* 31 (18 January 1889): 47.

9. See Nathan Rosenberg, *Perspectives on Technology* (Cambridge: Cambridge University Press, 1976); George Wallis and Joseph Whitworth, *The American System of Manufactures* (1854), edited with an introduction by Nathan Rosenberg (Edinburgh: University of Edinburgh Press, 1969); Sigfried Giedion, *Space, Time and Architecture* (Cambridge, Mass.: Harvard University Press, 1941); and John A. Kouwenhoven, *Made in America* (Garden City: Doubleday, 1962).

10. James Bain, "American Locks," *Architect* 17 (30 June 1877), 413.

11. Anton Poschacher, "Architektur und öffentliche Bauten," in *Bericht über die Weltausstellung in Philadelphia 1876*, no. 14 (Vienna: 1877), 8.

12. César Daly, "Maisons américaines," *Revue générale de l'architecture et des travaux publics*, 4th ser., 13 (1886): 23.

13. Leopold Gmelin, "American Architecture from a German Point of View," *Forum* 27 (August 1899): 698.

14. Paul Sédille, "American Architecture from a French Standpoint," *American Architect* 20 (11 September 1886): 123.

15. P.P. [Paul Planat], "L'architecture américaine," *La construction moderne*, 2d ser., 1 (12 October 1895): 15.

16. Hans Schliepmann, "Amerikanische Architektur," *Kunstwart* 7 (August 1894): 339–40.

17. M. Brincourt, "États-Unis," *Encyclopédie de l'architecture et de la construction* 4, pt. 2 (1888–95): 423.

18. Marcel Daly, "L'architecture américaine," *La semaine des constructeurs*, 2d ser., 6 (23 April 1892): 515.

19. Robert Kerr, "Architecture Thirty Years Hence," *British Architect* 23 (13 February 1885): 82.

20. Kern, 82.

21. "English Industries and American Competition," *Engineering* 26 (9 August 1878): 115. This long article, appearing in *Engineering* between 5 July 1878 and 18 April 1879, was an excellent analysis of attitudes and approaches in the two countries. In "An American Block of Offices" (*Engineering* 48 [15 November 1889]: 564), the editors wrote, "In America the inevitable is accepted with far better grace than in this country. When changed conditions demand new methods we resist their introduction as long as possible, and when at last they can be deferred no longer, we suffer them under protest, until the recollection of their novelty is lost in daily use. But across the Atlantic a new idea, or an improved method, is treated with the generous reception due to a newcomer of whom no one knows any ill."

22. For example, in "The United States Exhibition of 1892" (*Engineering* 49 [7 March 1890], 305), the journal's editors claimed the United States was the place where Europeans could learn more in a shorter period than anywhere else in the world, and that Chicago, at least if one listened to its citizens, was its most instructive city.

23. According to Paul de Rousiers, widespread desire for self-improvement in the United States produced "superb confidence," stemming from two main factors: individual energy and the faith of Americans in eventual success. And no city in the United States, he added, was more accustomed to success than Chicago. Paul de Rousiers, *American Life*, trans. A. J. Herbertson (Paris: Firmin-Didot, 1892), 73–74.

24. Chas. Heathcote, "Comparison of English and American Building Methods," *British Architect* 37 (11 December 1903): 432.

25. *America and the Americans from a French Point of View* (New York: Charles Scribner's Sons,

1897), 265. Written anonymously to avoid offending American friends, the book is opinionated but perceptive, particularly on American processes.

26. Quoted in Rousiers, 437.

27. Matthew Arnold, *Civilization in the United States* (Boston: Cupples and Hurd, 1888), 129.

28. At this meeting Andrew T. Taylor, an associate member who established an architectural career in Montreal, Canada (1883–1904), spoke for a segment of his colleagues when he said that despite its accompanying disorder, the "go-ahead" mentality was better than self-satisfaction and lethargy, "for even in this 'unrest' lies, I am convinced, the 'power and the gateway' of great things in the future." Arthur J. Gale, "American Architecture from a Constructional Point of View," *Royal Institute of British Architects, Transactions* (1882–83): 56. Following the 18 December 1882, lecture by Arthur Gale, several members of the RIBA commented on the report of his architectural tour in the United States.

29. W.S., "Ein amerikanisches Miethaus," *Deutsche Bauzeitung* 18 (27 September 1884): 461. See also Br. Stephany, "Zwanglose Briefe aus Amerika," *Wochenblatt für Architekten und Ingenieure* 3 (6 May 1881): 184.

30. "The Godwin Bursary 1882: Tour in the United States," *Royal Institute of British Architects, Proceedings* (21 December 1882): 45.

31. He remarked, "It is here [Chicago], indeed, that the American 'go-ahead,' the idea of going always forward without useless regrets and recriminations, with an eye to the future, fearless and calm—it is here that it attains its maximum intensity." Rousiers, 73.

32. Dankmar Adler, "Engineering Supervision of Building Operations," *American Architect* 33 (4 July 1891): 12.

33. F. T. Reade, "The Application of Iron and Steel to Building Purposes," *Royal Institute of British Architects, Transactions,* n.s., 6 (1889–90): 35.

34. Henry Ericsson and Lewis E. Myers, *Sixty Years a Builder* (Chicago: A. Kroch, 1942), 106.

35. Chicagoans were quick to adopt the telephone in the 1870s and viewed its social consequences in a positive way. Though Boston opened the first central exchange in May 1877 and New Haven the first commercial exchange the following January, the Chicago Telephone Exchange, granted a franchise in September 1878, grew more quickly and was more experimental than franchises in other cities. Robert H. Glauber, "The Necessary Toy: The Telephone Comes to Chicago," *Chicago History* 7 (Summer 1978): 76.

36. Walter Marshall, *Through America* (London: Sampson Low, Marston, Searle, and Rivington, 1882), 100.

37. Max O'Rell [Paul Blouët] and Jack Allyn, *Jonathan and his Continent* (New York: Cassell, 1889), 232.

38. Richard Müller-Frienfels, "The Mechanization and Standardization of American Life," in *America in Perspective,* ed. Henry Steele Commager (New York: Random House, New American Library, 1947), 188.

39. Ernst von Hesse-Wartegg described a device on the wall beside his bed at the Auditorium Hotel, enabling him to make specific requests. Above the arc of the movable pointer were words identifying available services, including towels, stationery, shoes polished, dinner, ice water, newspaper, whiskey, and soda. When he needed something, he turned the pointer to his selection, pressed the button, and soon a youth appeared at his door with what he had ordered. "Just as in 'Bellamy,'" he added (a reference to Edward Bellamy, *Looking Backward, 2000–1887,* 1888). Ernst von Hesse-Wartegg, *Chicago: Eine Weltstadt im amerikanischen Westen* (Stuttgart: Union Deutsche Verlagsgesellschaft, 1893), 22–23.

40. "Very Tall Building," *Architect* 30 (15 September 1883): 155.

41. Kern, 214.

42. *America and the Americans from a French Point of View,* 83–98.

43. Rainer Hanns Tolzmann, "Objective Architecture: American Influences in the Development of Modern German Architecture," (Ph.D. diss., University of Michigan, 1975), 176.

44. Chas. Heathcote, "Comparison of English and American Building Methods," *British Architect* 37 (4 December 1903): 413.

45. Hermann Maier, "Einige Wand- und Deckenkonstruktionen in den amerikanischen unverbrennlichen 'Stahl-Rahmen-Gebäude,'" *Deutsche Bauzeitung* 28 (23 May 1894): 253.

46. Dankmar Adler, "Some Technical Reflections on Tall Buildings," *British Architect* 36 (17 July 1891): 54.

47. Adler, "Engineering Supervision of Building Operations," 11.

48. Paraphrased in Gustave Rodrigues, *The People of Action* (New York: Charles Scribner's Sons, 1918), 36.

49. Reade, 36.

50. Adler, "Engineering Supervision of Building Operations," 11.

51. Adler, "Some Technical Reflections on Tall Buildings," 54.

52. Adolphe Bocage, "L'architecture aux États-Unis et à l'exposition universelle de Chicago," *L'architecture* 7 (13 October 1894): 338.

53. Giuseppe Giacosa summarized the latter point well when he declared that those who ignored Chicago did not know the nineteenth century, for the city had become its ultimate expression, an insight I have quoted in the introduction. See Bessie Louise Pierce, *As Others See Chicago* (Chicago: University of Chicago Press, 1933), 276.

Part Two

Chicago: Modernity Materialized

Discovering
5 Chicago's
Architecture

EUROPEANS first became curious about multistory office buildings in New York City in the 1870s,[1] but their curiosity did not extend to Chicago's commercial architecture until 1882, when Arthur John Gale reported to the Royal Institute of British Architects (RIBA) about his recent study tour of the United States. A decade later the architectural establishment in Paris and Berlin, in addition to that of London, knew the meaning of "Chicago construction," even though many architects, builders, and critics abroad continued to downplay its significance. Until 1893 the British were better informed about Chicago's revolutionary architecture than were continental observers, a consequence of the close cultural ties between Britain and the United States and the obvious advantage of a common language. During the Columbian Exposition and in the years immediately following it, French and German professionals demonstrated greater curiosity about this new type of architecture and produced the best-researched and most-informative criticism.

Until 1893, when many European critics saw the tall buildings of the Loop for the first time, their primary sources of information about early skyscrapers were architectural journals published in the United States that circulated in Europe.[2] The practice of reprinting or editorializing on material from American sources began shortly after the founding of the *American Architect* in 1876. At first, American journals were commended for their verbal content, later for both illustrations and text. Architectural circles abroad responded favorably to the *American Architect*'s special edition of gelatine prints—full-page plates of historic buildings and monuments in Europe—which it began to issue in 1884. Encouraged by the warm reception within the country and beyond, the journal's editors in March 1886 launched an international edition—the "Imperial"—each volume to contain forty gelatine prints from nature and thirty-six double-page photolithographic plates. At the turn of the decade articles appeared in journals in Britain, France, and Germany citing the quality of architectural reporting and illustrations in the United States, particularly in the *American Architect* and the *Inland Architect* of Chicago. In 1889 the RIBA library in London subscribed to seven American architectural journals.[3]

If architects in the three European countries had created attractive, functional architecture that was also up-to-date, they would have paid much less attention to developments in the United States. But this was not the case. Frustrated by failure to develop a satisfying contemporary architecture, they began to take American work more seriously in the mid-1880s, not to imitate its final forms but to study its priorities and the factors that shaped them.

British Architectural Criticism before 1893

The restlessness of architects in Western Europe was evident in the major architectural journals published in the three countries. The sense of frustration revealed in the articles and editorials in the *British Architect* of London during these years typified the attitude of the British press. Between the early 1880s and the early 1890s its editors expressed a mixture of impatience and resignation about the state of architecture in Great Britain, while gradually becoming more curious about theory and practice in the United States. Earlier in the 1880s the journal's articles and editorials referred to "a sense of impending change," but also to a "time of felt uncertainty," of "stranded purposes," and of hopes that "came to nothing." The journal's writers complained that the past no longer provided guidance while the present was still too vague for architects to read with assurance. According to Basil Champneys in the 9 December 1887 issue, every practitioner had become "a law to himself." Some commentators contended the British profession could get back on track if it could learn how to address practical problems better. Others cited the decline of an appreciation of "the beautiful" as the source of the problem. In their summary of British architecture for the year 1887, the editors of the *British Architect* claimed there were only a "few good architects in Britain." In their review of 1890 they referred to an "uneventful record," one that showed little progress in either the art or the science of building. The journal recognized the "utilitarian spirit of the present age" but wondered how "ruthless utilitarianism" could lead to an original development in art. Though its editorial policy endorsed the importance of the functional side of architecture, the journal's plates usually featured cultural, religious, or governmental buildings, not utilitarian or commercial ones.[4]

Like other journals in Britain, the *British Architect* had a high opinion of the technical quality of American architecture. In the early 1880s it often published notes about ventilating systems, elevators, or fireproofing schemes that had first appeared in journals in the United States. This reflected its staff's conclusion that Americans, naive in art, were, nevertheless, practical people whose purposeful products merited examination, a conclusion the journal held until the end of the century. On the other hand, American design, at moments refreshing, was not sophisticated; it lacked proportion, refinement, and harmony, qualities the *British Architect* found in contemporary British work. Its editors thought free-standing houses represented the best of American work and, on one occasion in 1890, stated that these designs served the future better than did comparable architecture in Britain. The journal published little about tall office blocks in the United States and missed the growing importance of iron and steel in their construction until about 1891. These summarized reactions of the *British Architect* were fairly representative of the British profession between 1880 and the early 1890s.[5]

One of the concerns voiced, but not addressed well, by the *British Architect* was the weakness of the British profession on the functional side of architecture. The creation of the Godwin Bursary in 1881, the fund that underwrote John Arthur Gale's three-month tour of the United States the following year, was a formal expression of that concern. Established by George Godwin, editor of *Builder,* and administered by the RIBA, the Godwin Bursary was a yearly competitive prize enabling young British architects to study modern techniques of construction, drainage, water supply, heating, and ventilation outside of Great Britain. Winners were obligated to spend at least five weeks in a chosen foreign country and to submit oral and written illustrated reports to the RIBA on their return. Gale and five of the next twelve recipients of the bursary chose to visit the United States.[6] Gale's reports, delivered at the Institute in November and December 1882, were systematic investigations resulting from on-site inspection. George B. Post gave him a tour and a set of plans of his Mills Building in New York (fig. 28), and P. B. Wight in Chicago explained to him why modern fireproofing was required for the protection of all constructive iron work.[7] His lecture on 18 December 1882 at the institute in London provoked a spirited discussion among members, several of whom applauded studying methods of construction in other countries.

Gale's findings were less enthusiastically received in the British architectural press. Granting that new commercial architecture in the United States was shaped by necessity, not whimsical factors, the editor of the *Architect* nevertheless urged readers to oppose talk of erecting similar tall structures along the streets of London. He predicted that in America such edifices would soon convert streets into "narrow gorges, as inaccessible to the light and air as they must be concentrative of the increasing noise and dirt of incessant money-spinning."[8] However, he was not worried that this would soon occur in London because its business people would oppose the introduction of both elevators and telephones on the grounds they were inimical to the English style of doing business.

The section of Gale's report that drew the crispest press reaction was his explanation of the use of iron in constructing office buildings. He referred to two different structural systems he had noticed on his tour—one, a skeleton of iron surrounded by a relatively thin exterior wall, and the other, an iron facade that did not necessarily contain an interior metal skeleton. Of the two, Gale thought the former was more effective because its supports were better protected from fire. His description of this system was brief.

> The foundation wall of the front is brick, carried-up in piers to receive the round cast-iron columns which are the vertical members of the skeleton. Across these, at the first-floor level, are rolled-iron riveted girders, and above are columns again. On the floors above the first, channel irons as lintels, laid with the back downwards, are placed, all bolted together. The columns are cased with brickwork, leaving a space between the outside of the brick and the ironwork shell; on the lintels or channel irons too is 12–inch brickwork as high as the window-sills. The columns are con-

tinuous in height, and have brackets for the reception of the channel iron, which in its turn carries the floors, which are anchored to the front.[9]

This was probably the first clear explanation of an American building supported by an internal metal framework published in the British press. Though Gale was ambiguous about the extent to which the exterior was a bearing wall and said little about the possi-

Figure 28. Mills Building, New York, 1881–83, George B. Post (*L'architecture américaine*, 1886).

bilities of flexible interior planning, he described a fireproofed skeleton in which the floors rested on iron girders that, in turn, were supported by metal columns.

Complying with the requirements of the Godwin Bursary, Gale concentrated on the structural aspects of iron and did not explain the relationship of metal framing to purpose or appearance. His conclusion that this system produced a stronger, safer structure was ignored by British critics. His apparent endorsement of iron concealed behind street facades, however, was not ignored. Concluding that Gale had described a dependent wall, the editor of the *Architect,* admitting his traditional prejudices, stated that this would not be acceptable in London. He could not conceive of meaningful architecture along its major streets in which the ornamental facade was supported by "metal framing filled in with panels of whatever handy material may best serve a cheap decorative purpose." The result would still be a box, not architecture, "even if the panels were of the choicest marbles and the 'skeleton' of silver and gold."[10] Though acceptable for the outer walls of temporary or industrial buildings and permissible as supports within interior walls of public buildings, iron, either as sheets or as bearing columns, would be rejected for use in the facades of significant street architecture by any cultivated architect, the editor asserted.

Metal had been used extensively in nineteenth-century utilitarian structures such as docks, mills, railroad sheds, and bridges. By midcentury, iron columns were increasingly used in greenhouses, libraries, theaters, and markets. Gerald Larson has argued that iron framing in Europe anticipated by at least ninety years the skeleton of William Le Baron Jenney's Home Insurance Company Building in Chicago and, furthermore, was more advanced in France in 1884 than it was in Jenney's structural system.[11] English architects of the day could find claims for the usefulness of iron in building in the writings of Viollet-le-Duc, Louis-Auguste Boileau, or William Fairbairn. Around 1880 John Belcher had constructed a store for Messrs. Rylands in the City in London that employed a frame of iron columns and rolled iron joists.[12] The *Architect* was not objecting to the use of iron, a material widely accepted in Britain in the 1880s, but to the Americans' failure to employ it appropriately.

Convinced that "American ingenuity is clearly on the wrong track," the editor of the *Architect* returned to the question of the acceptable deployment of iron in architecture in an editorial of 22 March 1884. Claiming to speak for responsible architects within the British profession, he declared that, as far as fine architecture was concerned, iron was "a cheap expedient to be kept strictly under control." He was disturbed by American designers who exploited iron for practical and economic reasons, calling the trend an "inadvertency of the multitude" that threatened the "enduring majesty" of the grand art. The editor was proud the British still trod the nobler path. "In other words, the contempt for sham, which with us is now provoked so unreservedly amongst people of taste when cast-iron (of all things in the world) takes the liberty of offering an imitation of the outward presentment of superior materials and workmanship, appears comparatively unknown to the Transatlantic public."[13] Whether the Americans tried to make iron sheets look like "superior materials" or whether they tried "to attach by means of screws an outer cuticle of slabs, of terra-cotta or whatever other artificiality of extreme tenuity" to bearing columns, they committed a major sin by compromising that part of a building entrusted with the primary role of architectural expression.

For critics of the day, no aspect of a public building communicated "enduring majesty" more effectively than its main facade. The quality of a facade—its design, proportion, ornament, materials, sense of purpose—determined to a significant degree a critic's opinion about the quality of the entire building. The principal facade was also expected to convey assurances of strength, ethical purity, and moral inspiration. To express these qualities effectively, this part, more than any other part of a building, had to be free from compromise and subterfuge. By employing disguised iron panels or concealed iron framing in street fronts, the architects in the United States occasionally drew charges that they were disregarding two rules by which the game of architecture was normally played in Europe. First, they showed disrespect to the maxim "design in beauty, build in truth," which assumed the coherence of art and strength. A proper facade preserved the interconnectedness of design and support; or, to put it another way, ornament was an artistic expression of the strength of a material. An iron-framed system, denying the double role of traditional materials, led to a semidependent or totally dependent outer surface. In the view of certain critics, this affected the wall's integrity and reduced its significance, realizations that challenged their traditional assumptions. Secondly, the architects of these new buildings were also thought in some quarters to have been irresponsible because they hid bearing columns of iron behind piers that appeared to be load-bearing elements. What one saw was not the structural reality that insured a building's stability. A few critics in Britain considered this a base practice, an unfortunate consequence of buckling to economic expediency. Yet objections in Britain to hiding the metal skeleton were mild. Despite the claim of the *Architect's* editor to speak for responsible architects, the cry of "sham" in Great Britain in the early 1880s came from a minority. And even he granted that "if iron is to be developed as a building material, art will inevitably find its way to it and make it its own."[14] On the other hand, though more open-minded, this statement was also revealing for it assumed art would own iron rather than iron owning art.

High buildings became a topic of conversation again when John B. Gass, the second recipient of the Godwin Bursary to visit the United States, gave his public lecture at the RIBA on 15 March 1886.[15] Unlike German and French designers, informed through no comparable catalyst like the bursary and for whom journal literature and illustrations became the primary source of news about American work in these years, Gale and Gass saw the new commercial architecture in context and explained it a few months later to key members of the British profession. The reactions of RIBA members to the reports of Gale in 1882 and Gass in 1886 enable us to measure shifts in British thinking about contemporary architecture in the United States.[16]

More convinced than ever about the importance of utilitarian aspects of architecture, the RIBA's members in 1886 expressed stronger praise for Godwin's idea. Several speakers also commended Gass's choice of the United States, claiming it was the place to go to observe the latest in structural approaches and new equipment. "Nobody can pass through any city in America without learning at every step," said Ewan Christian, president of the institute. The members were also better informed about the individuals who had influenced recent trends in American education and design. Some commended William Robert Ware, first professor of architecture at the Massachusetts Institute of Technology and later head of the Columbia School of Architecture, for creating curricula some considered superior to the training British students received, while others commented positively on the work of Henry Hobson Richardson.

One reason for the greater specificity in the commentary that followed the address by Gass was an extensive exhibition of 112 drawings and photographs of recent work from the United States—plus a few from Canada—that he hung at the RIBA. Formerly predisposed to view the architecture of the United States in general terms, institute members now had an opportunity to study specific buildings by named architects. This exhibition, which included 27 plates of buildings by Richardson, 7 by Richard Morris Hunt, 4 by Peabody and Stearns, and a small sampling of the work of Adler and Sullivan, Burnham and Root, W. L. B. Jenney, Cobb and Frost, and S. S. Beman in Chicago, was considered by some members in 1886 to be the best survey of recent architecture in the United States ever displayed in London.[17]

Gass and his respondents were hard on the antiquarians of the British profession, much more so than participants in the Gale discussion had been. Several commended American designers in their verbal attacks on historicism. "There architects have thrown aside survivalism and have worked according to their own ideas," contended Thomas Rickman, son of the better-known architect of the same name who was active in the first half of the century. Designers in the United States had often been reprimanded in the British press because they had followed their own ideas, but by 1886 a portion of the British profession, revising earlier verdicts, saw some advantages to yesterday's impudence. Their views about American architecture were changing because basic criteria for evaluating architecture were changing. Earlier, revisionists had not been very effective in questioning the primacy of art, but in the mid-1880s their contention that even art must adjust to changing realities no longer seemed so radical. Gass expressed this position when he said he had seen in the United States "new combinations, dictated by and growing out of the necessities of the building." Compared to British design, he continued, American work is "accordingly more living and interesting, less the production of a dry-as-dust archaeology, and more in accordance with the true principles of all great architecture." Seldom had any European critic or architect come so close to stating that American designers, traditionally labeled as flagrant abusers of the Grand Tradition, had become its latest defenders. Though his remarks reflected emerging attitudes among some London architects, they did not reflect the majority of British professionals in 1886.[18]

To explain the construction of tall buildings, Gass chose examples primarily from Chicago. In his initial talk before the Council of the RIBA in October 1885, he explained that most of the recent office buildings in the Loop had been built according to the same system and then chose William Le Baron Jenney's Home Insurance Company of 1883–85 to explain how they were constructed.

> The outer walls are of brick with stone or terra cotta dressings. In the Home Insurance Company's building, iron columns run up the full height in the centre of brick piers; iron window lintels rest on the columns. It is of fire-proof construction, with cast iron columns and wrought iron girders encased in terra-cotta; the floors are arches of hollow tile, wooden flooring on sleepers above. Internal partitions are of hollow tile, which being light can be set on floors at any point, and the offices are divided and made the size required by tenant.[19]

The membership may have concluded the building's exterior walls were self-supporting, for he said nothing further about the relationship of the brick walls to the iron framework. He discussed the use of hollow tiles for internal walls and illustrated hollow-tile flooring, which, he added, was also being used in England. Gass also illustrated the fireproofing of an iron column, a girder, and a hollow tile arch (fig. 29), but he was not explicit about internal supports and did not elaborate on their role in flexible planning. However, he included three plans of the entrance, second, and third floors of the Home Insurance Company Building (fig. 30) and wrote on two of them, "partitions can be changed to suit." He also referred to the Home Insurance Building when explaining briefly that isolated foundations were used to control and minimize the settlement of heavy structures on Chicago's soft subsoil.

By 1886 architects in London had heard about the iron framing system used in the Home Insurance Company Building, had studied drawings showing its hollow-tile flooring and fireproofing of its girders and columns, and also knew of its exterior appearance from an illustration published in the 15 May 1886 issue of the *Irish Builder* (fig. 31). However, the British response to America's multistory commercial structures remained mixed. Some critics would have concurred with Gass that this type of architecture should be studied because it was determined by contemporary conditions, or they might have agreed with the editors of *British Architect,* who published a plate of the Studebaker Building (1885) in Chicago by S. S. Beman and commented, "This is certainly the work we should apply for were we in need of an architect for a London street" (fig. 32).[20] Yet the majority of British professionals remained cautious, acknowledging the correlation between office blocks and needs but also wondering if necessity's triumph meant architecture's retreat in the form of disquieting scale, restricted artistic expression, and the intrusion of iron into street facades.

By the late 1880s, British attitudes toward America's new commercial architecture were clearly different from earlier reactions in England. One viewpoint was expressed by Alexander Graham, an active member of the RIBA who served as its vice-president from 1893 to 1897. He remarked in 1888, "It is in the erection of offices and business premises, rather than of public edifices and private dwellings, that the American architects show the greatest promise."[21] Observers in Britain began to view the multistory office block as a type pertinent to their architectural discussions instead of treating it as a novel but distant American product. Categorizing these buildings as a "new and independent departure," Graham concurred with an unnamed French critic who had said, "We may cavil at details, but we must doff our hats to the result." In these years British professionals also decided this new type of building could be studied best in Chicago. Charles Brodie, a young British architect who had spent winter through spring of 1887/88 in the United States, declared:

> I have seen nowhere, either in this or our own country, or on the Continent, such a truly noble lot of buildings as Chicago possesses, and buildings at the same time so original in treatment. There is an almost total lack of conventional stuck-on-look-

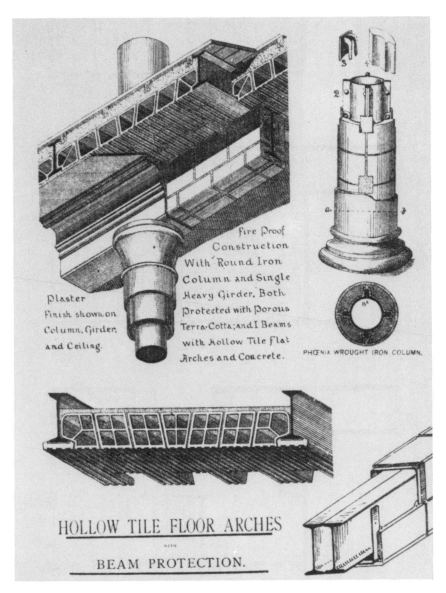

Figure 29. Hollow tile floor arches with beam protection (*Royal Institute of British Architects, Transactions*, 1885–86).

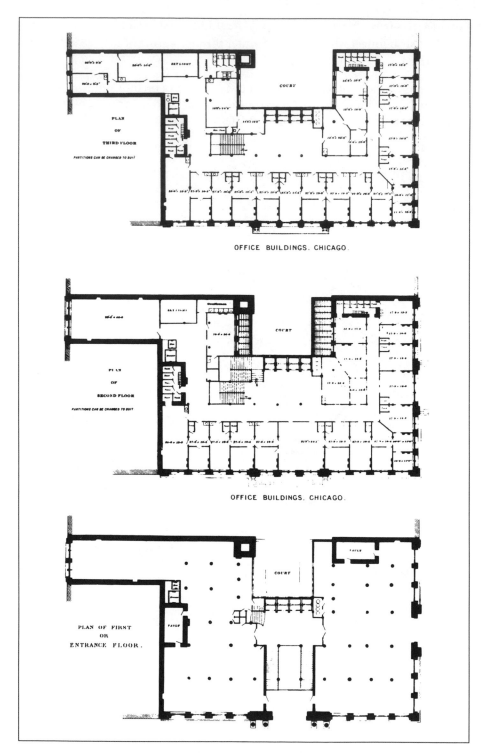

Figure 30. Plans of the first, second, and third floors of the Home Insurance Company Building, Chicago, 1884–85, William Le Baron Jenney (*Royal Institute of British Architects, Transactions*, 1885–86).

Figure 31. Home Insurance Company Building, Chicago, 1884–85, William Le Baron Jenney (*Irish Builder*, 15 May 1886).

Figure 32. Studebaker Building, Chicago, 1885, S. S. Beman (*British Architect*, 29 January 1886).

ing column and pilaster treatment. There they stand, what you see carrying them, with little ornament, but that little good, a credit to their designers and constructors, and to the enterprising citizens who laid out their money in allowing these "to design in beauty" and massiveness and "to build in truth."[22]

However, British critics were vague about the causes of tall office buildings until 9 July 1892, when the *Builder* published its exceptional article entitled, "New Business Buildings in Chicago," criticism that I will discuss in the last chapter.

The rise of the skyscraper in Chicago was not the only architectural news British journals published about the city during the decade. Aware that Chicago had become symbolic of American vigor and daring, the *Architect* of London, despite its attack on the use of iron in street fronts, gave persistent support to the Western Association of Architects (WAA) from its founding in Chicago in 1884 until its merger with the older American Institute of Architects (AIA) at the end of the decade. Responding to the WAA's 1886 convention, the *Architect*'s editor stated its meetings were always important events because the issues addressed were pertinent to those facing professions in all Western countries but then added that English architects always followed American theory and practice more closely than they did the architectural activities on the Continent.[23] The *Architect*'s annual reviews of WAA conferences were positive until the 1888 meeting when its members discussed the possibility of merging with the older and more prestigious American Institute of Architects. The London-based journal opposed this action, complaining that in the United States as in England there was a contemporary push toward centralization inimical to the expression of independent thought. Previously the journal had approved the WAA's relatively open membership policy, including its acceptance of women.

> It is difficult for a stranger to understand both sides of the question of consolidation, but apparently the Western Association is risking everything that is characteristic by the leap in the dark which it is about to undertake. For the reflected respectability which is supposed to come from the union with the older Society, it will have to sacrifice the liberty which has already produced so much good. We know of no Society with so short an existence that can produce a more creditable record than the Western Association, and yet the future is to be jeopardized; perhaps it would be nearer the truth to say that the Association is not to have a future, because there are some men who believe in a mammoth Society in which the members will be compelled from their numbers to leave the government to a few.[24]

On 27 December 1889 the *Architect*'s editor denounced the merger that had been formalized on 21 November, regretting that it meant the termination of a society more individualistic, self-assertive, and enthusiastic about architecture than the institute that remained. Thus, a journal in Britain warned about the consequences of homogenization at a time when Chicago's architects and builders believed their independence was assured.

In the first years of the 1890s, British journals, notably *Engineering* and the *British Architect,* published articles on construction methods and materials employed for tall buildings, a subject last addressed in detail by John Gass in 1885–86.[25] The *British Architect* reissued, sometimes in abridged form, articles by William Le Baron Jenney and

Dankmar Adler that had first appeared in American publications.[26] In December 1891 the *British Architect* carried Jenney's address to the American Institute of Architects on October 29 entitled "The Chicago Construction, or Tall Buildings on a Compressible Soil," in which he defined the phrase. "DEFINITION.—What is now generally known as the Chicago Construction consists of a fireproofed steel skeleton so arranged that all the load including the walls and partitions are carried story by story on the columns. The foundations as far as practical are on isolated piers."[27] Technical articles like these were influential because they diverted attention from the issue of art, where reservations were stronger, to the practical realm, where British architects and critics could more easily empathize with American colleagues facing new challenges, even if they were still disinclined to imitate them.

Most architects in Great Britain probably had a fair understanding of skeleton construction by 1892, but few of them would have advocated "Chicago construction" for new business buildings along London's major streets. Nevertheless, they were better informed about Chicago's technical revolution at this time than were designers and critics in France or in Germany. Furthermore, they heard about new developments in Chicago almost as quickly as did Americans who lived on the East Coast. On 30 November 1891, the *New York Times* reported, "Probably a majority of those people in the East who have read of the new high buildings in Chicago suppose that these buildings have self-sustaining walls."[28] On 19 December 1891, the *American Architect* stated that the average professional in the United States "generally" knew that the outer walls of many of Chicago's high buildings were thin shells attached to a metal skeleton of floor beams resting "even at the outside ends" on iron columns. The paper given by Jenney at the AIA convention in October 1891, in which he reviewed the history of "Chicago Construction" and explained the role of both columns and foundations, was reprinted in the *British Architect* four months before it was published in America's major architectural journal, the *American Architect,* whose editors apologized for losing the initial galley on the cutting-room floor.[29]

Continental Architectural Criticism before 1893

In France and Germany architectural critics prior to the Columbian Exposition knew about tall buildings primarily from information published in American journals. From the Franco-Prussian War in 1870–71 until the end of the century, the German press regularly carried reports about technical developments in the United States. Unlike the British, who often recognized advantages in American innovations but tended to resist their adoption for the sake of art or social convention, or the French, who viewed American developments from a lofty, philosophical vantage point, the Germans, especially those in the fields of manufacturing, engineering, and architecture, openly approved of steps to cut costs and increase efficiency, speed, simplicity, convenience, and comfort. They were more curious than either the British or the French about American purposefulness.

German architects also learned of American practices in the mid-1880s from the reports published regularly in the *Centralblatt der Bauverwaltung* and occasionally in the *Deutsche Bauzeitung* that had been filed by the technical attaché assigned to the government's embassy in Washington, D.C. Franz Lange, trained in architecture but an authority on railroads, held the position from 1882 to 1884 when he was replaced by Karl Hinckeldeyn, a graduate of the Berlin Academy of Architecture, who had been working as a lead writer for the *Centralblatt der Bauverwaltung*. Hinckeldeyn, the more informative and influential of the two, remained in the United States until 1887. Like Lange, he focused on utilitarian aspects of American architecture during his tenure in Washington, in part because he thought designers in the United States were artistically weak.[30]

Shortly after he arrived in the United States, Hinckeldeyn went to Chicago, where he attended the organizational meeting of the Western Association of Architects in November 1884. At one of its sessions, Daniel Burnham had likened Chicago to Athens, contending both cities profited from the presence of people from other countries. If this advantage could be utilized, Burnham predicted, the architecture of the region could become the most practical, distinctive, and beautiful the world had yet known. Reacting like a sage to the sincere but innocent proclamations of youth, Hinckeldeyn warned that parochial overvaluation would only delay the appearance of sound architecture. To assume that self-confidence and isolated ingenuity could compensate for an historically based understanding of the complexities of architecture was foolish in his judgment. The tall office buildings of Chicago were sufficient evidence of the failure of this approach; before them "the Muse of Architecture must silently veil her head." He urged architects in Chicago to take lessons from their colleagues in Eastern cities, where "the ship of time is laden more heavily with European ballast" and sails more surely into the seas ahead (translations mine).[31]

Hinckeldeyn was a major reason why the German profession learned little about American commercial work during the 1880s. Though he called new office buildings the "sum and substance" of advanced construction, he was not impressed by them because he thought they were ugly and inapplicable to German problems. He preferred the tall buildings of the East over Chicago's, which he claimed were harmed by "an affected aboriginality, not to say brutality,"[32] but even the skyscrapers in eastern cities did not move him as did attractive detached houses. Considered Germany's leading authority on American architecture during the 1880s, he returned to the United States in 1893 to cover the Columbian Exposition for his government's *Centralblatt der Bauverwaltung*. His occasional comments on tall buildings between visits were neither precise nor current.

The architectural community in Berlin was much less informed about multistory commercial buildings in the United States at the beginning of the nineties than were architects in London. The *Deutsche Bauzeitung,* Germany's most progressive architectural journal, did not publish its first article on the subject until 21 November 1891, when it discussed F. P. Dinkelberg's unexecuted project for a twenty-six-story building for the west side of lower Broadway in New York (fig. 33). At this time, the *Deutsche Bauzeitung* considered tall buildings to be characteristic, but unattractive, examples of recent American architecture, "which, in other respects [domestic architecture] is beginning to exert an influence on our latest architecture that should not be underestimated."[33] The *Baugewerks-Zeitung* may have published the first illustration of a Chicago office building in a German architectural journal when it issued a plate of the Schiller Building by Adler and Sullivan in March 1892 (fig. 34).[34] When they finally focused on the new architecture of the Loop—about 1893—German critics produced studies that were more detailed than those published in either Britain or France.

The first significant acknowledgment of early skyscrapers in France was the unexpected publication in 1886 of *L'architecture américaine,* three volumes of excellent photographs of recent American work taken by Albert Lévy.[35] Reflecting current French interest in American domestic design, two of the three volumes featured recent urban and suburban houses. In the first volume, however, more than half of the plates illustrated new commercial buildings. From New York, Lévy included George B. Post's Mills Building (1881–83, fig. 28) as well as the Produce Exchange (1881–84). From Chicago, he chose Adler and Sullivan's Rothschild Store (1880–81, fig. 35), its main facade extensively of glass; the National Bank of Illinois (1885) and the Insurance Exchange Building (1884–85, fig. 36) by Burnham and Root; and the Mallers Building (1884–85) by J. J. Flanders, the first twelve-story office block in Chicago (fig. 2). *L'architecture américaine* apparently did not lose money, since its publishers announced a sequel, *Villas américaines,* two years later.[36]

La semaine des constructeurs endorsed the merger of the Western Association of Architects with the American Institute of Architects, arguing that the WAA would invigorate the more complacent AIA with its midwestern "practicality and enterprising spirit." Consistent with the current French inclination to overstate admired qualities of American architects, the journal editor described the meetings of the WAA as "nothing academical; no phrases; no mystical burned incense; no flow of words that mean nothing. They only speak when they have an idea to give or objection to make, and this in a few words. Rhetoric is not considered, but what is said is substantially to the point."[37] In addition to exaggerating the qualities of American architects in order to goad their colleagues, French critics in the years around 1890 probably overstated because few had traveled to the United States for on-site inspections.

When French critics first commented on America's multistory commercial architecture—approximately two years before the Columbian Exposition—their reaction tended to be calm, reflective, and encouraging. Initial French commentary was itself lofty, as if expressed from a vantage point with assurance and generosity. *La construction moderne* took the lead. Between 1888 and the exposition it published a series of both signed and anonymous articles on the subject that were surprisingly consistent in tone and position.[38] Unsupported by specific references, the journal had a penchant for overarching pronouncements about the meaning of these buildings for the current age. The staff called them expressions of contemporary needs but never specified what those needs were or precisely how they reflected them. It urged readers to be open-minded, to suspend concern about whether this architecture represented moral progress or decadence, be-

Figure 33. Unexecuted design for a twenty-six-story building, New York, 1891, F. P. Dinkelberg (*Deutsche Bauzeitung*, 21 November 1891).

Figure 34. Schiller Building, Chicago, 1891–92, Adler and Sullivan
(*Baugewerks-Zeitung*, 5 March 1892).

cause it was probably a foretaste of the urban landscape of tomorrow. Often *La construction moderne* would cite a tall building in the United States, not to analyze it carefully but to reinforce an editorial position. This architecture, readers were told repeatedly, was bold, original, utilitarian, and built on rational thought, but the journal provided little concrete information to allow its subscribers to judge for themselves. Of the three nationalities, the French were the critics most inclined to interpret office buildings in social and economic terms and to ponder their cultural significance.

Figure 35. Rothschild Store, Chicago, 1880–81, Adler and Sullivan (*L'architecture américaine*, 1886).

The Olympian declarations of the *La construction moderne* before the Columbian Exposition differed markedly from the detailed inspections of skyscrapers carried out by numerous German observers during and just after the event. The French journal published few details, floor plans, or even illustrations of the main facade of an office building and often identified visual material indifferently. It was also incurious about

Figure 36. Insurance Exchange Building, Chicago, 1884–85, Burnham and Root (*L'architecture américaine*, 1886).

the technology that made these buildings possible, virtually ignoring the role of the steel skeleton. Despite its lack of specificity, *La construction moderne* preferred the new buildings of Chicago to those of New York and considered the Auditorium by Adler and Sullivan the most impressive of the Loop's new architecture. Its editors did not think the commercial architecture of the Loop was beautiful but commended designers for stressing the majesty of vast facades as their primary artistic element.

Hesitation, Confusion, and Denial

We may be inclined to think that initial responses to the radical departures of yesterday may have been more sympathetic and reasonable than, in fact, they were. Though intending to search for the contradictions and ambiguities inherent in reception at such times, we may, possibly because we have come to terms with the threat ouselves or need to simplify the story for the sake of narrative concision, gloss over them. In 1941 Sigfried Giedion was searching for pivotal moments in the evolution of modern architecture when he proclaimed that "from 1880 to the time of the Columbian Exposition of 1893 the 'Loop' area in Chicago . . . was the center of architectural development not merely for the United States but for the whole world."[39] His remark may leave the impression that the Loop commanded the focused and unified attention of the international architectural community, its members aware in these years of the zone's implications. On the contrary, Europeans were caught off guard by instantaneous Chicago and its challenging architecture. Before returning to the strands of that narrative, we need to look briefly at the ways in which they dealt with a development for which many were not well prepared.

When news of an unexpected break-through in a discipline circulates, especially a development challenging some of that field's fundamental assumptions, the compulsion to react—to have an opinion—may exceed the knowledge and understanding needed to respond in a competent manner. Continental critics were in a particularly disadvantaged position, for they attempted to comment about strange architecture in a distant land about which the best information was printed in another language. Not surprisingly, their reactions, especially those published between the late 1880s and 1892—when the difference between rumor and fact was often blurred—were sometimes naive or erroneous. For example, the *Schweizerische Bauzeitung,* attempting to convey to its readers the size of these buildings, claimed they contained as many habitable rooms as some small cities.[40] Even the cosmopolitan *Deutsche Bauzeitung* had to struggle to explain "Chicago construction." Its editorialist maintained, "The entire inner core would topple over as a solid iron object, it cannot collapse; an earthquake can overthrow it, it would fall as a solid block of iron."[41] The awkwardness of these two reactions reveals the partial vacuum in which these German-speaking critics were caught in 1891. In such a vacuum misinformation thrives. In three separate articles the *Wiener Bauindustrie-Zeitung* described the Masonic Temple by Burnham and Root (fig. 37) as a building containing fourteen, twenty, and twenty-two stories. Perhaps encouraged by the rumor that any-

Figure 37. Masonic Temple, Chicago, 1891–92, Burnham and Root (*Engineering*, 21 April 1893).

thing was now possible in Chicago, continental journals before 1893 were more inclined to exaggerate than to understate quantitative information about skyscrapers. The *Wiener Bauindustrie-Zeitung* claimed the roof garden of the Masonic Temple was large enough to hold thirty thousand people. Though misinformation and exaggeration in continental criticism may have been caused, in part, by inaccurate translations, they also may reflect the scrambling of foreign editors to cope with the unexpected.

Misinformation also characterized accounts in France and Germany of the history of "Chicago construction." British architects and engineers, informed by reprints of technical papers published in the United States, thought the system had originated in Chicago and had been refined there during the 1880s and early 1890s through the collective effort of the city's architects and engineers. Many continental professionals, however, believed its inventor was Leroy S. Buffington of Minneapolis.[42] Buffington claimed his description for a twenty-eight-story building project and his design (fig. 38), published in the *Inland Architect* in July 1888, were "copied all over the world." He was partially correct. His drawing was not as widely known in Europe as he assumed, and foreign critics who mentioned it sometimes focused on its appearance rather than on its structural features, but it was cited on several occasions. His sketch first appeared abroad in an article that Francis Osborne, a professor of architecture at Cornell University, wrote for *La construction moderne* in September 1888.[43] Early European references to the scheme sometimes contained mistakes. Osborne called it an office building already standing in Minneapolis. The *Wiener Bauindustrie-Zeitung* published a sketch in 1890 of a twelve-story hotel in New York, attributing it to Buffington; but the journal confused it with his twenty-eight-story building project and explained that the hotel's twelve visible floors actually contained twenty-eight interior levels.[44] Despite mistakes in reporting Buffington's claim to have invented the steel frame, pre-exposition articles published on the Continent tended to assume it was legitimate. Prior to 1893 only one continental observer contradicted Buffington's claim by stating that a complete, wall-bearing skeleton had been erected in Chicago as early as 1886.[45] In his article on tall buildings for *Zeitschrift des oesterreichischen Ingenieur- und Architekten-Vereines* in 1893, Fritz von Emperger corrected the impression that Buffington's design had been executed, but added more confusion by identifying Buffington as the father of the skyscraper, while explaining that his claim did not carry the weight of an invention because this type of construction had already developed organically.[46] Because Emperger's five-part article was widely read and quoted on the Continent, some German and French writers as late as 1895 still believed the skeleton system came to Chicago from Minneapolis in 1889 (Emperger had cited the wrong date for the patent). By the middle of the decade, however, continental professionals were becoming suspicious of Buffington's role.[47]

We may want to assume that a new idea in history, especially one that profoundly affected later developments and to us now seems useful and inevitable, would have been welcomed and given a thoughtful hearing when it first appeared. Yet dramatic challenges to existing thinking often do not receive inquisitive receptions, even in this case where a new architecture had been long awaited. Early reactions, those before the exposition,

Figure 38. Unexecuted design for a twenty-eight-story building, 1888, Leroy S. Buffington (*Inland Architect*, July 1888).

to tall commercial buildings were frequently hesitant or negative. Those who resisted the new architecture seldom declared that it had appeared for artificial or unnecessary reasons. The large majority of these critics publicly supported the notion of progress but were often unable to accept some of its manifestations. As a result, they might praise the realistic attitudes of the shapers of Chicago, but then claim the forces transforming the city were inapplicable to Europe; or they might justify their opposition to tall buildings at this time by citing the nervousness of American fire insurance companies over rising building heights, adding that safety must always take precedence over innovation. Prior to 1893 strategies of denial were probably more common than genuine curiosity about this revolutionary architecture.[48]

Finally, departures from habit were easier to endorse in theory than to accept in practice. In their musings about new developments in architecture, editorial staffs in Britain and on the Continent were inclined to be open-minded in the abstract. This was certainly true of their reactions to the tall building. For example, the *British Architect* published an article on elevators in February 1887 in which it praised American models and then challenged British architects to try new approaches, especially those that might convince their clients that the value of their property would be enhanced by the adoption of lifts. "We confess we should like to see a greater interest manifested by the profession at large in discovering for themselves the merits of this or that building material, or the advantages to be derived from the employment of this or that patent invention."[49] When high-toned recommendations came home to roost, however, the forms they took were often less appealing. In 1890 the *British Architect* denied the spirit of its 1887 exhortation when it objected to rumors of a proposed American-style hotel for the Waterloo House site in London. "It is a splendid site and worthy of something more cultured in the way of architectural adornment," wrote the journal's editor.[50] There were reasons why critics rejected in practice what they had advocated in editorials. Familiar architecture limited the imagination's ability to conceive of different architecture. When the new arrived, it was not necessarily what was expected or wanted. Desiring change was one thing, enjoying its unintended consequences another. Some had not realized that their generous call for technical or structural innovations would have an effect on art; they had assumed it was possible to make fundamental changes in one aspect of architecture without necessitating fundamental changes in others.

Notes

1. See William Fogerty, "On the Conditions and Prospects of Architecture in the United States," *Irish Builder* 17 (1 June 1875): 146–48; "*Tribune* Building," *Building News* 28 (16 June 1875): 796; "Cast-iron Construction in the United States: Messrs. Lord & Taylor Dry-Goods Store, Broadway, New York," *British Architect* 5 (18 February 1876): 88; James Montgomery, "Description of the New Offices of the 'New York Tribune,'" *British Architect* 6 (14 July 1876): 19–21; "Marble, Iron, and Zinc Palaces in New York," *Builder* 36 (27 April 1878): 422–23; and "The Women's Hotel, New York," *Builder* 36 (18 May 1878): 505.

2. In the early 1890s, less than six weeks elapsed between the appearance of an article in an American journal, principally the *American Architect and Building News* of Boston and the *Inland Architect and Builder* (renamed the *Inland Architect and News Record* in 1887) of Chicago, and the date when it was reprinted or acknowledged in European professional journals.

3. See "Notes on Current Events," *British Architect* 32 (4 October 1889): 232; "English Praise of American Architectural Journals," *American Architect* 26 (26 October 1889): 200; "Aus dem technischen Vereinsleben Amerikas," *Deutsche Bauzeitung* 24 (15 January 1890): 25–30; and "Les journaux d'architecture aux États-Unis," *L'architecture* 3 (20 December 1890): 614–16. The seven American journals available at the RIBA were *American Architect* of Boston, *Engineering and Building Record* and *Building* of New York, *Inland Architect* and *Building Budget* of Chicago, *Western Architect* of Denver, and *California Architect* of San Francisco.

4. See the following articles from the *British Architect*. "Retrospective—1884," 23 (2 January 1885): 1–2; J. D. Sedding, "The Modern Architect and His Art," 22 (14 November 1884): 232–36; Basil Champneys, "Victorian Architecture and Originality," 28 (2 December 1887): 409–19 and (9 December 1887): 427–28, 437; "Eighteen Hundred and Eighty-Seven," 29 (6 January 1888): 1–5; Alfred Darbyshire, "Modern Secular Architecture," 33 (17 January 1890): 53–54; and "Eighteen Hundred and Ninety," 35 (2 January 1891): 1.

5. Among the articles from the *British Architect* referred to in this paragraph are: "House at Narragansett Pier," 24 (25 December 1885): 281; "A Modern American House," 25 (5 February 1886): 129; "An American Gymnasium," 26 (24 December 1886): 619; "A House at Nahant, America," 26 (17 September 1886): 264; "Eighteen Hundred and Eighty-Seven," 29 (6 January 1888): 1–5; "Tall Building in Chicago," 30 (12 October 1888): 270; "American Architecture," 31 (18 January 1889): 47; "Our Illustrations: American Domestic Architecture," 33 (24 January 1890): 60; W. L. B. Jenney, "Economy in the Use of Steel in Building Construction," 33 (7 February 1890): 111; and T. Claxton Fidler, "Iron and Steel Considered as Building Materials," 35 (23 January 1891): 76–77, (6 February 1891): 113–14, and (13 February 1891): 129–30.

6. John B. Gass, 1885; Alfred A. Cox, 1890; Banister Fletcher, 1893; A. W. Cleaver, 1895; and A. N. Paterson, 1896.

7. Arthur J. Gale, "American Architecture from a Constructional Point of View," *Royal Institute of British Architects, Transactions* (1882–83): 45–56. He arrived in the United States 28 April 1882 and departed 19 July, spending half of his time in New York City and the bulk of the remaining in Philadelphia, Baltimore, Chicago, and Boston. See also Arthur John Gale, "The Godwin Bursary: Report of a Tour in the United States of America," *Royal Institute of British Architects, Transactions* (1882–83): 57–64.

8. "Very Tall Building," *Architect* 30 (15 September 1883): 155.

9. Gale, "American Architecture from a Constructional Point of View," 53.

10. "Iron Architecture in the United States," *Architect* 28 (30 December 1882): 407.

11. Gerald R. Larson, "The Iron Skeleton Frame: Interactions between Europe and the United States," in *Chicago Architecture, 1872–1922: Birth of a Metropolis,* ed. John Zukowsky (Munich: Prestel-Verlag, 1987), 39–55.

12. Alastair Service, *London 1900* (New York: Rizzoli, 1979), 23.

13. "The Architectural Employment of Iron," *Architect* 31 (22 March 1884): 185.

14. "The Architectural Employment of Iron," 186.

15. John B. Gass, "Some American Methods," *Royal Institute of British Architects, Transactions* 2 (1885–86): 129–44. On his three-month tour Gass visited New York; Boston; Newport; Philadelphia; Washington, D.C.; Chicago; Buffalo; Albany; and Saratoga in addition to major Canadian

cities. He later called the experience "the best time I ever had in my entire professional career. It was exciting to meet those who were making a new civilisation tick."

16. John B. Gass, "Some American Methods," *Royal Institute of British Architects, Journal of Proceedings* 2 (18 March 1886): 182–88.

17. "The Seventh Ordinary Meeting," *Royal Institute of British Architects, Journal of Proceedings* 2 (4 March 1886): 161–62. These two pages contain the names of architects and buildings included in the exhibition.

18. Gass, "Some American Methods," *Royal Institute of British Architects, Journal of Proceedings* 2 (18 March 1886): 184 (Rickman quote); idem, "Some American Methods," *Royal Institute of British Architects, Transactions,* n.s., 2 (1885–86): 144 (Gass quotes).

19. John B. Gass, "The Godwin Bursary: Portions of Report of a Visit to the United States of America and to Canada," *Royal Institute of British Architects, Transactions,* n.s., 2 (1885–86): 145.

20. "Our Illustrations: A Chicago Building," *British Architect* 25 (29 January 1886): 102.

21. Alex. Graham, "Architecture in the United States," *Royal Institute of British Architects, Journal of Proceedings,* n.s., 6 (8 March 1888), 194.

22. C.H.B. [Charles H. Brodie], "Jottings about the United States," *American Architect* 23 (19 May 1888): 235. In his article Brodie said he planned to send a collection of photographs of the Loop's office buildings to the Architectural Association in London to help members understand why he was so taken with them, but he warned that the scale of these structures could be appreciated only by standing in front of them.

23. Two weeks later the *Architect* commented on the major papers of the 1886 meeting. Of Louis Sullivan's ethereal "Essay on Inspiration," the journal observed that the architects of the Midwest were quicker-witted than those on English soil if they could understand what Sullivan was saying. Referring to John Root's paper in which he described the United States as "the country of the great architectural go-as-you-please," the staff writer admitted he felt a twinge of envy. Half a decade earlier the jubilant remark of Root would probably have prompted a reprimand from the British press. For articles on the WAA meetings during 1884–86, see "An Architects' Convention in America," *Architect* 32 (27 December 1884): 413–14; "American Architects in Congress," *Architect* 35 (29 January 1886): 56–57; "The Chicago Convention," *Architect* 36 (24 December 1886): 360–61; "The American Style of the Future," *Architect* 37 (7 January 1887): 3–5; and "An American Convention of Architects," *British Architect* 26 (31 December 1886): 623–24.

24. "The Architects of Western America," *Architect* 40 (28 December 1888): 359.

25. *Engineering* published "An American Block of Offices [Drexel Buildings, Philadelphia]," 48 (15 November 1889): 564–66; "The Auditorium Building, Chicago," 51 (3, 24 April 1891): 400, 490; and "The Masonic Temple, Chicago," 52 (7 August 1891): 150–52. Relying on information and illustrations supplied by Dankmar Adler, the journal focused on the foundations of the Auditorium. With the aid of numerous figures, it explained innovations of the Masonic Temple from its foundations to its heating system. These studies may have been inspired by the visit to the Windy City of the joint delegations of the British Iron and Steel Institute and the Verein Deutscher Eisenhüttenleute on 13–15 October 1890. W. L. B. Jenney reported the group had been impressed by the quality and application of steel in the buildings of the Loop. At the end of the article on the Masonic Temple, *Engineering* included a detailed discussion of the structural system used in the Tacoma Building in Chicago by Holabird and Roche.

26. In February 1890 it reprinted Jenney's piece on "Economy in the Use of Steel in Building Construction," which had appeared a month earlier in the *Inland Architect.* Jenney wrote the article to argue the advantages (cost, strength, and quality) of using steel rather than iron and to

explain how the demand for tall, fireproofed buildings had transformed work within the offices of Chicago's firms. See *British Architect* 33 (7 February 1890): 111. In July 1891 the *British Architect* extracted from the previous month's *Inland Architect* Adler's forthright statement about the temporary nature of each successive foundation system that had been tried in Chicago in recent years. See "Some Technical Reflections on Tall Buildings," *British Architect* 36 (17 July 1891): 54. In May and June of 1890 the *Architect* and the *British Architect* had also made available to their readers the American architect Henry Van Brunt's essay on "Architecture in the West," which had appeared in the December 1889 *Atlantic Monthly*. He contended that the new architecture of Chicago, frankly based on science and invention, had "redeemed the waning influence of this noblest of the arts" by rescuing it from the studio and treating it as a living craft.

27. W. L. B. Jenney, "The Chicago Construction, or Tall Buildings on a Compressible Soil," *Inland Architect* 18 (November 1891): 41. The paper appeared in Britain with the title "Tall Buildings on a Compressible Soil," *British Architect* 36 (4 December 1891): 416.

28. "Chicago's Veneered Buildings," *New York Times,* 30 November 1891, 4.

29. W. L. B. Jenney, "The Chicago Construction or Tall Buildings on a Compressible Soil," *American Architect* 36 (16 April 1892): 44–45.

30. For a list of Hinckeldeyn's reports, see Arnold Lewis, "Hinckeldeyn, Vogel, and American Architecture," *Journal of the Society of Architectural Historians* 31 (December 1972): 276–90.

31. [Karl] Hinckeldeyn, "Die Begründung eines Verbandes der 'Architekten des Westens' in Nordamerika," *Centralblatt der Bauverwaltung* 5 (24 January 1885): 38–40.

32. C. [K.] Hinckeldeyn, "A Foreigner's View of American Architecture," *American Architect* 25 (25 May 1889): 243.

33. H., "Die amerikanischen Thürmhäuser," *Deutsche Bauzeitung* 25 (16 January 1892): 30. The author of this article was Albert Hofmann, assistant editor of the journal.

34. "Das Deutsche Haus in Chicago," *Baugewerks-Zeitung* 24 (5 March 1892): 214. Increasing curiosity in Germany about the skeleton system of framing and its effect on the time required for building was also evident in M., "Ueber die ausserordentlich rege Bauthätigkeit und einige bauliche Sonderheiten in Chicago," *Centralblatt der Bauverwaltung* 12 (17 September 1892): 412.

35. A French national, Lévy was a commercial photographer who maintained a residence in New York from 1871 until about 1890 when he apparently returned to France. I am indebted to Barbara E. Reed and Keith Morgan for this information. The 120 plates in this title represented the first book published in Europe exclusively devoted to American architecture of the 1870s and 1880s and contained plates of equal quality but was broader in scope than George William Sheldon's photographic study *American Country-Seats* published in Boston in 1886. Each volume of *L'architecture américaine* contained forty identified plates plus a table of contents but no plans, dates, descriptions, or text. *L'architecture américaine,* 3 vols. (Paris: André, Daly, 1886). This title was republished as *American Victorian Architecture* (New York: Dover, 1975), with an introduction by Arnold Lewis and notes by Keith Morgan.

36. However, contemporary as well as twentieth-century historians have seldom mentioned either publication. The *American Architect,* always attentive to foreign praise or reproof, evidently was unaware of the 1886 venture for it printed no acknowledgment of it. The journal did comment on its sequel—"The new firm of architectural book publishers in Paris, Messrs André, Daly and Cie. have just published a book on 'Villas américaines' in which the work of the profession here seems to be fairly represented." See "American Architecture Winning Attention in Europe," *American Architect* 23 (17 March 1888): 122. I have been unable to locate a copy of *Villas américaines.*

37. Quoted in "Comments upon the Consolidation Movement," *Inland Architect* 13 (February 1889): 2.

38. The following were published in *La construction moderne* between 1888 and 1893. C. Francis Osborne, "La construction moderne aux États-Unis," 3 (3 March 1888): 241–43 and (15 September 1888): 577–80; "Maison à quinze étages," 4 (17 November 1888): 72; R., "L'architecture américaine," 6 (13 December 1890): 109–11; B., "The Pulitzer Building," 6 (7, 21 March 1891): 257–59, 285–87; R.E., "Les grandes constructions américaines," 6 (5 September 1891): 568–69; E.R., "Les hautes maisons américaines," 7 (14, 21 November 1891): 69–72, 82–84; "Le temple maçonnique à Chicago," 8 (5 November 1892): 50–52; No Day., "À propos du dôme central de l'exposition de Chicago," 8 (31 December 1892): 145–46; and "L'architecture américaine," 8 (1, 28 July 1893): 459–60, 498.

39. Sigfried Giedion, *Space, Time and Architecture* (Cambridge, Mass.: Harvard University Press, 1941), 10.

40. "Amerikanische Häuserbauten," *Schweizerishe Bauzeitung* 17 (23 May 1891): 134.

41. W.G.R., "Das Riesenhaus am Broadway in New-York," *Deutsche Bauzeitung* 25 (21 November 1891): 565.

42. Buffington published a description of a metal skeleton that carried the load of a building in *Northwestern Architect* in March 1888, obtained a patent for it in May 1888, and published an ink perspective of his twenty-eight-story scheme based on "Buffington's Patent Iron Building Construction" in the *Inland Architect* in July 1888. His explanation of his system contained almost all the basic elements Jenney had in mind when he referred to "Chicago construction." See "Our Illustrations," *Inland Architect* 11 (July 1888): 89.

43. Osborne, 577–80. Osborne included the sketch not because of its internal skeleton but to convince French readers of the advantages of mixing styles on the exterior.

44. F.X.K., "Das Haus der Zukunft," *Wiener Bauindustrie-Zeitung* 7 (12 June 1890): 396. This article was reprinted in Germany in *Innen-Dekoration* 1 (10 July 1890): 109.

45. M., "Ueber die ausserordentlich rege Bauthätigkeit und einige bauliche Sonderheiten in Chicago," *Centralblatt der Bauverwaltung* 12 (17 September 1892): 412. The author did not name any buildings constructed on this system.

46. F. v. Emperger, "Eiserne Gerippbauten in den Vereinigten Staaten," *Zeitschrift des oesterreichischen Ingenieur- und Architekten-Vereines* 45 (14 July 1893): 398–99.

47. According to Julius Meyer, a German, the so-called steel skeleton building appeared and developed rapidly from the middle of the eighties, particularly in Chicago. Julius Meyer, "Zwei new-yorker Geschäftstürme," *Ueber Land und Meer* 73 (1895): 247. After listing several types of supporting systems Henri Nodet in 1897 declared that the type that is truly modern was Chicago's approach, known as "skeleton construction." H. Nodet, "The Modern Office Building," *La construction moderne,* 2d ser., 2 (13 March 1897): 283. Twentieth-century historians have continued to comment on Buffington's claim. See "Father of Skyscraper," *Architect and Engineer* 105 (April 1931): 138; E. M. Upjohn, "Buffington and the Skyscraper," *Art Bulletin* 17 (March 1935): 48–70; Hugh Morrison, "Buffington and the Invention of the Skyscraper," *Art Bulletin* 26 (March 1944): 1–2; Dimitris Tselos, "The Enigma of Buffington's Skyscraper," ibid., 3–12; Muriel B. Christison, "How Buffington Staked His Claim," ibid., 13–24.

48. The wary response to tall buildings by some journals was well expressed in a series of articles that appeared in the *Wiener Bauindustrie-Zeitung* between 1888 and 1893. D.B., "Technische Mittheilungen: Feuersichere Eisenconstruction," 5 (16 February 1888): 246; F.X.K., "Das Haus der Zukunft," 7 (12 June 1890): 395–96; "Die neuesten Bau-Curiositäten in Chicago," 8 (15 January 1891): 172; F.X.K., "Ein amerikanisches Haus in Wien," 9 (8 July 1891): 435–37; F.X.K, "Markante Beispiele amerikanischer Bauweise," 9 (1, 8 October 1891): 1–2, 13–15; "Ein neues Bauwunder in New York," 9 (11 February 1892): 195; "Gegen die Höhen amerikanischer Wohnhäuser," 9 (21 April 1892): 30; J. S—r, "Die 'höhen Häuser' in Amerika," 10 (22 June 1893): 448; idem, "Amerikanische Schnellbau-

ten," 19 (10 August 1893): 531–32; and O., "Der 'Freimauer-Tempel' in Chicago," 11 (12 October 1893): 13–14.

    49. "The Elevator System," *British Architect* 27 (18 February 1887): 132.

    50. "A 'Real' American Hotel for London," *British Architect* 33 (10 January 1890): 19.

The
Uniqueness
6
of the
Loop

CHICAGO'S reputation abroad as the materialistic shock city of the late nineteenth century reached its high point about 1893, coinciding with the international attention given to the Columbian Exposition, which opened in May of that year. Many Europeans intrigued with the city came from business, the social sciences, engineering, and architecture, fields that were usually more accepting of "progress" than the disciplines of higher culture. Increasing economic interdependence of the Old and New Worlds had stimulated foreign curiosity about the United States. In 1894 Leopold Gmelin argued that the pursuit of profits had now "achieved the most influential position in the thoughts and feelings of men" on both sides of the Atlantic.[1] After 1890, inquisitive foreign observers increasingly named Chicago the prime urban example of the country's economic surge. Ernst von Hesse-Wartegg wrote, "I have lived long enough in America and have traveled the two halves of the New World for years. I can say unhesitatingly I consider Chicago the greatest wonder of America, the *Urtypus* of the distinctive American essence, the most American city of this huge land, much more so than New York or Boston or Philadelphia. It is perhaps the most powerful human creation of all time."[2] Returning critics advised audiences and readers they could save time and money touring the United States if they just concentrated on Chicago. Gmelin thought it now represented the contemporary age of materialism as Hildesheim had once expressed the age of faith.[3] In no other American city could visitors find such dramatic demonstrations of power and change crystallized so conveniently for them as they were in the small but overwhelming Loop.

In the early 1890s no European observer questioned calling the Loop a commercial zone. Occasionally, a visitor would refer to its cultural institutions, sometimes to point out that theaters, such as the Auditorium and Schiller, were incorporated in office buildings to insure the speculative success of the property. They also noted that churches in downtown Chicago were selling their land and using the profits to build new edifices in outlying districts. Visitors quickly understood that the business of the Loop was business. Observers not only discounted contrary evidence, they described capitalism's permeation of the district with metaphoric flair. Paul Bourget wrote, "You divine, you feel the hot breath of speculation quivering behind these windows. This it is which has fecundated these thousands of square feet of earth."[4] However, capitalism's presence in this zone was not as startling or as illuminating to those who considered the city, as Hesse-Wartegg put it, "das Museum der Neuzeit," as was the Loop's efficiency in processing the objectives of capitalism. Never before had Europeans encountered a central district more focused and efficient in serving trade. Critics who reached this conclusion explained that Chicagoans had defined their city center in the narrowest and most prosaic of urban terms and then proceeded methodically and with little distraction to integrate its essential elements—streets, transportation, towering buildings, concentrated in a small area crammed with swift-moving people—for the sake of speculation and commerce. Anything was justifiable there, explained Paul de Rousiers, as long as it made a useful contribution to the success of business.[5] For those who considered the Loop instructive around 1893, its major lesson was its daily demonstration of a singular purposefulness. Unrivaled for succinct and graphic effect was the author and publisher Paul Lindau's summation: "A gigantic peepshow of utter horror, but extraordinarily to the point."[6]

Numerous accounts of European visitors who walked into this concentrated zone in the first half of the 1890s convey their shock at encountering its focus, intensity, noise, pulse, and scale. Within this territory of business, strange to them but normal to natives, they came to sudden insights challenging previous assumptions and expectations. The jolt of experiencing something new triggered their imaginations and their realism, giving clearer meaning to shifts sensed earlier but not fully grasped. For many, no message of the Loop was more basic than the principle of developing everything only insofar as it was fitting to its purpose.

In studying American architecture, foreign observers valued its practicality above other characteristics and claimed in countless articles, especially in the last quarter of the nineteenth century, that this priority was the most important contribution designers in the United States had made to the international community.[7] Practicality in Chicago meant architecture limited by the objectives of investors and executed by designers who, suspending their own desires and ulterior programs, attempted to carry out these narrow specifications. Some foreign observers, disturbed by the subjugation of talent to economic pressure, charged Chicago's architects with capitulation. Others believed their actions were realistic and even admirable, further evidence that diverse elements in Chicago could collaborate in pursuit of a mutually beneficial goal.

"The Rhythm of the Metropolis"

In May 1888 the *Tribune* sent a reporter to the corner of State and Madison Streets to record the flow of activity during a normal working day.[9] He took his post at 6:00 A.M., when dawn was breaking and the two streets were virtually deserted. Occasionally a cable car or horse car arrived from the suburbs, dropping off janitors, porters, and female cooks and picking up night watchmen and policemen who were going home to sleep. By 6:30 the window washers with long-handled brooms were at work. Suddenly the street was filled with cars and the sidewalks crowded. Most of the people had walked. The men carried food buckets; the women, smaller packages wrapped in brown paper. They ranged in age from preadolescents to the elderly. At 6:59 they were moving rapidly to begin a day that would not end for most until 6:00 in the evening. Many workers were employed in printing shops, book binderies, box companies, cigar factories—the light industry located in the upper floors of downtown buildings.

After 7:00 A.M. there was a lag, enabling the janitors to sweep the walks. Men set up clothes dummies in front of stores or displayed bolts of cloth and goods on packing crates stacked on the sidewalks. As 8:00 approached, the crowd again grew, this time composed of shop girls and saleswomen who were better dressed than those who had arrived an hour earlier. The dry-goods stores opened at 8:00 A.M. Wagons appeared bringing loads of merchandise from wholesale stores or from the freight depots. The din rose and remained high for the next ten hours. The density of the vehicles and pedestrians increased dramatically around 9:00 when the professional people, office employees, shopkeepers, and early shoppers arrived. Cars approached full and departed empty; between three hundred and four hundred people passed a given spot at this intersection each minute.

After 9:00 the morning shoppers appeared, most of them women who were more elegantly dressed than the sales people who served them. The crowds remained fairly constant until noon, when the clerks emerged for lunch, usually for three-quarters of an hour except on busier days—Mondays and Saturdays—when they were given fifteen minutes less to eat. Shortly after 1:00 P.M. the afternoon shoppers arrived, five hundred to six hundred pedestrians per minute, or thirty thousand per hour, passing a specific location.[9] By 3:00 P.M. that count rose, but the numbers declined gradually toward 4:00 when many of the women shoppers departed for home and a larger percentage of quicker-moving men was seen. Though the store clerks were still busy, few people arrived by the cars between 5:00 and 6:00. The final rush of the day occurred at 6:00 when the workers, who had arrived between 7:00 and 9:00 in the morning, made their mass exodus from the buildings. Almost all of them left the district, either walking home or fighting for a place on the overcrowded cars. Though a small percentage stayed to eat in restaurants or to go to the theater, the activity at State and Madison essentially ceased with the close of the business day.

The reporter for the *Tribune* had described the rhythm of a typical workday in Chicago observed from its busiest corner. This daily pattern of swelling and shrinking crowds moving through this intersection would be repeated with little variation from block to block, month after month, the year round. Unexpected incidents might alter normal procedures for brief periods of time, but they could seldom interrupt the efficient rhythm of central Chicago for long. Predictable activities in the crowded sections of a modern metropolis tended to be reassuring. They were also informative, for they revealed a city's particular metabolism. That the *Tribune* devoted considerable space to such a survey in the Loop in 1888 or that an influential drama critic and conservative journalist, Francisque Sarcey, wrote a long article three years later on the daily cycle of life on the boulevards of Paris[10] is symptomatic of the growing interest in the "rhythm of the metropolis."[11] Not surprisingly, the *Tribune*'s reporter chose a major intersection of the Loop and Sarcey the liveliest boulevards of Paris to describe a "typical day" in their respective cities. The corner of State and Madison was a spot where the priorities and tone of Chicago's business district could be effectively observed. Likewise, the boulevards expressed qualities central to the image of contemporary Paris. In all probability, foreign visitors to both cities in the years around 1890 would have gone to the same locations to observe the characteristic scenes of each city.

But a brief comparison of Sarcey's view of the boulevards with the *Tribune*'s description of State and Madison also reveals significant differences. According to Sarcey, the boulevards of Paris came to life at 8:00 A.M. when the street-cleaning crews were finishing their work. At 9:00 the cafés opened, but the boulevards did not fill until 10:30 when the regulars appeared to sip apéritifs and black bitters. At midday the restaurants and taverns were crowded. At 1:00 P.M. it was time for coffee and cigars before returning to work at 2:00. Traffic remained heavy through the afternoon. Boulevardiers read the newspapers at 4:00, drank vermouth and played dominoes at 6:00, and went to dinner at 7:30 followed by the theater at 9:00 and a late supper afterward. The boulevards, frequented by all classes in society in the evening, did not become quiet until 3:00 A.M. Sarcey depicted an environment where citizens responded slowly to the rising sun but became more lively as the day progressed. There, predictable types and even known characters appeared at regular times of day to sit, read, and socialize with friends. Though the boulevards were enriched by work and play and, in the late evening at least, frequented by "all classes of society," Sarcey assumed their primary function was social, and their "regulars" members of the upper classes.

The rhythm of central Chicago was not determined by either specific individuals or one class but by the daily requirements of commerce and trade, and its pervasive activity was not leisure but work. The hours of shops and offices, not the habits of *flâneurs*, determined its cycle. The Loop's day began earlier, affected the lives of larger numbers of people, and was faster paced though less exuberant. Varying little from street to street between morning and evening, its requirements permitted few opportunities for relaxation, idle conversation, or unproductive pleasure. Signs of cultural expression in this sea of transactions were rare; even daytime discussions in the lobbies of the main hotels were dominated by talk of buying and selling. Ending approximately twelve hours after it had begun, the life of this quarter was also shorter than that of the boulevards of Paris.

Visitors from abroad were intrigued with the masses of people in the Loop, flowing back and forth on the narrow sidewalks or swelling at the intersections. By their standards the crowds were large, their size directly affected by the tall buildings of the district, some of which accommodated more than three thousand employees who served an even larger transient population. No period was more memorable for outsiders than the early evening, when the firms and shops closed and employees burst from the hourglass entrances of multistory structures and department stores. They poured onto the sidewalks to walk home or onto the streets to catch cabs and cable cars for more distant destinations, a scene caught well in an 1893 painting by A. Castaigne (fig. 39). This moment etched in their memories, Europeans may have underestimated the numbers remaining on the downtown streets after the evening rush was over.

The scene of thousands of people in the Loop, each with personal foibles and the potential for unpredictable behavior, motivated by different kinds of self-interest yet functioning with an uncanny uniformity appropriate for this impersonal zone, was memorable. The ebb and flow of humans, undistinguished by class or rank, most attempting to complete predetermined missions in a reasonable amount of time, gave new and prophetic meaning to the phrase "rhythm of the metropolis." In central Chicago the rhythm was determined by investment capital's definition of time, which stressed how precious it was and how important it was to take quicker and quicker advantage of it. This rhythm was affected by the mechanization of life, by labor-saving innovations, by conspicuous clocks to monitor the pace, by mass production and the assembly line. Paul de Rousiers observed regularized movements at stations in the Union Stock Yards where laborers had elevated their simple, repetitive movements nearly to the level of an art form. At Pullman, where workers assembled sleeping cars, he reported, "Everything is done in order and with precision; one feels that each effort is calculated to yield its maximum effect, that no blow of a hammer, no turn of a wheel is made without cause."[12] As a production machine, the Loop was noticeably less efficient than the stockyards or the shops at Pullman, and the actions of its workers less manageable, but compared to the flow of throngs in large European cities, the rhythm of Chicago seemed metronomic. Jacques Hermant thought he detected a new urban phenomenon in Chicago in which "an entire people move with the most perfect precision."[13]

Although foreign visitors were fascinated by the crowds of the Loop, many did not feel comfortable in their midst, in part because their reasons for being there were different. While access to the hierarchical turf of the boulevards of Paris was determined to a degree by rank and style, access to the space of the Loop usually depended on one's mission. Those who facilitated or required its services—salespeople, secretaries, laborers, clerks, managers, shoppers, clients—were at home there. Though the majority of them may not have been important people, they knew this district could not function without them. Their public masks of preoccupation discouraged Europeans from interrupting them; no visitor, to my knowledge, ever reported a conversation on the streets with a named individual. Preoccupation was often interpreted as impoliteness. Possibly with fond memories of London in mind, George Warrington Steevens, an Oxford-trained journalist, complained, "The truth is that nobody in this rushing, struggling tumult has any time to look after what we have long ago come to think the bare decencies of civilisation."[14] Steevens focused on the social inadequacies of people who were acting congruently with the Loop's primary purpose. Chicago had become an instructive arena in

Figure 39. A Chicago street in the evening, painted by A. Castaigne (*Century Magazine*, September 1893).

which assumptions, workable abroad, collided with its daily routine. Today we are more accustomed to the unsympathetic city and may even welcome the security of its impersonal face, but in the late nineteenth century most Europeans were not prepared for the social code of Chicago's busiest streets. The factors that have taught us to suspend our instinctive generosity or thoughtfulness as a means of self-preservation in the modern city had already affected Chicagoans in the 1890s.

Despite their impatience over perceived incivility on the downtown streets, visitors were still concerned about the welfare of individuals in the Loop. The *Times* of London for 29 August 1892 thought Chicagoans had pushed themselves to the point of collective collapse. Foreign observers commiserated with those who depended on this quarter because they could not imagine themselves enduring its pressures for the rest of their working days. They were concerned about its effects on the spirit as well as on the body. One onlooker expressed his consternation: "Men! The word is hardly correct applied to this perplexing city. When you study it more in detail, its aspect reveals so little of the personal will, so little caprice and individuality, in its streets and buildings, that it seems like the work of some impersonal power, irresistible, unconscious, like a force of nature, in whose service man was merely a passive instrument."[15] The author of this remark, Paul Bourget, wondered if the daily inhabitant of the district had become a puppet—"a passive instrument." He alluded to a new form of human subjugation—the loss of will. He was not worried about poverty, working conditions, or labor's toll on the body, common themes in nineteenth-century writings, but about the possibility that forces now out of human control had mechanized thought. If the city could destroy the body and the spirit in the age of steam, could it quash idiosyncrasy and whim for the sake of efficiency in an age of electricity? Chicagoans may have been proud of their endorsement of progress and their willingness to march accommodatingly to its steady beat, but Europeans often read compliance as docility. Apparently unaware of or unimpressed by reform efforts, Hesse-Wartegg claimed the only people who ever complained about the Loop were outsiders.

Most foreign observers were less worried than Bourget. Evaluating the people on the streets of downtown Chicago at a more prosaic level, they tended to view them as materialists rather than as passive tools. These hordes were too "intent on winning fortune or fame, to admit of mere loungers or passing tourists to step between them and the goal to which they were hastening."[16] The majority of visitors from abroad regarded Chicagoans as realists who accepted the disruptive transformations of modern life, and as opportunists who acted out of self-interest. These citizens of the city adjusted to the necessities of change consciously, assuming their compliance would bring material benefits.[17]

Participatory Architecture

Alert to the instinctive ways of Chicagoans in the Loop, observers noted responsibilities natives assumed in order to make it function. For example, they were responsible for their own safety when walking past debris on the sidewalks, open manholes, or unguarded railroad crossings. They were also given responsibilities Europeans would have considered privileges at home. These were exercised primarily in areas linking private and public spaces. As early as 1876 Emil Dietrich, who covered the Centennial Exhibition in Philadelphia for the *Deutsche Bauzeitung,* noted that public buildings in the United States "appear as though they are always under control of the citizens."[18] He had observed that pedestrians in major cities walked into commercial and municipal buildings without showing identification, a letter of introduction, or being checked by a guard. The right of the citizens to enter, regardless of mission, seemed to be honored as long as they behaved properly. Travelers to Chicago were intrigued by the hospitality of semiprivate spaces in their hotels. These caravansaries were accessible; anyone could walk from the sidewalk into spacious lobbies surrounded by comfortable parlors. Managers outfitted interiors as if they were tempting pedestrians to take a break. No one asked those who entered why they were there.[19] Semiprivate space in Europe had become semipublic space in the United States.

In Chicago and other American cities the private sector also assumed more responsibility for municipal problems than was true of cities that were much more centralized and regulated, such as Paris. Adolphe Bocage referred to this when he noted that in the United States private initiative replaced administrative direction.[20] Though cooperation was expected from the private sector, it was not always prompt, adequate, or sufficiently integrated, one reason why the housekeeping of the city was so atrocious.

In the lobbies of tall buildings Europeans observed how personal responsibility replaced administrative control in order to make the processes of the Loop more efficient. Bocage described what happened when a client entered an office building for an appointment.

> If we follow a visitor entering the lobby of one of these edifices, we'll see him looking for the name of the person he wishes to see on a long list placed near the elevator. He'll note the number printed beside that name, telling him which floor to stop at. If it is the fifteenth floor, for example, he will take the direct elevator which doesn't stop at the lower stories for there are local and express cars. Furthermore, he will consult a special indicator, a kind of *manomètre,* placed at the base of each elevator to show its movements, that allows him to select the one to take him most quickly to his destination, and the elevator operator will stop at the floor corresponding to the number.[21]

A visitor then stepped into a corridor, identical to corridors on most of the other floors, as shown in the illustration of the interior of the Chamber of Commerce Building of 1888–89 by Baumann and Huehl, published in the September 1893 issue of the *Gazette des beaux-arts* (fig. 40). Since no concierge had given instructions or alerted a representative of the desired firm, the newcomer was responsible for finding the correct office, but this was easy because all offices were numbered. The egalitarian treatment of office doorways was also surprising. "On all the floors the plan is the same, the cells are similar, the doors have the same frosted glass window with the number, and . . . that's all."[22]

Figure 40. Light court, Chamber of Commerce Building, Chicago, 1888–89, Baumann and Huehl (*Gazette des beaux-arts,* September 1893).

There was little variation in the size of the lettering, and rarely any titles or special credentials. Sometimes office doors were open, permitting views into interiors, but without having been announced and feeling uncomfortable in this world without idleness, foreign visitors often hesitated to walk right in.

This practice of anonymous people taking responsibility for finding their destination within private space intrigued observers. In Western Europe pedestrians did not normally enter buildings containing offices and bureaus without credentials or an appointment. This space, especially in France and Germany, was usually a protected territory accessible only to those who worked there and also to their clients. Since certain people were encouraged to enter and others were not, it was necessary to monitor the traffic entering and leaving business premises. The person entrusted with this responsibility, the doorman, concierge, or *Pförtner,* also showed visitors how to reach their desired destinations within the building. This practice, small in scale, highly personalized,

Figure 41. "Just arrived in Chicago—
Trying to see the tops of buildings" (*Chicago
Tribune*, 12 July 1892).

and rich in etiquette, was effective because the line between private and public space was
both clear and respected and the number of visitors to be served was relatively small. In
Chicago, French visitors, in particular, noted the absence of a figure of authority. With
so many people coming and going—there were six hundred offices in the Rookery Building of 1885–86 by Burnham and Root and nine hundred in the remodeled Chamber of
Commerce Building (fig. 16)—it would have been impossible to check the credentials
of each, let alone alert requested offices to the arrival of a specific client. This would have
complicated procedures, a result diametrically opposed to the purposes for which these
buildings had been designed.

Ironically, business buildings in Europe, particularly on the Continent, looked more
attractive and less intimidating on the outside than did comparable structures in the
Loop. Foreign visitors were disarmed by the towering spare flanks twelve to sixteen stories above the sidewalk, as suggested in the *Tribune's* sketch, "Just arrived in Chicago—
Trying to see the tops of buildings" (fig. 41), and were not encouraged by the relatively
blunt entranceways that looked "crushed beneath the weight of the mountain" above.[23]
Nevertheless, they entered these buildings without letters of introduction. The new architecture of Chicago was less inviting in appearance to visitors but more accessible and
easier to use. Furthermore, developers of office buildings had included services needed
by people on the sidewalks. The Masonic Temple (fig. 37) contained more than most
structures. Inside were a two-thousand-seat restaurant in the basement, elegant fashion
and speciality shops on the first three floors, seven floors of retail stores—described by
a German visitor as a bazaar similar to the Bon Marché in Paris—five floors of offices,
upper stories reserved for Masonic activities and administration, a nineteenth-floor
barber shop, and, at the top, a cabaret, small theaters for lantern shows, and a glass-cov-
ered conservatory (fig. 42). The variety of services and entertainment opportunities reduced the need to leave. Several critics mused about the idea of the skyscraper as a self-

contained vertical city—"a population of 3,000 inhabitants who are able to be independent of the outside since they have there the restaurant, the bootblack, the newspaper hawker, and the hairdresser, the baths, and the Club"[24]—but none elaborated this possibility in the early 1890s.

Chicagoans seemed to adjust easily to the new technology and buildings that had made the Loop such an efficient environment for business. Europeans watched local citizens, old hands at reading mechanical indicators or the vertical tubes of colored liquid, move toward certain elevators before the doors opened.[25] Such spontaneous actions reminded observers of the differences between the style of doing business there and the way in which it was conducted at home. The instinctive manner in which Chicagoans functioned left some foreign tourists feeling they were inept in this modern atmosphere. Yet the novel responsibilities Chicagoans accepted as a matter of course were not complicated. Dropping a letter in a glass-enclosed mail chute located in the center of a building, requiring employees to walk a short distance and clerks in the basement to collect the day's letters with little effort, was not an act that required training. Self-initiated procedures could be mastered quickly, and many contained their own instructions. At the Central Post Office in Chicago, Charles Croonenberchs reported that,

Figure 42. Conservatorium, Masonic Temple, Chicago, 1891–92, Burnham and Root (*Inland Architect*, December 1892).

at each side there are two doors. Push one, it resists; push the other, it opens. The opposite happens when leaving; the first door will push in and the second will resist. . . . Upon entering you read in English, "stamp sales, card sales, mail boxes, letters in transit, orders, late postage, small package service, registered letters. . . ." Writing is everywhere. Also, information bureau, inquiry office, letter boxes for the East, boxes for the South, etc., boxes for printed matter, newspapers, books.[26]

The public thus participated in limited acts by making choices and doing work clerks would not have to duplicate. Because some steps in this operation were carried out by thousands of people who received no pay for their contribution, the process was both faster and cheaper. Once Europeans participated, the mystique began to fade and so did their initial reaction that Chicagoans were a breed apart, uniquely equipped to deal with a changing world.

Reservations about American labor-saving devices were invariably stronger before rather than after Europeans had encountered them. In Chicago they commented positively about equipment to increase convenience and comfort, for example, in hotels, where typewriters were available in the parlors, room service could be called by pushing electrified buttons, and pneumatic tubes provided communication with the main desk.[27] However, it was in the new architecture of the Loop that they discovered how much employees depended on electrified and mechanized equipment and how at home these clerks seemed to be with their telephones, typewriters, speaking tubes, bells, and fans. Technology had also created a pleasant interior atmosphere, much to the surprise of many who expected the opposite, given the relatively graceless facades of office blocks, their subdivision into hundreds of cells, and their prosaic objectives.[28] Devices to increase interior comfort and convenience were more centralized than in business premises in Britain, France, and Germany. Adolphe Bocage called attention to this centralization in the basement of the Masonic Temple, to the boiler room with its seven steam pumps distributing water to the different stories, to the pumps that expelled the sewage, and to the dynamos and the central heating system.[29] Steam radiators fed from below, not open grates, kept offices in the new buildings at a steady temperature in winter. The source of illumination was also centralized. On dark days and during the winter, rooms could be illuminated by electric bulbs, sometimes "cunningly arranged on the desks so that their light will fall upon the books and papers rather than upon the eyes." Flush toilets were available on certain floors. Some offices contained washbasins with hot or cold running water. Critics concluded that owners had placed a high priority on systems for the maintenance of health—heating, ventilating, plumbing, and sanitation—and that designers had been ingenious in working them into the plan.[30]

A few critics noted the ability of Chicago's architects to create environments in which mechanical and electrical devices facilitated human efforts to meet business objectives. One wrote:

Packages and letters are quickly thrown by minor employees into the box placed on each floor. They are sent on their way to the general reception room on the first floor where the mailman picks them up. Others pick up letters and journals sent up from the first floor by means of pneumatic tubes. Through open doors one sees girls typing letters dictated to them shortly before by the employer; at the same time he is pushing all the electric buttons placed near his feet and hands, necessary fixtures in his office which is large but very simple.[31]

Some visitors had assumed that the opposite would be true, that an office would become more hectic as each new labor-saving device was added. In the buildings of the Loop, however, both Adolphe Bocage and Jacques Hermant discovered an unexpected integration of humans, machines, and architecture. Electrical and mechanical devices seemed to hum in concert with human energy instead of intruding as discordant elements. Acknowledging the ability of Americans to make work as pleasant and as untiring as possible and to create an architecture ideal for this purpose, Hermant treated these "temples of labor" as profound barometers of culture.

> Just as in the architecture of antiquity we find the temples, the basilicas, the baths and the circuses corresponding to the primary needs of the people of Greece and Italy; just as later we find the church, the feudal castle and the town hall symbolizing the three major elements of the middle ages: religion, feudalism and the towns; just as we find in the great imperial and royal chateaus the expression of the omnipotence of the absolute monarch, so in the architecture of the most American of all cities we find particular buildings expressing the need to work—the very essence of the American genius.[32]

Hermant's excitement about the Loop stemmed from his conclusion that its new architecture was a frank revelation of a new context, the kind of intimate relationship between causes and results that he believed had been essential for the creation of great architecture in the past.

Of all the labor-saving devices incorporated into the Loop's skyscrapers, the elevator received the closest attention from European critics in the first half of the 1890s. They recognized its crucial role in making floors above the walk-up level attractive to renters as well as its revolutionary impact on internal traffic. Elevators also fascinated visitors because they could watch, feel, hear, and ride these cages, discovering personally the difference between a modern office block in Chicago and a traditional six- or seven-story business structure in London or Paris. The experience of using an efficient elevator usually was enough to overcome prejudices against their implementation. Fritz von Emperger, an engineer who worked in New York during 1891–94 before returning to Vienna, observed:

> With us the most common bias is our unwillingness to live high in the air, not only because of stair climbing but also because of the elevator. However, we should remember that this prejudice had to be overcome in America also. Now it has passed and the contrary is true. This can be proven best by giving a European who has been living in America for only a short time the choice of living on a lower floor, the first or second, and climbing the stairs or on the fifth of tenth floors and using the elevator.[33]

When searching for examples of *Zweckmässigkeit,* the word the Germans used for the "purposefulness" of the Loop, the elevator was often chosen.

The fourteen passenger elevators in the Masonic Temple by Burnham and Root, the most in any Chicago building at the time of the exposition, made a deep impression on several visitors. After seeing so many arranged in an arc opposite the main entrance, some understood, as never before, the implications of this internal transportation system.[34] In the Masonic the elevator had not extracted piecemeal concessions from architecture, it had transformed architecture. It also provided the city with another transportation system, a vertical one that rivaled both the speed and the capacity of transportation systems on the ground. The building's hydraulic elevator system could accommodate approximately four thousand people per hour, even though electric elevators made it obsolete by 1893. Leopold Gmelin pointed out that at 750 feet per minute, or almost nine miles an hour, one could now travel in the Masonic's elevators more quickly than one could move in street cars through congested city centers.[35] Banister Fletcher, the British critic and architectural historian, drew an analogy between the elevators of the Masonic and tracks at a large station, each "under the charge of a guard with a head-guard over all sending these vertical-train loads of people 'on time' express to such or such a floor."[36]

Elevators, particularly in the Masonic Temple, helped visitors comprehend the priorities of this architecture, priorities that seemed questionable until they saw a tall commercial building and the Loop in operation. They verified a harmonious, purposeful relationship between architecture and profit, architecture and art, architecture and technology, architecture and people. After seeing elevators and riding them, Europeans usually concluded that the purposeful objectives of these buildings would have been impossible without them. Furthermore, elevators convinced some visitors that modern equipment did not have to be inimical to art; "our English designers might learn a good many lessons in the way they are fitted up, especially in the iron or copper screens with which they are enclosed," Fletcher wrote.[37] The elevator was also evidence of the importance accorded convenience in the Loop's new architecture. Though human dependence on mechanical or electrical equipment may have been difficult for some to welcome intellectually, its benefits for the body were obvious, prompting Wilhelm Bode to argue that an architecture of comfort and accommodation had been better developed and artistically expressed in the United States than it had been in Germany, France, or England.[38] In January 1889 William Le Baron Jenney declared that "the practical is at the bottom of the whole and underlies all that makes claim to architecture."[39] However, the refined *Zweckmässigkeit* of the Loop would have been impossible without the endorsement and participation of those who worked there.

Notes

1. Leopold Gmelin, "Architektonisches aus Nordamerika," *Deutsche Bauzeitung* 28 (15 September 1894): 453.
2. Ernst von Hesse-Wartegg, *Tausend und ein Tag im Occident* (Leipzig: Carl Reissner, 1891), vol. 1, 160–61.
3. Gmelin, 453.

4. Paul Bourget, *Outre-Mer* (New York: Scribner's Sons, 1895), 118.

5. Paul de Rousiers, *American Life*, trans. A. J. Herbertson (Paris: Firmin-Didot, 1892), 61.

6. Paul Lindau, *Altes und Neues aus der neuen Welt* (Berlin: Carl Duncker, 1893), 375.

7. For example, William Fogerty, a Fellow of the RIBA who had practiced architecture in New York City for approximately three years before returning to Ireland in the winter of 1874/75, meant by "American practicality" the comfort of carpeted churches, or the greater control architects exerted when they included closets, shelves, and built-in furniture in their domestic plans. William Fogerty, "On Some Differences between British and American Architectural Practice," *Architect* 13 (6 March 1875): 140–42; "On the Conditions and Prospects of Architecture in the United States," *Irish Builder* 17 (15 May 1875): 132–34 and (1 June 1875): 146–48; and "Hints from American Practice," *Builder* 34 (26 February 1876): 189–91. For the *Builder*, which reviewed American approaches to hospital planning in December 1879, practicality meant giving priority to patients' needs and curbing the spread of germs instead of to historical styles or one's reputation. "Hospital Construction and Organization," *Builder* 37 (27 December 1879): 1419. This article was a reaction to a book of five essays, *Hospital Plans* (New York: W. Wood, 1876), written by American doctors for the Johns Hopkins Hospital in Baltimore. To Karl Hinckeldeyn in 1887 Americans were practical when they incorporated refinements in heating, ventilating, plumbing, and sanitation equipment quickly, the reason, he claimed, they now led the Western world in this respect. Hinckeldeyn, "Hochbau-Construction und innerer Ausbau in den Vereinigten Staaten," *Centralblatt der Bauverwaltung*, 7 (12 March 1887): 117. Paul Gout, editor of the *Encyclopédie d'architecture*, saw practicality in the relationship between use and design. "The form is simply what the function of the structure permits it to be. The profiles are marked out in accordance with their destination without betraying a more precious conception of the model." Paul Gout, "Maison à Boston," *Encyclopédie d'architecture*, 4th ser., 1 (1888–89): 133. Rainer Hanns Tolzmann, who studied the image of America in the *Deutsche Bauzeitung* in the late nineteenth century, claimed the publication's staff focused almost exclusively on issues of practicality in American society and architecture. Rainer Hanns Tolzmann, "Objective Architecture: American Influences in the Development of Modern German Architecture" (Ph.D. diss., University of Michigan, 1975), 154. Tolzmann's research has been valuable for me, not only because it confirmed my conclusions about German attitudes toward American practicality but also for his argument that American architecture reflected a congruency of factors rather than a privileged regard for art.

8. "A Day on State Street," *Chicago Tribune*, 6 May 1888, 25.

9. This may be an inflated estimate. Homer Hoyt reported that 7,500 people passed hourly from Madison to Monroe on State Street at the height of pedestrian activity in 1890. Hoyt, *One Hundred Years of Land Values in Chicago* (Chicago: University of Chicago Press, 1933), 172.

10. Francisque Sarcey, "The Boulevards of Paris," *Scribner's Magazine*, June 1891, 663–84.

11. This phrase is taken from Klaus Strohmeyer, "Rhythmus der Grossstadt," in *Die Metropole: Industriekultur in Berlin in 20 Jahrhunderts*, ed. Jochen Boberg, Tilman Fichter, and Eckhart Gillen (Munich: C. H. Beck, 1986), 32–51.

12. Rousiers, quoted in Bessie Louise Pierce, *As Others See Chicago* (Chicago: University of Chicago Press, 1933), 264.

13. Jacques Hermant, "L'architecture aux États-Unis et à l'exposition universelle de Chicago," *L'architecture* 7 (20 October 1894): 343. According to Adolphe Bocage, everything in Chicago seemed to be moved by electricity. Adolphe Bocage, "L'architecture aux États-Unis et à l'exposition universelle de Chicago," *L'architecture* 7 (13 October 1894): 334.

14. G. W. Steevens, *The Land of the Dollar* (New York: Dodd, Mead, 1897), 151.

15. Bourget, 117.

16. William Smith, *A Yorkshireman's Trip to the United States and Canada* (London: Longmans, Green, 1892), 195–96.

17. Many employed in this district were, by international standards, well paid. They had chosen to work there despite the availability of jobs in other parts of the city; spent eight to ten hours in warm, furnished offices and stores working alongside managers and owners at tasks that were not backbreaking, though they could be repetitive; and then departed in the early evening for more varied and personalized domestic environments. In 1888 the city's bricklayers earned $21.00 per week compared to $8.00 for their English counterparts; carpenters enjoyed a $15.00 to $7.50 advantage, and the edge for masons was $21.00 to $8.00, for plumbers, $18.00 to $8.00, and for plasters, $21.00 to $7.50.

18. Tolzmann, 444–45.

19. Leopold Gmelin, "Architektonisches aus Nordamerika," *Deutsche Bauzeitung* 28 (17 November 1894), 567.

20. Bocage, 338.

21. Ibid., 334. Another step-by-step explanation of how to find an office in a skyscraper, specifically in the Masonic Temple, appeared in "Die Kolumbische Weltausstellung in Chicago," *Schweizerische Bauzeitung* 21 (13 May 1893): 125–26.

22. Jacques Hermant, "L'art à l'exposition de Chicago," *Gazette des beaux-arts* 73 (September 1893): 247.

23. Bourget, 118.

24. H. Nodet, "The Modern Office Building," *La construction moderne,* 2d ser., 2 (20 February 1897): 242.

25. Hesse-Wartegg, 84.

26. P. Charles Croonenberchs, *Les États-Unis* (Paris: Delhomme and Briguet, 1892), 122–23.

27. Leopold Gmelin was impressed by circular food-vending machines—"upon punching a button and moving a pointer at the desired selection," one is served "instantly, like a magic table." Quoted in Tolzmann, 173.

28. A few observers expressed concern. André Chevrillon charged that only the worker, not the owner or the dilettante, had to endure the gadgetry of these offices. Chevrillon, "La vie américaine," *Revue des deux mondes* 62 (1 April 1892): 564. In "Bricks and Mortar" (*Builders Journal* 4 [16 December 1896]: 299), the anonymous author implied that working conditions decreased in quality as the height of the buildings increased. Other critics told a different story. According to Marcel Baudouin, away from the bustling lobby the corridors above seemed strangely quiet, a silence he likened to that of a balloon floating above a busy city. Baudouin, "Les maisons hautes et les maisons qui marchent aux États-Unis," *Revue scientifique,* 4th ser., 9 (22 January 1898): 111.

29. Bocage, 334.

30. Auguste Joseph Lutaud, *Aux États-Unis,* 2d ed. (Paris: Ernest Flammarion, 1897), 80. The American love affair with technology had enabled designers and contractors in the United States to produce a distinctive architecture of convenience and comfort in the last half of the nineteenth century. Their creation of a somatic architecture—one sensitive to the needs of the body—was one of their significant contributions to contemporary building, though its importance has not been stressed by twentieth-century historians.

31. Bocage, 334.

32. Hermant, "L'art à l'exposition de Chicago," 243.

33. F. v. Emperger, "Eiserne Gerippbauten in den Vereinigten Staaten," *Zeitschrift des oesterreichischen Ingenieur- und Architekten-Vereines* 45 (6 October 1893): 528. He was referring to apartment buildings in New York.

34. British and German professional journals began publishing notes and articles on American elevators in the mid-1880s. This publicity led to commissions for American firms in Europe, particularly in Great Britain where the Otis Company of New York opened a London office to market the Standard Hydraulic Elevator and install it in new buildings erected in England and Scotland. In 1890 German authorities claimed American elevators set the standards for the industry in terms of rapidity, smoothness, and their excellent accident record. When comparing lifts manufactured in the United States with those made in Europe, British critics attributed the success of American models to a business community that grasped their potential value and tried to take full advantage of it. "Not so in England, however. We still cling to our stairs and low-rented top storeys as a national institution," complained the *British Architect* on 18 December 1885. The top floors of a six-story business building in London at this time produced half the rent of the first two stories. Professionals who promoted the elevator pointed out that the best rents in tall commercial buildings in the United States came from the first and top floors, the latter renting first. Business premises with elevators became more profitable in London in the later 1880s, increasing the rental value over those without from 40 to 200 percent by the end of the decade. This encouraged others to follow suit, particularly when they realized some renters were moving out of buildings where stairs provided the only access to upper floors. Nevertheless, old habits died slowly in Britain. Some architects there were reluctant to reduce the size of the main stairway, traditionally a focal point of the entrance level, or to place the elevator in a conspicuous location. Change came, but usually step by step. After patrons responded positively to the installation of a lift, a second one was often added to an existing building to improve service. Though the second elevator was sometimes installed in a different part of the building, clients soon realized it was more effective to place them together in a central location. See "The Elevator System," *British Architect* 27 (18 February 1887): 132–33; J. Slater, "New Materials and Inventions," *Architect* 37 (6 May 1887): 268–70; and C. E. Gritton, "Lifts," *Architect* 43 (25 April 1890): 257–59.

35. Gmelin, "Architektonisches aus Nordamerika," *Deutsche Bauzeitung* 28 (20 October 1894), 520.

36. Banister F. Fletcher, "American Architecture through English Spectacles," *Engineering Magazine* 7 (June 1894): 319.

37. Ibid.

38. Wilhelm Bode, "Moderne Kunst in den Vereinigten Staaten von Amerika," *Kunstgewerbeblatt*, n.s., 5 (1894): 118.

39. W. L. B. Jenney, "A Few Practical Hints," *Inland Architect* 13 (February 1889): 7.

The
7 Domain
of
Women

THE FUNDAMENTAL difference between the heart of Chicago and the central districts of European cities was its single-minded focus on commercial activity. One could easily argue there were other features of this zone that set it apart from comparable zones in Europe—the height of its buildings or its relentless crowds—but these attributes were consequences of centralizing the trade of America's most prosperous city in a small, defined area. Though there were activities in the Loop not directly related to commercial transactions, one could not find in the Western world an urban quarter in which this function was more honored or concentrated. It was concentrated not only in terms of space, but also in terms of time—from morning until six in the evening. At the beginning of each workday thousands of people entered this spatial-temporal container, focusing their attention on and devoting their energies to its dominant purpose. Because the restricted space of the district intensified the impression of their numbers and their movements, and because employees took their jobs seriously, many Europeans concluded Chicagoans were preoccupied only with work. Convinced that no person could survive such a steady cadence for long without serious consequences, visitors regularly advised Chicago's citizens to slow down and to remember that labor was only one aspect of life.

Concerned observers sometimes failed to realize that for personal gain employees had consciously suspended their private habits and whims and assumed a public style appropriate for functional buildings, right-angled streets, unvaried sidewalks, and fast transportation. Even those who did understand wondered if these workers at the end of the day could set aside its strain, take delight in poetry and art, and drop their public masks of indifference to attend to the welfare of family and friends. In short, could they reclaim those aspects of personality they had willingly suspended in order to serve the tempo of commerce and industry? Chicagoans thought they could and attempted to do so by splitting their lives into two parts—a world of work and a world of leisure. Without the regenerative residential neighborhoods to look forward to when work was finished, the form and the pace of the downtown would have been different.

In calling Chicago the "City of Contrasts, just as the United States is the Land of Contrasts," James Fullarton Muirhead, author of the 1893 Baedeker guide to the United States, cited as evidence the difference between its business district and its residential areas.[1] Accustomed to the practice of intermingling commercial offices, retail stores, professional services, governmental and cultural buildings, and apartment blocks in the central districts of their own cities, visitors were intrigued but not necessarily persuaded by the American practice of separating the commercial center from the districts where people lived. This division was consistent with tendencies in the United States to subdivide operations into discrete steps or parts, as was true of processing hogs at the stockyard or constructing balloon frame houses. In European cities the apartment and the place of business were each influenced to an extent by the proximate presence of the other. In Chicago, however, the office block evolved in an area increasingly reserved for commercial transactions while the freestanding house evolved in a setting where speed was much less important. Each architectural form was thus freer to develop without adjustments to the function of the other, resulting in building types shaped more narrowly by respective requirements. Europeans made much of the visible architectural differences in these two environments. Many believed this contrast was more evident in Chicago than elsewhere, not only because of its restricted business quarter but also because its residential districts covered a larger area and contained more detached houses than any city in the United States.

Suburban Chicago was also a spatial-temporal container, and, like the Loop, fulfilled needs in an effective manner. However, it differed in a number of respects from the core it surrounded. Spatially, its boundaries were less clear; in fact, suburban areas continued to expand, even beyond the formal limits of the city, while the business district remained geographically defined despite its constant transformation. Temporally, the suburbs functioned twenty-four hours a day instead of ten. Though the residential neighborhoods were marked by daily patterns of activity, their events were less predictable than those of the Loop. Decentralized to a greater extent in both time and space, residential neighborhoods provided a semirural alternative to the city's urban core. European observers emphasized the physical and psychological differences between the two sectors. To them, the suburbs seemed soft, open, intimate, attractive, manicured, comforting, and safe while the central district seemed hard, cramped, overscaled, ugly, unkempt, jarring, and dangerous. Nevertheless, the suburbs and the Loop, though dissimilar, were also interdependent spatial-temporal containers, their relationship reflecting "the ecosystem notion of exchange and 'natural balance.'"[2] From a European perspective, the Loop wasn't a city at all, but only a half city that required another half city radically different in temporal, spatial, and functional qualities to make Chicago whole.

Typical European travelers of the years around 1890 came to Chicago to confirm for themselves the legendary tales they had heard about the city, not to study its suburbs, areas that, in many respects, seemed to contradict the thrust of its international reputation. With few exceptions, foreign observers did not examine the nature of the city's residential life thoughtfully until the time of the Columbian Exposition. The differences between the Loop and the suburban neighborhoods provoked opinionated commentary from numerous visitors during and immediately after 1893, though most of them continued to slight the latter and to base their generalizations about Chicago primarily on the former. Those curious about its residential life tended to focus on several themes—the dual lives of business people, the importance of home ownership, the suburb as an expression of middle- and upper-class social confidence, and the rising influence of women.

Dual Lives of Businessmen

The male employed in the Loop divided his life into two distinct parts, one devoted to work and the other to his family or bachelor existence. Between the two there was normally no connection. From eight in the morning until six in the evening he worked in the business district, and from six in the evening until the following morning he concentrated on his family or himself in locations often miles from the center. For some years land developers had promised frequent, fast train service to new towns more than thirty miles from the Loop. The quality and nature of life in these two environments differed, and to function effectively in each the businessman developed two distinct personal styles. At work he subordinated his needs to those of a thriving commercial system. He was considered a valuable employee if he appeared to put the welfare of the firm first, labored conscientiously until quitting time, and handled responsibilities in a decisive and efficient manner. The successful employee did not publicly object to this hard-driving atmosphere in which his effectiveness could be measured. At the end of an eight-to-ten-hour workday he departed his office world of typewriters, pneumatic tubes, bells, contracts, letters, deadlines, undergoing an emotional and mental transformation during which, in the words of the French traveler Jean Landry, "the merchant is replaced by the man."[3] He returned to his family as a human being, no longer a cog in the gears of capitalism.

No foreign writer described the transformation experienced by a businessman leaving the Loop and arriving at his home, but a few recounted their own experiences as they climbed aboard public transportation and headed for the suburbs. The most expressive account was written by Jacques Hermant.

> As the foreign visitor, overwhelmed, tired, and prey to that dizziness that seizes one in the midst of crushing masses, goes off in search of a little rest and gets into a "car" to go to the north or south of Chicago, he is happily surprised before long by the complete change that occurs in the look of the city. Trees line the streets, and the houses are lower and spaced out; these are the elegant districts, inhabited by the families of all those big businessmen seen just minutes before, wearing the traditional round hats and walking with a quick and jerky step, as indifferent to every-

thing that surrounds them as if they were moving about in a desert. Little by little
the vise, that just a moment ago gripped the mind, loosens. Smiling and happy
thoughts take over once again, and the influence of woman is felt. We are in her
domain; she is the sovereign mistress here; everything is made for her and to satisfy her love of comfort and elegance.[4]

Hermant stressed several points in this commentary. He was overwhelmed by the scale and
frenzy of the Loop, needed the suburbs to recover his sense of well being, associated their
healing qualities with woman, and considered this part of Chicago her jurisdiction.

European critics of the early 1890s never claimed the hard, competitive Loop was
male and the reassuring, delightful suburbs were female, but they did associate men with
the function of the Loop and women with the function of the home. Despite the female
secretaries found in most offices by the mid-1880s, the young women who clerked in the
department stores, and the suburban women who shopped in them mornings and af-
ternoons, the dominant sex on the streets of the Loop was male, as Hermant implied.
The man was the go-between, the one who made the Loop churn during the day and
who fulfilled his family responsibilities when he returned in the evening. However, foreign insights about the two Chicagos still relegated him to inferior roles in his own
spheres, subordinate to an economic system in the Loop and subordinate to the woman
who managed his family in the suburbs. Though husbands earned the money that made
the single-family home or "castle" possible, a few of the best informed observers concurred with the opinion of Adolph Bocage: "The house—the 'home'—is made for the
wife, who reigns there like a queen and takes charge of everything."[5] The development
of two essential but very different Chicagos, the realm of work and the realm of family
and leisure, had consequences for the male who linked them. In the villages of yesterday
where the places of work and hearth were identical or closer together, when hand crafts
flourished, and housewives were not the carriers of culture their later sisters were to
become, the responsible male had been more directly influential. But, in the judgment
of a few observers, Chicago's separation of functions had altered his roles and eroded
his authority in both spheres.

The City's Domestic Neighborhoods

Foreign visitors usually commented favorably about the residential districts that radi-
ated from the Loop. Even when satirizing Chicago as the only metropolis in the world
where one could shoot wolves within city limits, they envied its spaciousness. In his
Exposition internationale de Chicago en 1893, Camille Krantz called attention to Chicago's geographical area by comparing it with a similarly scaled map of Paris (fig. 43). Travelers sometimes complained about interminable car and cab rides to the outskirts where
they saw big plans but little development—identified but undeveloped streets in fallow
land on which horse-car tracks had already been laid. The discovery of future neighborhoods, miles from the center, was further evidence of the hope, confidence, and imagination of the citizens.[6] The silence of the unbuilt streets of future Chicago and the hours

required for the return trip to downtown hotels were impressions that remained vivid for several writers. On their return they rode through successive stages of fulfillment of the dreams of young couples. First came the free-standing wooden cottages, usually on lots twenty-five feet wide, then substantial structures on tree-shaded streets, and finally broader avenues flanked by impressive mansions of stone or brick (fig. 44).

Europeans sometimes commiserated with couples forced to begin married life in cottages on Chicago's periphery but not with those who lived on more established streets flanked by sidewalks, lawns, and one-family houses constructed of wood, brick, or stone. These semibucolic settings in which individual families could function in harmony with but independently of neighbors impressed them as an ideal domestic environment not only for Chicagoans but also for the citizens of French and German cities. Several architectural writers tried to convince journal readers at home of the advantages of this kind of living arrangement. Although they had praised the Anglo-Saxon suburb throughout the last quarter of the century, continental critics made a greater effort around 1890 to distinguish between the British and American versions. The following attempt by Marcel Daly in *La semaine des constructeurs* was representative. "First of all, what is the American house like? Is it related to the small French town house or to the English cottage? To neither, at least not completely, but its relationship to the latter is undeniable. The predominant type isn't the town house, neither is it the retreat in the country. It is

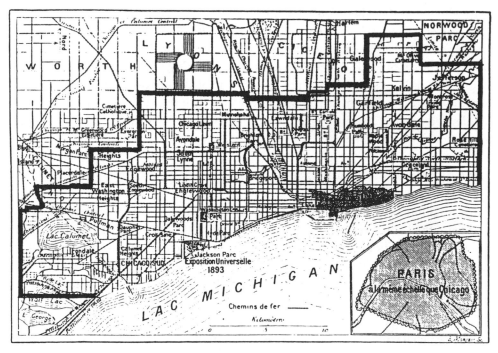

Figure 43. Comparison of the areas of Paris and Chicago; district burned in 1871 has been shaded (Krantz, *Exposition internationale de Chicago en 1893*, 1895.

the *maison de faubourg,* the 'suburban house,' as the American calls it."[7] Some thought the term "villa" suitable, but it seemed more applicable to the costlier houses constructed of stone or brick than to the predominant type in wood. While recognizing that mansions marked by ostentatious display were to be expected in "a country in which wealthy parvenues play the major role,"[8] critics noted basic similarities in plan between moderate and more expensive houses. They tended to see domestic architecture more in terms of family life than of expressions of private wealth and power.

In Chicago and other major cities in the United States, couples looked forward to moving into separate houses in surroundings that were pleasant and reassuring. This objective struck a chord among some foreign critics dissatisfied with current European housing options. According to Karl Mühlke, writing in the *Centralblatt der Bauverwaltung* in 1887,

> The Germans, especially, ought to study these arrangements because the American country house illustrates so well the idea of "one's own home" and embodies the saying, "My home is my castle." We have understood the meaning of the latter only vaguely, and our attempts to construct detached houses have been rare despite our awareness of the troubles and poor conditions we face in apartment buildings which increase in size and number each year in the larger German cities.[9]

French writers were much more cautious than the German in urging their readers to

Figure 44. A residential street in Chicago (*Deutsche Bauzeitung,* 3 October 1894).

emulate specific examples of middle-class detached houses in the United States, preferring instead to compliment American designers for their *esprit* or common sense. Even
Marcel Daly, more informed and enthusiastic than most architectural critics in France,
hesitated: "perhaps it [frame construction] could be adapted advantageously . . . in temporary constructions for housing railroad workers."[10]

Separate family dwellings would not have sprung up across the United States unless cheap houses were available and couples were unashamed to move into dwellings
unpretentious in size and appearance. By comparison, it was unlikely that young continental couples would commission unassuming wooden houses erected on the balloon
frame system in order to live independently of parents and neighbors. Wood was not
considered a proper building material in most cities in France and Germany, and, compared to genuine carpentry, balloon framing was regarded as a cheap expedient. European professionals also wondered why a caring husband in a country known for its violent storms and frequent fires would enclose his family in a flimsy-looking envelope of
joists and studs covered with clapboard or shingle siding. American couples were also
aware of these dangers but wanted their "castles" immediately, not in twenty years. Despite reservations, some German critics commended quickly built domestic architecture
of wood, arguing that its advantages of cheapness and speed were worth the struggle of
rethinking traditional attitudes about materials and vernacular methods.[11]

Evidence of aggressive individuality in family efforts to secure private sanctuaries was
only one indicator that Chicagoans in residential neighborhoods and Chicagoans in the
Loop acted differently. On the city's commercial streets, pedestrians fashioned protective
demeanors, seeking anonymity by melting into the crowd. In their own houses, however,
they often expressed family personalities through exuberant architectural gestures. They
also trusted their neighbors far more than they trusted people on the streets of the Loop,
announcing this publicly by not walling their lots. The reaction of Europeans to this was
mixed. Granted, free-standing houses in natural settings were attractive and provided a
healthy environment for family life, but, in the words of A. S. Northcote, who studied
Chicago's suburbs in 1893, "more privacy would seem desirable to an English mind than
can be afforded by the utter absence of all substantial boundaries" to each property.[12] Often only a few trees stood between the house and strangers on the sidewalks, a condition
evident in the photographs of Chicago houses in *Neubauten in Nordamerika,* published
in 1897 (fig. 45). Furthermore, the grass around one house imperceptibly became the grass
of a neighbor's. "One would think these were country houses, placed on the lawns of some
common property where everyone knew each other and had no reason to seek privacy,"
Jacques Hermant remarked.[13] Children who play outdoors, girls as well as boys, are unrestricted; even the road in front of the house is open to them, he noted. Unswayed by such
trust in an unreliable world, most foreign observers did not urge fellow Europeans to follow suit. Different in many respects, the suburbs and the central city seemed to condition
the attitudes of their respective inhabitants, inducing foreign writers to chide Chicagoans
for being too trusting at home and too absorbed at work. Visitors on short inspection tours
exaggerated observed behavior in the two quarters. Their overstatements about the effects

Figure 45. House of R. Alders, Chicago, 1890, Frank Burnham (*Neubauten in Nordamerika*, 1897).

of locale on character were also reflected in their collective amazement that Chicago's two halves were so linked yet so different.

That the Americans really did have confidence in their suburban neighborhoods in the 1890s was confirmed by the architecture itself. Between the "castle's" interior and the public street, designers had created a middle ground for the family to enjoy during the warm months of the year. The verandah or porch was a symbol of social confidence, a place where families could sit, play, eat in full view of unknown people on the sidewalks. This was true of the Evanston house of Dr. E. H. Webster by Holabird and Roche, also included in *Neubauten in Nordamerika* (fig. 46). From the porch, family members could observe the activity of the street, not because this zone needed watching but because watching enriched their lives. From the front porch one entered directly into the interior, an area that was usually central to the horizontal and vertical movement within the house. French and German visitors were startled to discover that immediately behind the front door was family space where children might play and from which one could look into the dining and living rooms or which even could be part of the living room. This planning rejected the continental vestibule where husband or wife could halt the advance of salesmen, thus protecting family and friends from unwanted intrusions. Admiring the spirit of openness and trust implied by these characteristics of the Amer-

Figure 46. House of Dr. E. H. Webster, Evanston, 1889–90, Holabird and Roche (*Neubauten in Nordamerika*, 1897).

ican home, most French and German critics were uneasy with them, preferring house planning that guaranteed greater privacy and security.

The exterior appearance of freestanding houses often amused visitors. If the commercial buildings of the Loop were taciturn, confusing the difference between utilitarian structures and works of art, the houses of the suburbs, including those constructed of stronger materials than wood, were expressive. Though the trend was slowing in the 1890s, owners still wanted animated exteriors proclaiming their energy, confidence, and good will. Combinations of projecting volumes, beguiling voids, and variegated surfaces appealed to some architectural editors abroad who commended them to their readers as proof of the American architects' independence, vitality, and imagination (fig. 47). Editors, concerned about professional stagnation in France and Germany, often praised American detached houses for their verve, even when by European standards they failed as coherent or logical designs.

A few critics thought these detached houses revealed family habits in a more specific sense because they discovered a connection between internal choices and exterior appearance. Several French and German observers claimed the basic intent of houses on both sides of the Atlantic differed. "All houses [in the United States] are planned to suit family life and not receptions, and form a sharp contrast to our Parisian houses," wrote

Figure 47. House of Theodor Krüger, Chicago, 1892, Frommann and Jebsen (*Neubauten in Nord-amerika*, 1897).

Paul de Rousiers.[14] By this he meant that the principal social spaces of the main floor—the dining room, the parlor, and the living room—were designed primarily to serve the immediate family and not the purposes of public entertainment or display. Wilhelm Bode went further, arguing that owners wanted rooms reflecting their family's habits and interests, a priority less noticeable in German interiors.[15] For example, a husband and wife who loved nature might insist upon a living room with a bay window facing a wooded part of their property. These houses were more effective than representative German types, Bode continued, because the personality of the owners was stamped on the principal rooms, and because the Americans designed their houses from the inside outward. Leopold Gmelin compared the perimeter walls of the first and second floors of a Chicago house to illustrate the external consequences of centrifugal interior volumes (fig. 48). Interior rooms, shaped by use rather than by the symmetry of formalism, determined the perimeter, resulting in what Karl Hinckeldeyn called "a propitious relationship between interior purposefulness and exterior effect."[16] Thus the design of an American detached house could appear to be imaginative while, at the same time, reflecting pragmatic concerns of its inhabitants. To some abroad this was not a reassuring development. If functional interior volumes could shape exterior form, voyeurs on the sidewalk would be tempted to read exteriors for clues to the personalities within.[17] The picturesque exteriors of American single-family houses appealed to foreign professionals bored with conventional practice, but a few of them became uneasy at the thought that external appearance might reveal too much about private matters.

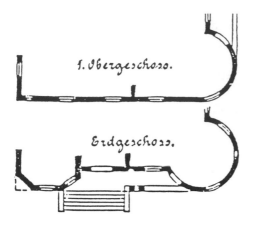

Figure 48. Contrast between the first- and second-floor exterior walls of a small house in Chicago (*Deutsche Bauzeitung,* 3 October 1894).

Her Influence on Interior Design

In Jacques Hermant's account of his trip from the Loop into the suburbs, he wrote that he was entering a territory under the control of women. For decades Europeans who analyzed American life had noted the respect accorded women in the United States and also their influence within the home. James Bryce thought there was no country in which the domestic power of women was greater. The German *Hausfrau,* he claimed, was too preoccupied with being an efficient housewife. The British wife tended to defer to her husband, who assumed his pleasures and concerns took precedence. In some countries on the Continent women appeared to gain their objectives, but only through flattery or manipulation. In America, by contrast, "the husband's duty and desire is to gratify the wife and render to her those services which the English tyrant exacts from his consort."[18] Chicago's businessmen-husbands perplexed several observers who wondered how they could be so aggressive in the pursuit of profits and apparently so accommodating in their secondary roles at home. Though almost all visitors disliked the self-absorbed businessman of the Loop, they were often empathetic to the husband of the suburbs. Madame Léon Grandin of Paris, who resided in Chicago for nearly a year in the early 1890s, observed:

> Here the husband is neither a sultan who disdains abasing himself to a woman's caprice, nor a tyrannical master, at times brutal and avaricious, who exploits the wife's labor as a manager does that of his workers. The American man asks only to make his wife and family happy. He wants their welfare to be his work, and it is that that motivates all his actions; it is the goal of his feverish activity, of his inimitable boldness, his road to fortune; he is tenacious, but seldom vainglorious.
>
> He is the founder of the family, of the house, the born protector of the woman, and if this is a fault, he is guilty.[19]

She was also critical of the women in Chicago who took his domestic efforts for granted and who did not understand the fortunate position they enjoyed among the women of Western nations.

> Used to this happiness, the woman is not appreciative enough, I think, but is satisfied to return his devotion.
> He brings her everything: affection, well-being, tranquillity; he keeps from her, taking upon himself, the pains, the trials, the cares; and it is only rarely that she thinks of showing gratitude; she by no means gives him all the sweetness of family life or the intimacies of home.[20]

Grandin's criticism, in addition to Hermant's reference to satisfying "her love of comfort and elegance," may suggest that foreign visitors viewed the Chicago woman as indolent and vain, a queen who expected her husband to rush home after a hard day's work to attend to her requests. If some did consider her spoiled, more commended her for her perceived role in the city's cultural development.

Foreign visitors began to comment on the cultural importance of the city's women in the early 1890s. Women played a more significant role in the World's Fair than in any previous international exposition, a fact mentioned in a number of foreign accounts. Women were also commended for their efforts to make Chicago a cleaner and more attractive place. However, for some observers, even the refining hand of woman could not prevent the ultimate triumph of boorishness in Chicago, a place "without soul and ideal, with its interminable dinners with their ranks of champagne bottles circulating among the evening coats, its drunkenness without gayety, its hypocritical luxury, its vulgar courtesies, its celebrations in which there is more flare than intelligence."[21] Despite the truths of such a charge, the women of Chicago fared well in foreign commentary. They were considered more than queens in insular domestic courts; they read books, learned languages, and studied art. Husbands, on the other hand, often exhausted by the day's work, enjoyed talking business but seemed bored or uninformed about other topics.[22] Did this prove what British observers, in particular, had worried about, that the absence of a leisure class plus a national preoccupation with business would render the country "uninteresting?" Not necessarily, was the verdict of many who had socialized with the women of the city. "My hostess attended twice a week a Plato club, and the winter before, so she told me, she had attended a similar class in Browning," reported a French intellectual.[23] Though Europeans sensed that the male leadership of the city wanted it to be known for its university, libraries, museums, and parks, they were more convinced of its cultural vitality and promise after conversations with Chicago's upper- and middle-class women.

In the judgments of several observers, the suburban housewife in Chicago had been given a unique opportunity and had used it well. The clear separation between the residential neighborhoods and the Loop meant a clear separation of responsibilities between husband and wife. He earned the money—and good money it was—while she cared for the children and managed the house. Her record of handling these responsibilities increased her husband's respect and her independence. Madame Léon Grandin referred to her envied international status in a poignant farewell to Chicago where she herself had been respected for her abilities.

I had tasted the fruit of independence, of intelligent activity, and I revolted at returning to the passive and inferior role that awaited me. I had enjoyed the consideration and respect accorded to women, and I would recover the scorn, the disdainful pity which masculine superiority heaps on women in France.

After seeing the women, my sisters, treated with consideration, relieved of life's burdens by their husbands, and in exceptional cases where women had to bear them, admired and helped by the man, I would return to see them treated either as beasts of burden or beasts of luxury, their moral value and intelligence held in contempt.

An old proverb calls Paris "the Paradise of Women!"

No, Paris is hell for women of spirit, the feminine paradise is America![24]

The "women of spirit" in Chicago had not only used their talents in trying to improve the housekeeping of their city, they had also been primarily responsible, from a European perspective, for a new kind of environment in which to raise a family. Journals abroad emphasized the appeal of these houses by publishing illustrations of them surrounded by trees and bushes with children playing in the yard, mothers waving from the porch, and smoke curling from the chimney.

In the early 1890s, half a decade after they had first taken notice of suburban and country houses,[25] several French and German architectural critics reiterated Karl Hinckeldeyn's 1889 insight that "the great development of dwelling-house architecture in this country is largely due to the refining and ennobling influence" of its women.[26] After visiting a number of houses in Chicago, Jacques Hermant declared, "One must look to her for cultivation of the mind, a feeling for taste and distinction, respect for and love of beauty. It is she, we will even say she alone, who is capable of understanding the infinite joy of daily contact with beautiful things." Though the majority of visitors to Chicago in 1893 said nothing about this possibility, they were surprised by the interior attractiveness of homes because they expected something else from the houses of "prosaic moneymen."[27]

In their expansive but vague praise, these critics commended architects for their planning, the natural woodwork around doors and windows, and the ingenious built-in furniture, but they also implied that the woman of the house was responsible for the character of its major spaces. By stressing comfort rather than propriety or pretentiousness, and by selecting furniture that served the body rather than the intellect, most women had created an environment for the family rather than for display. She was also given credit for encouraging steps that increased convenience and saved time, freeing her to attend to her loved ones or to the restlessness of her mind, for welcoming the open plan that undermined the concept of hierarchical territories and mandated freer interaction among of all members of the family, and for attractive interior decoration.

Once foreign observers had studied the residential districts of Chicago, the Loop made more sense. They realized that those who worked in this zone could not have kept up with its demanding pace unless they could leave it to spend other hours of their days in a qualitatively different environment. They also realized that residential districts allowed the function of Chicago's downtown to be more narrowly defined, further clarifying the meaning of *Zweckmässigkeit*. Like work at the stockyard, life in Chicago was affected by a division of labor, the male primarily responsible for the hardness and efficiency of the business district and the female for the softness and attractiveness of its residential neighborhoods. Though many Europeans regarded this split between the downtown and the suburbs as strange or arbitrary, they nevertheless believed Chicagoans had acted in the present, pushing aside their light history, questioning artistic conventions, and reconsidering social patterns to make it happen.

Notes

1. James Fullarton Muirhead, *The Land of Contrasts* (Boston: Lamson, Wolffe, 1898), 207.

2. Elizabeth Grosz, "Bodies-Cities," in *Sexuality and Space,* ed. Beatriz Colomina (New York: Princeton Architectural Press, 1992), 243.

3. Jean Landry, *Hommes et choses d'Amérique* (Paris: J. Lefort, 1897), 148.

4. Jacques Hermant, "L'art à l'exposition de Chicago," *Gazette des beaux-arts* 73 (November 1893): 418.

5. Adolphe Bocage, "L'architecture aux États-Unis et à l'exposition universelle de Chicago," *L'architecture* 7 (13 October 1894): 336.

6. Homer Hoyt reported that at the end of the 1880s thousands of laborers and clerks were pooling their money and forming syndicates to purchase acres of suburban tracts. Hoyt, *One Hundred Years of Land Values in Chicago* (Chicago: University of Chicago Press, 1933), 164.

7. Marcel Daly, "L'architecture américaine," *La semaine des constructeurs,* 2d ser., 6 (23 April 1892): 515.

8. Emil Deckert, "Das amerikanische Haus," *Gegenwart* 32 (30 July 1887): 68.

9. Karl Mühlke, "Das amerikanische Landhaus und die Preisbewerbung des *American Architect,*" *Centralblatt der Bauverwaltung* 7 (8 January 1887): 11. This excellent two-part article (the second on 15 January) was inspired by the 1885–86 competition for a $5,000 detached house initiated by the *American Architect.*

10. Marcel Daly, "Les constructions en bois aux États-Unis," *La semaine des constructeurs,* 2d ser., 3 (1 September 1888): 112.

11. See Mühlke, 12, and Arnold Lewis, "Hinckeldeyn, Vogel, and American Architecture," *Journal of the Society of Architectural Historians,* 31 (December 1972): 276–90.

12. A. S. Northcote, "American Life through English Spectacles," *Nineteenth Century* 34 (September 1893): 480.

13. Hermant, 418.

14. Paul de Rousiers, *American Life,* trans. A. J. Herbertson (Paris: Firmin-Didot, 1892), 291. On the other hand, foreign observers noted that adjacent rooms in an open plan could be treated as a single space for large social events. Among the more informative discussions of domestic interiors were Marcel Daly, "L'architecture américaine," *La semaine des constructeurs,* 2d ser., 6 (23, 30 April, 7 May 1892): 515–17, 532–33, 544; Leopold Gmelin, "Architektonisches aus Nordamerika," *Deutsche Bauzeitung* 28 (29 September, 3, 6 October 1894): 481–83, 485–87, and 495–96, 498; and G. Diercks, *Kulturbilder aus den Vereinigten Staaten* (Berlin: Allgemeiner Verein für Deutsche Litteratur, 1893), 332–45.

15. Wilhelm Bode, "Moderne Kunst in den vereinigten Staaten von Amerika," *Kunstgewerbeblatt,* n.s., 5 (1894): 115–17.

16. Paul Graef, *Neubauten in Nordamerika,* intro. Karl Hinckeldeyn (Berlin: Julius Becker, 1897), 2.

17. CL., "Arch.- und Ing.- Verein zu Hamburg" [talk by H. Wolbrandt], *Deutsche Bauzeitung* 28 (24 January 1894): 43.

18. James Bryce, *Social Institutions of the United States* (New York: Chautauqua Press, 1891), 138–39.

19. Madame Léon Grandin, *Impressions d'une Parisienne à Chicago,* (Paris: Ernest Flammarion, 1894), 313–14; anonymous translation attached to copy in Chicago Historical Society.

20. Ibid., 314.

21. "A Frenchman's Impressions of Chicago Itself," *American Architect* 41 (16 September 1893): 176, from remarks by Octave Uzanne in *Figaro* of Paris.

22. This reaction is not surprising since many who led Chicago's economic development had left school to make their fortunes. Their children, the first generation of wealth to attend colleges and universities in large numbers, were more impressive in their table conversation.

23. *America and the Americans from a French Point of View* (New York: Charles Scribner's Sons, 1897), 254. Browning claimed more of his books were sold in Chicago than in any other American city. See Charles Dudley Warner, "Studies of the Great West," *Harper's Magazine,* May 1888, 878. Generalizations about women in Chicago conform to the popular image abroad of "the American woman," a subject on which European males wrote at length in the late nineteenth century. Charles de Varigny's 1893 characterization was representative. The American woman was independent, determined, adaptable, everywhere at ease, could laugh at her weaknesses, scorned social conventions, had luxurious tastes but was not afraid of work, and sustained American culture. "She is to-day . . . the most finished work of the country's two centuries of civilization." M. C. de Varigny, "The American Woman," *Popular Science Monthly* 43 (July 1893): 386. According to James Bryce, there were three main reasons why her "average of literary taste and influence" was higher than that of European women: educational opportunities and facilities, equality of the sexes in social and intellectual life, and the leisure they have compared to men. Bryce, 143.

24. Grandin, 313.

25. News and commentary about American detached houses increased noticeably in the architectural literature of the Continent in the last half of the 1880s. French writers concentrated on their exteriors, often finding in them the verve they thought was missing in house design in France, while German observers were more impressed by the spatial and functional aspects of interiors. The British studied American detached houses and their bucolic surroundings less often, probably because they appeared to be similar to their own practice. Citing American work for its informality, functionalism and pleasantness, continental critics sometimes held it up as an example for their readers. "I ask myself with shame, why can't we do this also?" wrote Hans Schliepmann after seeing illustrations of American suburban homes in the May, June, and October 1890 issues of *Scribner's Magazine.* Hans Schliepmann, *Betrachtungen über Baukunst* (Berlin: Polytechnische Buchhandlung, 1891), 96.

26. [Karl] Hinckeldeyn, "A Foreigner's View of American Architecture," *American Architect* 25 (25 May 1889): 244. See also Bocage, 336; Hermant, 417; Gmelin, 483; and R.E., "Les grandes constructions américaines," *La construction moderne* 6 (5 September 1891): 569.

27. On return from the exposition, Victor Champier gave a lecture illustrated by lantern slides of domestic interiors at the Conservatoire des Arts et Métiers in Paris. Commenting on the lecture, *La semaine des constructeurs* observed, "What harmony, what original and unexpected pleasantness, what a wealth of good taste in all these interiors! . . . One can understand the disgust of a Frenchman, returning from Chicago, to find again in the Parisian apartments the naked walls, the staring curtains, the monotonous wooden floors, and, especially, the universal whitewash which everywhere covers the ceilings." See "The Industrial Arts of America Criticized by M. Victor Champier," *American Architect* 43 (31 March 1894), 146.

The 8 World's Columbian Exposition

WHEN THE World's Columbian Exposition opened in Jackson Park on Chicago's south side in May 1893, it was the largest of all of the great nineteenth-century international exhibitions, containing approximately three times the roofed space of the acclaimed Paris Exposition of 1889. The European press called the effort behind Chicago's fair unprecedented in the history of these periodic celebrations of material progress. It also considered the appearance of the buildings and grounds spectacular. The central area of the exposition was an integrated complex of walkways, lawns, woods, waterways, and spacious exhibition halls designed in variations of Roman, Romanesque, and Renaissance styles and finished in "staff"—a blend of plaster of Paris and water reinforced by jute—painted white to simulate marble. Chicago had once again amazed Europeans, but this time for reasons Chicagoans did not expect. Assuming the products of a dynamic mechanical and electrical age would be exhibited in architecture reflecting that age instead of in buildings that looked backward for stylistic inspiration, foreign visitors were mystified. Furthermore, the sprawling White City, as the complex was also called, seemed to have little in common with the compact, vertical Loop, which had been instrumental in shaping Chicago's international image. Though Europeans had been shocked time and again by the city, they had rarely been confused by its expressions, but now they were.

Pre-Exposition Confusion

Many thought the success of the exposition in Paris in 1889 had set new standards that would be difficult for later international events to equal. Henry Trueman Wood, secretary of the British Commission for the Columbian Exposition, contended this challenge had only roused the competitive spirit of the Yankees. "France had had the best and biggest exhibition. America must have a better, and, above all, a bigger one."[1] In 1889 in Paris over thirty-two million people had visited the Champ de Mars to climb the Eiffel Tower and to experience the breadth of space in the Galerie des Machines, where iron was used without apology to demonstrate, in the words of Eugène-Melchior de Vogüé, a fundamental concept of art, namely, beauty derived from the integration of form and destination.[2] The buildings of the 1889 exposition in Paris seemed to be further evidence of an impending age in which engineers and architects would collaborate to take advantage of new materials. Because engineers and architects had also collaborated in the Loop, foreign observers reacted positively to the decision of the American Congress on 25 February 1890 to name Chicago the host city for the international exhibition commemorating the four-hundredth anniversary of the discovery of the New World by Columbus.

European critics who commented on the forthcoming exposition expected its planners to create a setting reflecting recent tendencies in American design and construction.[3] In articles announcing the selection of Chicago, European commentators sometimes offered advice, the thrust of which was to be yourself; don't try to rival Paris, for this would be impossible. Be as "rash" in conceiving the grounds of the exposition as developers had been in creating the topography of the Loop. Express the ample space of the United States by designing an exhibition park on a generous scale, thus avoiding the overcrowded buildings of 1889. Make the setting imposing for the occasion because Europeans who make the journey will not want to be disappointed. Above all, use this opportunity to communicate to the rest of the world what it wants to know—how a young country has applied technology to exploit the resources of nature with greater productivity and efficiency than any other people. Though critics abroad had often advised American architects to water their wine, for this occasion they urged Chicago's planners to act like Yankees by "licking all creation." After all, reasoned the editors of *Engineering* in December 1890, this was a temporary festival, therefore, new ideas should be "set forth by novel methods, and in ways never yet attempted."[4] The consensus held that the choice of Chicago was appropriate for there was no city in a stronger position to summarize the astounding achievements of a marvelous century.

Word spread quickly in Britain and on the Continent that the Parisian exposition would look like "a mere village fair next to the colossal exhibition" Chicago was preparing.[5] In addition to lubricating rumors of the exposition's immensity, the European press carried reports and illustrations of imaginative, if not absurd, schemes for exposition structures that American newspapers had been quick to publicize. The *Chicago Tribune*, in a gesture of euphoria in the early days of planning for Chicago's fair, did its part to stir "tower fever" by inviting designers on 20 October 1889 to submit "plans and suggestions for a World's Fair tower, arch, or monument." The newspaper repudiated its invitation on 15 June 1890, however, when it published an editorial entitled, "The Columbian Exposition Cranks." Despite the *Tribune's* second thoughts reflecting its increasing concern that Chicago be a responsible, rather than a risk-taking, host city, it published illustrations of more than forty imaginative schemes.[6] Though invariably taller, the tower projects were less graceful and less unified than the Eiffel; the proposal of W. L. Judson is a good example (fig. 49). Some editors of professional journals abroad expressed skep-

Figure 49. Comparison of the Eiffel Tower and the proposed tower by W. L. Judson for the Columbian Exposition (*La semaine des constructeurs*, 5 April 1890).

ticism about the tower phase of the exposition's planning. "We are familiar with the early suggestions, which should not be taken seriously, to build a tower higher than the Eiffel Tower. For example, the one which pivots on a horizontal axle [see fig. 50]. Visitors would enter the platform which always remains horizontal and would be lifted gradually into the air, enabling them to admire the changing landscape as if they were ascending in a balloon."[7]

Anticipating a spectacular monument and knowing Chicagoans could probably pull off anything they set their minds to, a few foreign journals treated unrealistic projects with more respect than they deserved. Though informed it would not be built, the *Zeitschrift des oesterreichischen Ingenieur- und Architekten-Vereines* published the pedantic scheme of F. Ingoldsby of Chicago, "Freedom Raising the World" (fig. 51).[8] The publicity given to wild schemes increased fears abroad in the last half of 1890 that planning for the exposition was in disarray and later to resentment when visitors, such as Otto Mueller, an Austrian, found no "wonderful, colossal figure by Ingoldsby" and no tower by the Plaisance Tower Company at Jackson Park. These were never serious undertakings, Mueller complained, only lies that served the purposes of advertising.[9] Other tower designs, such as the one by George Morison (fig. 52), were touted, but increasingly European journals paid less attention to the rumored projects.

If professionals in Britain, France, and Germany had specific forms in mind for the "truly American" construction the majority called for, they did not describe or illustrate them. However, the positive foreign reaction to the unexecuted tent tower by E. S. Jenison and Company, the only scheme to win widespread European endorsement, may give us some indication of their expectations. The project of this Chicago firm consisted of a 1,100–foot central steel tower supporting at the height of 700 feet radiating cables anchored at ground level in a circle 3,000 feet in diameter (fig. 53). Under the structure's glass and corrugated metal roof, illuminated at night by electric lights, there would be 193⅔ acres of usable space. Possibly influenced by the endorsement of Jenison's scheme by the respected American publication *Engineering News* (15, 29 March 1890), several European journals commented positively. Intrigued by its "daring grotesqueness," *Engineering* of London thought it original, ample—providing more than twice the exhibit space of Paris in 1889—and a challenge American engineers could master.[10] This scheme struck a positive chord abroad because it was innovative, relied on steel and glass, was daring but simple, was spacious enough for exhibitors, would be graceful without being arty, was inexpensive ($36 per covered acre compared to $75 at Paris), could be sold later for scrap, and, in theory at least, could be built. After appearing to support the Jenison plan, believing Chicago's real estate community was pleased with it, the *Tribune* opposed it in editorials, arguing that such a structure would violate good taste, would become an artistic eyesore, and could not support its weight.[11]

These preparatory steps seemed uncharacteristically confused and indecisive for Chicago. They may have encouraged Gustave Eiffel to cable authorities in Jackson Park on 4 August 1891 to ask for the opportunity to design a tower that he promised would be higher than the one he had designed for the 1889 exposition.[12] But the futile noise

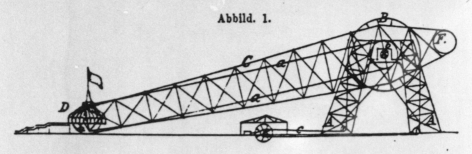

Eine massive Wandmauer würde das Ganze umgeben. Die Drahtseile würden gleichzeitig zur Verankerung der Mittel-

Abbild. 1.

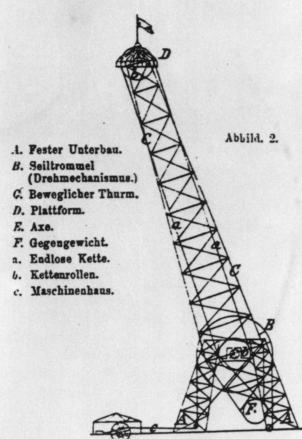

A. Fester Unterbau.
B. Seiltrommel (Drehmechanismus.)
C. Beweglicher Thurm.
D. Plattform.
E. Axe.
F. Gegengewicht.
a. Endlose Kette.
b. Kettenrollen.
c. Maschinenhaus.

Abbild. 2.

stütze dienen. so dass diese nur stark genug gebaut zu sein branche, um senkrechte Press-ungen aufzunehmen. Spannseile, in verschie-denen Ebenen zwischen Zelt - Peripherie und Mittelstütze ange-bracht, würden seit-liche Ausbauchungen des Zeltdaches unter dem Einflusse des Windes verhindern.

Der ganze Innen-raum würde also nur eine Theilung durch die Mittelstütze erfah-ren und sich im übri-gen dem Blicke frei öffnen, also entschie-den einen großartigen Eindruck machen. Durch Galerien in ver-schiedener Höhe könn-ten schöne Ueberblicke über den Raum gewon-nen werden. Die kreis-förmige Grundriss-Anordnung ermöglicht einen übersichtlichen Aufbau der Ausstellungs-Gegenstände, indem, wie bei der Pariser

Figure 50. Project for a pivoting tower by Timothy Bernard Powers for the Columbian Exposi-tion (*Deutsche Bauzeitung*, 14 May 1890).

Figure 51. Project, "Freedom Raising the World," by F. Ingoldsby for the Columbian Exposition (*Zeitschrift des oesterreichischen Ingenieur- und Architekten-Vereines,* 18 March 1892).

about towers was less worrisome to interested international exhibitors than the inability of American commissioners to decide where the celebration was going to be held. The possibility of a dual site—Jackson Park and the lakefront east of the Loop—was debated for almost a year before the lakefront site was dropped in favor of the single site. In May 1891 *Engineering* asked, "How is it possible that this vast amount of construction, greatly exceeding that of the Paris Exhibition of 1889, will be ready in two years?"[13] Construction on the first buildings did not begin until 3 July 1891. On 21 February 1892 the *Chicago Tribune* published an air-view sketch of the progress of construction on the major exhibition halls (fig. 54).

The inefficient process by which the final site was chosen provided Eastern skeptics, particularly New Yorkers, with additional ammunition to argue that the exposition would be a failure. Chicago was still a provincial town in their eyes, too parochial to represent the country with the class their city would have guaranteed. Newspapers in the East predicted Chicago's fair would be big, boorish, and unattractive to Europeans, who would not be interested in traveling great distances to see a vast cattle show. Their depiction of Chicago as a crass metropolis also fed stereotypes abroad that its moneywise citizens

Figure 52. Proposed tower by George S. Morison for the Columbian Exposition (*Engineering*, 20 November 1891.

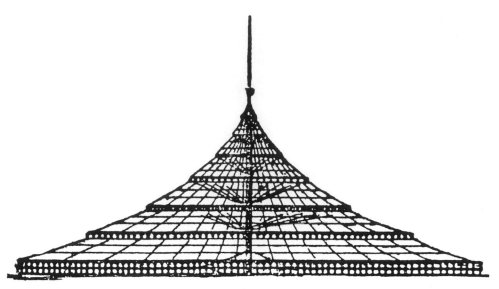

Figure 53. Proposed tower by E. S. Jenison and Company for the Columbian Exposition (*Chicago Tribune,* 9 March 1890).

would take advantage of innocent visitors. Furthermore, the timing of the McKinley Tariff in 1890 could hardly have been worse since the consequences of the tariff were inimical to international cooperation. Denounced throughout Europe, the tariff inspired angry responses from some manufacturers who announced they would not participate in the exposition. However, the disadvantages of a boycott convinced influential leaders to endorse the exposition. "The way to show that England was in many branches supreme would be to show what we could do in a public-spirited way, even if we did not derive as much pecuniary benefit from it as we otherwise might have done," reasoned Sir Richard Webster before the Society for the Encouragement of Arts, Manufacturers, and Com-

Figure 54. "The World's Fair Buildings showing the progress made" (*Chicago Tribune,* 21 February 1892).

merce in London.[14] Late in 1891 the *New York Times* also altered its editorial policy—"the failure of the fair or anything short of a positive and pronounced success would be a discredit to the whole country, and not to Chicago alone."[15] Decisions to participate did not allay fears abroad that Chicago was attempting too much with too little time remaining. Foreign commissioners tried to calm nervous prospective exhibitors by reminding them that "Chicago is accustomed to speed in the construction of big buildings, and her best building contractors are working in Jackson-park." Thus, foreign commentators drew from the standard image of the city to counteract the emerging image that the exposition was being managed in an un-Chicago-like manner. On opening day foreign visitors found numerous exhibits still in their packing cases.[16]

Unexpected Architecture

European architectural journals began to respond to the published designs of the major exhibition halls in the fall of 1891. The *Builder* of London noted that what was expected, architecture designed in the modern Romanesque style, was missing except for Adler and Sullivan's round-arched Transportation Building, which it called simple and suitable for a temporary exhibition structure. The journal called the designs of the major halls pleasing but uninspired. The Administration Building by Richard Morris Hunt (fig. 55), for example, lacked the vigor French designers could impart to modern variations on historic styles.[17] An anonymous writer for *Centralblatt der Bauverwaltung* was more positive, commending planners for inviting the best architects of the country to participate.[18] Another of Germany's major professional journals, the *Deutsche Bauzeitung,* reacted negatively. Prefacing his criticism with the observation that what American architects had been able to accomplish independently through the free study of Western art had been remarkable and that the *Deutsche Bauzeitung* had tried to point this out on numerous occasions, Albert Hofmann, the assistant editor, concluded reluctantly that the architectural designs for the exposition proved that even the independent Americans could not resist the seduction of historicism.

> Roman and Italian influences, at times eclectically mixed with motifs from various Renaissance and other styles, completely dominate the architectural appearance of the exhibition. We see this in the Administration Building, the Manufacturers Building, the Machinery Building, the Palace of Fine Arts, etc. Even the Woman's Building, the result of female initiative, is not exempt.
>
> One could have expected a certain distinctiveness in American art. Because of its peoples' impressive talent in construction, purposefully directed, because the country has no historical monuments, and because, like Old Egypt, it is isolated, it, more than any other country, seemed destined for an autochthonous development of art, and to a degree this has been successfully shown. But the exhibition will betray this expectation. . . . Perhaps we shall have to modify this judgment in some respects after we have been able to study the completed details; the main impression, however, will still be that of a traditional, antiquarian, backwards-looking exercise in art.[19]

Figure 55. Administration Building, Columbian Exposition, 1893, Richard M. Hunt (Jaffe, *Die Architektur der columbischen Welt-Ausstellung zu Chicago, 1893*, 1895).

Reflecting continental reaction but not necessarily the response of British architects, Hofmann felt betrayed. His sense of loss revealed the degree to which some German professionals had counted heavily on the exposition's version of contemporary architecture.

The first substantial reaction in France appeared in *La construction moderne* in December 1892. Like Hofmann, the unidentified writer was disappointed. We have daydreamed, he admitted, wondering "what wouldn't the enterprising and innovative American genius produce for our astonished eyes when given full freedom!" Perhaps bold-shaped pavilions, rational construction, purposeful decoration, in short, a preview of the architecture of the twentieth century. After all, he continued, this was an exposition where designers could exercise license they were normally denied and was located in the city that rebuilt itself in no time after its destructive fire, where fifty-one railroad lines converge, where citizens embody the American "go-ahead." Though faulting his colleagues for expecting too much, he reached the same conclusion as Hofmann about the implications of the designs for Western architecture.

> Isn't the first plate published in *La construction moderne* [Administration Building by Richard Morris Hunt, fig. 55] rather disappointing? We have seen this done

smaller and larger many times before; these *torchères* and this Ionic porch at the second level are obligatory for school-designed Pantheons. The ground floor and the rostral columns are familiar, oh so familiar, and so hackneyed! May God forgive me for I am showing disrespect for the milk which has nourished us all. And not only the central dome, but also, judging from the color prints displayed everywhere, all the other major buildings of the exposition seem to spring from the same prejudices.

In 1889 the architects of old Europe had searched for a new path by justifying the use of iron, panels more or less colored, etc. Yet Chicago in 1893 resuscitates forms with which we wanted nothing more to do.[20]

His advice to French readers traveling to the exposition: ignore the contrived work at Jackson Park; pay attention to the commercial buildings of the city, to the pretty villas on Greenwood and Michigan Avenues, to the massive Auditorium, for these buildings, though naive, were sincere.

Despite the delays, indecisiveness, bad press, erroneous reports, and resentment over the tariff, despite the sense of betrayal voiced by some architectural authorities abroad, the White City, particularly its Grand Basin and surrounding buildings, named the Court of Honor (fig. 56), stunned European visitors. Just as early illustrations of tall buildings had not prepared critics for the reality of the Loop, the illustrations of the buildings and waterways of the exposition had not prepared them for the enchanting, fairy-tale park they found. Ironically, Daniel Burnham, chief of works; Frederick Law Olmsted and Harry Codman, who planned the grounds; Frank Millet, the supervisor of color and decoration; and the architectural firms responsible for the designs of the major buildings had collaborated to create an environment that seemed more like a vision than a reality. Intended to house the products of contemporary science and industry, the complex seemed unreal, immaterial, a creation beyond ordinary time and place. Even critics who ultimately condemned the result, such as Jacques Hermant, could be momentarily silenced by the incomparable scene. Hermant recalled a "temptation to forget all criticisms in the face of the truly magnificent impression which results from this dream so audaciously conceived and naively realized."[21] Under its mesmerizing spell, critics tended to replace critical judgment with extravagant comparisons. "No other scene of man's creation seemed to me so perfect as this Court of Honour," wrote James Fullarton Muirhead.[22] Prose took flight. "The great white city which rose before me, silent and awful, seemed to belong to an order of things above our common world. It was a poem entablatured in fairy palaces, only to be done into human speech by the voice of some master singer. It was a dream of beauty which blended the memory of classic greatness with the sense of Alpine snows."[23] Compliments came not only from lay observers but also from established architects. Walter Kyllmann, of the Berlin firm of Kyllmann and Heyden, a member of the International Jury on Architecture at the exposition, claimed the rulers of Assyria, Egypt, Byzantium, and Rome as well as Charlemagne and Napoleon had failed to create monuments of equal beauty.[24] To a significant extent initial disappointment over the failure to further the cause of iron melted before the visual splendor of the White City. Referring to a gathering of European architects, artists, and critics at the Century

Figure 56. Court of Honor, Columbian Exposition, 1893 (Jaffe, *Die Architektur der columbischen Welt-Ausstellung zu Chicago, 1893,* 1895).

Club in New York, Wilhelm Bode reported all were full of admiration except for an unnamed French architect.[25] Europeans also complimented planners for the breadth and imagination of their conception and the herculean labor required to complete it. In the past, foreign writers had often scolded or satirized ambitious Chicagoans; this time they thanked them sincerely for their effort.

The Columbian Exposition confirmed or clarified a number of European presuppositions about the United States and its heterogeneous society. Visitors from abroad noted a connection between the vast space they experienced on trains between New York and Chicago and the amount of space (685 acres) that overwhelmed them within the official grounds. The United States was big; furthermore, its people, at home with spatial amplitude, planned with confidence in large, if not extravagant, terms. European countries had not conceived of an international event on the scale of Chicago's, nor would they attempt to in the near future, the majority predicted. The exposition also confirmed that Americans commanded powerful means and knew how to use these means to turn their expansive conceptions into realities. Many argued that the exposition was a clarifying moment in contemporary history, waking up people on both sides of the Atlantic to the "power, progress, and importance" of the United States.[26]

Late nineteenth-century expositions were considered by many contemporary observers to be concentrated expressions of the culture of the host nation.[27] No one applied this argument more thoroughly or influentially to the expositions of 1889 and 1893 than the Marquis de Chasseloup-Laubat, a representative of the Société des ingénieurs civils who was in Chicago from July to mid-October 1892.[28] Like France, a country in which space was precious, he reasoned, the exposition of 1889 was compact. Within limited space its exhibition buildings were carefully placed and vistas between them emphasized to remind visitors of the total plan. These decisions were an expression of the orderliness of French culture, regulated by the heritage of Roman laws and the codes of Napoleon, and expressed in experienced artistic language derived from proven principles. Characteristic of a centralized state, the exposition in Paris had been planned and managed by a national administration, not by a city or a region. At Jackson Park the marquis found a contradictory approach. Chicago's version was gigantic, asymmetrical, without strong central control, and highly diversified. Its vast grounds located approximately seven miles south of the Loop in an undeveloped part of the city reflected the size and the openness of American space. Furthermore, the initial formality and order of the Court of Honor dissolved into picturesque asymmetry around the Lagoon to the north, transforming a somewhat systematic plan into one that "leaves so considerable a portion to each one's whim, that it is hardly visible." Yet this was similar to America's federalized system in which each state, marked by distinctive climate, products, customs, and populations, was tied to others by loose political bonds. Unlike France, the United States was a nation of many peoples. "The buildings at Jackson Park constitute a nation of exhibitions rather than a single and homogeneous exhibition." Finally, Chasseloup-Laubat argued that mature France had taken independent artistic steps in 1889 but the United States, a society still too young and too fluid from immigration, lacked that confidence in 1893. His assumption of a close correlation between the international image of the United States and selected characteristics of its exposition was not uncommon among European observers.

Although Europeans praised the visual impact of the White City, few recommended it be repeated. For the purpose of displaying the material progress of the world, this architectural wonderland was too ephemeral. The first impression, so magical that it inevitably received poetic treatment in otherwise prosaic accounts, was a profoundly optical experience. The eyes of visitors reported what their minds resisted—the presence of an ancient city in contemporary time. Not alone, Friedrich Dernburg admitted he was afraid to close his eyes for fear that when he reopened them, "all will disappear as in a dream."[29] There was another sense in which this was a visual experience. Once touched, in order to know what deceptive marble felt like, these buildings, composed of attached planes, a vast Hollywood stage set before Hollywood, were read as surfaces rather than as plastic forms or functional containers. Painted white, their facades glistened in the sun. Reflected light was so bright visitors complained they could not stare for long, yet they could not easily avoid doing so, surrounded as they were by long flanks separated from one another by vistas revealing more surfaces of white, many of them mirrored in rippled water. Unable intellectually to control the complex and dazzled by the competing luminosity of its parts, observers experienced it optically as a series of fragments. Wittingly or unwittingly, the designers of the exposition, despite employing styles from a distant past, affirmed a contemporary sensibility—the shift from absolutism to relativism, from the tactile to the visual. They had created a contradiction in terms, an architecture more suggestive than substantive, which, like the ballet scenes of Degas and the Paris streetscapes of Pissarro, implied greater sensitivity to movement and temporal multiplicities, phenomena too evanescent for the promotion of material progress. The delights the setting offered to the eyes upstaged the delights it offered to the mind.

The creators of the scene had been successful in making a real mirage, the initial impact of which foreign visitors recalled as their most vivid experience at the Columbian Exposition. From a manufacturer's standpoint, a mirage was antithetical to the interests of international trade. The spectacle kept fairgoers outside instead of inside. It transfixed viewers, encouraging them to fantasize instead of investigate. They doted on something unattainable instead of something tradable. Ecstatic about the beauty of the architecture, one European visitor, the French novelist and critic Madame Blanc, confirmed the fears of manufacturers when she declared, "I do not care to know what these buildings contained. It displeases me to think that they had a useful purpose—or any purpose whatever."[30] Some writers claimed the effects of electric lights at night made the scene more magical. The most common literary reference used to describe the White City, "A Thousand and One Nights," was often inspired by Jackson Park after sundown.

Since the Crystal Palace of 1851, international expositions had displayed the fruits of science and industry in settings that were often innovative. Manufacturers needed distinctive-looking buildings at these events to attract crowds, but they were concerned that the framework not divert attention from their exhibits. Furthermore, they demanded effective display areas as a condition of participation. At Jackson Park, authorities threatened this delicate balance in two ways. First, they made their event, in the judgment of James Dredge, editor of *Engineering,* the "most magnificent of all International Exhibitions, so far as the buildings and grounds are concerned,"[31] and, secondly, they provided exhibitors with more space than ever before. This complicated the relationship between exterior art and interior function. The public was dazzled by spectacular facades while exhibitors struggled with huge interiors of varying effectiveness. Some exhibition halls were large enough to provide viewing room around exhibits without appearing to be cavernous; Dredge thought the Mines and Mining Building by S. S. Beman and the Transportation Building by Adler and Sullivan were the best in this respect. Others were less effective. The worst match occurred in the mammoth Manufactures and Liberal Arts Building (385 feet wide, 1140 feet long, and 200 feet high in the center) by George B. Post (fig. 57), where the displays of jewelry, fashions, and furniture were "piteously lost in this immensity,"[32] in the judgment of the French aristocrat S.-C. de Soissons. In addition to upsetting the relationship between art and usable space by trying to set records in both categories, the Americans compounded the problem by beguiling the crowds with the

Figure 57. Manufacturers Building, Columbian Exposition, 1893, George B. Post (Jaffe, *Die Architektur der columbischen Welt-Ausstellung zu Chicago, 1893*, 1895).

possibility of an earthly paradise obtainable through idealistic planning and the collaborative efforts of business, science, and art.

Though commentators in Britain, France, and Germany credited those responsible with having demonstrated a new kind of setting for international expositions, they often added, "please don't do this again." In addition to being too seductive on the outside to the disadvantage of exhibitors, Chicago's vast halls were criticized for poor ventilation, leaking roofs, and galleries that increased exhibition space but detracted from the internal unity and darkened the exhibit area underneath. Critics also objected to the dimensions of the exposition, a predictable outcome Soissons attributed to the Americans' "hypertrophy of sight." Countries would not want to host a future world's fair if the current escalation of size continued, critics believed, for they would be unable to raise the 19.5 million dollars that Chicago's celebration cost (which was five times that of the Paris Exposition of 1889). Europeans also had reservations about the Midway Plaisance, larger and more diversified than the Street of Nations at the exposition in Paris. They were not concerned about its racial implications, as recent twentieth-century historians have been, but worried that this sideshow, a response to the crowds' need for diversion, might "establish a dangerous precedent" by undermining the traditional purpose of expositions. In short, foreign critics thought the Columbian Exposition had "Americanized" these occasions. By this they meant it had expanded the scale of expositions, increased the importance of architecture, drawn attention away from the intellectual content of the exhibits, and placed a higher value on entertainment. Though publishing his plea a year before the White City opened, Friedrich Reusche, in a book on old and new directions in exposition planning, summarized European sentiment by recommending a return to greater simplicity and to the original purpose of these international events.[33]

Implications for American Architecture

European critics interpreted the designs of the major buildings at Jackson Park as a sign of a change in American architecture. There were a few writers, usually those displeased with the reversion to historic styles, who urged their readers to discount the significance of the fair's buildings, claiming they were created as temporary halls for an artificial purpose and thus were unreliable indicators of the current thinking of the profession in the United States.[34] The majority, including those pleased and displeased, took the opposite view. There was also a small number of critics, foremost among them Wilhelm Bode, Karl Hinckeldeyn, and Banister Fletcher, who contended or implied that both the practical strain so evident in the Loop and the triumph of old art at the White City were compatible contemporary expressions of American culture. But the desire for a simpler handle was greater, and this accounted for the two basic conclusions: the unexpected buildings at Jackson Park meant American designers were becoming more moderate—a positive turn—or the designers of the fair's buildings had lost their independence, courage, and sense of direction—a negative turn. The former conclusion was more popular in 1893 but lost adherents with time.

These two positions, the one claiming the architecture of the exposition was good for the United States and the other claiming it was unfortunate, were in at least 90 percent of the cases predictable, based on an individual critic's reaction to the Loop and to the image of American work in general. If foreign observers objected to the tall commercial buildings at Chicago's center, though not necessarily to the principles behind them, they almost always praised the major exhibition halls in Jackson Park. Conversely, critics who called the skyscrapers responsible examples of contemporary work were less inclined to see the exposition as a triumph for architecture.

Positive assessments of the fair's buildings were briefer and more superficial than contrary reactions. This may be explained, in part, by background. A much larger proportion of older and lay observers—diarists, essayists, and popular writers without training in architecture—dominated this group, which also included architects and architectural critics from these Western European countries. Shying away from analysis of individual buildings, nonprofessionals tended to generalize about the setting, and they often rhapsodized about it not in architectural terms but in the language of literature. One would have expected closer scrutiny of specific buildings from professional critics and architects, both those pleased and displeased by the major halls. However, only a handful attempted to judge the quality of each or most of the major buildings.[35] Regardless of their conclusions about the implications of this architecture for the United States, Europeans had trouble concentrating on individual buildings because the total effect was so strong. Furthermore, both groups agreed the quality of the architecture of the Columbian Exposition was higher when the halls were judged as an ensemble than when they were judged separately.

How could the Americans, who were not known for their skill in adapting classical architecture to contemporary needs, have created such a soul-satisfying panorama? Could this be explained by plagiarism? "Doubts were expressed by a number of artists as to the bulk of the work having been designed and executed by Americans, seeing that it is so infinitely superior to anything done in the general buildings of the large towns," wrote William Emerson of the British delegation.[36] Convinced this was true, Jacques Hermant charged Charles B. Atwood, designer of the Palace of Fine Arts (fig. 58), with lifting ideas from *Grand Prix de Rome* projects.[37] Emerson's more reflective response cited three reasons for the surprising results: it was easier to create pleasing academic facades for open interiors requiring none of the rooms, stories, and hallways normal architecture required; the plans had been submitted to a committee of the whole, which could improve weaknesses in individual designs; and the collaboration among architects, sculptors, and painters increased prospects for an integrated spectacle. Others linked the results to the extraordinary effort, particularly that of Chicagoans, to prove to Europeans the United States was not a cultural backwater.

Another explanation held that the United States, a country in which growing affluence and leisure was creating an aristocracy of wealth, was becoming increasingly vulnerable to European artistic influences. Apologists for the White City often cited evolutionary change. The period of survival, when the "rough ways must be made smooth," had passed. No longer subordinate to necessity (the opposite argument had been used by admirers of the Loop), citizens looked to higher goals in life. Now they were developing a finer appreciation for beauty and greater respect for history's contributions to art. Thus, the surprising architecture at Jackson Park was considered not just the result of a remarkable collective effort, not just a compensatory act by people embarrassed by

Figure 58.   Palace of Fine Arts, Columbian Exposition, 1893, Charles B. Atwood (Jaffe, *Die Architektur der columbischen Welt-Ausstellung zu Chicago, 1893*, 1895).

their material progress, not just a consequence of the determination to please, but also the result of a national maturation. Europeans also saw this process at work in individual Americans they observed. One journal claimed, "To the laborious people of the Western wheatfields, familiar with what surely seems to us the dullest and dreariest form of human existence, absolutely ignorant of the arts and luxuries of life, the exhibition was a revelation."[38] Foreign descriptions of people at the fair, though not flattering, were hopeful. With rare exceptions, American visitors were depicted as innocents compulsive about seeing everything and awed by everything they saw—an entire population on the verge of self-realization through education. Numerous European writers saw the White City as more than a complex of buildings and waterways. It was also a special moment in American history, simultaneously a culmination of settlement and the beginning of a new stage of national culture inspiring poorly educated but eager citizens to higher levels of existence. Many European observers turned the opportunity for architectural analysis into musings about moral, intellectual, and aesthetic improvement.

The reactions of the British, French, and Germans to the exposition were not identical, even though lay and trained observers in all three countries praised it, often for the same reasons using similar phrases. Differences in nationally based criticism were evident in foreign reactions to the buildings of the Loop, or, for that matter, to American architecture in general; however, they were more conspicuous in the respective responses to the exposition's halls. British architectural journals were noticeably more complimentary than those on the Continent. They acknowledged that these buildings were not as innovative as expected but praised the effort and predicted, in the representative words of the *Builder,* that the exposition "may possibly be a starting-point on which the Americans will found an expression of their national aspirations for a higher and nobler phase of architectural art."[39] Condemnations of the exposition's architectural choices were rare in the British press. The sharpest comment may have been the warning—not a repudiation—by Banister Fletcher about the possible misapplication of its success.

> Let us hope, however, that the imitative element will not cause the great classical designs of the Chicago fair to be reproduced for town halls, museums, etc., but that American architects, already advancing so rapidly along certain new lines of departure, will value the lessons they teach without copying the forms which they present to his eye; if not, we shall see a great classic revival which will go far beyond any craze we have had in England and do more to retard the true progress of art in America than if no exposition had been held. . . .
>
> The great styles must of course be studied and well studied, not for the forms with which they abound, but deeper still, for the principles which they inculcate, in the same way that one studies the literature of the past, not to be able to talk in a dead language, but the better to be able to do so in a living one. If this is done, and done with the earnest intention which a true artist has of producing works which shall reflect the hopes, needs, and aspirations of the life and character of the age in which he lives, a good result must be assured.[40]

Though British critics were inclined to look for positive signs in the buildings and grounds of the White City, the Germans and the French were less so, and a number of them were openly critical.

Continental Disappointment

Displeased continental professionals usually regretted that an opportunity to define a skeleton style of architecture at the exposition had been missed, despite the fact that Chicago's architectural firms were already doing so in the Loop. Counting heavily on a progressive demonstration in 1893, they expressed their reactions more angrily than did the British, who issued carefully worded expressions of disappointment. Arthur Vierendeel, a Belgian engineer, charged, "We have been profoundly deceived."[41] "The immense success known as the 'White City' will precipitate a plague for rationalism," claimed a French engineer, Antoine Grille.[42] Julius Lessing argued that the Americans should have realized "iron construction has won the right to a completely independent artistic life."[43] Most of those who felt betrayed did not try to explain why the Americans had depended on historic styles. They simply criticized the decision as a blow to the cause of modern architecture. Three of them, however, Hans Schliepmann, Albert Hofmann and Jacques Hermant, did try to explain the implications of Jackson Park's historicism. Their theses counterbalanced the contention of numerous British critics that the White City revealed a United States artistically more sure of itself.

Schliepmann was so impressed by the practicality of American architects, especially in their domestic and commercial designs, that he tried to argue that the classical thrust of the exposition was an isolated phenomenon, but he could not quite convince himself this was true. His tug of war between personal insights and hopes was not uncommon among critics for whom the exhibition halls were a disappointment.

> It is possible that this "accomplished project for a master architect's examination in Berlin," as the outward appearance of the large buildings could be called, may exert an ominous influence which will encourage over there, as well, the fatal conclusion that only the antique constitutes true taste. Then these imposing structures will look even stranger beside the houses which are the products of the native talent of American architects. The picturesque and individualistic treatment of these houses is tied too intimately to the practical aspects of the problem to enable formalism and schematism to get a foothold.
>
> Nevertheless, we may be forced into the conclusion that the culture over there has not become sufficiently independent to deal with ideological problems in such a way that indigenous tendencies are respected and even encouraged. The American betrays a certain fear of his own coarseness in his almost uncritical acceptance of the influence of old Europe in undertakings which are prodigious, uncommon, and not exclusively utilitarian.
>
> Our ground, however, is not firm enough for such presumptuousness.[44]

Schliepmann was one of a few critics to imply that American architects were caught in a bind. In assignments in which practical answers were required, as in domestic and commercial work, they created buildings more inspiring technologically and artistically than current work in Europe. When they strayed from challenges "not exclusively utilitarian," they lost their confidence and direction. His point that American culture was too young to protect the United States from seductive influences was made more passionately by Hofmann, and his implication that necessity was the source of America's progressive architecture was made more effectively by Hermant.

Hofmann developed his explanation in three articles published in the *Deutsche Bauzeitung* between 1892 and 1895.[45] He argued that the architecture of the Columbian Exposition was a profound revelation of cultural change in the United States, not an incident that should be dismissed as artificial or transient. Europeans had been foolish to have asked so much of Chicago's planners. They should have been smarter, realizing a young country could not withstand the centralizing tide of Western development. Applied to art, "the old doctrine of President Monroe, 'America for the Americans,' was no longer true." The exposition had revealed that architecture in the United States was only partially independent of Europe. It was independent in its structural daring and in the magnitude of its spatial conceptions but not in art, where it remained a "colony." This explained the exposition's "contradiction between the magnificence of the thought and the dependence of the form. The thought was grand, the form was borrowed." The Americans had not yet been able to find an artistic expression suited to the modernity of their scale and advanced technology. Henry Hobson Richardson had partially succeeded by drawing on robust Romanesque forms. At the exposition, Adler and Sullivan in the Transportation Building and Henry Ives Cobb in the Fisheries Building (fig. 59) had also been inspired by architecture of the medieval period, but "against the natural course of things, the strength and designs of individuals are weak," Hofmann contended. By "the natural course of things," he meant the decreasing isolation of the United States from Europe. He predicted, "America will have to get used to the idea that it is no longer a remote country which can erect a Chinese Wall along its borders and fashion a culture and an art untouched by all natural foreign influences." American architecture had now entered a second phase, he argued, the first being the Richardsonian Romanesque, a living art reflecting the needs and habits of the country. The architect principally responsible for defining the second phase was Richard Morris Hunt, who had studied at the École des Beaux-Arts and became a mentor to Americans who later became students there. "A substantive part of the Monroe Doctrine was absorbed in Richardson's art. Nothing of it, however, can be found in Hunt's artistic career." For Hofmann, Richardson was the hero and the cosmopolitan Hunt the one primarily responsible for squandering the country's independent birthright. "Genius is solitary; polished grace is sociable," he concluded. Instinct had given way to proper manners, and the trend for the immediate future was irreversible. The buildings of the Columbian Exposition, including Hunt's Administration Building, had made clear that the United States, too young and too insecure about its art, could not escape the Europeanization of its architecture.

Jacques Hermant agreed with several of Hofmann's conclusions. The exposition

Figure 59. Fisheries Building, Columbian Exposition, 1893, Henry Ives Cobb (Jaffe, *Die Architektur der columbischen Welt-Ausstellung zu Chicago, 1893*, 1895).

revealed the artistic youthfulness of the country, it was not a positive development for Western architecture, and trying to create variations on classical prototypes was an unwise course for American designers to follow. However, Hermant disagreed with Hofmann on two major points. The White City revealed little about the current state of American architecture. Secondly, he blamed the disappointing exhibition buildings on questionable necessity and a skewed process rather than on the country's loss of isolation. Don't give too much thought to the hasty structures at the fair, Hermant advised readers. "They correspond to no precise necessity of life and are only the results of a very accidental situation created by a few clever men in order to attract the public and present a gigantic advertisement for the city which already considers itself Queen of the World."[46] The exhibition halls did not mean American architecture had lost its progressive edge. Go to the cities, particularly the cities of the Midwest, he urged; there one can see serious architecture corresponding to the needs and customs of the people.

The firms selected to design the major halls, Hermant explained, had been lured from their strongholds where they created useful architecture shaped by necessity to play a game for which by practice and instinct they were unprepared, but their internationally acclaimed successes in domestic and commercial architecture had convinced them they were equal to any challenge. Thus, they could not resist the opportunity to

> play the *Grand Prix de Rome* at home, piling entablatures on columns and arcades, multiplying porticos, balustrades, statues and groups, setting up vast ensembles like those conceived by ancient Rome, with the wave of a wand building a dozen school

projects united in one immense Piranesian composition, and then, turning to their poor French comrades, who back from Rome, were stagnating in modest positions as inspectors of civil buildings, pointed out, "You study them! We build them!"[47]

But instead of putting designers of the Old World in their place, the Americans had exposed their inexperience and naiveté in creating buildings that "make the European artist, trained for many years to respect pure form, grit his teeth." The White City represented a "debauchery of architecture"—facades weak in proportions, details of disturbing banality, strange stylistic combinations in an ensemble that aspired to unity. The Manufacturers Building by Post (fig. 57) was marred by "a monotonous succession of simple arcades," and the Electricity Building by Van Brunt and Howe of Kansas City, by disconcerting campaniles unrelated to the restful lines of the lower section. Even the Administration Building by Hunt (fig. 55) failed because the height of its dome, with dimensions larger than that of the Panthéon in Paris, was undermined by the scale of the four corner pavilions. There was a difference between knowing, and knowing about, the classical language of architecture, argued Hermant, and the Americans, though they didn't realize it, were guilty of the latter.

In addition to inexperience, he believed questionable objectives and the process by which the exhibition halls were designed and built guaranteed poor architecture. Through artistic means the planners of the exposition hoped to surpass France, through scale they intended to demonstrate that the United States was the greatest country in the world and Chicago the greatest city, he wrote. Unnecessary and contrived goals, they led to forced results. To accomplish these objectives, Uncle Sam, a good businessman, needed a large number of huge booths and called on the best talent in the country to plan and decorate them. The architects didn't take the assignment very seriously. Some spent barely three weeks for which they were each paid ten thousand dollars. They were encouraged to create astounding fantasies on the outside in order to hide the necessary barrenness of the interiors. Then the drawings were turned over to an architect-in-chief and a central staff to supervise the construction in the absence of the responsible firms. At this moment, when adjustments to the original designs were required in order to harmonize the conception, changes were entrusted to an army of recent graduates from new schools of architecture. Inorganically developed from flawed objectives and procedures, the intended unity never materialized, Hermant contended. This retrospective art failed to impassion sensitive viewers. These failures—artificial objectives, a process without integrity, and architects whose designs exceeded their expertise—were not characteristic of the kind of American architecture that had attracted attention abroad. In fact, he argued, the real American architecture was marked by converse tendencies.

Convinced the architects of the United States had found the means by which a new architecture could be created, Hermant searched the grounds of Jackson Park for signs of them. He looked for decoration that was distinctive, for effects closely related to purpose, for facades that were fresh, for "some corner where emotion seizes one," for something that was not predictable. Away from the academic halls around the Grand Basin, he found some work that caught his attention. Of the Transportation Building by Adler and Sullivan, he wrote: "It isn't in the best taste, not very pure nor logical, but, in the midst of the old arsenal of columns and pediments that the designers of works we have been reviewing have ground out, it would be wrong not to take special notice of this attempt by artists desirous of leaving the beaten path."[48] Hermant focused on the building's surfaces and color (a lively red accented by yellow, orange, and green) that conveyed an "Oriental but frankly modern feeling." Its central entrance, the Golden Door (fig. 60), was an assertive composition, astoundingly rich on the one hand and blunt on the other. "Cela n'est pas banal," he concluded. Hermant was also pleased by the Fisheries Building by Cobb (fig. 59), not for its coarse energy or round arches, but for its charm, delicacy, sureness of touch, and for the wonderful details of sea plants and fish that decorated its capitals and columns. "One little expects to find here such a wealth of skill and knowledge of composition coupled with such unerring good taste."[49] Like the Transportation Building, the Fisheries exterior was a variation of the modern Romanesque, a revival style no less than Hunt's Administration Building, yet one that seemed more characteristic of American independence than classically inspired architecture.

However, Hermant was grabbing for straws. He had come to Jackson Park expecting to find practical architecture that utilized new materials to address contemporary requirements but ended up approving of decorative, polychromatic surfaces and admiring an artist (Cobb) "who, above all, wants to shock no one." The Transportation and Fisheries Buildings did not support Marcel Daly's expansive assertion that "the sponta-

Figure 60. Golden Door, Transportation Building, Columbian Exposition, 1893, Adler and Sullivan (Jaffe, *Die Architektur der columbischen Welt-Ausstellung zu Chicago, 1893,* 1895).

neous genius of the American is repulsed by copying, even by adaptation." Other Europeans, who counted on new forms at the exposition, scrambled to make the best of their disappointment. For a few years Sullivan profited because his work looked different; S.-C. de Soissons called the Transportation Building a bloody spot on a field of snow. Between 1893 and 1895 some critics raised the possibility that Sullivan's revolutionary color might energize contemporary architecture. To the jaded eyes of Europeans, its chromatic punch was refreshing, claimed Banister Fletcher.[50] European excitement over the Transportation Building's color lasted until about 1895.

In later evaluations, not necessarily written by individuals who had been stunned by the Court of Honor, awed by the scale and rapidity of the transformation of the site, or thankful for partial heroes, judgments became sharper. The Austrian aesthetician and art historian Richard Streiter in 1898 did not exonerate Sullivan or Cobb when he concluded, "What was expected, above all, from the World's Exposition Buildings on Lake Michigan, originality, daring, and independence of architectural form, was precisely what was missing."[51] In *Stilarchitektur und Baukunst* of 1903, Hermann Muthesius, a prolific author of architectural studies and an authority on British work, wrote: "To the astonishment of the world, Chicago, from which contemporary events were expected, had nothing better to do than to hang the familiar, antique disguises over the iron skeletons of its exhibition halls. Perhaps the fairy picture which was created was bewitching, but for artistic progress this regressive performance scored no more than zero."[52] European critics around 1900 were much more likely than their predecessors in 1893 to regard the architecture of the Columbian Exposition as unexpected and disappointing. Uninterested in the exposition's contributions to the city's reform movements and its influence on American urban planning, restless professionals in Europe increasingly interpreted the fair as a lost opportunity—in Chicago of all places—on the road to modern architecture.

Critics who attacked the planners of the Columbian Exposition for not furthering the cause of iron and steel may have assumed that the relationship between exposition architecture and everyday or nonexposition architecture on both sides of the Atlantic was the same. This was not true. To a greater extent than in Western Europe, American architects and engineers experimented daily, questioning current theory and practice in their efforts to meet changing requirements and mounting pressures. Their need for a special moment granting them license was less urgent than for their counterparts abroad. In the Loop they had already shown how they could collaborate to create a functional commercial architecture dependent on new demands, materials, and procedures. Intent upon taking advantage of the golden opportunity the exposition afforded, its planners stressed something new rather than something old by celebrating culture rather than the latest in architecture and engineering. Europeans who were disappointed with the major buildings of the fair frequently urged their readers to disregard the artificial White City in preference for the functioning Black City of the Loop.

Marcel Daly's image of American designers as incorruptible, forward-striding modernists was shared by many European professionals, particularly on the Continent, when the fair opened. They expected the Columbian Exposition to confirm, and thus publicize more widely, the reasons for their extravagant praise. The image they had inflated was intended primarily for home consumption, as a weapon with which to attack lethargy and historicism in France and Germany and to a lesser degree in the United Kingdom. They looked for evidence in American work that reinforced this myth and overlooked evidence that refuted it. Their prime exhibit was the architecture of Chicago's Loop. Instead of reinforcing this useful image, the White City confused it, demonstrating some anticipated characteristics—the enormity of the conception and the speed of its execution, for example—but also mingling this evidence with unexpected historicism and technological restraint. Europeans who went to Chicago in 1893 left with a clearer understanding of the Loop's purposefulness and its implications for urban development, but they no longer assumed American architects were immune to the temptations that had undermined the search for an up-to-date architecture in Britain, France, and Germany. The image of the clear-eyed, practical Yankee designer was compromised. A few foreign critics admitted they had asked too much, that they had been unrealistic in assuming the momentum of the Monroe Doctrine would also insure cultural isolation. Hermant predicted Chicago would not be able to resist for long the influence of historicism and European fashions, already evident in New York, but in the short run thought the city's artistic independence would be protected by its distance from the Atlantic Ocean.[53]

Between the fair and 1895, critics abroad continued to monitor architectural developments in the United States but with a lowered level of curiosity. The reputation of Chicago as the most progressive, though certainly not the most beautiful, livable, or admired metropolis, continued for a few years; however, its aura as the world's materialistic wonder city, a place where miracles really happened, became less distinct in the second half of the decade. In this age of "quick transformations" judgments also changed. The doubts about the contemporaneity of American architects that surfaced abroad in the mid-1890s would have been rare in the early 1890s. On the other hand, if the architecture of the White City disappointed restless European professionals in 1893, the architecture of the Black City of the Loop in 1893, the subject of the next chapter, did not.

Notes

1. Henry Trueman Wood, "Chicago and Its Exhibition," *Nineteenth Century* 31 (April 1892): 558.

2. Eugène-Melchior de Vogüé, "Impressions made by the Paris Exposition," *Chatauquan* 10 (October 1889): 68. The article was translated from the *Revue des deux mondes.*

3. The unidentified author of an article in *La construction moderne* published in late 1890 characterized recent American work, referring to an architecture that, if not new, was at least independent, bold in temperament, forceful and rough in its expressions, exhibiting a frankness Europe had begun to lose. R., "L'architecture américaine," *La construction moderne* 6 (13 December 1890): 109–11.

4. "The Columbian Exposition," *Engineering* 50 (5 December 1890): 667.

5. R.E., "Les grandes constructions américaines," *La construction moderne* 6 (5 September 1891): 568.

6. The *Tribune* published illustrations and comments about proposals for exposition towers and monuments on the following dates: 12 October 1889, 12; 24 October, 2; 26 October, 9; 2 November, 9; 3 November, 11; 9 November, 9; 10 November, 26; 16 November, 9; 7 March 1890, 1; 9 March, 11; 3 April, 1; 4 April, 4; 6 April, 12; 10 May, 12; 19 May, 6; 24 May, 9; 9 November, 5; 23 November, 9; 24 January 1891, 9; 5 March, 5; 7 March, 2; 29 March, 39; 4 April, 7; 16 July, 7; 16 August, 8; 25 August, 8; 12 September, 12; 17 October, 12; 24 October, 12; 11 May 1892, 9; 9 July, 13; 23 July, 13; 5 December, 10; 25 February 1893, 9; 28 February, 8; 18 June, 25; and 9 July, 26. See also Robert Jay, "Taller than Eiffel's Tower: The London and Chicago Tower Projects, 1889–1894," *Journal of the Society of Architectural Historians* 46 (June 1987): 145–56.

7. Fr.E., "Die geplante amerikanische Welt-Ausstellung 1893," *Deutsche Bauzeitung* 24 (14 May 1890): 234. The pivoting tower, designed by a mechanic, Timothy Bernard Powers, was published in the New York *Tribune*. It was republished by the *Chicago Tribune* (26 October 1889, 9).

8. R. Volkmann, "Die Columbische Weltausstellung in Chicago," *Zeitschrift des oesterreichischen Ingenieur- und Architekten-Vereines* 44 (18 March 1892): 198. On the ground floor of the complex was a theater seating 15,000. The globe supported by the rising figure was to be 450 feet high. It contained two levels, the lower for restaurants and galleries and the upper covered by a star-filled sky exactly as it was on the night Columbus discovered America.

9. Otto H. Mueller, "Skizzen von der Weltausstellung in Chicago," *Zeitschrift des oesterreichischen Ingenieur- und Architekten-Vereines* 45 (1 September 1893): 484.

10. "The United States Exhibition," *Engineering* 49 (14 March 1890): 334–35. A writer for the *Deutsche Bauzeitung* predicted the impression of the interior would be magnificent and could be viewed from galleries at various heights. Furthermore, the circular plan would permit the exhibits to be arranged in radiating rings as was done at the Parisian exhibition of 1867. See Fr.E., 235. The radiating system of display also appealed to the editors of *British Architect*, where it was discussed in an article entitled "'A Truly American Way'" (*British Architect* 33 [4 April 1890]: 237).

11. See the following in the *Chicago Tribune:* "All under One Roof," 3 April 1890, 1; "The Circus Tent Plan," 4 April, 4; "The World's Fair in a Tent," 6 April, 12; and "Ideas Anent the Fair," 10 May, 12.

12. See "Eiffel Wants a Chance," *Chicago Tribune,* 5 August 1891, 7, and "M. Eiffel's Proposition," ibid., 25 August 1891, 8.

13. "The Chicago Exhibition of 1893," *Engineering* 51 (1 May 1891): 522.

14. Reported in "England and the Fair," *Chicago Tribune,* 24 January 1891, 9.

15. "New-York and the World's Fair," *New York Times,* 6 November 1891, 4.

16. "German and French Complaints touching the World's Fair," *American Architect* 41 (1 July 1893): 1.

17. "Chicago Exhibition Buildings," *Builder* 61 (8 August 1891): 102–3.

18. B., "Die Weltausstellung in Chicago 1893," *Centralblatt der Bauverwaltung* 11 (31 October 1891): 431–34.

19. H., "Die Columbische Weltausstellung in Chicago," *Deutsche Bauzeitung* 26 (7 May 1892): 218.

20. No Day., "À propos du dôme central de l'exposition de Chicago," *La construction moderne* 8 (31 December 1892): 145.

21. Jacques Hermant, "L'art à l'exposition de Chicago," *Gazette des beaux-arts* 73 (November 1893): 425. See also, "What the Foreign Commissioners Say of the Columbian Exposition," *Chicago Tribune,* 26 June 1893, 1.

22. James Fullarton Muirhead, *The Land of Contrasts* (Boston: Lamson, Wolffe, 1898), 205.

23. F. Herbert Stead, "An Englishman's Impressions at the Fair," *Review of Reviews* 8 (July 1893): 30. Reverend Stead was the younger brother of William Thomas Stead, editor of the *Review of Reviews* and author of *If Christ Came to Chicago!*

24. "Official Praise of the World's Fair Buildings," *American Architect* 42 (28 October 1893): 51. Franz Jaffe, a Regierungsbaumeister and the author of the most comprehensive German study of the exposition's architecture, claimed the buildings and grounds of Jackson Park marked the high point of the history of festival decoration from the time of Alexander and Caesar to the present. Franz Jaffe, *Die Architektur der columbischen Welt-Ausstellung zu Chicago, 1893* (Berlin: Julius Becker, 1895), ix.

25. Wilhelm Bode, "Moderne Kunst in den vereinigten Staaten von Amerika," *Kunstgewerbeblatt* 5 (1894): 113.

26. See Pierre de Coubertin, *Souvenirs d'Amérique et de Grèce* (Paris: Hachette, 1897), 3–19, and "The World's Columbian Exposition," *Engineering* 56 (3 November 1893): 544.

27. S.-C. de Soissons, *A Parisian in America* (Boston: Estes and Lauriat, 1896), 131.

28. Marquis de Chasseloup-Laubat, *Voyage en Amérique et principalement à Chicago* (Paris: Société des ingénieurs civils de France, 1893). Excerpts from his report in the minutes of the society were published in "A Frenchman on the World's Fair and America," *American Architect* 39 (28 January 1893): 58–60 (the source of the quotations in the next paragraph). Because he made his simplistic but persuasive comparison to the society on 21 October 1892, well before the French press had focused on the fair, and then turned his report into a book, his views were often paraphrased by later critics.

29. Friedrich Dernburg, *Aus der weissen Stadt* (Berlin: Julius Springer, 1893), 22.

30. "Impressions of the World's Fair," *Critic* 23 (25 November 1893): 331.

31. James Dredge, *A Record of the Transportation Exhibits at the World's Columbian Exposition of 1893* (London: Office of *Engineering*, 1894), 56.

32. Soissons, 133.

33. Friedrich Reusche, *Chicago und Berlin: Alte und neue Bahnen in Ausstellungswesen* (Berlin: Carl Ulrich, 1892), 21.

34. See No Day., 145–46, and [Karl] Hinckeldeyn, "Von der Weltausstellung in Chicago," *Centralblatt der Bauverwaltung* 13 (30 September 1893): 405–8, and (14 October): 425–28.

35. For articles and books in which professional authors discussed each or most of the major buildings at Jackson Park, see "The World's Columbian Exposition, 1893," *Engineering* 55 (21 April 1893): 503–96; "American Architecture at the Chicago Exhibition," *British Architect* 40 (29 July 1893): 73; "The Chicago Exhibition: A General View," *Builder* 65 (1 July 1893): 1–4; "The Greater Buildings at the Chicago Exhibition," *Builder* 65 (15 July, 5, 19 August 1893): 39–41, 95–97, 131–33; William Emerson, "The World's Fair Buildings," *Royal Institute of British Architects, Journal,* 3d ser., 1 (1893–94): 65–74; Jacques Hermant, "L'art à l'exposition de Chicago," *Gazette des beaux-arts* 73 (November, December 1893): 416–25, 441–61; Hinckeldeyn, "Von der Weltausstellung in Chicago," *Centralblatt der Bauverwaltung* 13 (30 September 1893): 405–8, plus five more parts; "Die Kolumbische Weltausstellung in Chicago," *Schweizerische Bauzeitung* 21 (6 May 1893): 114–18, plus seven more parts; R., "Skizzen von der Chicagoer Ausstellung," *Schweizerische Bauzeitung* 22 (7, 14 October 1893): 92–93, 100–101; and Franz Jaffe, *Die Architektur der columbischen Welt-Ausstellung zu Chicago, 1893* (Berlin: Julius Becker, 1895). The most informative were by Hinckeldeyn, Hermant, Jaffe, and the anonymous studies published in *Builder* and *Engineering*.

36. Emerson, 72.

37. Hermant, "L'art à l'exposition de Chicago" (December 1893), 448. In a 1987 Harvard sem-

inar paper, "European Reaction to the World's Columbian Exposition," Linda S. Phipps claims the portico for the Palace of Fine Arts was similar to an 1867 *Grand Prix* project by E. Bénard.

38. "The Chicago Exhibition," *Architect* 51 (25 May 1894): 23.

39. "The Chicago Exhibition: a General View," *Builder* 65 (1 July 1893): 4.

40. Banister F. Fletcher, "American Architecture through English Spectacles," *Engineering Magazine* 7 (June 1894): 321.

41. Arthur Vierendeel, *La Construction architecturale en fer et acier* (Brussels: Lyon-Claesen, 1902), 249, quoted in Sigfried Giedion, *Space, Time and Architecture* (Cambridge, Mass.: Harvard University Press, 1941), 210.

42. A. Grille quoted in Michel Vernes, "Le gratte-ciel toujours recommencé," *Archi-Créé* 211 (April–May 1986): 58.

43. Julius Lessing, "Neue Wege," *Kunstgewerbeblatt*, n.s., 6 (1895): 3.

44. Hans Schliepmann, "Amerikanische Architektur," *Kunstwart* 7 (August 1894): 339.

45. See the following articles by Albert Hofmann in the *Deutsche Bauzeitung:* "Die Columbische Weltausstellung in Chicago," 26 (7 May 1892): 217–18; "Das künstlerische Ergebniss der Weltausstellung in Chicago," 28 (28 April 1894): 209–10; and "Richard Morris Hunt," 29 (7 December 1895): 605–7.

46. Hermant, "L'art à l'exposition de Chicago" (November 1893), 422.

47. Ibid., 423.

48. Ibid., 450.

49. Ibid., 451.

50. Fletcher, 320–21. According to the *Builder,* "As a purely colour scheme, thought out and designed from its very commencement for polychromatic decoration, this building is as important, and perhaps more so, as any erected in recent years." "Colour Decoration at the Chicago Exhibition," *Builder* 65 (26 August 1893): 152. In the opinion of Franz Jaffe, only the future would determine if Sullivan's experiment with color had been a harbinger of something new in American work, perhaps in international architecture. Jaffe, 60–63. See also Pbg., "Architekten-Verein zu Berlin," *Deutsche Bauzeitung* 29 (13 March 1895): 130; "Die farbige Behandlung des Verkehrsgebäudes auf der Weltausstellung in Chicago," *Centralblatt der Bauverwaltung* 15 (10 April 1895): 152; and André Bouilhet, "L'exposition de Chicago," *Revue des arts décoratifs* 14 (1893–94): 68–70.

51. Richard Streiter, "Nordamerikanische Architektur," *Allgemeine Zeitung,* 6 June 1898, 5.

52. Hermann Muthesius, *Stilarchitektur und Baukunst* (Mülheim/Ruhr: K. Schimmelpfeng, 1902), 42.

53. Hermant, "L'art à l'exposition de Chicago" (December 1893), 451.

9 International Implications of the Loop's Architecture

D ESPITE RISING INTEREST in Britain, France, and Germany about multistory commercial buildings, the quality of the foreign commentary about them was poor. The first profound European analysis of this new type of building appeared in July of 1892 when the *Builder* published "New Business Buildings of Chicago" as its lead article. This thoughtful study of the office blocks of the Loop was a surprise. In the previous five years the journal had published numerous articles and illustrations about American free-standing houses but had almost ignored the rise of office buildings in American cities.[1] Judging from the unidentified author's informed comments about a number of new buildings in Chicago, it was probably written by someone who had recently visited the city. Since it was the lead article of the issue, it could have been written by the journal's editor, Henry Heathcote Statham, but his subsequent attacks on the concealment of metal framing behind a street facade does not square with the article's praise for the responsible actions of Chicago's architectural firms. We might also assume that the *Builder,* having featured this type of architecture, was ready to embark on an editorial policy endorsing the practicality of tall buildings, but this did not happen. In fact, "New Business Buildings of Chicago" was the high-water mark of British journalistic analyses of Chicago's commercial architecture during the 1890s. In the remaining years of the decade the *Builder,* as well as the *Building News,* the *British Architect,* the *Architect and Contract Reporter,* and the *Royal Institute of British Architects, Journal,* published little about American skyscrapers.

Though anonymous, the *Builder* article was exceptional; no other European critic had written by this date such a perceptive, accurate, and inquisitive study of the early skyscrapers of the Loop. Fundamental to the value of this article was its author's insistence on two points. First, that "Chicago architecture must be estimated by the Chicago standard." By honoring this approach throughout, its writer rejected the common inclination to judge these buildings according to prevailing European notions of good architecture. In 1893 and 1894 a number of critics followed suit, insisting this new type be judged according to the criteria that had determined it. Second, the *Builder's* writer pointed to the logical and purposeful process by which office blocks had been created. A number of later critics agreed, citing the process as the most useful lesson demonstrated by the new buildings of Chicago. This is what Wilhelm Bode was referring to when he wrote that the great value of American work for German architects was its incomparable *Zweckmässigkeit.*

In order to reach just conclusions about this architecture, the author urged readers to clear their agendas of irrelevant issues, particularly their personal feelings about the boisterousness of the city and its preoccupation with money. They should also not blame designers for meeting the requests of clients. The author of the article pointed out, "The Chicago architect does not build high because he likes it, but because the problem presented to him forces him to do so, and his success lies in his frank and business-like treatment of the buildings." Furthermore, the creators of these office blocks, lacking choice, wisely turned restrictions into responsible architecture. The primary restrictions cited by the author were the limited space in the Loop and the clients' stipulation that these buildings be created for revenue, not for art. Realizing their "programme was unalterable," the Loop's designers, more than those in other American cities, set aside precedent, enabling them to create a distinctive business architecture modern in every sense of the word. "If architecture be simply an ornamental art of ornamental construction, then perhaps the Chicago buildings may not come within its scope, but if architecture be the meeting of conditions in building in a manner suited to the conditions, regardless of what might have been done under other circumstances, and for other purposes, they are clearly architecture, and very good architecture to boot."[2] However, this definition of good architecture was not recognized by the majority of European critics who passed judgment on the skyscrapers of the Loop in the early 1890s. By contrast, they were more inclined, consciously or unconsciously, to rest judgments on a richer variety of factors, among them the transforming role of the architect, the primacy of beauty, and the nobility of purpose.

The author also claimed the form and even the treatment of the facade of these buildings were predetermined by the nature of the program; to disregard or attempt to doctor the appearance of this inevitable form was foolish. Unlike the architects of tall buildings in New York (unnamed), the majority of those in Chicago "recognized the utter impossibility of 'making' facades, and have suppressed all unnecessary ornamentation and architectural features, leaving their buildings simple walls relieved only by windows, or, perhaps, by bow windows." In the author's judgment, not all designers of buildings in the Loop had followed this course. The Manhattan Building (fig. 61) by W. L. B. Jenney, for example, was a composed, and thus less successful, street front. On the other hand, the Monadnock Block (fig. 62) by Burnham and Root epitomized Chicago's artistic resolution of the problem. This building had been left in its "natural state," proclaiming its commercial mission. Recent tall buildings of the Loop were not identical in

Figure 61. Manhattan Building, Chicago, 1889–91, William Le Baron Jenney (*Builder*, 9 July 1892).

his critics, or both
us error. Modern
fly commercial, and
es are erected for
es. It, as was
revious archi-
de to fit the
building
itecture.
of the
ng the
ior is
points
hitect-
riking
s and
of its
of pro-
tudied
of the
ciples
an
en
on
he
ic
e,
of
d,
e
is
e
of
en
d,
ly
s,
oned
e is
lot,
may

Figure 62. Monadnock Building, Chicago, 1889–91, Burnham and Root (*Scribner's Magazine*, March 1894).

appearance, the author granted, but, as by-products of similar requirements and priorities, their exterior designs were essentially the same. Too tall to be treated in a traditional
manner, their facades had been divided into a few sections accented with limited detail.
"For typical Chicago buildings impress by mass, not by detail. Their finest quality is that
of immensity, and the less the fronts are broken up, the less the walls are interrupted by
piers and by strings, the more imposing the structure and the more tremendous the effect."[3] To appreciate the impact of the mass, the building had to be seen. The Masonic
Temple (fig. 37) by Burnham and Root was "one of the least satisfactory structures in
the world on paper," but when standing in front of it one could appreciate the "genuine
merit" of its immensity. With the exception of the placement of light courts, the author
found fewer opportunities for originality inside business buildings where the obligation
of architects to create numerous well-illuminated offices restricted their freedom. The
Builder's critic thought the unique feature of each floor was its openness, enabling tenants to act independently of architects by arranging spaces to suit their needs.

Later critics who concentrated on the process rather than on the appearance of the
finished office blocks tended to be more positive about Chicago's new buildings. They
also were more inclined to argue that their designers had been responsible. On the other hand, critics who focused on the dimensions and style of the Loop's architecture, usually the ones who also discounted causal factors, tended to downplay the significance of
these buildings. Expecting art to play a dominant or transforming role, the latter were
also less pleased with the compliance of Chicago's architectural firms. The reaction of
critics was usually affected by what they considered important in architecture. In Kan-
dinsky's analogy, some saw the shell, some saw the nut, some focused on style and the
creativity of designers, some focused on purpose and process. The influential editor Paul
Planat, for example, for whom the role of art in architecture was primary, was so unset-
tled by the appearance of tall buildings that he glossed over their innovative features. After
reporting millions of francs had been spent on the Masonic Temple to accommodate
five thousand tenants on twenty-plus floors served by seventeen elevators, he added, "But
can we be quite sure that the total expense has much effect on the beauty of the edifice?"[4]

However, both the troubled and the intrigued European professional shared one
conclusion—these buildings looked alike, not necessarily because they were identical but
because their characteristic appearance was so different from that of representative business premises in Britain, France, and Germany. The stylistic variations among them
seemed incidental compared to fundamental differences of function and form between
these buildings and similar types on the other side of the Atlantic. Focusing on the typical rather than the particular, critics usually did not identify by name the examples from
which they generalized. The most frequent exceptions were the Monadnock Block (fig.
62), the simplicity of which attracted the attention of several critics, including the author of "New Business Buildings of Chicago"; the Masonic Temple (fig. 37), mainly for
its height; and the Auditorium (fig. 63), for its size and diversified functions. Foreign
observers were even less curious about the name of the architect or firms responsible
for a commercial block in the Loop. Their focus on an anonymously designed proto-

Figure 63. Auditorium Building, Chicago, 1887–89, Adler and Sullivan (*Engineering*, 3 April 1891).

type contrasts with the attention twentieth-century historians have paid to the stylistic differences distinguishing one of these buildings from another and to the personalities responsible for them.

Ironically, several Europeans who comprehended the Loop's modernity went to Chicago looking for something new but found there something old. Jacques Hermant confirmed this when he spoke at the annual meeting of the Société centrale des architectes français on 10 May 1894. American architects, he contended, had not created works that sprang fully formed from the inspiration of genius, nor had they devised answers antithetical to public custom. Instead, they had proceeded logically in devising "a system of buildings based on the techniques of the past and the progress of science, a system adapted to its needs by men who reason and who know how to respond to the consequences of modern art."[5] Hermant attributed the growing international importance of American architects to their understanding of context, their openness to new developments in technology, and their insistence on practical steps directed by purpose. These priorities were old, not new, yet the results in Chicago were, paradoxically, startling, an architectural revolution all the more profound, he claimed, because it had invented nothing but had drawn logically from all that went before. "It is scientific art, and we are not afraid to say that this is why it is the art of the future." Then he challenged his audience: "Let us hope that having let America find the formula for the art of the future by our side, we shall not let her develop and perfect it alone."[6] Though the tall buildings of the Loop were dramatic, the real eye-opener for Hermant was the process by which they were formed. This process, familiar rather than invented, reaffirmed for him the notion that healthy architecture was not an artistic lid superimposed on the cauldron of change but was a consequence of evolving conditions.

One reason professionals in Britain, France, and Germany had not yet developed an architecture that really reflected contemporary shifts in European culture was their habit of asking the question, When will the new style arrive and what will it look like? Professionals who cast the coming chapter in architecture in terms of style credited designers with considerable power to shape appearance. In musing about the role of architects in this impending revolution, professionals did not ignore functional issues but did slight them. Of course these architects would be responsible, adapting their designs to the conditions and demands of the shifting contemporary scene. However, "responsible" carried degrees of meaning, as the *Builder* had acknowledged in an article about hospital plans in December 1879.

> And we fear the fact is, that architects who are asked to carry out such buildings do not really grapple with the problem. They get some general rules and look at some existing hospitals, and then make a building with pilasters and cornices, or mullions and arches, in the orthodox arrangement, and an interior adequately ventilated and sufficiently convenient in its general working arrangements, but destitute of those score or so minor details which go to make the difference between a real solution of the problem of a perfect hospital, and the mere random shot at it.[7]

Though all might agree that "commodity, firmness, and delight" were essential for good architecture, too many designers in Western Europe had been trained to and continued to enjoy privileging "firmness," and especially "delight," at the expense of "commodity." This habit affected the way in which they envisioned the next development in Western architecture.

When significant change appeared, as it did in the Loop, and the visual evidence of this change did not conform to the artistic revolution they anticipated, many were caught off guard. Paul Planat was one. In 1895 he was reluctant to agree with unnamed members of the French profession who had claimed architects in the United States had "been able to unnest the *merle blanc* that everyone is seeking and no one is achieving anywhere: complete originality in architecture."[8] For Planat "complete originality" meant artistic originality, in effect, the ingenuity of designers attempting to protect art. Confused by a new form that could not easily be encompassed by his aesthetic visions, Planat asked for more time before deciding if the "students have surpassed their masters." The questions the architects of the Loop asked about responsibility and the questions critics like Planat asked were not necessarily the same questions.

That new conditions and needs required new architectural answers made sense in theory but the premise was difficult to apply. European professionals of all persuasions endorsed this notion. They often cited historical evidence confirming the tie between new forces and fresh architectural responses, sometimes to reassure audiences that the present malaise in Western architecture would not last forever. Hadn't the cultural transformation of the Greek city-state required continuous refinements in temple architecture? Didn't communal and theological requirements in the thirteenth century outgrow the form and style of Romanesque churches of the twelfth century? History was full of examples of evolving conditions' changing architecture. Overnight the Loop provided a contemporary demonstration of this. The firms of Chicago, responding to fresh economic pressures, had acted as responsible architects in history were supposed to have acted. What had been self-evident in the past had become self-evident in the present. This did not mean, however, that the challenge of fulfilling the logic of this maxim for European designers was necessarily easier, as Banister Fletcher admitted in 1894.

Fletcher, the Godwin Bursary recipient of 1893, seconded the logic of this relationship but cited reasons why it could be applied more easily in the United States than in the United Kingdom. He argued that the architects of the Loop had been responsible, justifying his point by simulating a moment from British history.

> Can you imagine a medieval architect (or master-builder, or chief workman, whichever he styled himself) uttering his laments and casting up his eyes to heaven when his lord told him that he was tired of sleeping in the common hall in the midst of his retainers and that he must have a "solar," yes, a private sleeping chamber for himself and wife!—thus starting all the development of domestic play? What would the modern antiquarian-architect have said? Why this: "I can see no precedent for a private-sleeping chamber; your father had none and it would spoil the symmetry of your old Norman keep if I tack on chambers, with drawing-rooms and offices!"[9]

To make his case about responsible architecture in history, Fletcher had manipulated his evidence. He had reduced a slow, irregular process from the British past to a discrete, exemplary moment. Dismissing the controversies of that earlier day, he treated the appearance of the private sleeping chamber as an inevitable development. Looking into history he had no difficulty finding an example to illustrate his belief that architecture must change when conditions changed.

Fletcher also had no hesitation in citing this principle when discussing the relationship between the causes of the Loop and its commercial architecture. Unlike the "modern antiquarian" and like the master builder of centuries ago, Chicago's firms had created "a product of the age," he contended. However, detecting the principle in history and recognizing it in Chicago were easier acts for Fletcher than stating how it could be expressed in contemporary British work. He wrote, "In respect to new problems, new wants, and new difficulties to be overcome, the American has a great advantage in that he has to solve them in a new way and therefore should not fail to be able to present new forms, while we over here generally have to design buildings which are to be used for the same purpose as hundreds of others and yet we are expected to do something strikingly original, which, if done, is usually very bad."[10] In other words, the architects of Chicago enjoyed an advantage their British colleagues were denied.

Fletcher's transatlantic perspective enabled him to isolate conditions in the United States that his up-close vision prevented him from seeing in Great Britain. Perhaps the "new conditions" of one's own time and place were too elusive to agree upon, and "new architecture" could be responsibly disqualified by reaffirming the dependability of old habits. Perhaps the realm of unconscious biases was murkier and more powerful than those calling for change realized. In any case, though the Loop was recognized as an operative demonstration of a much-cited causal relationship, the principle was still easier to proclaim than to apply to one's own contemporary scene.

In 1893 and 1894 the Loop inspired, and it also confused. What a gold mine for those worried that too many European architects were only paying lip service to their obligation to honor change. What a disappointment these bare-looking buildings must have been for those who had hoped the New World might devise an appropriate but attractive dress for an architecture of modern life. Ironically, both groups shared a reaction. Neither embraced the tall building, the latter because it did not conform to their stylistic expectations, the former because it directed them to something more useful, its reason and means for being. The perceptive looked through or beyond the new form to study how architects in Chicago's "laboratory of the present" had dealt with their charge and, in doing so, rediscovered basic principles of architecture.

These principles reminded them that architects must be realists who dealt with life as it was, not as it was supposed to be, realists who respected limits to their desires to manipulate, who realized their primary obligation was to create buildings meeting the requirements of clients, who had to cooperate with engineers and builders to produce economical buildings in a new age. Chicago's architects also reminded foreign observers that fundamental architecture was created for specific reasons that must be respected at every stage of planning and building. Their architectural purposefulness made a profound impression on a number of critics. According to Wilhelm Bode, the best-known German art authority to come to the United States for the exposition, the new office buildings of the Loop gave German architects many new ideas, "above all, purposefulness itself."[11] He did not mean that German architects had ignored purpose; he meant that the designers of office blocks in Chicago had taken this obligation so seriously that their execution of a familiar responsibility had transformed its meaning. These architects had not apologized for function; they had acted as if architecture facilitating a prosaic goal (profits) could still be responsible architecture. To make effective "temples of labor," they had created efficient, convenient, and comfortable working environments. Critics also discovered that the architects of Chicago had questioned the exclusivity of art. Instead of employing art as a veneer to hide purpose, these designers had incorporated it with purpose, making it an integrated rather than a privileged element of the program.

These realizations, most of them explained in articles in French and German architectural journals between 1893 and 1895, were essentially the same reached by the anonymous author of "New Business Buildings of Chicago" in 1892. However, critics who found merit in the Loop underscored different aspects of its purposefulness. Stressing the architects' respect for and close reading of requirements, Adolphe Bocage claimed Chicago's commercial architecture was new because it was "dictated by needs."[12] "G.M.J.," author of an extended article that appeared in *La semaine des constructeurs* between November 1893 and April 1894, focused on its revelations about resulting form, arguing that the makers of offices buildings had devised a style that would last longer than work determined by momentary fashion "because it has its roots, not in the rumination of traditions, henceforth sterile, but in the nature of things."[13] Architecture rooted in the "nature of things" was an architecture congruent with place, purpose, means, and art. Characterizing American commercial work as systematic and relatively devoid of sentiment and romanticism, Albert Hofmann of the *Deutche Bauzeitung* called these buildings an art of "cool calculation," not an art of feeling.[14] Hans Schliepmann singled out focus and consistency. "It is the clear-sightedness of the Yankee which is his greatest advantage and is expressed even in the repugnant excesses of American cities."[15] Certainly, evidence for these priorities could have been observed in commercial and even domestic work erected in other cities in the United States, but it was the spatially concentrated Loop that became for foreign critics the ultimate arena of revelation and clarification in the early 1890s, provoking many of them to fresh insights and deeper realizations about the nature of contemporary architecture.

The Changing Role of Architects

Critics who credited the new office buildings with directing them to old principles of architecture were open-minded and imaginative enough to find virtue in a disturbing setting. Most observers were less generous, and for good reasons. The hesitant ones might approve in theory the self-effacing courage of Chicago's firms, their contemporaneity, or their sustained practicality, but still object to the architecture they had designed and to its implications for the profession. The office blocks of the Loop carried personal and cultural costs most foreign professionals were not yet ready to approve. Few of them were prepared to make the sacrifices the architects of the Loop had made. They were not willing to define purposefulness in such narrow terms. Purposefulness was not determined solely by functional or economic considerations, they contended, it was also defined by history, tradition, habits, aesthetics. Architects abroad might profit from studying the direct response of their colleagues in Chicago to a dominant demand, but this did not mean they suddenly objected to the richness, variety, and texture of their own city centers. To the contrary, they were proud their European cities had put up stiffer resistance to economic pressures. Though critics seldom charged the designers of tall buildings with selling out to capitalism—after all, they were only being realistic—nevertheless, the Loop's architects had collaborated in making Chicago's center the first in modern history unabashedly speculative. Even when praising them as realists, some critics wondered if they had given up the high ground of the profession too quickly. Why had they been so ready to surrender their moral authority to serve those who wanted larger and faster profits?[16] Once they had agreed to this compact, their course was determined. Since time was money, the quicker the office building could be completed the better. But this was not how great art in the past had been created. For the first time, inhabitable architecture— the largest on record—was being made by the clock. Would time of construction now take its place beside harmony and proportion as a measure of a great building? Building faster also required the continuous incorporation of quicker procedures, forcing architects to experiment in the transient present instead of relying on time-honored means. Furthermore, nothing seemed to be stilled long enough to permit reflection, let alone time for refinement, a challenging act that in history had often separated good architects from the herd. Jacques Hermant described Chicago as "a city built from day to day, dedicated solely to meeting immediate requirements."[17] If immersing architecture in the mire of circumstance was appropriate for Chicago, it was not necessarily appropriate for Paris, or London, or Berlin.

European observers who concentrated on the shell, the resulting form, instead of the nut faced another problem. What could one do with these buildings? Suitable for the style by which business was conducted in Chicago, they would have been inappropriate for the personalized, formal, and more deliberate style of transactions in the Old World. Furthermore, they were ugly—ugly in Chicago and even uglier if erected abroad. The thought was ludicrous. Henbest Capper of McGill University in Montreal asked his readers to try to "imagine the Acropolis of Athens girt round with buildings like those of Broadway. Imagine Siena, her valleys enriched with 'tall buildings' spouting high above that fair Duomo which so nobly crowns her highest rock!"[18] Even professionals who respected Chicago's architectural realism and tried to convince colleagues of its relevance faced ridicule if they suggested transplanting tall structures to European soil. Adolphe Bocage was sensitive to this when he spoke about his experiences in Chicago to the Société centrale des architectes français in 1894. Sensing resistance to his prediction that skyscraper apartments would become popular if erected in the parks of Paris, thus anticipating Le Corbusier's gardens in the sky of the early 1920s, he offered the suggestion with diffidence, "at the risk of being reproached for Utopian thinking."[19] He also waited until the end of his talk to float his idea. In the early 1890s professionals abroad believed their own cities could adjust to increasing industrial-commercial pressures without having to replace their business buildings with American-style office blocks.

If a critic had been converted by the lessons of the Loop, that individual could more easily justify or discount their consequences for the architects involved. However, Europeans who had missed, or who had been less convinced of, the zone's message—a majority, though not an overwhelming one—often expressed their concern. When standing before a multistory building, which to most visitors looked much like other multistory buildings in the district, troubled observers often were confused about the role of architects. Should they admire these designers or feel sorry for them? Should they be viewed as pacesetters with an eye for the heart of the problem, or were they good soldiers who had been handed the onerous task of producing huge containers for prosaic purposes? Judging from the stark fronts of these blocks, the term "architect" did not seem to carry the same meaning in the Loop as it did in London, Paris, or Berlin. In European cities the word implied inspired individuals who created memorable designs. They were freer to be imaginative, to impose their artistic skills on the project, but designers of tall buildings were discouraged from soaring above circumstances. In fact, as Henbest Capper pointed out, their options had already been restricted by numerous specifications before they even began their drawings.[20] The new architecture of the Loop also provoked questions that a current survey of new commercial work in Europe was less likely to provoke. A few abroad wondered if these facades signified an end to the image of the garret genius, or the demise of the privilege of artists to use their talents to make function appear sweeter than it was, or the drying up of opportunities for imaginative critics to point out what the design might have been. Architecture, once idealized as an art form personalized through the skills of the designer, had become in Chicago the outcome of a process over which designers exerted limited control.

A few critics contended the real designers of tall buildings were the clients who had gained a reputation for knowing precisely the kind of business building they wanted and when they wanted it. Some architects of Chicago complained about the limitations imposed on them.

> We would like to construct buildings with some of the features of the Owings or Woman's Temple [fig. 64] Buildings. . . . Our clients, however, demand buildings after a commercial style of architecture. They do not care to discuss lines, angles, domes, turrets, and recessed windows. They are willing to confer with us in regard to floor space, light shafts, steel frames, or pressed brick. In building residences these same clients are anxious to secure artistic effects and spare no expense to produce picturesque homes.[21]

Though most foreign professionals, believing the Loop's architects had little choice, commended them for creative responses to difficult charges, several depicted their role in ambiguous language. Paul Bourget's reference was a good example. "The architect who built them, or rather, made them by machinery, gave up all thought of colonnades, moldings, classical decorations. He ruthlessly accepted the speculator's inspired conditions,—to multiply as much as possible the value of the bit of earth at the base by multiplying the superimposed 'offices.'"[22]

Of all the new buildings, the Monadnock Block (fig. 62), its relatively unornamented stories repeated over and over, probably inspired more speculation about the designer's role than any another building in Chicago. "Here there is no longer the slightest care for arrangement and form. It is no longer the work of an artist responding to particular needs with intelligence and drawing from them all of the possible consequences. It is the work of a laborer who, without the slightest study, superimposes fifteen strictly identical stories to make a block and then stops when he finds the block high enough."[23] Architects in Chicago were seldom depicted as mechanical processors or as puppets controlled by their clients, yet these possibilities, the thought unacceptable to all critics, were raised by a few of the most perceptive—Bourget, Bocage, and Hermant.

Some also asked if Chicago's architects had lost stature because they worked so closely with engineers. An unidentified writer for the *Deutsche Bauzeitung* in November 1891 went further, claiming, "The engineer plays the principal role in these gigantic buildings."[24] Professionals opposed to skyscrapers sometimes played up the contribution of engineers to strengthen their claims these buildings were not genuine architecture. Alarm about the encroachment of the engineer and the assumed demise of the importance of the architect was more common when these buildings were judged from Europe than when they were studied in the Loop.[25] First-hand knowledge tended to reduce apprehension and encourage more open-minded investigations of this interdependence.[26] Although Banister Fletcher called the engineer, not the architect, the real builder of the nineteenth century, he believed a modern architecture, exemplified by the steel-framed buildings of Chicago, could not have been created without the cooperation of both of

Figure 64. Woman's Temple, Chicago, 1891–92, Burnham and Root (*Rand, McNally and Co.'s Pictorial Chicago*, 1893, 1898).

them.[27] Henri Nodet's remark in 1897 was illustrative of the increasingly positive attitude toward teamwork in the criticism of the last half of the decade: "if this sympathy is going to give us the style of the twentieth century and the formula of new art," then it would be wise for continental professionals to follow suit.[28] Impressed by Adler and Sullivan's Union Trust Building in St. Louis (fig. 65) and Stock Exchange in Chicago, he had attributed the effectiveness of these buildings to the collaboration of engineer and architect.

By extolling the wonders of "architectural engineering," critics acknowledged, sometimes unwittingly, the changing responsibilities of architects, but in the early 1890s they did not analyze well how Chicago's designers, though less heroic, now exercised more

Figure 65. Union Trust Building, St. Louis, 1892–93, Adler and Sullivan and C. K. Ramsey (*La construction moderne,* 5 November 1892).

challenging supervision. Foreign observers tended to underestimate how essential a co-ordinating head was in designing and executing buildings that were becoming more and more complicated. Granted, engineers had developed floating raft foundations, the iron and steel skeleton, elevators, fireproofing, and, internally, the electrical, heating, ventilating, plumbing, and sanitary systems, but it was the architects who planned and integrated all of these essential elements for the benefit of the thousands who used these buildings. Dankmar Adler, admired for his technical expertise, understood this. "You cannot leave the designs of the plan of a building to one person, the devising of its structural features to another, and its artistic development to still another." Compartmentalized supervision guaranteed bad buildings, he insisted.[29] The designers of the Loop's commercial buildings cast a paradoxical light on the meaning of "architect" in the early 1890s; they had lost considerable freedom but assumed control of the most complex projects in history. In the early 1890s many professionals abroad did not fully understand this and interpreted the changing roles of these designers as a setback for the profession.

Facades: "Compose" or Leave Simple?

Europeans were more accepting in 1893 and 1894 of the logic of the density of the Loop than they were of its consequences for the exterior design of office blocks. It was not uncommon for critics to second the architects' realism about unalterable conditions and approve of their collaboration with engineers, but fewer were willing to live with the consequences of this system for art, even when recognizing the logic of these consequences. The unsentimental reasoning of Hans Schliepmann's "What is ugly, must be ugly"[30] was not typical. More representative was the double conclusion brilliantly summarized in the previously quoted remark of Paul Lindau, "A gigantic peepshow of utter horror; but extraordinarily to the point." The open mind that granted concessions about purposefulness and teamwork tended to close when art was humbled. One can almost hear some of these critics, suspended between theory and impact or contemporaneity and attachments, even between head and heart, saying, "Yes, but . . ." Drawing such a line in the sand could be awkward. Leopold Gmelin admitted his predicament. "Indeed, when we contemplate these towering structures of twenty stories, their smooth surfaces of brick and even, rectangular windows, and consider their finished appearance and high adaptability to present requirements, we are almost inclined to forget all our scruples."[31] "Scruples," an encompassing word, referred to all he had been taught, what he had learned through practice, his understanding of architectural history, the assumptions he shared with others making conversations about architecture possible. It referred to the belief that good architecture was unified, humane, and attractive. "Scruples" meant artistic, moral, and ethical standards leading to buildings edifying and inspiring. The other two challenges to the expectations of Europeans—the purposefulness of the Loop and the redefinition of the role of the architect—were challenges from the practical realm. Art, however, spoke for architecture's ideals and aspirations, those dreams of designing life as it was supposed to be, that had inspired people through the ages to pick up their pencils in the first place. Practicality and quantity were admirable, but the quality of a culture was still measured in its thought, poetry, and artistic achievements. European opinion, more surprised than opposed to the changing role of architects and the Loop's intensified purposefulness, splintered over the artistic implications of the district's street fronts.

Objections to the design of skyscrapers were published in all three major Western European countries, though the continental reaction tended to be milder than judgments in Great Britain. The French, more curious than either the Germans or the British about the cultural implications of the Loop, were less disturbed by the appearance of tall buildings, possibly because they considered their own architecture and educational system without rival in the Western world. German critics, of the three the most eager to know how these buildings worked, devoted more of their attention to planning and applied technology than to exterior appearance. Of the three, the British seemed most preoccupied with the spare look of tall buildings and expressed more reservations about it. Between the lines of some British commentaries one senses a certain irritation, as if skyscraper designers had been unfair by not playing by the expected rules. The following anonymous quote appeared in London's *Architect and Contract Reporter* in May 1893. "We must admit that if all we have learned to call architecture, from prehistoric times till today, and which attained its epitome of perfect beauty of fitness and proportion in Greece, is one thing, then the modern ten or twenty storey building is another; if Athens and Rome and the Middle Ages and the Renaissance and Paris is one thing, in their monumental dignity, symmetry and repose, then New York and Chicago and the spirit of the age is something else which is not dignity, symmetry nor repose."[32] The sudden rise of tall buildings in American cities helped to focus the current debate in Western Europe about the definition and nature of contemporary architecture. Was architecture "dignity, symmetry and repose?" Was it, as the author of "New Business Buildings of Chicago" had contended, the effective meeting of specific conditions regardless of what had been done under other conditions? Critics in all three countries in the early 1890s struggled with these questions, their hearts tugging in one direction, their heads in another. The author of the above quote seemed to imply the advisability of a double standard until the interchange between old assumptions and new realities had acquired at least a patina of familiarity. This accommodation, intended to make sense and buy time in a confusing period, was not uncommon; many began their observations with prefatory phrases such as, "according to our understanding," or, "by our aesthetic taste."[33]

Their reactions to art within these buildings were more positive than their comments on exteriors. Foreign visitors often expressed surprise at the lavish surfaces inside, a display of richness some expected to find on the outside. The floor of a skyscraper lobby was often laid in mosaic or ornamental tile, as indicated by the photograph of the New York Life Building's entrance hall from the *Inland Architect* (fig. 66). Announcements to prospective renters sometimes promised lobbies finished with "tessellated Roman floor," "mosaics of Italian manufacture," or walls covered with marble imported from Massa, Carrara, or Mexico. The mosaic work of the Old Colony Building was designed by the

Tiffany Studios in New York. White marble was preferred in dim lobbies and, in addition to white porcelain brick, was used in light courts for its reflective properties. John Kendall, an English traveler, likened the effect of illumination from the skylight of the Masonic Temple on the marble walls below to light animating the walls of a cathedral.[34] For doorways, elevators, and railings, bronze was the favored metal (fig. 67). Publicity about the new Unity Building in November 1891 claimed its metal surfaces were covered

Figure 66. Entrance hall, New York Life Insurance Company Building, Chicago, 1893–94, Jenney and Mundie (*Inland Architect*, October 1894).

Figure 67. Stairway and landings, Masonic Temple, Chicago, 1891–92, Burnham and Root (*Inland Architect*, December 1892).

with "a triple plate of silver." Despite the growing dependence on elevators, the main staircase in most lobbies was finished in marble or metal with marble treads. Corridor floors, commonly of maple laid on cement, were in some buildings—the Rookery, Schiller Theater, and Masonic Temple, for example—finished in mosaic or marble. The corridor walls of the most luxurious buildings were also faced with marble.

Pleased with the ambience of these interiors and impressed by the amount of money spent on them, some observers wondered why owners denied the public the art and expenditures they gave their clients.[35] The *Tribune* answered this question on 29 November 1891. "It has been proved that tenants are willing to pay for improvements in this line. The fine office buildings which are now in course of construction will all be marvels of interior finish." Thus, interior and exterior purposefulness did not lead to similar visual results. However, the favorable response of Europeans to interior finish was not unanimous. In subjugating art to advertising, wrote Paul de Rousiers, Chicago's entrepreneurs exposed their bad taste. Offended by the glittering surfaces, he asked if clients actually believed this "barbaric luxury" was attractive.[36] On the other hand, Wilhelm Bode, who studied Chicago's office buildings in 1893, concluded that the close relationship between design and profits was the principal reason commercial architecture in the United States was better than the country's cultural or governmental architecture.[37] Though critics abroad gave interiors higher marks, they also paid less attention to them than to exteriors.

The Auditorium Building by Adler and Sullivan (fig. 63) was dedicated on 9 December 1889 with the president and the vice-president of the United States, Benjamin Harrison and Levi P. Morton, in attendance and Adelina Patti as featured soloist (fig. 68). It became Chicago's best-known building internationally in the late nineteenth century, symbolizing the city's postfire regeneration. Diversified in function, it contained a 17–story tower holding 136 offices, a 400–room hotel, dining facilities, a recital hall, and a theater seating 4,237. Critics often cited the building when searching for an example of Chicago's imagination, daring, technological resourcefulness, or limitless wealth. Though they had frequently chided Americans for spouting statistics, numerous foreign writers succumbed to their convenience when describing the Auditorium, while a few, tired of hearing the litany of its facts and figures, resorted to sarcasm.[38] Nonetheless, Europeans admired the largeness of the thought behind the Auditorium. "Never before were opera house, hotel and business block projected under one roof." They also interpreted the building as a sign of the city's cultural aspirations. Though reserved about its grave exterior, critics were quite enthusiastic about its interior, crediting Sullivan with a decorative originality "that helps the architecture without overloading it or becoming intrusive."[39]

Negative reactions to the appearance of tall buildings in the Loop were rarely systematic or detailed. Displeased observers may have assumed reasonable people would know this new form was aesthetically deficient. The less said the better. Though their

Figure 68. Adelina Patti singing at the dedication ceremonies, 9 December 1889, for the Auditorium Building, Chicago, 1887–89, Adler and Sullivan (*Chicago Tribune*, 10 December 1889).

displeasure was provoked primarily by artistic features, critics also found fault with other aspects of this architecture. Safety was one. No foreign visitor, to my knowledge, was injured by structural failure in these buildings in the early 1890s, but periodically visitors raised the question of danger. Appearances may have fed their suspicions. Given the height of many facades, the modest entranceways at street level were not reassuring. Also, the sight of a clerk on the fourteenth floor, working inches away from a broad sheet of glass, made observers below nervous. Even the old attack on "sham," which briefly flourished in the British press in the early 1880s, was renewed a decade later. London's *Builder* charged dishonesty on several occasions in the 1890s. Opposed to hiding a metal skeleton behind a robust-looking but dependent wall, the journal in September 1893 endorsed the views of an Australian architect who had argued that to cheapen "beauty, grace, and grandeur" by relying on this structural system was to dethrone architecture from "her high estate, to disestablish her as an art, and to relegate her to the rank and file of the mechanical crafts."[40] This minority viewpoint was rarely voiced so bluntly. Critics were more likely to express reservations about the skeleton system by condoning the "misuse" of brick, stone, or terra-cotta in order to obscure it. Also, some observers still worried about the impact of this new business environment on people. "However it may be humanized later, man will always feel diminished there by the scale of these temples of work, overwhelming indicators of the power of money, that symbolize the mother idea under the rule of which an entire people moves with the most perfect precision."[41] The early skyscraper provoked emotional reactions abroad for many reasons. Critics could acknowledge the numerous innovations and the lessons they learned from this architecture and still wish it had never materialized. Chicago's office blocks announced in blatant terms a more vulgar world, one that was seldom welcomed abroad in the first half of the 1890s.

Among the artistic criticisms, the following were common. These buildings were too large, their height discounting the notion that public architecture should be related to human scale. The difference between human and constructed height was caught well in Orson Lowell's painting of a shopper with the Chamber of Commerce Building behind him (fig. 69). The exaggerated relationship of height to width in a typical elevation looked ungainly. A few writers stated flatly that it was impossible for any designer to make a narrow form of more than ten stories look attractive.[42] There were many comments about the brutality or emptiness of street fronts, and, when sparely decorated facades were joined along a block, critics sometimes complained of the monotony of the extended flank. How ironic that the most complex structures of modern architecture looked "like books in a loan library."[43] To European eyes, these buildings seemed interchangeable, a conclusion reinforced not only by the repetitious treatment of floors but also by the division of the exterior into three basic parts—the base, central section, and the cornice. The erroneous but understandable conclusion, "if one has seen one of these facades, one has seen all of them," undoubtedly infuriated those who had designed them. Although some critics tried to convince their readers that, given the circumstances, architects in Chicago had designed these buildings as well as could be expected, and Samuel Bing,

Figure 69. Chamber of Commerce Building, Chicago, 1888–89, Baumann and Huehl, painted by Orson Lowell (*Scribner's Magazine,* June 1895).

German born but a naturalized French citizen, reminding readers Americans were still babes in art land, told them to be thankful the results were not worse than they were,[44] the majority probably would have agreed with Leopold Gmelin when he called the pace-setting skyscraper the most objectionable feature of American architecture.[45]

In the early 1890s Europeans hesitated to tell American firms how to design this new kind of architecture. Why? Since journals abroad carried few illustrations of early skyscrapers prior to the Columbian Exposition, the tall building was still regarded abroad as a novel development in 1893 and 1894. Though curious, and often quick to state whether or not they believed the office block an important contribution to Western architecture, most critics withheld artistic advice. Those who believed this new form was irrelevant to problems facing European cities did not waste their time recommending steps to refine it. Empathizing with American designers caught between the Grand Tradition and a paycheck, some foreign professionals were reluctant to second guess their colleagues abroad. If, on the one hand, they were hesitant to pick up a pencil to illustrate their suggestions for artistic improvement, several did refer to certain buildings, the designs of which they considered better or worse than others, but they offered no new design ideas in these years. Their judgments were reactive, triggered by their likes and dislikes of what American architects had already done. These judgments can be categorized. A smaller number of critics urged Chicago's architects to leave street fronts simple.[46] A larger number encouraged them to "compose" street fronts to make them more interesting and/or to reduce the impression of the building's height.

Critics in the former group agreed with the anonymous author of "New Business Buildings in Chicago" who claimed Chicago's architects had realized the futility of "'making' facades." One British visitor, J. R. Creed, explained why this was a wise decision. The canvas on which these designers worked was too large. Since artists would never think of carving a filigree pattern on a mountainside, he reasoned, why attempt to do the same on a tall building? His conclusion: "The simpler the buildings were that I saw, the more they impressed themselves on my memory."[47] Those who preferred the plainer street fronts of Chicago did not address well the question of the degree to which an exterior should reflect its supporting steel frame but did advise designers to respect the constraints it imposed on their creativity. They urged them not to try to compete with the extensive amount of glass demanded by renters. Instead they would be better off treating windows as primary elements in the composition. By keeping them simple and similar in size, unlike current practices in New York, they could take advantage of a realization confirmed for a number of foreign professionals in Chicago—repetition could be an effective artistic tool. The repetition of like forms—windows, sills, mullions, spandrels—could be satisfying when spread regularly over an extensive facade. Maintaining simplicity was the only way to maximize the impact of the most distinctive visual feature of office blocks—their size. Ugly or not, these buildings were, nevertheless, imposing works of architecture. By leaving them "in their natural state," architects could promote their inherent power as the dominant artistic element. Chicago's designers, aware that intervention and manipulation could be counterproductive, had turned their limitations into virtues.

Critics impressed by "grandeur" or "majesty" sometimes cited the Masonic Temple (fig. 37) and the Monadnock Block (fig. 62), the former for its size and the latter for its spareness. Despite its twenty-plus stories, however, the Masonic Temple did not provoke the clarifying realizations spurred by the Monadnock. This stark sixteen-story building became a litmus test for European professionals, separating those who seconded Chicago's revolutionary architectural message from those who did not. No building was more disturbing to some or inspiring to others. Its brick surface above the first floor was varied only by splaying at the second level and the attic and by bays running from the third through the fifteenth floors. The building's reductiveness confounded European observers. One pointed out, "The 'Monadnock,' for example, has a series of windows alternating with shallow bow-windows, without ornament of any kind, no strings or piers, or even hoods or sills, to the windows, which are all of one design and almost of one size. The larger front of this building contains 389 window openings approximately of one kind."[48] Some of the sharper critics struggled with this building. Alternately struck by the clarity of its logic and the strangeness of its appearance, Jacques Hermant thought it prototypical of the Loop's new architecture but balked at its implications for creative designers. From a few observers the Monadnock won grudging respect for the consistency with which the firm of Burnham and Root had carried out its spare agenda. Banister Fletcher, who credited it with helping him realize the limits of decoration for this type of architecture, added, "The great charm of the building is its simplicity, and I would suggest to every one designing a building of this size to 'let it alone' and allow it to tell its tale by its boldness of mass and proportion, and not fritter away the dignity which size can give by an unlimited and totally unnecessary crowding of small detail."[49] The Monadnock was a classic case of a form so extreme in its revelation of a new concept that it revealed meaning not grasped in the study of other examples. J. R. Creed admitted its bluntness prodded his imagination. "In Chicago, where a severely commercial style of architecture is *de rigueur,* stands the Monadnock Building, which is certainly the plainest structure of its size in the world. I have heard it described as a band-box. In its photographs it looks hideous. Yet as you stand before it, you feel respect for its sombre dignity. Its strength impels your admiration; its magnitude leaves you lost in wonder."[50] Creed claimed the Monadnock expressed a dignity that, by contrast, made other buildings appear pedestrian. In a period of rhetorical design, a building so constrained became a memorable anomaly.

The multistory office building exacerbated a problem architects had struggled with for centuries—how to make the lower and the upper floors of a building appear to be parts of a unified composition. Leaving a facade in "its natural state" did not necessarily guarantee visual integration. Among discussions of both simplicity and unity, the most thorough came from Banister Fletcher, who believed no tall building would look unified if the horizontality of its central stories were emphasized. "Variety in unity, if you will, but you must have unity," he insisted. He found his prototype in history. The classical column, from which no part could be removed without destroying its harmony, represented in miniature a three-part unit ideal for multistory buildings.[51] Accordingly, the first two stories should convey the impression of solidity. In order to imitate the molding of a column's base, he recommended these floors of a skyscraper be designed as prominent horizontal bands. The middle stories should be treated like the shaft of an order, the windows and mullions analogous to its flutes and arrises. Finally, boldly expressed upper stories should terminate a tall building in a manner similar to the abacus of the Doric order. Not the originator of this analogy, Fletcher developed it more thoroughly than other foreign critics. Julius Meyer also advocated a three-part composition but chose the pilaster rather than the column as his prototype because office fronts were flat.[52] The building of the Loop that Fletcher thought met his criteria better than any other, a structure he considered not only the best designed in Chicago but the finest in the country, was the Schiller Theater Building (fig. 34) by Adler and Sullivan. He praised the horizontality and fine proportion of the second-floor balcony, the recessed windows suggesting the concavity of a flute, and the building's pronounced cornice. He also liked the central section, which soared like a proud tower above the lower sections on either side. In his judgment, the Schiller Theater was to tall buildings what the Parthenon had been to the architecture of classical Greece.[53]

Critics who disliked facades that were relatively spare tended to favor New York's versions of the tall building to those of Chicago. Or they singled out buildings in the Loop—usually the Masonic Temple (fig. 37) and the Woman's Temple (fig. 64) by Burnham and Root, the Owings Building by Cobb and Frost, or the Columbus Memorial Building by W. W. Boyington (fig. 70)—that had been made more "interesting" by stronger compositional breaks, more ornament, or references to earlier styles. Their preference for aggressively composed street fronts was understandable. Decorated facades seemed more familiar, less strange. They reassured some foreign observers that there were architects in the United States attempting to express themselves, to elevate "grim utilitarianism," to reconnect their buildings with Western architecture's glorious past. However, the principal reason many professionals abroad called for greater intervention was to reduce the impression of height in these early skyscrapers. Many of the new office blocks in the Loop were at least twelve stories, often twice or more than twice the height of business buildings in European cities. The size of these buildings shocked visitors regardless of whether they endorsed or decried them. Grandeur could be inspiring; it could also be intimidating. Lightly articulated facades could look inexpressive, and the crenellation of a block's skyline, fourteen-story buildings separated by six-story structures, was ungainly to the artistic eye. Buildings on which designers had emphasized mullions at the expense of spandrels required only a quick glance to assess the distance between the street level and the cornice, depriving them of tactile security.

Like many, Leopold Gmelin preferred the tall buildings of New York to those in Chicago.[54] In New York, designers had been more effective in carrying out a practice he endorsed. They had tried to counteract the impression of a building's height, employing compositional devices to make a tall street front look as if it contained fewer stories than it did. According to Gmelin, this could be done by pulling down the cornice to mask upper stories or by including the last story within a slanting roof. At the top of the build-

Figure 70. Columbus Memorial Building, Chicago, 1892–93, W. W. Boyington (*Rand, McNally and Co.'s Pictorial Chicago*, 1893, 1898).

ing, he favored a solution employed by Henry Hobson Richardson in the Marshall Field Wholesale Store (fig. 71) and by Adler and Sullivan in the Auditorium Building (fig. 63). They had increased the number of windows in a bay, quickening the rhythm and reducing the appearance of weight in the upper wall. The impression of height could also be countered at street level if a number of lower floors were grouped to form a substantial base. In the middle section of a facade, Gmelin urged designers to combine several floors

Figure 71. Marshall Field Wholesale Store, Chicago, 1885–87, Henry Hobson Richardson (*Deutsche Bauzeitung*, 27 October 1894).

Figure 72. Union Trust Company Building, New York, 1889–90, George B. Post
(*Deutsche Bauzeitung,* 20 October 1894).

within a unified register. George B. Post had done this on the facades of the *Times* and Union Trust Company Buildings (fig. 72) in New York. This compositional device reinforced a building's verticality while periodically interrupting its upward sweep. The effectiveness of the bay-wide arch in subordinating stories to a dominant unit was one reason Gmelin favored the modern Romanesque style for tall buildings. Many would have seconded Gmelin's suggestions.

However, there was one type of tall building in New York that did not appeal to European critics—buildings that were extremely narrow. Chicago's wider street facades, for example, those of the Rookery, Chamber of Commerce, Home Insurance Building, Manhattan Building, Ashland Block, or Woman's Temple, were considered preferable to towerlike buildings in New York such as the *Mail & Express* by Carrère and Hastings, eleven floors on a base twenty-five feet wide.[55]

An indication of how the French in 1892 might have altered the appearance of tall buildings appeared in *La construction moderne* in February of that year when the journal published one elevation and two plans of the winning entry in an unexpected and unproductive competition held at the École des Beaux-Arts. As a thoughtful gesture to its sponsors, former American students who had established a yearly *Prix de reconnaissance des architectes américains,* École administrators chose a fourteen-story skyscraper as the theme for the 1892 competition. This was an unrealistic choice for participants. At that time French students had probably seen a few illustrations of tall buildings and knew that their interiors were divided into numerous offices, but they had limited knowledge of causes, construction, and internal complexity. The specifications for the competition suggested those in charge were not well informed either.[56] Stipulations for the main facade were minimal and loose. Entrants were permitted to add a few more stories to this "fourteen-story building" to round out their composition. They were instructed to include a bold cornice and an artistically attractive roof while the central section could be varied through orders, balconies, loggias, windows, towers, and turrets "to give the character of a grand composition . . . while insuring the unity of the whole." The scheme of M. Deperthes, one of nine entrants, was judged the best (fig. 73). His exterior design contained several features critics of 1892–94 tended to recommend to American designers to make their tall buildings more attractive. He attempted to minimize the impression of height by dividing his facade into horizontal sections, each comprising a number of floors, and by placing the main cornice slightly below the midpoint of its approximate height of 275 feet. He tapered the upper half, transforming a rectangular facade characteristic of the Loop's buildings into a pyramidal shape to increase the appearance of stability. His main facade appeared heavily inflected with projections, cavities, and details derived from history. Its composition was unrelated to the rectilinearity of an internal metal skeleton. His plans of the first two floors indicated he did not realize Americans erected multistory buildings because of the high cost of urban property. Without identified elevators, stairs, and functions, the plans submitted by Deperthes were academic exercises in the symmetrical distribution of vast spaces. This student project in 1892 should be taken lightly. The faculty's specifications were a better measure

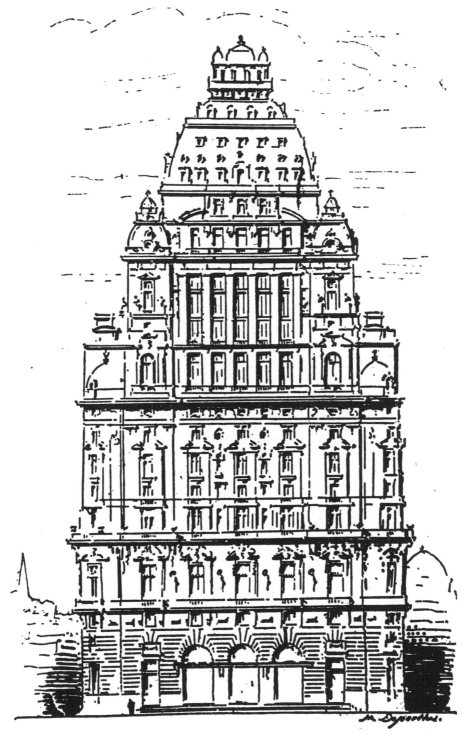

Figure 73. Winning design by M. Deperthes for *Prix de reconnaissance des architectes améric-ains*, 1892 (*La construction moderne,* 13 February 1892).

of initial French thinking prior to the more thoughtful investigations of 1893 and 1894. What the scheme of Deperthes does imply is that the tall, blunt, and rectangular office block did not appeal to French academic tastes.

Styles versus Style

The assumptions of foreign visitors about contemporary cities had been shaped by their urban experiences at home. However, these experiences did not necessarily prepare them for their encounters with the Loop. The purpose, pace, and appearance of this unique zone were the results of criteria many did not favor and of choices many would not have made. Put simplistically, the key did not fit the lock. Was the key the fault or was it the lock? Should visitors discard their assumptions, or had Chicago taken a destructive turn? The question is too simplistic because assigning discrete fault is unrealistic. The visitors were right; Chicago was right. In an exciting period of "quick transformations" the established and the innovative became awkward but interdependent colleagues. Not all visitors understood this. Some practiced denial, dismissing a city sufficiently important to host an international exposition in 1893. Some championed Chicago's contemporary realism, citing it as a better route to the future than the conservative adjustments evident in their own countries. Fortunately, many critics compromised. They tried to make sense of the new while respecting the lessons of the old. But the gamut of compromise was wide. Some compromised with more curiosity, others with greater skepticism; curiosity sometimes led to fresh insights, skepticism to the reaffirmation of familiar practices. How tightly or loosely critics held to their assumptions had much to do with their conclusions about the architecture of the Loop in the early 1890s.

The inclination of some to declare and others to inquire affected the language they used in attempting to relate these buildings to their understanding of architecture. Those who declared tended to believe good buildings should be beautiful buildings, their facades harmonious, graceful, and enlivened by ornamental details well chosen and thoughtfully placed. These critics were inclined to slight the effectiveness of a building in fulfilling its requirements, preferring to focus on the appearance of its facade as the primary criterion of its quality. To judge quality, they referred to history and the architectural language of previous styles. In effect, they attempted to stretch this language to include the business blocks of American cities. Architects in New York and Chicago had given them reason to do so. Chicago's firms had raided the treasuries of historic styles for compositional ideas and details. Their buildings displayed Gothic oriels and gables, Doric columns, Renaissance cornices. Leopold Gmelin maintained that fronts organized in a series of superimposed Romanesque arches were the most satisfying.[57] The tendency of many critics to think of these buildings as "Gothic" or "early Renaissance" also revealed their architectural predispositions. Such terminology reflected a belief that architecture was art, the quality of which was largely determined by the principal facade of a building. Many foreign critics in the early 1890s stopped at the surface of tall buildings and declared them more or less satisfactory according to current artistic criteria.

For a smaller number of observers, this approach and the language used to explain it were now passé. Suspending declaration, they inquired, and in the process looked beyond the facade to study the factors responsible for it. This group was more willing to view architecture as the author of "New Business Buildings in Chicago" did. Substituting for stylistic acceptability the effectiveness of a response to specific requirements, they argued that old terminology failed to get to the heart of this new architecture. Though an "early Renaissance" skyscraper might display elements reminiscent of fifteenth-century facades, the connection was irrelevant. The "styles" of history "can be applied only to the details, to the decoration" of these structures, claimed Fritz von Emperger.[58] In the opinion of G.M.J., who wrote about tall buildings for *La semaine des constructeurs,* these structures had turned the art of classifying architecture according to earlier styles into "an exercise of words."[59] This had occurred because the architects of these buildings had paid close attention to function. They had integrated art with purpose, dislodging it from its lofty perch. Old styles had been replaced by architecture responding to new criteria. This shift was explained well in 1897 by Karl Hinckeldeyn in his introduction to Paul Graef's *Neubauten in Nordamerika.* In the modern world, he argued, the importance of specific styles had been pushed into the background. Judgments of its architecture were now based on three factors: had the architect used his means of expression effectively, had the building answered its intended purpose, and had this purpose been expressed in characteristic form?[60] In the early 1890s the office blocks of the Loop played a catalytic role in Western architecture in helping to focus the international debate about the responsibility of architects to the past, and to the present, and the debate about the nature of contemporary architecture.

Throughout the last half of the nineteenth century, dissatisfied architects and critics in Western Europe had been asking when the new style of architecture would arrive and what it would look like. Did the appearance of the tall office building in the United States mean their wait was over? A few critics thought so. Julius Meyer even gave it a name—*Profanbautenstyl* (secular building style), an appropriate term for a period in which materialism was pushing idealism aside. His criterion was originality. The tall building was so different from all previous architecture that he had no choice but to designate it a new style.[61] Though adding more reasons, B.-H. Gausseron came to the same conclusion: "To imagine a mode of new construction, which corresponds to new needs, which has no model elsewhere, and which is able to utilize in its proper principle, without help from abroad, the variations of its form and the motifs of its ornamentation, what is this then if it is not the creation of a style?"[62] However, those who claimed a new style had arrived did not go beyond generalizations. In 1893 and 1894 none of them explained their reasoning in detail nor the extent to which this "new style" affected Western architecture. For example, P. Germain, a French engineer who had made a study tour of the United States in 1891, wrote, "I am convinced that we are now witnessing the birth of a new style [in the United States], which will characterize its age as our cathedrals and castles characterized the Gothic epoch."[63] Critics who made such pronouncements did not make clear if "new style" applied to all of Western architecture, referred only to business buildings, or only to American work. Their vagueness was understandable; they had not had sufficient time to put this new form in perspective. European critics often acknowledged its contemporaneity—Fritz von Emperger called it the architectural achievement of the age[64]—but hesitated to predict its long-term consequences. Leopold Gmelin referred to "incontrovertible evidence of a most important cultural development" but could not say precisely what that development was.[65]

There were several reasons why most observers in the first half of the 1890s resisted calling the multistory office building a new style of architecture. It was too new. Critics abroad had been surprised by its sudden appearance. They needed more time to determine its significance. Expecting the new style to arrive in more attractive clothing, some resisted on artistic grounds. Others hesitated because this new type of building was intimidating in scale. Some hesitated to welcome the future in a building type so tainted by speculation. Furthermore, the office block was a solution to problems of large American cities, not necessarily an answer for urban planners in Europe. Finally, some considered the skyscraper too narrow a conception to be regarded as an authentic revelation of a cultural moment. According to Alphonse de Calonne, a French novelist and prolific commentator on politics, literature, and art, "It is all in vain to claim that the satisfaction arising from the adaptation to need, from the exterior manifestation of utility or from the expression more or less exact of the manners, the uses, the habits, even the eccentricities of an epoch or of a nation is sufficient to constitute an art and to impress upon it the character of beauty."[66] Profound architecture, even in the modern period, expressed a culture's traditions and aspirations as well as its material preoccupations. These reservations merged in the minds of most critics in the first half of the 1890s to disqualify the Loop's office buildings as the embodiment of a new style.

Architects and critics in Britain, France, and Germany found a new kind of building in Chicago but valued it as a by-product clarifying a process that had become confused in Western Europe. Though they did not necessarily discover a new style in the Loop, they agreed these buildings worked extremely well. Ugly, disquieting, and crass, the office blocks of the Loop nevertheless served their purposes with unprecedented efficiency, convenience, and even comfort. If this architecture frustrated foreign artistic expectations, its revelation of a logical connection between demands and architectural answers was consequential, convincing some observers it represented the "formula of the art of the future." By respecting the context in which they designed, the architects of Chicago restructured for a number of European critics the definition of contemporary architecture.

Notes

1. The journal did publish illustrations of the Brooklyn Life Insurance Company Building (1889:208) and the United States Trust Company Building in New York (1890:304).
2. "New Business Buildings of Chicago," *Builder* 63 (9 July 1892): 23.
3. Ibid., 24.

4. P.P. [Paul Planat], "L'architecture américaine," *La construction moderne,* 2d ser., 1 (12 October 1895): 14–15.

5. Jacques Hermant, "L'architecture aux États-Unis et à l'exposition universelle de Chicago," *L'architecture* 7 (20 October 1894): 343.

6. Ibid.

7. "Hospital Construction and Organization," *Builder* 37 (27 December 1879): 1419. Reviewing *Hospital Plans* (New York: W. Wood, 1876), the journal on page 1417 cited American attention to construction and planning. "When they are in earnest about these matters, they go more systematically to work than we do, and with a more defined determination to get at the best way of doing the thing."

8. Planat, 15.

9. Banister F. Fletcher, "American Architecture through English Spectacles," *Engineering Magazine* 7 (June 1894): 318.

10. Ibid., 314–15.

11. Wilhelm Bode, "Moderne Kunst in den vereinigten Staaten von Amerika," *Kunstgewerbeblatt* 5 (1894): 118.

12. Adolphe Bocage, "L'architecture aux États-Unis et à l'exposition universelle de Chicago," *L'architecture* 7 (13 October 1894): 335.

13. G.M.J., "Les grandes bâtisses aux États-Unis," *La semaine des constructeurs,* 2d ser., 8 (10 March 1894): 442. The other parts of the article appeared on (11, 18 November, 2, 9, 16 December 1893): 232–33, 244–45, 269–70, 281, 291–92 and (3, 10 February, 7 April 1894): 379–80, 387–88, 487.

14. H., "Amerikanischen Thurmhäuser," *Deutsche Bauzeitung* 26 (16 January 1892): 29.

15. Hans Schliepmann, "Amerikanische Architektur," *Kunstwart* 7 (August 1894): 338.

16. The architect Alfred-Lambert Vaudoyer warned readers of *L'architecture* that cities in France would soon be tainted by Yankee speculation. Our God will become a "calf of gold," he prophesied, unless intellectuals interceded to protect French culture. A. Vaudoyer, "L'enquête sur l'architecture moderne," *L'architecture* 9 (11 January 1896): 12. Though he believed the recent architecture of the United States contained valuable lessons for German firms, Hans Schliepmann was skeptical that Germans could overcome sufficiently their condescension about American culture to appreciate its architectural originality. Schliepmann, 340.

17. Jacques Hermant, "L'art à l'exposition de Chicago," *Gazette des beaux-arts* 73 (September 1893): 242.

18. S. Henbest Capper, "The American Tall Building from a European Point of View," *Engineering Magazine* 14 (November 1897): 252.

19. Bocage, 338.

20. Capper, 243.

21. "Two Types of Office Buildings," *Chicago Tribune,* 29 November 1891, 25.

22. Paul Bourget, *Outre-Mer* (New York: Charles Scribner's Sons, 1895), 117.

23. Hermant, "L'architecture aux États-Unis et à l'exposition universelle de Chicago," 343.

24. W.G.R., "Das Riesenhaus am Broadway in New-York," *Deutsche Bauzeitung* 25 (21 November 1891): 565.

25. No one can comprehend the tall building, claimed Marcel Baudouin, unless that person understands the Americans, and "in order to understand a people and their customs, the first thing to do is to study them . . . on the premises." Marcel Baudouin, "Les maisons hautes et les maisons qui marchent aux États-Unis," *Revue scientifique,* 4th ser., 9 (22 January 1898): 110.

26. The firm of Burnham and Root, for example, set aside a large office for its chief engineer, who was assisted by a consulting engineer for structural matters and by a sanitary engineer

who supervised the drainage, plumbing, ventilation, and heating. It also maintained a separate office for those who served as superintendents or clerks of works—usually engineers previously employed by the firm—who were selected by the architects but paid by the clients.

27. Banister Fletcher, "The Influence of Material on Architecture," *Builder* 73 (4 September 1897): 181–83. In a footnote at the end of the article, Henry Heathcote Statham, editor of the *Builder*, distanced himself from Fletcher's contention that material, rather than historicism, should mold style.

28. H. Nodet, "The Modern Office Building," *La construction moderne*, 2d ser., 2 (3 April 1897): 319.

29. Dankmar Adler, "Engineering Supervision of Building Operations," *American Architect* 33 (4 July 1891): 12.

30. Schliepmann, 338.

31. Leopold Gmelin, "American Architecture from a German Point of View," *Forum* 27 (August 1899): 701. This article was a drastic abridgement in English of his eight-part article that had appeared in the *Deutsche Bauzeitung,* September–November 1894.

32. "High Building in Baltimore," *Architect* 49 (26 May 1893): 349.

33. The first phrase came from W.G.R., "Das Riesenhaus am Broadway in New York," 565, and the second from Paul de Rousiers, *La vie américaine*, vol. 1 (Paris: Firmin-Didot, 1899), 100.

34. John Kendall, *American Memories* (Nottingham: E. Burrows, 1896), 181.

35. For reliable information about interiors in this period, see Daniel Bluestone, *Constructing Chicago* (New Haven: Yale University Press, 1991).

36. Michel Vernes, "Le gratte-ciel toujours recommencé," *Archi-Créé* 211 (April–May 1986): 53.

37. Bode, 117.

38. See R.E., "Les grandes constructions américaines," *La construction moderne* 6 (5 September 1891): 569.

39. "New Business Buildings of Chicago," 24. The editor of the *Architect* was impressed with the Auditorium's interior color scheme. "The Chicago Auditorium," *Architect* 43 (21 February 1890), 126. The vast theater of the building attracted the most commentary. See Paul Lindau, *Altes und Neues aus der neuen Welt* (Berlin: Carl Duncker, 1893), 378–79; Jacques Hermant, "L'art à l'exposition de Chicago," *Gazette des beaux-arts* 73 (September 1893): 252; H. E. von Berlepsch, "Kunstleben in Amerika," *Kunst für Alle* 12 (15 April 1897): 214; "The Auditorium Building, Chicago," *Engineering* 51 (3, 24 April 1891): 400, 490; "The Chicago Auditorium," *Architect*, 126; Bocage, 334; and Samuel Bing, *Artistic America, Tiffany Glass, and Art Nouveau*, intro. Robert Koch, trans. Benita Eisler (Cambridge, Mass.: MIT Press, 1970), 90.

40. G. Allen Mansfield, "The Architect, the Engineer, and the Contractor," *Builder* 65 (16 September 1893): 205. The author had made this point in a lecture before the Institute of Architects in Sydney, Australia. The *Builder* added, "We have already very decisively expressed the same opinion." See also "Steel and Iron Frame Construction in the United States," *Builder* 63 (15 October 1892): 296. One of the few to continue the attack on "sham" architecture in the last half of the 1890s, Henry Heathcote Statham, editor of the *Builder*, wrote the following: "This simple treatment, in buildings of such great scale and height, would have a very powerful effect if it were all genuine masonic architecture. The knowledge, however, that the apparent masonry exterior is only a veneer concealing an interior construction of steel, robs such a structure, to my mind, of all its impressiveness; it is a vicious method of building, contrary to all true architectural principle; and it is to be hoped before long the Americans, architects and building-owners alike, may come to recognize this, and give up a method of building which, besides being a gigantic architectural sham,

is not without its element of danger." Henry Heathcote Statham, *Modern Architecture* (London: Chapman and Hall, 1897), 262–63. Other British critics who addressed the problem of covering a metal skeleton were Capper, 246, and A. N. Paterson, "A Study of Domestic Architecture in the Eastern States of America in the Year 1896," *Royal Institute of British Architects, Journal*, 3d ser., 5 (23 April 1898): 319–20.

41. Hermant, "L'architecture aux États-Unis et à l'exposition universelle de Chicago," 343.

42. See Gmelin, 701; and J.S., "Die 'hohen-Häuser' in Amerika," *Weiner Bauindustrie Zeitung* 10 (22 June 1893): 447.

43. Lindau, 380.

44. Bing, 79.

45. Gmelin, 700. Octave Uzanne claimed their lack of moderation and harmony shocked visitors. Octave Uzanne, *Vingt jours dans le nouveau monde* (Paris: May and Motteroz, 1893), 166. S.-C. de Soissons called them "artistic horrors." S.-C. de Soissons, *A Parisian in America* (Boston: Estes and Laurait, 1896), 166. William Emerson, who became president of the RIBA a few years later, thought office blocks advanced the cause of engineering but were destructive to the cause of art. William Emerson, "The World's Fair Buildings, Chicago," *Royal Institute of British Architects, Journal*, 3d ser., 1 (1893–94): 73. The British artist Frederick Villiers declared, "There is nothing beautiful, artistic, or worthy of being imitated by us or any other nation in these sky scrapers." Frederick Villiers, "An Artist's View of Chicago and the World's Fair," *Journal of the Society of Arts* 42 (8 December 1893): 50.

46. Among those who sympathized with this position were Wilhelm Bode, Albert Hofmann, Ernest von Hesse-Wartegg, and Hans Schliepmann in Germany; Jacques Hermant, Adolphe Bocage, Paul Bourget, Paul de Rousiers, and B.-H. Gausseron in France; and Banister Fletcher and J. R. Creed in Great Britain.

47. J. R. Creed, "Sky-Scrapers," *Pearson's Magazine*, August 1897, 187. Henbest Capper also felt strongly about simplicity. "The buildings are themselves so large and so imposing that they do not require enrichment to give them interest: mere surface ornament becomes unmeaning and superfluous; when used on so large a building, it becomes mere frittered labour, painful from its ineffectiveness." Without naming them, he claimed there were several tall buildings in New York on which generous ornament had compromised their potential grandeur. Capper, 247.

48. "New Business Buildings of Chicago," 23.

49. Fletcher, "American Architecture through English Spectacles," 319.

50. Creed, 188.

51. Fletcher, "American Architecture through English Spectacles," 318–19.

52. Julius Meyer, "Zwei New-Yorker Geschäftstürme," *Ueber Land und Meer* 73 (1895): 246–47. Meyer called for stronger relief at the bottom and the top of the main facade for two reasons: these were the sections pedestrians tended to notice, and robust modeling at the base would reassure the public the building was solidly constructed. Meyer did not discuss Chicago's buildings. S. H. Capper seconded Fletcher's insistence on artistic elaboration at the base of skyscrapers, not because he agreed with Fletcher that the exterior was compositionally akin to a column but because he believed, like Meyer, the walls of the first floors were the ones people on the sidewalk saw. He also thought skyscrapers ought to have a cornice as powerful as the partially completed cornice of the Strozzi Palace in Florence but acknowledged this was impossible. The higher the building, the bolder the cornice, he wrote; however, this system would eventually lead to projections that could not be supported. Consequently, he recommended bold projections be replaced by cornices of vertical depth at least one story in height. Capper, 248.

53. Jacques Hermant and Karl Hinckeldeyn also praised the Schiller Theater Building. Call-

ing it the most successful from an aesthetic standpoint, Hermant thought the Schiller would exert considerable influence on future design. Impressed by the fervor and imagination of its designer, Louis Sullivan, he wrote, "we think we should draw very special attention to this name which will certainly play a large role in the history of art in America." Hermant, "L'architecture aux États-Unis et à l'exposition universelle de Chicago," 342. Hinckeldeyn considered the Schiller and the Wainwright Building in St. Louis, also by Adler and Sullivan, the most satisfying facades he had seen for metal-supported architecture. See Pbg., "Architekten Verein zu Berlin," *Deutsche Bauzeitung* 29 (13 March 1895): 130.

54. Leopold Gmelin, "Architektonisches aus Nordamerika," *Deutsche Bauzeitung* 28 (20, 27 October, 17, 24 November 1894): 520–22, 532–34, 566–70, 582–83. Gmelin illustrated numerous buildings from New York—the Union Trust, Morris, Metropolitan Life Insurance, Mills, and Mutual Reserve Fund Life Association, plus hotels Imperial, Waldorf, New Netherland, Savoy, and San Remo—but only two from Chicago, the Auditorium and the Marshall Field Wholesale Store.

55. Henbest Capper, like Leopold Gmelin, argued for designs emphasizing the horizontality of each story. If the skyscraper had evolved from a tower, he contended, there would be historic reasons for continuing to treat it as such. However, the spacious interiors containing thousands of workers were quite different from traditional towers. He urged American architects to call attention to these roomy, well-lighted interiors by designing office blocks in horizontal sections. This orientation would also reflect the horizontal rectangles of the metal frame. To deny structural layers in the outward expression of a building, he maintained, was dishonest. See Capper, 239–52.

56. They called for a free-standing structure on a lot 125 feet wide by 200 feet deep. The first floor was to accommodate offices for the supervision of the building, restaurants, billiard rooms, and necessary services. The height of this story, which would include a mezzanine, was to be at least thirty feet. The second level, with space for club facilities and rooms for concerts, dining, library, and cards, was to be at least 25 feet but not over 40 feet. Above this level there were to be three to five stories, each from 9 to 25 feet in height, for banks, stores, and offices. There were no requirements for the remaining floors of the project. *La construction moderne* was highly critical of both the theme and its minimal requirements. See U.A., "École des beaux-arts," *La construction moderne* 7 (13 February 1892): 219–21.

57. Gmelin favored the Modern Romanesque for tall buildings for another reason. He thought the architecture of the eleventh and twelfth centuries—strong, primitive, simple—expressed a raw power appropriate for the United States at this stage of its development. He was not the only German observer to overstate in these years the popularity of the Modern Romanesque in the United States while ignoring the rising classical revival. The source of German enthusiasm for this style was Karl Hinckeldeyn, who wrote the only continental obituary of Henry Hobson Richardson, in *Centralblatt der Bauverwaltung* 6 (5 June 1886): 221–22. He gave Richardson credit for the improvement in American architecture in the 1880s and also declared the Richardsonian style ideal for the United States. More convinced of this than either the French or British, the German press made exaggerated and outdated claims about its continuing influence in the 1890s. Franz Jaffe, author of *Architektur der columbischen Welt-Ausstellung zu Chicago, 1893,* insisted as late as 1895 that the real national style of the United States, controlling both interiors and exteriors, was the Modern Romanesque. See Jaffe, "Amerikanische Innen-Dekorationen," *Innen-Dekoration* 6 (July 1895): 105. The only architect that Hinckeldeyn mentioned in his introduction to Paul Graef's *Neubauten in Nordamerika* (Berlin: Julius Becker, 1897) was Richardson. Most of the plates depicted buildings designed in the Modern Romanesque style.

58. F. v. Emperger, "Eiserne Gerippbauten in den Vereinigten Staaten," *Zeitschrift des oesterreichischen Ingenieur- und Architekten-Vereines* 45 (6 October 1893): 527. B.-H. Gausseron made

the same point, pointing out that though the Gothic was a type of vertical style, even the most fervent medievalists knew its theory and practice had little to do with skyscrapers. B.-H. Gausseron, "Maisons hautes aux États-Unis," *Le monde moderne* 1 (April 1895): 548.

59. G.M.J., "Les grandes bâtisses aux États-Unis," *La semaine des constructeurs* (10 March 1894): 440.

60. Graef, 2. This conclusion was quite different from his initial comments on Chicago. In 1885 he scolded the city's architects for not appreciating the importance of architecture's "eternal rules." Disturbed by their disregard and misuse of former styles, particularly in their recent commercial buildings, he likened their attempts at art to "a jargon which reminds one of Pennsylvania Dutch." See [Karl] Hinckeldeyn, "Die Begründung eines Verbandes der 'Architekten des Westens' in Nordamerika," *Centralblatt der Bauverwaltung* 5 (24 January 1885): 40.

61. Meyer, 247.

62. Gausseron, 548. He was reacting to a viewpoint expressed by the American writer Barr Ferree (*Scribner's Magazine,* March 1894). Gausseron thought Ferree was being too modest when he wrote that the designers of skyscrapers had not yet created a distinctive style.

63. P. Germain, "Correspondance: Maisons colossales aux États-Unis," *Le génie civil* 19 (3 October 1891): 377.

64. von Emperger, "Eiserne Gerippbauten in den Vereinigten Staaten" (14 July 1893), 396.

65. Gmelin, "American Architecture from a German Point of View," 694.

66. Alphonse de Calonne, "High Buildings in England and America," *Chatauquan* 19 (July 1894): 431.

Postscript

A S THE summer months of 1893 passed, Chicagoans looked forward to the end of the exposition. Citizens assumed that after the fair closed in October they would catch their breath, reread the glowing tributes foreigners and even New Yorkers had written about their triumph, and then return to the challenge of making their city the nation's first. But they were to find that these hopes would be difficult to realize.

There were several reasons for this. More exhausted from hosting the exposition than they thought they would be, the makers of Chicago did not immediately demonstrate the collective energy that had marked their efforts earlier in the 1890s and attracted the attention of foreign observers. Citizens were demoralized over the assassination of Mayor Carter Harrison by a disgruntled office seeker on the exposition's last day. The nation-wide recession that began in 1893 hit Chicago harder than cities along the East Coast. New York, for a brief period upstaged by the Windy City, recaptured its international reputation as the country's most dynamic metropolis. Chicago's architectural influence abroad also declined. Foreign professionals who had treated the Loop as a classroom did not have to keep returning to it to make use of its lessons. Furthermore, the foreign press disapproved of the growing classical revival in American architecture. American work lost its earlier appeal; radical Chicago seemed less radical by 1900 as European modern-ism gained ground. In the last years of the century British editors, who had been sup-portive of the historicism in the designs of the exposition halls, often warned American architects to stop imitating the French.[1]

In this postscript I will not explain all these reasons in detail but will review quickly two developments that affected the commercial architecture of the Loop, the achieve-ment for which the city was best known abroad in the early 1890s. First, construction in the Loop was severely curtailed by the recession, and, second, efforts to limit the height of tall buildings in Chicago had a temporary effect on its skyline.

Signs of Chicago's depressed economy had been noted before the exposition even opened. The monthly surveys of building conditions in the city, published in the *Inland Architect,* tracked the deteriorating opportunities for architectural firms. In May 1893, even as the exposition began, the journal reported it was difficult to find any architects who were busy with new work in the city. By September Chicago was "full of unemployed draftsmen." Investment capital had disappeared, all branches of industry and business had been affected, and unemployment and tension mounted. On 21 August, with the exposition still open, four hundred men gathered under Mayor Harrison's office in the city hall, shouting, "We want work," before police dispersed them. Year-end statistics confirmed how disastrous 1893 had been. In the previous year the estimated cost of new construction in Chicago had been 63 million dollars, 4 million more than New York's total, but in 1893 it dropped to 28 million. The depression continued month after month. In virtually every volume of the *Inland Architect* during 1894 the staff concluded that the economy was so poor it had to rebound in the near future. Hunger and homelessness increased, as did worker frustration. On 11 May 1894 employees of the Pullman Sleeping Car Company at Pullman struck over layoffs (2,200 since the previous July), slashed wages, and unreduced rents in the company's model town. After the American Railway Union effectively joined forces by boycotting railroads using Pullman cars, federal troops were called and strikers died. Violence also spread to the building industry, where fewer jobs and declining wages prompted strikes by trade unions. In a practice that had begun years before 1893, scabs, hired by the day, were often attacked by union employees either on the job site or on their way to or from work. At least two deaths and thirty injuries occurred in late 1894 as a result of a strike at the Marquette Building, one of the few major projects still under construction in the Loop.[2] The panic of 1893 devastated Chicago more than eastern cities because it dragged on longer. Homer Hoyt reported that foreclosures at the Chicago Real Estate Board did not reach their peak until 1898.[3]

Under these depressed conditions, there was no great demand for additional office space or large hotels in downtown Chicago. Only a few commercial structures ten stories or higher were erected in the Loop during the last half of the decade, just slightly more than the seven office blocks and one fourteen-story hotel that had opened in one month (May) of 1892. Furthermore, Loop skyscrapers built between 1895 and 1899 were no higher than those erected earlier. The architectural press in Britain, France, and Germany published more information in the last half of the decade about tall buildings in New York than they did of skyscrapers in the Loop.[4] In 1898, when the twenty-six-story Park Row Building by Robert H. Robertson was rising in New York, Marcel Baudouin declared Chicago's day was over.[5]

The movement to make Chicago a more responsible and livable city also affected skyscraper development in the postexposition nineties. The tall commercial buildings of the Loop had been created by investment capital, modern technology, and ingenuity. The municipal government and the public had not objected successfully during the 1880s to the increase in the number of floors over a piece of valuable property. Chicago was fortunate to have had capable architects and engineers, who, despite rewriting the rules instead of obeying them, created buildings of new scale and complexity that were relatively safe. However, around 1890, in Chicago and in other cities in which tall buildings had been erected, individuals and groups, believing capitalism's needs must be subordinated to the needs of the larger community, were becoming more effective in making their point that tall buildings were potentially dangerous buildings. They were concerned primarily about fire and to a lesser extent about the dependability of skeleton construction.[6]

The power brokers of Chicago were reluctant to curb vertical expansion. When the issue of a height limitation came up in Chicago's city council in June 1889, both the *Inland Architect* and the *Tribune* opposed it. According to the journal, proposals like this were introduced now and then by some alderman lacking in public spirit who did not understand the damage it would cause. "There is no sense, no utility and no necessity to limit the height of buildings in the city of Chicago, and we do not believe there is anyone who will honestly advocate the passage of such an ordinance."[7] During the next two years national organizations, including the American Institute of Architects and the National Board of Underwriters, debated the wisdom of setting limits on high buildings. In May 1891 representatives from various groups decided to pressure state legislatures to pass restrictions. In Chicago, however, architectural and business circles remained opposed. The *Inland Architect* attacked another proposed ordinance in council in October 1891, denouncing its sponsors as blockers of the "wheels of progress and metropolitan growth."

To this point, the *Chicago Tribune,* a representative voice of the city's power structure, had opposed height restrictions because firms continued to demand more and more space in the Loop. Its editorial policy was directed by the belief that what was good for business was good for Chicago. In the last months of 1891, however, the *Tribune* changed its position. This was a pivotal moment in the evolution of communal consciousness in Chicago. That it came during the period of intense self-examination in preparation for the Columbian Exposition was not surprising. Freewheeling capitalism had made Chicago's recent reputation; now, the *Tribune* decided, it must also bear its share of responsibility for making Chicago a safer and more pleasant city. The catalyst for the editorial reversal was the assertion in October 1891 by Brigadier General Charles Fitz-Simons, an influential local engineer, that Chicago was practically afloat on soil so fluid he would not invest a cent in any of the office blocks currently under construction.[8] The loss of confidence in the floating raft foundation system by such an authority was troubling. His warning galvanized those in Chicago who had opposed unrestricted building heights. Chief Denis Swenie of the fire department supported their cause when he told the council there was little his men could do to help people trapped in the upper floors of a burning sixteen-story building. If the rescue squads were hampered at this height, they would be ineffective trying to save victims from the proposed Odd Fellows Building, a thirty-four-story project by Adler and Sullivan (fig. 74), an illustration of which the *Tribune* ran below the remarks of Fitz-Simons.

In November 1891 Chicago's real estate board announced it would back an ordinance limiting the height of office buildings to 180 feet and mercantile buildings to ten stories. The Builders and Traders Exchange also encouraged the city council to enact a ceiling. Doctors expressed concern about the consequences of packing tall buildings together, fearing a rise of consumption due to the "growth of microbe life" from reduced sunlight as well as contaminated air at street level. Then Chief Swenie dropped a bombshell by claiming he had proof that even fireproofed metal would expand and contract from intense heat and cold water, dislodging attached materials. This prompted the *Tribune*

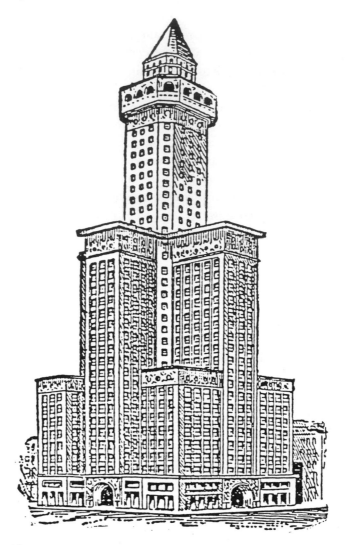

Figure 74. Unexecuted design for Odd Fellows Building, Chicago, 1891, Adler and Sullivan (Kendall, *American Memories,* 1896).

to proclaim editorially on 19 November 1891 that greed was out and civic responsibility was in. "The desire of gain is innate in man. The progress he has made is due to it largely, but when the lust for profit becomes excessive and its gratification endangers the lives or the property of others then it is the right and the duty of the community to apply the curb."[9] The newspaper continued to gloat over every new skyscraper that was finished before the exposition and, speaking to the outside world, boasted that no other metropolis could rival Chicago's architectural wonders, but for entrepreneurs the *Tribune* now had a different message: facilitating trade and providing jobs were important but, henceforth, corporate self-interest must be challenged for the good of the community. Endorsing a cap on building heights was a more difficult decision for the *Tribune* than its unsuccessful campaign to reduce smoke pollution, because reducing smoke did not inhibit the rise of the skyscraper, the ultimate symbol of Chicago's modernity.

This debate became academic on 16 December 1891 when the Chicago Fire Underwriters Association adopted a resolution denying coverage at reasonable rates to any future fireproofed building higher than 1.5 times the width of the fronting street or for buildings higher than 120 feet facing streets with widths exceeding 66 feet. Without insurance policies as security, investors could not borrow money for major construction. Within twenty-four hours of the announcement of the resolution, two contracts for tall buildings were canceled. The association also reevaluated upward the cost of insurance for each existing building that exceeded these limits. Foreign journals followed these developments closely, often predicting the end to "Babylonian" heights.

A number of the city's architects spoke out strongly against restrictions—Henry Ives Cobb, Dankmar Adler, and William Le Baron Jenney. Jenney argued that "the safe limit in height of buildings is not measured by feet but by the skill of the architects, the engineer and the builders erecting them."[10] In effect, those who protested asked why they should be doubted when they had never failed. However, their cause was then undermined by another former ally. Speaking before an engineering class at the University of Illinois on 31 March 1892, General William Sooy Smith, a bridge engineer, expressed doubts about the reliability of steel. Claiming a metal skeleton became "a creeping, crawling thing" when exposed to temperature fluctuations, Smith concluded metal supports could not be adequately fireproofed. Persuaded by the uneven floors of the tower of the Board of Trade Building, he also declared the floating raft system for foundations suspect. Though Jenney and P. B. Wight politely told Smith his data and conclusions were questionable,[11] and a blaze of a pile of eighty thousand feet of lumber stored in the unfinished Chicago Athletic Club vindicated their claims that proper fireproofing did protect metal from heat, Smith's fears carried weight with the public. Increasingly concerned about the image of Chicago, the *Tribune* pressured the city council. Under the heading "As Others See Us: The Council Refuses to Limit the Height of Buildings or Greed of Landlords," the paper published a cartoon on 3 July 1892 exaggerating the height of the Schiller Theater by Adler and Sullivan (fig. 75). On 8 March 1893 the city's aldermen by a vote of 37 to 3 passed an ordinance limiting future construction to 130 feet or ten stories, and, to strengthen enforcement, created a Department of Buildings. The ordinance was more symbolic than effective (in 1902 the limit was reset at 260 feet), but its passage discouraged for several years the continued rise of tall buildings.

Chicago's days as the shock city of the Western world would soon be over. The economy that had made possible the city's extraordinary boom would temporarily fail it, forcing developers for the remainder of the decade to reduce their demands for new office space. Citizens also wanted their city's center to be more than an experiment station for material progress. Having demonstrated how contemporary conceptions of time, purpose, venture capitalism, modern technology, art, and ingenuity could produce a futuristic business district, they took more seriously the challenge of making the center of Chicago a safer and more humane environment.

Figure 75. "As Others See Us: The Council Refuses to Limit the Height of Buildings or Greed of Landlords," caricature of the Schiller Building, Chicago, 1891–92, Adler and Sullivan (*Chicago Tribune*, 3 July 1892).

Notes

1. See "Concerning Things American," *Builder* 70 (28 March 1896): 267; "American Architects and Contemporary Architecture," *British Architect* 48 (9 July 1897): 33; "An American Architectural School," *Builder* 75 (16 July 1898): 51; "The Future of American Architecture," *British Architect* 51 (17 February 1899): 107; "Some American Architectural Designs," *Builder* 76 (8 April 1899): 338; "A Retrospective Review of the California University Competition," *Builder* 77 (9 December 1899): 523–526; and "Outre Mer," *Builder* 79 (28 July 1900): 69.

2. "Assaulted Workmen in Chicago Strike Back," *Inland Architect* 24 (December 1894): 41–42.

3. Homer Hoyt, *One Hundred Years of Land Values in Chicago* (Chicago: University of Chicago Press, 1933), 181.

4. The Reliance Building of 1894–95 and the Fisher Building of 1895–96, both by D. H. Burn-

ham and Company, were the only Chicago buildings erected after the exposition to gain much attention abroad. After 1895, foreign journals published more illustrations of New York office buildings (particularly the *World* Building, United States Trust, Manhattan Life Insurance, American Surety Company, Union Trust Company, Tower Building, *Times* Building, and St. Paul Building), than of the contemporary buildings of the Loop.

5. Marcel Baudouin, "Les maisons hautes et les maisons qui marchent aux États-Unis," *Revue scientifique,* 4th ser., 9 (22 January 1898): 110.

6. Before the exposition there were periodic major fires in tall buildings in Chicago: the Grannis Block (February 1885), McGrath Building (April 1887), Dale Block (January 1888), Chicago Opera House (December 1888), and Cooper, Siegel and Company Store (August 1891). There were also several smaller fires, some during the construction process, in the Montauk Block, Ryerson Building, Home Insurance Building, and Ashland Block. The most publicized accident was the fall in February 1889 of a 2,700-pound water tank that was too heavy for the partially finished tenth floor of the Owings Building. The tank fell to the basement, destroying a portion of all floors in between. For an account and illustration, see *Chicago Tribune,* 18 February 1889, 3; and 19 February, 8.

7. "A Proposed Ordinance to Limit Height of Buildings," *Inland Architect* 13 (June 1889): 81.

8. See "Chicago's Building Foundations," *Chicago Tribune,* 11 October 1891, 12; and "It's a Serious Problem," *Chicago Tribune,* 11 October 1891, 13.

7. "The Fire Risk of Sky-Scraper Buildings," *Chicago Tribune,* 19 November 1891, 4.

8. W. L. B. Jenney, "Chicago High Buildings," *Inland Architect* 20 (October 1892): 24.

9. "High Building Plans," *Chicago Tribune,* 4 April 1892, 9; and "Gen. William Sooy Smith's Paper on High Buildings Criticised," *Inland Architect* 19 (April 1892): 34–36. P. B. Wight responded to Smith's paper at the request of the *Inland Architect.*

Biographical Appendix

The Europeans who have been included in this biographical appendix published the most informative commentaries on Chicago and the urban development of the United States in the late nineteenth century. Approximately 80 percent of these individuals have been mentioned in the text. This list includes professionally trained observers as well as commentators without particular fields of expertise. Their observations and criticism appeared in popular magazines and technical journals, in books accounting for travel experiences and books analyzing specific themes, and in reports sent back to London, Paris, and Berlin by governmental representatives.

ARCHER, WILLIAM (1856–1924)—Educated at Edinburgh University, he worked as drama critic of the *World* from 1884 to 1905. In *America To-Day* (1899) Archer claimed Chicago was a much-changed city from the one he had seen on a trip to the United States in 1877. Despite his celebrated description of the city's smoke, he predicted the "young giant" would soon become a wonderful place, its culture matching its astounding buildings. He detected evidence of Chicago's "thirst for beauty" in the marble lobby of the Rookery Building. He was more complimentary about American art and literature than British critics tended to be.

AUBERTIN, J. J. (1818–1900)—He traveled through Canada and the United States between June 1886 and April 1887 and published his experiences in *A Flight with Distances* (1888). The book reflected the growing interest in Chicago in the last half of the 1880s among British visitors. With its noise, daring, and energy, the city had become more representative than New York.

BARE, H. BLOOMFIELD (d. 1912)—Liverpool architect who went to Philadelphia to establish an architectural practice but returned to Liverpool about 1904. One of several young British architects who served as links between the professions on either side of the Atlantic in the early 1890s (*Royal Institute of British Architects, Journal* [1894–95]: 394), Bare discussed American commercial blocks and the conveniences of freestanding houses before the Manchester Society of Architects, 5 March 1895.

BARTELS—Talked about the physical development of Chicago and some of its major buildings at a large gathering of the Architectural Society of Berlin on 8 April 1878 (*Deutsche Bauzeitung*, 13 April 1878). This may have been the first time an architectural organization in Europe devoted a session to the city's architecture.

BAUDOUIN, MARCEL (1860–1941)—A graduate of the Faculty of Medicine in Paris, he wrote on diverse subjects. He was editor of both *Bibliographia medica* and *L'homme préhistorique*. A visitor to the United States in 1893, Baudouin discussed American hospitals in *Aux bureaux des archives provinciales de chirurgie* (1894). In the 22 January 1898 issue of *Revue scientifique* he focused on the new skyscrapers of the United States. Drawing heavily on his knowledge of New York, he claimed these structures were sensible responses to the needs of modern business districts. However, he concluded Europeans were not taking this revolutionary architecture seriously enough.

BENFEY, GUSTAV—A correspondent for the *Baugewerks-Zeitung* of Berlin who wrote several articles from Chicago (1896: 615, 1195; and 1897: 945) about house building and moving. In 1896 (1195) he also discussed the construction of the Fisher Building, documenting its rise with dated photographs.

BERLEPSCH [BERLEPSCH-VALENDAS], HANS EDUARD VON (1849–1921)—German architect and painter associated with the Munich Sezession. He was quite active as a critic at the turn of the century calling for renewal in German architecture and decorative arts. He reviewed Samuel Bing's *La culture artistique en Amérique* (1896) for *Kunst für Alle* (vol. 12, nos. 14 and 15). Identifying architecture as the most instructive contemporary art of the United States, Berlepsch stressed the functional effectiveness and attractive interiors of skyscrapers, citing, in particular, the Auditorium by Adler and Sullivan.

BING, SAMUEL (1838–1905)—Born in Hamburg but a naturalized French citizen, Bing was instrumental in introducing the decorative arts of Japan and the United States to Paris through his Salon de l'Art Nouveau. His study of the arts of the United States, *La culture artistique en Amérique* (1896), its preface dated 1895, was the most thorough survey of American painting, sculpture, architecture, and industrial arts published abroad during the 1890s. Bing reported that in no branch of art had the Americans been more successful than in architecture, in part because they had been able to separate the functional from the aesthetic. Endorsing designers in the United States who experimented to find new forms, he also praised Richardson for adopting a style from an earlier period and then transforming it to meet contemporary needs. His comments on tall buildings were general but perceptive, addressing such issues as the new sense of scale, the relationship between art and function, the rapidity of change, and the goal of maximum results from a minimum sacrifice of time. Excerpts of his book appeared in *Le moniteur des architectes,* between 1896 and 1898, and in *Revue encyclopédique Larousse* (vol. 7, no. 223).

BLACK, FREDERICK—In an article on skyscrapers in New York in *Chamber's Journal* (9 July 1898), Black described the reasons for the rise of these buildings and argued that they resulted from the need for greater speed and concentration in business. He was impressed by this new architectural type, calling it one of the great wonders of the nineteenth century and stressing its cleanliness, conveniences, and efficiency. However, he was also troubled by this new architecture, concerned about its durability, fireproofing, and artistic impact. His article reveals the difficulty of trying to cope with a sudden marvel of technology.

BLANC, MARIE-THÉRÈSE [TH. BENTZON] (1840–1907)—French novelist, feminist, and travel writer. In 1895 she published *The Condition of Women in the United States* and in 1896 *Notes de voyage: Les Américaines chez elles.* Though she was not impressed by the architecture of the Women's Building at the Columbian Exposition, she described the appearance of the buildings and grounds at Jackson Park as unforgettable (*Critic,* 25 November 1893, 331). She depicted the Loop as a wondrous and terrifying sector, a common reaction, and underscored the marked difference between Chicago's business center and its surrounding residential areas.

BOCAGE, ADOLPHE (1860–1927)—Parisian architect who represented the Société centrale des architectes français at the International Congress of Architects at the Columbian Exposition. His report, delivered at the society's conference on American architecture, 10 May 1894 in Paris (published in *L'architecture,* 13 October 1894), was one of the most perceptive European accounts of Chicago's architecture, commercial and domestic, in the early 1890s. More inquisitive than most foreign critics, Bocage evaluated the city's architecture on its own terms rather than judging it by European criteria. Referring to the builders of Chicago as the "pioneers of progress," he tried to convince his resistant audience of the significance and implications of the complexity, scale, and technological innovations of the Loop's skyscrapers. Bocage was also one of the rare foreign professionals to recommend skyscrapers for European cities when he argued their advantages as isolated apartment buildings in parklike settings. He ended his report with a lengthy discussion of architectural education in the United States.

BODE, ARNOLD WILHELM (1845–1929)—Made the director of the sculpture section of the Berlin Museum in 1883 and then head of its Gemälde Galerie in 1890, Bode (von in 1914) became the museum's director in 1905. He was favorably impressed by the buildings of the Columbian Exposition, especially the Transportation Building by Adler and Sullivan. During his visit in 1893 he studied American household arts and architecture. Bode claimed that the relationship between their requirements and their resulting form was tighter and more rationally determined than was true of contemporary German work. Because furniture, silverware, ironwork, and other functional arts in the United States seemed to be designed so appropriately for their use, they were beautiful in a sense that differed from European products that were influenced to a greater degree by traditional styles. The most useful architectural lesson of the United States was *Zweckmässigkeit* (purposefulness), exemplified best by multistory commercial blocks. His position was well expressed in *Kunstgewerbeblatt* (1894:113, 137).

BOUILHET, ANDRÉ—A goldsmith who represented the Union centrale des arts décoratifs at the Columbian Exposition, he claimed American work in gold and silver was less inhibited by tradition than comparative work in Europe. He was taken with the designs of Louis Sullivan, especially the Transportation Building and the Auditorium Building. Bouilhet sent drawings, casts, and photographs of Sullivan's work to Paris for display. His criticism appeared in *Revue des arts décoratifs* (14 [1893]:66; and 15 [1894]:110, 136, and 167).

BOURGET, PAUL (1852–1935)—A prolific French journalist and novelist who pondered the implications of American developments and institutions with greater imaginative insight than most European observers of the early 1890s. Intrigued but disquieted by the Loop, Bourget depicted it as a reality difficult to believe, a zone of disconcerting noise and haste where the impersonal throb of business subverted individuality. Without elaborating, he claimed that the architecture of the Loop was the first sign of a new art, "an art of democracy made by the masses and for the masses, an art of science, where the invariability of natural laws gives the most unbridled daring the calmness of geometrical figures" (*Outre-Mer* [1895], 118). He arrived in the United States in August 1893 and attended the fair during its final ten days (*Chi-*

244 | Biographical Appendix

cago Tribune, 24 September). He wondered if the beauty of Jackson Park confirmed that democracy and science, shaping forces of the United States and considered inimical to art, could indeed underwrite beauty. He wrote about Chicago in *Outre-Mer* (1895) and contrasted it with the Columbian Exposition in *Cosmopolitan* (December 1893).

BOUSSARD, JEAN MARIE (1844–1923)—A French architect who specialized in tombs, post offices, *hôtels,* and tenement houses. He also wrote about architecture, publishing *L'art funéraire moderne* (1881) and *L'art de bâtir sa maison* (1887) as well as editing the journal *Le moniteur des architectes.* Between the mid-1880s and 1893, he often recommended American work to his readers, calling it a "curiously instructive" alternative to the formality and traditionalism of current French work.

BRINCOURT, EUGÈNE-MAURICE (b. 1857)—A Parisian architect who designed villas, *hôtels,* factories, and tenements. His survey of the architecture of the United States, published in Paul Planat's *Encyclopédie de l'architecture et de la construction,* was one of the best illustrated French surveys prior to the Chicago exposition. American work was useful, he contended, because it drew from numerous schools and styles to address needs of a new people. He praised designers in the United States for rejecting traditions incompatible with modern needs and for meeting requirements in a practical manner that did not forsake art. His survey was republished in *American Architect* (18, 25 July and 1 August 1891).

BRODIE, CHARLES HENRY (1859–1940/45)—He received his architectural training at the Exeter School of Art and at the Architectural Association in London. A fellow of the RIBA, he designed a number of London shops and banks as well as buildings at Doncaster, Taunton, Wellington, Swindon, and Ashton Gate. In the winter of 1887 and spring of 1888 he made a study tour of the United States, spending the bulk of his time in New York and Chicago. Brodie was one of the first British critics to claim, as he did in his report to the Architectural Association, that the office blocks of the Loop were not only practical but also effectively designed (*American Architect,* 19 May 1888). He also lectured on American frame houses at the Architectural Association (13 November 1891), receiving a negative reaction to his tacit endorsement of pattern-book designs (*Builder,* 21 November and 5 December 1891).

BRUWAERT, EDMUND (b. 1847)—French consul in Chicago in the early 1890s who published *Chicago et l'exposition columbienne* (1893) in collaboration with F. Régamey. In *Le tour du monde* (1893:294) he argued that the city of Chicago would be the main event of the Columbian Exposition.

BRYDON, JOHN MCKEAN (1840–1901)—Born in Scotland, he became a London architect whose characteristic style, free in plan but careful in detail, was a Georgian variation of the English Renaissance. He became a Fellow of the RIBA in 1881 and its vice-president in 1899. On 20 February 1899 he read a paper on American libraries at the RIBA, commending the Boston and New York Public Libraries and the library at Columbia University.

CALONNE, ALPHONSE BERNARD DE (1818–1902)—After studying law in Paris, he wrote for several political, literary, and art journals, besides publishing novels under the pseudonyms Max Berthaud and A. Bernard. His article for a general audience on high buildings in England and the United States for *Revue des deux mondes,* translated in *Chautauquan* (July 1894), was opinionated but not authoritative. His comments reflected the awkward position of foreign critics in the early 1890s who granted the necessity of tall buildings and predicted their inevitable technological refinement but, citing their unorthodox shapes, reserved artistic judgment.

CAMPBELL, JOHN KERR—His travel account *Through the United States of America and Canada* (1886) is a representative example of growing British interest in Chicago in the mid-1880s. Referring to Chicago as the "lightning city," he stressed the speed of the procedures and systems he observed there.

CAPPER, STEWART HENBEST (1859–1925)—Edinburgh architect and lecturer in architecture at Edinburgh University, he emigrated to Montreal in 1896 to become a professor of architecture at McGill University but returned to Britain about 1903. He taught architecture at Victoria University, Manchester, from 1908 to 1912. His article on skyscrapers (*Engineering*, November 1897) reveals the struggle of open-minded European critics to come to terms with certain aspects of this new architecture—the prominent and essential role of the engineer, the limits placed on architectural imagination, verticality versus horizontality in design, acceptable veneers for metal skeletons, and the limits of ornament.

CHAMPIER, VICTOR (1851–1929)—Studied law in Paris before turning to writing. He founded the *Revue des arts décoratifs* in 1887 and edited it until 1902. In 1901 he published *The Arts of the Nineteenth Century*. In 1893 Champier spoke to the Conservatoire des arts et métiers about industrial arts in the United States, illustrating his talk with lantern slides of American interiors. Citing the originality, comfort, and good taste he discovered in these houses, he exhorted his audience to reconsider current assumptions about interior decoration in France (*La semaine des constructeurs*, 3 March 1894, and *Inland Architect*, February 1895).

CHASSELOUP-LAUBAT, MARQUIS DE (b. 1863)—An aristocrat and engineer, he came to Chicago for a three-month stay in July 1892. Late in 1892, in a lecture before the Société des ingénieurs civils in Paris, he compared the expositions of 1889 and 1893, concluding that France was a mature country, centralized, confident, and strong in taste and theory, while Jackson Park proved the United States was still young, federated, unsure, and advanced in science (*American Architect*, 28 January 1893). Despite his admiration for American technology, he expressed an elitist apprehension about the country's material development. He published his experiences in the United States as *Voyage en Amérique et principalement à Chicago* (1893).

CHEVRILLON, ANDRÉ—His essay about the United States in *Revue des deux mondes* (1 April 1892) showed the extent to which Chicago had become for many European observers in the early 1890s the prime example of contemporary urban development in the United States.

CHRISTIAN, EWAN (1814–95)—A prolific London-based architect who built numerous churches and parsonages. He was a respected member of the British architectural profession, serving as vice-president of the RIBA and also as its president (1884–86). During the 1880s he spoke on several occasions at the institute as an advocate of the "go-ahead" spirit of the American architects he had observed while traveling in the United States in 1879.

COLIBERT, M. EUGÈNE (1832–1900)—A lower-level diplomat intrigued by the architecture of the past. For the exposition of 1889 he created models of the Bastille as it looked in the eighteenth century and La Cour des Miracles as it stood in the fourteenth century. As a correspondent for *Le Temps* in 1891, he wrote with mild derision about Chicago, its Loop, and the unfinished residential streets miles from it. He also satirized the facts and figures quoted to him about the Auditorium by Adler and Sullivan (*La construction moderne*, 5 September 1891).

COOK, JAMES HENRY (1861–1903)—A promising architect, he died at the age of forty-two. He went to the United States in April 1890, working for eighteen months with Richard Morris Hunt in New York, part of the time on the firm's Administration Building for the Columbian Exposition, and later with Frank Miles Day in Philadelphia. He attributed the high quality of work he observed to architectural training in the United States. On 5 March 1894 he gave a paper about his experiences at the Liverpool Architectural Society (*Royal Institute of British Architects, Journal* 1894:262). He may have returned to the United States, remaining there until the end of the decade.

COOK, JOEL—American correspondent for the *Times* of London, Cook wrote articles on Chicago in 1887 for the paper (21 October 24) and four articles in 1991 about the city and the coming exposition. The latter were republished by the Columbian Exposition's Department of Publicity and Promotion as *World's Fair at Chicago* (1891). He stressed the "prodigious energy" of Chicagoans and their ability to complete unprecedented undertakings in short periods of time.

COX, ALFRED ARTHUR (d. 1945–46)—The Godwin Bursary recipient in 1890, Cox emigrated to Canada in 1892, practicing in Montreal and Vancouver. He was made a Fellow of the RIBA in 1900. In the United States for almost three months in 1890, he spent most of his time in New York where he examined technical aspects of the Manhattan Athletic Club and the Marquand Residence on Madison Avenue. In Chicago, he concentrated on the foundations of the Rookery Building by Burnham and Root, but also examined the Auditorium, Tacoma, and Chamber of Commerce Buildings. His report was published in the *Royal Institute of British Architects, Transactions* (vol. 7, 351).

CREED, J. R.—In an article in *Pearson's Magazine* (August 1897), he argued that the tall building was a necessary consequence of evolving business requirements. One of the few foreign critics to recommend these buildings be left as simple as possible, he criticized architects of New York skyscrapers for trying to mask the structures' height through compositional means. Creed regarded the Monadnock Building the best designed of new skyscrapers in Chicago; minimizing compositional intervention, Burnham and Root had utilized simplicity to create an unexpected artistic effect.

DALY, CÉSAR (1811–94)—Architect, editor, author, and archaeologist, he made significant contributions to late nineteenth-century architectural theory. Founder and editor of the *Revue générale de l'architecture et des travaux publics,* he endorsed the experimental attitude of American architects but also warned them that work without moments of regenerative reflection and respect for beauty made Jack a dull boy. Though he was disappointed with the buildings of New York when he stopped there in 1856, he predicted in 1886 (*Revue générale*, 23–25) a bright future for architecture in the United States because its citizens were now beginning to consolidate their advantages without sacrificing their cultural independence.

DALY, MARCEL-ROBERT (b. 1860)—First son of César Daly. He studied architecture with his father and then wrote for both the *Revue générale* and *La semaine des constructeurs* prior to becoming assistant editor of the latter journal in 1892. Between 1886 and 1892 he wrote numerous articles in *La semaine des constructeurs* about architecture in the United States, mainly domestic, in which he claimed American architects, representing the future of architecture, had already left their counterparts in Europe behind. This position was expressed most forcefully in *La semaine* in a three-part article that began 23 April 1892. The firm of André, Daly, fils et Cie, in collaboration with the *Revue générale,* published the three-volume *L'architecture américaine* in 1886 and *Villas américaines* around 1888.

DALY, RAYMOND-AUGUSTE (b. 1862)—The second son of César Daly, he studied architecture with J. A. E. Vaudremer. In the obituary he wrote for Richard Morris Hunt in *La semaine des constructeurs* (24 August 1895), he called him the greatest American architect of the day and credited him with the influence French architecture now exerted in the United States.

DECKERT, FRIEDRICH KARL EMIL (1848–1916)—An economic geographer who retired as professor of geography at the University of Frankfort. His interest in the United States dated from 1884 when he made the first of many trips to the North American continent. By the turn of the century he was regarded as one of the premier German authorities on the United States. In his *Die neue Welt* (1892) he commented on the Palmer House and Chicago's parks and boulevards. His discussion of the American house (*Gegenwart,* 30 July 1887) was one of the most valuable foreign studies because he searched for the causes of specific architectural features. This article was particularly informative about the influence of nature on house planning and the relationship between American life and domestic design.

DERNBURG, FRIEDRICH (1833–1911)—A lawyer and member of the Reichstag from 1871 to 1881, he also served as editor in chief of the *National-Zeitung* of Berlin until 1890. He was feuilleton editor of the *Berliner Tageblatt* when he visited Chicago and the exposition. His accounts, carried by the *Tageblatt,* were collected under the title *Aus der weissen Stadt* (1893). He depicted Chicago as an unfinished and uncultured city, of interest only to the politician and the engineer. On the other hand, he regarded the exposition as an inspirational event but regretted it had not been held in Berlin where cultivated individuals really could have appreciated its message.

DESCHAMPS, PHILIPPE (b. 1848)—Based on his visit to the United States, he wrote *À travers les États-Unis et le Canada,* which had gone through three editions by 1896. His study of Chicago was lengthy and informative, including discussions of its history, cultural organizations, commercial architecture, Union Stock Yards, house moving, charities, and the Columbian Exposition.

DIETRICH, EMIL (1844–1912)—A graduate of the Berlin Academy of Architecture, he began work as a government engineer concerned with river and bridge construction. In 1882 he became a professor at the Technische Hochschule in Berlin. He reported on American architecture and the Philadelphia Centennial Exposition for the *Deutsche Bauzeitung* (July–November 1876) and later published his experiences in *Reiseskizzen* (1879).

DREDGE, JAMES (1840–1906)—Trained as an engineer, he began working for the new journal *Engineering* in 1866 and became one of its joint editors in 1870. As a result of close ties with American engineers, he was made an honorary member of the American Society of Mechanical Engineers in 1886. Dredge covered the expositions in Vienna (1873), Philadelphia (1876), and Paris (1878 and 1889) for *Engineering.* A member of the British Royal Commission for the Columbian Exposition, he helped to persuade British manufacturers to participate in the fair despite their anger over the McKinley Tariff (See *Engineering,* 5 and 12 December 1890; and *Chicago and Her Exposition of 1893,* a survey published in Chicago in 1892 based on a lecture given at the London Polytechnic Institute).

EMERSON, WILLIAM (1843–1924)—After studying with William Burges in London, he went to India at the age of twenty-one, where he designed numerous buildings in Bombay and Calcutta. Later he established a successful though conservative practice in London. He served as RIBA president from 1899 to 1902 and was knighted when his term ended. A member of the international architectural jury in 1893, his reaction to the architecture and setting of the Columbian Exposition was most positive (*Royal Institute of British Architects, Journal,* 1894:65.)

EMPERGER, FRITZ VON (1862–1942)—He studied engineering in Vienna and Prague until 1885. He went to Paris to observe the use of ferro-concrete in construction for the Parisian Exposition of 1889. In 1891 von Emperger landed in New York where he worked initially as an engineer for the Jackson Architectural Iron Works and later as a foreign representative of the Austrian railroad. Returning to Vienna in the mid-1890s, he lectured on engineering and completed in 1903 one of the first doctorates awarded in engineering in Austria. In 1902 he founded and edited the influential technical journal *Beton und Eisen,* first published in Vienna and later in Berlin. His profusely illustrated, five-part survey of the skeleton system of construction in the United States was published in the *Zeitschrift des oesterreichischen Ingenieur- und Architekten-Vereines* beginning 14 July 1893. This was the most thorough European discussion of the skeleton system and also the most influential; between November 1893 and April 1894 it was adapted for French readers in *La semaine des constructeurs* under the title "Les grandes bâtisses aux États-Unis."

FABRE, AUGUSTE—Primarily a writer on labor, economics, and socialism for the Bureau de l'Émancipation in Nîmes. In 1896 the bureau published his study entitled *Les Sky Scratchers, ou les hautes maisons américaines.* Though short, this was one of the rare foreign studies published in the 1890s in book or pamphlet form exclusively about the skyscraper.

FAUCONNET, RAOUL—A member of the French delegation of workers to the Columbian Exposition who published *Exposition internationale de Chicago* (1894). He also published *L'employé aux États-Unis* (1894), a short report in which he commented on factors affecting American labor, including the living conditions of workers.

FERGUSSON, JAMES (1808–86)—Scottish-born writer on architecture. After a brief business venture in India, he settled in London with enough savings to indulge his desire to write about architecture. He wrote initially about Indian architecture. In 1855 he published the *Handbook of Architecture* and in 1862 *A History of the Modern Styles of Architecture.* He thought American architects were free to choose a sensible style but probably would botch the opportunity because they lacked discipline and patience. He depicted them as builders more concerned about quantity than designers who valued quality.

FLETCHER, BANISTER (1866–1953)—Educated at King's College and University College, London, he studied architecture at the Royal Academy Schools and the Architectural Association. Though made a partner in his father's architectural firm in 1889, he was better known for his writing, publishing the first edition of his influential *A History of Architecture on the*

Comparative Method in 1896. As the Godwin Bursary recipient for 1893, Fletcher traveled to the United States, visiting New York, Philadelphia, Baltimore, Washington, Boston, and Chicago. He met Richard Morris Hunt, George B. Post, and Robert Swain Peabody. In Chicago he was most impressed with the work of Burnham and Root and Adler and Sullivan. On return to London, he submitted his Bursary manuscript on the Columbian Exposition to the RIBA and summarized his reactions to American architecture in *Engineering Magazine* (1894:314) in which he expressed the hope that the "imitative element" in the classical designs for the exposition's major buildings would not become a craze in American cities. Calling engineers the real builders of the nineteenth century, he urged closer cooperation between them and architects (*Builder,* 4 September 1897).

FOGERTY, WILLIAM (1834–78)—He was the best informed European critic of American architecture in the mid-1870s. An Irish architect, he was responsible for a number of buildings in Ireland and also in London where he settled for a short time before departing for the United States about 1871. He remained in the New York area until the winter of 1874–75, when he returned to Ireland, settling in Dublin. He was a Fellow of the RIBA and also served as president of the Royal Institute of Architects in Dublin. Fogarty died from small pox prevalent in Dublin in 1878. He gave three major addresses on current architecture in the United States (to the New York Chapter of the American Institute of Architects, 1 December 1874; to the Royal Institute of Architects in Dublin, 15 April 1875; and to the Architectural Association of Ireland, 27 January 1876) in which he emphasized practicality in American work.

FRAHM—A German government building contractor who published a well-illustrated, technical discussion of the role of metal in American tall buildings, focusing on those erected in Chicago (*Stahl und Eisen,* 1894:258, 303).

GALE, ARTHUR JOHN (d. 1928–29)—Gale influenced British architectural thinking about contemporary American architecture when, as the first recipient of the Godwin Bursary, he traveled in the United States from early May through mid-July 1882 and reported to the RIBA the following November and December (*Royal Institute of British Architects, Transactions,* 1882–83, 45). Although he concentrated on apartment buildings in New York City, he spent three days in Chicago studying fireproof construction and elevators. He was first to inform RIBA members about American experiments with an internal metal skeleton, his remarks prompting an attack by the *Architect* (30 December 1882). Three years later he discussed American work before the Leeds and Yorkshire Architectural Society (*Builder,* 19 December 1885), claiming its designers were finding new ways to unify the artistic and the practical, a resolution he attributed in part to architectural education at MIT and Columbia. Later in his career he became a principal in the firm of Smith, Son and Gale

GASS, JOHN BRADSHAW (1855–1939)—Member of the successful firm of Bradshaw and Gass of Bolton, which became Bradshaw, Gass and Hope in 1903. Also, a Fellow of the RIBA and of the Manchester Society of Architects, for which he served a term as president. The second Godwin Bursary recipient to select the United States, Gass arranged an exhibition of more than a hundred drawings and photographs of recent American work at the RIBA in the spring of 1886 (see *Royal Institute of British Architects, Journal of Proceedings,* 4 March 1886, for the complete list). Though stressing the work of Richardson, this exhibition introduced RIBA members to the names of specific designers and buildings in the United States, counteracting the tendency to generalize broadly about American work. He chose the Home Insurance Company Building by W. L. B. Jenney to explain how contemporary tall buildings were erected in Chicago. His reports appeared in the *Royal Institute of British Architects, Transactions* (1885–86, 129). He wrote about the United States again in 1896 (*Royal Institute of British Architects, Journal,* 229), concentrating on the influence of Richardson, Richard Morris Hunt, and the educator William Robert Ware.

GAUSSERON, BERNARD-HENRI (b. 1845)—He was respected as a translator of publications written in both French and English and as an author of minor studies on literature, art, and education. In *Le monde moderne* (April 1895) he commented at length on Barr Ferree's article on high buildings in *Scribner's Magazine* (March 1894), arguing that this new architecture represented a new style because it met the requirements of its time. He also commented on the Columbian Exposition in *La revue encyclopédique* (1 November 1893).

GERMAIN, P.—French engineer from Saint-Étienne (Loire) who traveled through the United States (c. 1891) studying construction projects. On return he wrote to *Le génie civil* to explain that the tall buildings he had seen represented a significant development, possibly a new style of architecture (*Le génie civil,* 3 October 1891, and *American Architect,* 5 March 1892).

GMELIN, LEOPOLD (1847–1916)—Called to the Kunstgewerbe Schule in Munich in 1879, he attempted to revitalize German and, particularly, Bavarian arts and crafts. Gmelin wrote five books on arts and crafts and architecture between 1883 and 1893. His eight-part study of American architecture, published in *Deutsche Bauzeitung* (15 September–17 November 1894), was one of the most thorough European discussions of these years. Like a number of German colleagues, he slighted the classical revival in the United States, in part because he was convinced the modern Romanesque was the appropriate style for a young but powerful country. Though he preferred the tall buildings of New York to those in Chicago, he claimed that Chicago stood for the spirit of the present day just as Hildesheim had characterized an earlier stage of Western development. An abridged, updated version of these articles appeared in English in *Forum* (August 1899).

GOUT, PAUL (b. 1853)—He was a successful Parisian architect trained at the École des Beaux-Arts. Editor of *L'encyclopédie d'architecture,* he endorsed the purposefulness, stylistic independence, and antiformal tendencies of American architects in his journal on several occasions (1888:132; 1891:20, 99).

GRAEF, PAUL (1855–1925)—Studied at the Academy of Architecture and the Technische Hochschule in Berlin. In 1879–80 he worked on the German excavation at Olympia. From 1887 to 1917 he was editor of *Zeitschrift für Architektur und Kunsthandwerk.* Graef published *Neubauten in Nordamerika* in 1897, a photographic study with an introduction by Karl Hinckeldeyn. The hundred plates, including some commercial and domestic buildings in Chicago, left the impression the modern Romanesque style was the dominant style in the United States at the end of the century.

GRAHAM, THOMAS ALEXANDER (1829–1912)—Designer of hospitals, warehouses, offices, and hotels, he was a member of the Council of the RIBA for twenty-two years and its Vice-President from 1893 to 1897. He published two articles on American architecture in the late 1880s in the *Royal Institute of British Architects, Journal* (8 March 1888 and 29 August 1889), arguing in both that the best work in the United States was now found in commercial buildings, not in detached houses as many earlier British observers had claimed. These buildings expressed an originality "too frequently absent" in British street architecture.

GRANDIN, MADAME LÉON—A Parisian who lived in Chicago with her husband from July 1892 until May 1893. Her spirited reaction to the city, published as *Impressions d'une Parisienne à Chicago* (1894), contains valuable insights about the city's life and customs from the perspective of a woman who discovered in Chicago greater social freedom and respect than she had known in Paris.

GRILLE, CHARLES JOSEPH ANTOINE—French civil engineer specializing in mines. He wrote *L'Architecture et les constructions métalliques à l'exposition de Chicago* (1894) in collaboration with Henri Falconnet and *Les travaux publics aux États-Unis* (1894) with Laborde. Both studies appeared in *Revue technique de l'exposition universelle de Chicago en 1893* (1894).

GRUNER, OTTO—Published a personal recollection of Henry Hobson Richardson in *Deutsche Bauhütte* (17 July 1902) in which he claimed to have worked for Richardson in New York in 1871, and that when they met later in Chicago, Richardson suggested the two establish a partnership. He was the author of two of the most informative statements published abroad in the 1870s about American architecture, "Der yankee-Styl" and "Über amerikanische Bauweise," in *Allgemeine Bauzeitung* of Vienna (1874:59, and 1875:77).

GUNESCH, RUDOLF VON—Member of the Society of Austrian Architects and Engineers who discussed American cities and frame construction at the society in March 1888 following his tour of the United States in 1887. In January 1890 he gave a technical lecture at the society on the Chicago Opera House, a ten-story commercial building by Cobb and Frost. His discussions appeared in *Wochenschrift des österreichischen Ingenieur- und Architekten- Vereines* (27 April, 4 May 1888, and 19 January 1890)

HEATHCOTE, CHARLES—A Fellow of the RIBA. He compared English and American building methods in a lecture delivered at the Society of Arts in London in late 1903. He stressed the advantages of time-saving and labor-saving approaches in American architecture and of treating each solution as a temporary achievement. The lecture was printed in the *British Architect* (4, 11 December 1903).

HEMS, HARRY—A prolific English decorator during the 1880s and 1890s, Hems visited the United States in 1881 and again in 1893. He criticized the Columbian Exposition for its size, architecture, and inefficiency. The city of Chicago also displeased him; he saw no improvement in the city since 1881. He thought the tall office blocks offered the average English architect nothing useful (*Building News,* 5 and 26 May, 1 December 1893).

HENRY, J. A.—Author of *Quelques notes sur l'exposition columbienne de Chicago* (1894) in which he claimed the exhibition buildings, though copies of older European models, could, nevertheless, serve as positive artistic examples for Americans.

HERMANT, RENÉ JACQUES (1855–1930)—Parisian architect who built utilitarian structures, stores, and private houses. Between 1889 and 1914 he represented his government and various French architectural organizations at several international expositions. His thoughtful and influential assessment of both recent American architecture and the Chicago exposition was published in three parts in the *Gazette des beaux-arts* (1893:237, 416, 441), excerpts of the first part appearing in *American Architect* (12 October 1893). He attempted to explain causes for the distinctive character of commercial and domestic architecture in the United States, work that he believed contained "the formula for the future." Surprised by the major halls of the Columbian Exposition, he urged his readers to discount their significance because they corresponded to no precise necessity, unlike the Loop, which was important for Western architecture because it did correspond to necessity. Hermant summarized his conclusions about American work at the annual meeting of the Société centrale des architectes français in May 1894 (*L'architecture*, 20 October 1894). See also, *Exposition universelle de Chicago en 1893, Comité 36, Génie civil. Travaux publics. Architecture. Rapport de M. Jacques Hermant, architecte de la ville de Paris* (Paris, 1894).

HESSE-WARTEGG, ERNST VON (1854–1918)—Prolific author of anthropological travel books, he published studies on China, Japan, Samoa, Siam, India, Korea, Tunis, and Egypt. Of his nine books on the New World, the best known were *Nord-America* (1881) and *Tausend und ein Tag im Occident* (1891). Though not well-known, his study of Chicago, *Chicago: Eine Weltstadt im amerikanischen Westen* (1893), was the most comprehensive European account of the city in the early 1890s. He attempted to explain why Chicago had become a *Weltstadt* so quickly and devoted specific chapters to its skyscrapers, commerce, park system, ethnic subgroups, women, and culture, as well as to Pullman and the Columbian Exposition. Hesse-Wartegg regarded Chicago—"das Museum der Neuzeit"—as a milestone in history, calling it "perhaps the most powerful human creation of all time." The city symbolized for him a new day in Western culture.

HINCKELDEYN, KARL (1847–1927)—Graduated from the Berlin Academy of Architecture in 1872. Won the Schinkel Prize for the design of a library in 1875 and two years later was appointed Königlicher Baumeister. After serving a year as chief writer for the *Centralblatt der Bauverwaltung*, he was named in 1884 as technical attaché of the German embassy in Washington, an assignment he held until 1887. He joined the Kulturministerium in Berlin in 1893 and then the Arbeitsministerium in 1896, heading its Hochbau Abteilung ten years later. He visited the United States only once, in the 1890s to cover the Columbian Exposition for the *Centralblatt*. Despite his failure to understand the depth of the classical revival, Hinckeldeyn's reputation as the foremost authority on American architecture in Germany remained unchallenged until the end of the 1890s. Between 1884 and 1895 he wrote more than three dozen articles or unpublished reports for the Ministry of Public Works in Berlin on the subject (see *Journal of the Society of Architectural Historians*, December 1972). His view of American architecture changed noticeably during the last fifteen years of the century. Initially, he criticized American architects for failing to understand and respect historic styles; in his introduction to Paul Graef's *Neubauten in Nordamerika* (1897), he commended them for knowing the difference between style and restatements of period styles.

HOFMANN, ALBERT (1854–1926)—Initially an architect in Baden, where he designed houses and churches, he became in 1886 the director of the Northern Bohemian Technical Museum in Reichenberg. Impressed by his writing, K. E. O. Fritsch, then editor of the *Deutsche Bauzeitung*, invited him to become his assistant editor in 1892, a position he held until he replaced Fritsch as editor in 1900. Well read and conscious of architecture's profound role in culture, he quietly encouraged new ideas. His comments about American architecture were perceptive; he sensed its strengths and vulnerability. Disappointed by the architecture at the Columbian Exposition, he argued that the White City had contradicted the myth about American cultural independence, proving instead that in a shrinking world, the United States was too young and artistically insecure to resist the seduction of Old World rhetoric. (See *Deutsche Bauzeitung,* 1892:29, 217; 1894:209; and 1895:605.)

Jaffe, Franz (b. 1855)—A painter, decorator, and architect, Jaffe was trained in Berlin at the Bau-Akademie and also at the Technische Hochschule in Charlottenburg. In 1886 he began his long association with the government, assuming responsibility for German exhibits at the world fairs in Melbourne (1888), Chicago (1893), and Paris (1900). He published *Neubauten in Grossbritannien* (1891) and *Ausstellungsbauten* (1906). As an archaeological restorer, his most important work was his decoration of the reconstructed Palace of Diocletian at Split. A member of the German delegation to the Columbian Exposition, Jaffe contributed a survey of recent American architecture to his government's *Amtlicher Bericht über die Weltausstellung in Chicago 1893* (1894) and also compiled a well-illustrated but undistinguished study of the major exhibition halls in Jackson Park, *Die Architektur der columbischen Welt-Ausstellung zu Chicago, 1893* (1895). Jaffe also wrote on American interior decoration in *Deutsche Bauzeitung* (1894:539) and *Innen-Dekoration* (July 1895). Some sources credit him as the author of *Türmhäuser in Nordamerika,* but I have been unable to verify this.

Kendall, John—British author of *American Memories* (1896), in which he wrote positively about Chicago's office blocks. He was one of the few European observers of the mid-1890s to discuss the atmosphere, materials, and artistic handling of interiors of the commercial buildings in the Loop. He focused on the Masonic Temple by Burnham and Root.

Kerr, Robert (1823–1904)—He studied architecture in his native Aberdeen. After a brief attempt to establish a practice in New York City, Kerr returned to Great Britain. By midcentury he had shifted from designing to criticism, advocating initially "unfettered originality" as a panacea for British architecture, but he became more conservative with age. In 1847 he was a founder of the Architectural Association and in 1864 published his most influential work, *The English Gentleman's House.* From 1861 to 1890 he was professor of the arts of construction at King's College, London, and for many years was the author of the lead article in the *Architect.* Kerr regarded himself as an American authority, often participating in discussions on the United States at the RIBA. His writings on American work, though supportive, as for example his editing of the third edition of Fergusson's *History of the Modern Styles of Architecture* (1891), also tended to be anachronistic, verbose, and overgeneralized. These weakness were evident in "The Problem of National American Architecture," *Architectural Record* (1893:121).

Kipling, Rudyard (1865–1936)—English author and winner of the 1907 Nobel Prize for Literature. His condescension toward the United States, expressed in his *American Notes,* provoked hostile criticism when published in 1891. He formed his initial opinions during a trip through the country in late 1889. Chicago symbolized for him the worst aspects of American urban life: greed, haste, incivility, lack of culture, monotony. Though he lived in Vermont from 1892 to 1896, after marrying a Vermont women he had met in London, his years in the United States were strained.

Kyllmann, Walter (1837–1913)—A government architect from Berlin, Kyllmann was a member of the International Jury on Architecture at the Columbian Exposition. He wrote a glowing tribute to Daniel Burnham and his staff for their work at Jackson Park, an example of the effusive praise expressed in some European architectural circles. Never, he claimed, had any civilization created architecture of such beauty, boldness, and size (*American Architect*, 28 October 1893).

LANDRY, JEAN—His *Hommes et choses d'Amérique,* with a preface written in 1894 though the book was not published until 1897, is a good example of French enthusiasm for American detached houses located along tree-lined residential streets. Though a nonprofessional foreign observer, he commented perceptively about American domestic life and architecture.

LANDSBERG, THEODOR (1847–1915)—From 1880 to 1907 he was a professor of architectural and engineering construction at the Technische Hochschule in Darmstadt. He traveled to the United States in 1893 to attend the Columbian Exposition and to visit major American cities. On returning to Germany he lectured frequently, sharing information he had acquired and arguing the future importance of iron in construction (*Centralblatt der Bauverwaltung,* 1894:165).

LANGE, KARL WILHELM FRANZ (1830–1916)—A graduate of the Berlin Academy of Architecture, Lange spent most of his life in Kassel working for the German government, primarily as a river engineer. Late in his career, he was responsible for dredging and constructing harbors along the Rhine. In 1882 he was named technical attaché at the German embassy in Washington, a post he held for two years. His lecture on constructional methods in the United States to the Society of German Architects and Engineers on 27 August 1884 (*Deutsche Bauzeitung,* 1884:550, 560, 571, 577), delivered also to the Architectural Society of Berlin on 22 and 29 November 1886 (*Deutsche Bauzeitung,* 1886:583, 595), signaled growing government interest in American approaches. In 1887 he published *Eigenthümlichkeiten im amerikanische Bauwesen.*

LEITHOLF, O.—Author of an article on technical aspects of tall buildings in the United States (*Zeitschrift für Bauwesen,* 1895:217).

LESSING, JULIUS (1843–1908)—An art history graduate of the University of Bonn, Lessing became the first director of the Museum of Industrial Arts in Berlin, writing on, among other subjects, Oriental carpets, porcelains, bronzes, Gothic and Italian furniture, and gold and silver. From 1871 to 1894 he also lectured at the Technische Hochschule in Berlin. In his comments on American architecture (*National-Zeitung,* 1893, no. 465), he underscored the importance of speed in the building process.

LINDAU, PAUL (1839–1919)—Studied philosophy and literature at the Universities of Leipzig, Halle, and Berlin before turning to journalism in the 1860s. Author of more than seventy-three books on diverse subjects, he also founded *Gegenwart* in 1871 and became publisher of *Nord und Süd* seven years later. After 1895 he became deeply involved in theater in Meiningen and Berlin. His comments about Chicago in *Altes und Neues aus der neuen Welt* (1893) are valuable for their insights and language. Lindau commented in detail about the Auditorium by Adler and Sullivan.

LOCKWOOD, H. W.—He may have worked for a period as an architect in a New York office. Lockwood spoke to the Sheffield Society of Architects and Surveyors in the winter of 1893–94 on "Architectural Practice in America," stressing the "extent to which the speed demanded from everybody in the States had affected the practice of architecture" (*Royal Institute of British Architects, Journal,* 1893–94:90).

LORDEREAU, GABRIEL—His travel account, *Du Havre à Chicago* (1894), is a good example of European opinion that judged contemporary American architecture as incoherent, insufficiently solid, and tasteless.

LUTAUD, AUGUSTE JOSEPH (b. 1847)—French physician who specialized in female medicine. He was editor of *Journal de médicine de Paris.* In 1896 Lutaud published *Aux États-Unis,* which contained frequent references to American architecture. Impressed by freestanding houses, he was opposed to the new commercial buildings, finding no justification for their development and fearing the influence they might exert on European cities. He interpreted the Columbian Exposition as a unifying experience for the United States.

MACRAE, DAVID (1837–1907)—A graduate of the University of Glasgow, he was a Scottish minister, a writer, and scholar. Macrae toured the United States in 1867–68, publishing his experiences and insights in *The Americans at Home* (2 vols., 1870). No visitor to Chicago in these years better understood the importance its citizens attached to speed and efficiency. His chapter on Chicago was entitled "The Lightning City."

MAIER, HERMANN—German writer, possibly an architect, who was impressed by the construction of walls and roofs in fireproofed office buildings (*Deutsche Bauzeitung,* 16 and 23 May 1894; 28 September 1895). Maier considered skeleton construction instructive but was disappointed that exposition planners had not used the event to demonstrate the advantages of iron and steel in architecture.

MAINARD, LOUIS (b. 1857)—A journalist and professor of literature in Paris, he wrote several books about the United States and Chicago: *Une cousine d'Amérique* (1891); *Livre d'or des voyages: l'Amérique* [1892]; and *Plus haut! Plus grand!! Le Chicago* (Paris, 1892), the last in collaboration with Paul Meyan (b. 1852), drama critic for *Le Pays.*

MEYER, JULIUS—Writing in *Land und Meer* (1895:246), Meyer credited American architects and engineers with the development of a new type of architecture that he called *Profanbauten.* His commentary was based on his study of tall buildings in New York City.

MEYER-BAESCHLIN, JOS.—He was an architect from Schaffhausen who collaborated with J. Lepori, an architect-engineer from Lugano, to write *Architektur, Baukonstruktionen und Baueinrichtung in nordamerikanische Städten,* published in Bern in 1894. Both were members of the Swiss delegation to the Columbian Exposition. The first book to be published on American architecture and construction in Switzerland, its contents are disappointing.

MONNIER, MARCEL (c. 1845)—Publicist and author, he was also a professor on the faculty of letters at the University of Geneva. As a correspondent for *Le Temps* (18 May 1893), he expressed the enthusiasm of many Europeans, particularly those untrained in architecture and engineering, about the poetic setting of Jackson Park.

MUELLER, OTTO H.—His reports from Chicago at the time of the exposition reflected the reactions of many Europeans. He considered the city dangerous, noisy, and dirty (*Zeitschrift des oesterreichischen Ingenieur- und Architekten-Vereines* (1 and 8 September 1893).

MUIRHEAD, JAMES FULLARTON (1853–1934)—For more than thirty-five years he was the English editor of Baedeker travel books. He authored the volumes on London, Great Britain, the United States, and Canada. Muirhead visited the United States in 1888 and then returned for a three-year stay, 1890–93. In 1898 he published *The Land of Contrasts,* in which he called Chicago the "city of contrasts," primarily because of the difference between its center and its residential neighborhoods.

MÜHLKE, KARL (b. 1851)—Berlin architect whose study of small, free-standing houses in the United States (*Centralblatt der Bauverwaltung,* 8 and 15 January 1887) was a major reason for the sudden rise in German interest in American domestic work during the last half of the 1880s.

NODET, ANTOINE-EUGÈNE HENRI (b. 1855)—A successful French architect with an office in Paris, he published a five-part study of the modern office building, relying heavily on Barr Ferree's *The Modern Office Building (1896)*. He encouraged closer cooperation between engineer and architect to develop a stronger connection between structure and design (*La construction moderne,* 1897:242, 256, 383, 309, 319).

PATERSON, ALEXANDER NISBET (1862–1947)—An architect who studied at the École des Beaux-Arts during 1883–86 and began independent practice in 1891 in Glasgow, where he designed banks, schools, churches, clubs, clinics, and office buildings. Active in numerous architectural societies, he was a member of Council of the RIBA and served a term as president of the Glasgow Architectural Association. Paterson was the Godwin Bursary winner in 1896, focusing on the technical aspects of domestic architecture in the eastern part of United States (*Royal Institute of British Architects, Journal,* 1898:309).

PITON, CAMILLE-MARIE (1842–1917)—Parisian architect and decorator who reported on the Centennial Exhibition in Philadelphia in 1876 for César Daly's *Revue générale de l'architecture et des travaux publics* (1877:167, 231, 254). He had a low opinion of American architecture, arguing designers in the United States paid too much attention to utilitarian questions and disregarded the lessons of the past.

PLANAT, PAUL (1839–1911)—Though active as a railroad engineer, he was more influential as an editor and lecturer on artistic and technical subjects. He founded *La construction moderne* in 1885 and edited it for twenty-six years. Between 1888 and 1895 Planat supervised the publication of *L'encyclopédie de l'architecture et de la construction* (13 vols.). He acknowledged change but welcomed it reluctantly. His *Encyclopédie* characterized American architecture as instructive, particularly in practical matters, but less successful in design. In an article in *La construction moderne* (12 October 1895), Planat asked if architecture in the United States was sufficiently original to be considered a new departure.

POSCHACHER, ANTON—He was an Austrian architect who wrote an informative, opinionated report on American architecture and the Centennial Exhibition in Philadelphia for his government in *Bericht über die Weltausstellung in Philadelphia 1876* (1877). At present, he declared, Europe had nothing to learn from the United States in architecture. America had developed too quickly and had been forced to build functionally. Necessity meant that architects devoted little time to "true architecture"; materialism had diverted their attention from higher goals. He predicted American architecture would not mature until the country had matured.

REUSCHE, FRIEDRICH—Author of *Chicago und Berlin: Alte und neue Bahnen im Ausstellungswesen* (1892). Objecting to the scale of the forthcoming Columbian Exposition, he called for greater simplicity and moderation in future international events.

RICKMAN, THOMAS MILLER (c. 1828–1912)—The son of the well-known architect Thomas Rickman (1776–1841), he was also an architect, but specialized in quantity surveying. Because he had visited the United States and Canada, he spoke as an authority on architecture in the New World at RIBA discussions in the mid-1880s. Rickman summarized his experiences in a fifty-six-page publication, *Notes on a Short Visit to Canada and the United States in August and September 1885*.

ROUSIERS, PAUL DE (1857–1934)—Respected French economist who focused on the modern industrial system, primarily in France, Britain, and the United States. He was interested in questions of trusts, labor, and the responsibility of the elite in contemporary societies. He was intrigued by the United States, not only because of its growing economic threat to Europe, but also because he believed business had become the determining factor in American culture. In *American Life* (1892), his principal study of the United States, Rousiers argued that Chicago and the Midwest, no longer the East, manifested the energy and confidence Europeans had grown to associate with the United States. He found ample evidence in Chicago reinforcing his contention Europe and North America were now in an age of "quick transformations" in which the imperative to act with dispatch took precedence over order, art, and history. In *American Life* he discussed the changing views of time, speed, and history that were fundamental to Chicago's meteoric rise as a commercial-industrial center in the late nineteenth century.

SADLER, JAMES HAYES (1827–1910)—Oxford-educated diplomat who served as British consul in France, Central and South America, and the United States. Stationed in Chicago during the early 1890s, Sadler filed numerous reports about the transformation of the Loop.

SAUVIN, GEORGES—In his *Autour de Chicago: Notes sur les États-Unis* (1893), Sauvin called Chicago the loftiest expression of American genius.

SCHLIEPMANN, HANS (1856–1929)—He was trained at the Berlin Bauakademie. Though he designed government, newspaper, and office buildings, as well as department stores, he was better known as a novelist, an aesthetician, and an art critic. His *Betrachtungen über Baukunst* (1891) was an inquiry into the architectural health of Germany. Schliepmann found the level of national taste higher in Britain and the United States. An outspoken advocate of simplicity and purposefulness, he commended recent American architecture, claiming that the future of Western design looked brighter there than in Europe, but he was not entirely convinced American architects, already insecure about their coarseness and beguiled by the artistic authority of old Europe, could continue to make practicality the determining criterion of their commercial buildings (*Kunstwart,* August 1894).

SÉDILLE, PAUL (1836–1900)—He was a well-known French architect and critic during the last three decades of the nineteenth century. His works included the Printemps department store in Paris, the lobby and foyer of the Theater of the Palais-Royal, buildings for the 1889 Parisian exposition, and numerous chateaux, villas, and apartments. He was honored as the vice-president of the Society of French Architects, as a gold medal winner of the society in 1889, and also served as an officer of the Legion of Honor. His most influential book was *L'architecture moderne en Angleterre* (1890). In the mid-1880s the *American Architect* invited him to comment on recent architecture in the United States (*American Architect,* 11 September 1886, and *Encyclopédie d'architecture,* 1886–87, 11). Impressed by detached houses in the United States, he thought American attempts at monumentality looked naive. Americans were wise to reject the "empty laws of symmetry," but they should not forget the wisdom of the past. One who had followed this course was Richard Morris Hunt; his buildings were both free and responsible.

SLATER, JOHN (1847–1924)—He was a respected London architect who served as president of the Architectural Association (1887–88) and vice-president of the RIBA (1900–1904). Though he had not visited the United States, Slater read journals to keep abreast of developments in American architecture and engineering. He was an enthusiastic supporter of the Godwin Bursary and commented positively during the discussions of the United States at the RIBA in the 1880s. He also called attention to the inventions and processes he thought were transforming American architecture (*Architect,* 6 May 1887).

SOISSONS, S.-C. DE (b. 1860)—The Count de Soissons was a committed aristocrat challenged by an age of social leveling and weakening traditions. His book *A Parisian in America* (1896) contains stimulating insights about American life, character, and architecture. He depicted Americans as impatient people insensitive to details and refinements. Eager to be up-to-date, which meant concerned with utility, comfort, and good sanitation, architects in the United States did not know history and gave lip service to beauty. The creators of skyscrapers exposed their naiveté by assuming that the obligatory luxury of their interiors compensated for this architecture's artistic deficiencies.

SPIERS, RICHARD PHENÉ (1838–1916)—He studied engineering at King's College, London, and architecture at the École des Beaux-Arts from 1858 to 1861. In Paris he made a number of American friends, including Henry Hobson Richardson. He also knew William Robert Ware, who established the architectural curriculum at MIT in Boston. In 1870 Spiers was appointed master of the Royal Academy architectural school and held the post until 1906. After 1870 he designed little but published several books on architecture and gained a reputation as a discriminating critic. On several occasions at the RIBA he commended architectural education in the United States and the importance of practicality in American work.

STATHAM, HENRY HEATHCOTE (1839–1924)—Though born and trained as an architect in Liverpool, Statham moved to London when he was thirty. He shifted gradually from designing to writing and in 1883 was named editor of the *Builder,* a position he held until 1908. He also wrote a number of readable books on architecture. His second field of interest was music, and he was an accomplished organist and music critic. Statham expressed his opinion of architecture in the United States in *Modern Architecture* (1897). He approved of the country's domestic architecture, noting its inventive planning, but had reservations about the primitivism of houses designed in the modern Romanesque style. He objected strongly to skeleton construction, contending concealed frames of iron or steel were not compatible with genuine architecture (*Builder,* 15 October 1892; 16 September 1893; and 4 September 1897).

STEAD, WILLIAM THOMAS (1849–1912)—Known for his feisty political responses and strong Christian beliefs, he became editor of the liberal *Pall Mall Gazette* in London in 1883 and in

1890 founded the popular *Review of Reviews.* His instinct for exposing wrongs made him a controversial journalist not only in England but also in Chicago. In 1894 he published *If Christ Came to Chicago!,* a scathing attack on the city's corruption, avarice, debauchery, poverty, and disregard of human life. Though his book annoyed city leaders, Stead presented evidence of a politically and socially soiled Chicago. In 1894 he also published *Chicago Today: The Labor War in America* as well as an article comparing Chicago and London in the *New Review* (May). In the *The Americanization of the World* (1901) Stead found merit in educational opportunities, new means and incentives for production, and the democratic institutions of the United States.

STEEVENS, GEORGE WARRINGTON (1869–1900)—A classical scholar at Oxford and Cambridge, he moved to London in 1893 to become a journalist, working initially for the *Pall Mall Gazette.* In 1896 he joined the *Daily Mail,* which sent him that year to the United States to cover the presidential contest between William Jennings Bryan and William McKinley. His articles from the United States formed the basis of *The Land of the Dollar* (1897). He called Chicago the "most amazing community in the world," stressing the dramatic contrasts of its ugliness and beauty and its state of perpetual flux. The last years of his short life were spent as a war reporter; he died of fever in the siege of Ladysmith, South Africa, during the Boer War.

STEPHANY, BRUNO (d. 1885)—He was one of the few professional German observers prior to the mid-1880s to comment on architecture in the United States. Calling Chicago the strangest American city he had visited, Stephany noted its citizens' energy, respect for speed, and practical outlook (*Wochenblatt für Architekten und Ingenieure,* 6, 13, and 20 May 1881). A Regierungsbaumeister, he died from a fall during construction at the University of Königsberg.

STEPHENS, A. G. (1865–1933)—Regarded as Australia's premier literary critic of the period between 1890 and 1930, Stephens wrote one of the more devastating foreign attacks on Chicago in his account of a trip through the United States, Canada, and Europe, published as *A Queenslander's Travel-Notes* (1894). With the exception of the exposition, almost nothing pleased him in the city. It was a squalid place unfit for human beings, filth was everywhere, the air laden with soot. He saw a relationship between "hustling" and the city's high suicide rate. The unflattering assessment of Chicago and the Columbian Exposition reprinted from the *Melbourne Argus* by the *Architect & Contract Reporter* of London (27 October 1893) was probably written by Stephens.

STRADAL, ADALBERT G.—He was an established Austrian engineer who published two articles about the United States in the *Zeitschrift des oesterreichischen Ingenieur- und Architekten-Vereines* in 1894, the first, a detailed account and explanation of the latest building regulations in both New York City and Chicago (16, 23 March), and the second, a summary of his address before the society on 26 April 1894, about American construction methods and materials (11 May).

TAYLOR, ANDREW THOMAS (1850–1937)—Born in Edinburgh, he studied architecture at the Royal Academy Schools and then practiced for a short period in London. About 1880 he toured Canada and the United States. This experience influenced his decision in 1883 to move to Montreal where he became one of Canada's most important architects until 1904 when he returned to London. Active in the RIBA, Taylor became a link between professionals on both sides of the Atlantic in the last two decades of the century.

TISSANDIER, ALBERT (b. 1839)—He was a French architect who studied at the École des Beaux-Arts. He was awarded the Croix de Chevalier for his ballooning exploits during the siege of Paris in 1870. Tissandier also traveled and sketched. His observations about American architecture in *Six mois aux États-Unis* (1886) were more perceptive than those of the majority of foreign travelers in the mid-1880s. He was impressed by Chicago's parks and by the efficiency of the cable car system and the meat-packing industry.

TOWNSEND, HORACE (1859–1922)—Townsend compared English and American architecture in the *Art Journal* (October 1892), arguing in a rambling manner that architects in the United States were producing better domestic and commercial work, while designers in Britain created better ecclesiastical and public buildings. He had resided in the United States from about 1879 until roughly 1891. On his return, he lectured at the Architectural Association in London (*Builder*, 4 April 1891) about houses in the United States and also to the RIBA (*Builder*, 19 December 1891) about American theaters.

UZANNE, LOUIS-OCTAVE (1852–1931)—He was a French writer, editor, and bibliophile. In 1880 he founded *Le livre: Revue mensuelle du monde littéraire*. Uzanne wrote a dozen books on varied subjects: art, fashion, women, book design. In 1893 he made a quick trip through the United States (*Vingt jours dans le nouveau monde*), concentrating on the major cities of the east and also Chicago. More pleased with New York, he considered Chicago a satanic, overpowering city.

VOGEL, F. RUDOLF (1849–1926)—He studied at the Technische Hochschule in Hannover. He evidently went to the United States during the 1870s, for he claimed to have worked there for Henry Hobson Richardson prior to his return to Hannover in 1879 or 1880. He published one of the earliest German studies on American detached houses for *Rombergs Zeitschrift für praktische Baukunst* (1880:325, 345). During his years as an architect in Hannover, Vogel designed a number of houses based on American prototypes. In 1897 he became chief editor of the *Deutsche Bauhütte*, a weekly journal that eventually concentrated on domestic architecture. In his effort to reform German domestic work, he used American work as an instructive example, publishing more than forty articles in the *Deutsche Bauhütte* about architecture in the United States (see *Journal of the Society of Architectural Historians*, December 1972). Though less impressed with American commercial work, he wrote occasional articles on the subject (*Zeitschrift des Architekten- und Ingenieur-Vereins zu Hannover* [1890:146] and *Deutsche Bauhütte* [22 and 29 September 1898]).

WATERHOUSE, ALFRED (1830–1905)—Considered one of Britain's leading architects during the 1870s and 1880s, he was president of the RIBA from 1888 to 1891. In 1888 he paid special tribute to Henry Hobson Richardson, explaining that his name had not been submitted for consideration for the institute's Gold Medal because of his premature death in 1886, before his work was fully appreciated by British architects (*Royal Institute of British Architects, Journal of Proceedings*, 9 February 1888). Several European architectural journals had acknowledged Richardson's death (*Architect*, 1886:306, 312, and 322; *Builder*, 22 May 1886; *Building News*, 21 May 1886; and *Centralblatt der Bauverwaltung*, 5 June 1886).

WILLS, HERBERT W. (d. 1937)—He designed numerous buildings in South Wales and in the London area. In the late 1880s he spent nine months in the United States, working for architectural firms in Boston and New York. Though he commended the energy of the American profession (*British Architect,* 6 December 1889), he thought British architects looking for fresh fields should first consider the countries of the empire. His career and advice were indicators of the increasing internationalization of architecture around 1890. After an active career, Wills became editor of the *Builder* (1913–18) and also the *Architect* (1918–26).

WOOD, HENRY TRUEMAN (1845–1929)—Educated at Cambridge, he went to work in the Patent Office in London in 1870 but two years later became editor of the *Journal of the Society of Arts.* From 1879 to 1917 he served as secretary of the society. He was a member of the royal commissions for the 1889 exposition in Paris and for the Columbian Exposition in Chicago. Wood deserves much credit for his efforts to convince British manufacturers to participate. They had been angered by the McKinley Tariff and made hesitant by rumors that the fair in Chicago was too ambitious an undertaking to be well organized or completed on time (*American Architect,* 7 June 1890; *Journal of the Society of Arts,* 26 September 1890; and *Nineteenth Century,* April 1892).

Bibliography

Because one of the themes of this study is when and where European curiosity about Chicago's Loop developed, the first section of the bibliography—books and articles published between 1860 and 1914—has been arranged chronologically and separated into four national-linguistic categories: English (United Kingdom), French (France and Belgium), German (Germany, Austria, Switzerland), and American (United States). Anything written by a European that was published, reprinted, or discussed in an American journal is included in the applicable European national-linguistic category. On the other hand, any American articles published or discussed in European journals are also included in the appropriate European category. Editorials are identified as such and are gathered under that key word within the alphabetical listings of article titles.

The unindexed *Chicago Tribune* in these years is an invaluable source of information. In the second section of this bibliography, sources pertinent to this study have been arranged chronologically and divided into seven thematic categories: A. Conditions, Environment, and Activities of Central Chicago and the Loop; B. Commercial Buildings and Real Estate; C. Concerns about Tall Buildings; D. Residential and Suburban Chicago; E. Image, Reputation, and Aspirations of the City; F. Business and Labor; G. Columbian Exposition.

The final section includes books and articles pertinent to the subject published since 1914.

Books and Articles, 1860–1914

1860–69

"A City Elevated." *Chamber's Journal of Popular Literature* 35 (26 January 1861): 49–50.

Deedes, Henry. *Sketches of the South and West*. Edinburgh and London: William Blackwood, 1869.

Gérard, A. G. *Itinéraire de Québec à Chicago*. Montreal: C. O. Beauchemin and Valois, 1868.

"New Paris." *London Quarterly Review* 29 (January 1868): 330–62.

Peto, S. Morton. *The Resources and Prospects of America*. London and New York: Alexander Strahan, 1866.

Zinke, Barham. *Last Winter in the United States*. London: John Murray, 1868.

1870–74

"Amerikanischer Feuerwachthurm." *Baugewerks-Zeitung* 6 (15 February 1874): 95.
"États-Unis: La tour gigantesque." *Gazette des architectes et du bâtiment,* 2d ser., 3, no. 6 (1874):
    47–48.
"Exposition universelle de Philadelphie en 1876." *Gazette des architectes et du bâtiment,* 2d ser.,
    3, no. 1 (1874): 6.
Fergusson, James. *History of the Modern Styles of Architecture.* London: John Murray, 1873.
Frignet, Ernst, and Edmond Garrey. *États-Unis d'Amérique: Les états au North-West et Chi-
    cago.* Paris: Imprimerie Jouaust, 1871.
Greenwood, Grace. *New Life in New Lands: Notes of Travel.* New York: J. B. Ford, 1873.
Gruner. "Der Yankee-Styl." *Allgemeine Bauzeitung* 39 (1874): 59–62.
H.A. "House Architecture in America." *Irish Builder* 16 (15 August 1874): 230–31.
Hall, Newman. *From Liverpool to St. Louis.* London: George Routledge, 1870.
Kist, Leopold. *Amerikanisches.* Mainz: Franz Kirchheim, 1871.
Macrae, David. *The Americans at Home.* 2 vols. Edinburgh: Edmonson and Douglas, 1870.
Malézieux, Ém. *Souvenirs d'une mission aux États-Unis d'Amérique.* Paris: Dunod, 1874.
"Proposed City Hall, Chicago." *Builder* 32 (25 July 1874): 628–29.
Robertson, William, and F. W. Robertson. *Our American Tour.* Edinburgh: Privately printed,
    1871.
Watson, John. *Souvenir of a Tour in the United States and Canada.* Glasgow: Privately print-
    ed, 1872.

1875

English

"Architects in America." *Builder* 33 (18 September 1875): 845.
"The Centennial International Exhibition of Philadelphia for 1876." *Building News* 29 (8
    October 1875): 383–84.
Fogerty, William. "On Some Differences between British and American Achitectural Prac-
    tice." *Irish Builder* 17 (1, 15 March 1875): 68–69, 82–84. Also in: *Architect* 13 (6, 13 March
    1875): 140–42, 162–63.
———. "On the Conditions and Prospects of Architecture in the United States." *Irish Build-
    er* 17 (15 May, 1 June 1875): 132–34, 146–48. Also in *Practical Magazine* 6 (1876): 77–82.
"The International Exhibition of 1876." *Engineering* 20 (30 July, 6 August 1875): 89–92, 123–
    25.
"Mr. Gladstone on Art." *Architect* 14 (20 November 1875): 285.
Robson, E. R. "Design in America and England." *Builder* 33 (9 October 1875): 913.
"[*Tribune* Building, New York]." *Building News* 28 (16 June 1875): 796.

French

"L'exposition de Philadelphie." *Gazette des architectes et du bâtiment,* 2d ser., 4, no. 17, 18 (1875):
    131–32, 138–39.
"Exposition internationale de Philadelphie en 1876." *Gazette des architectes et du bâtiment,*
    2d ser., 4, no. 22 (1875): 174–75.
"A Frenchman in New York." *Appleton's Journal* 13 (3 April 1875): 431–34.

German

Funk. "Die Gebäude der internationalen Ausstellung zu Philadelphia im Jahre 1876." *Zeitschrift des Architekten- und Ingenieur-Vereins zu Hannover* 21, no. 4 (1875): 445–68. Also in *Notizblatt des Architekten* 1 (1875): 38–48.
Grunner [Gruner]. "Über amerikanische Bauweise." *Allgemeine Bauzeitung* 40 (1875): 77–80.

1876

English

"Cast-Iron Construction in the United States: Messrs. Lord and Taylor Dry-Goods Store, Broadway, New York." *British Architect* 5 (18 February 1876): 88.
Davenport, M[ontague]. *Under the Gridiron: A Summer in the United States and the Far West.* London: Tinsley Brothers, 1876.
Fogerty, William. "Hints from American Architectural Practice." *Van Nostrand's Engineering Magazine* 15 (September 1876): 246–52.
———. "Hints from American Practice." *Irish Builder* 18 (1, 15 February 1876): 34–37, 47–48. Also in: *Builder* 34 (26 February 1876): 189–91; *Architect* 15 (26 February 1876): 126–27.
Lewis, Charles E. *Two Lectures on a Short Visit to America.* London: Privately printed, 1876.
Montgomery, James. "Description of the New Offices of the *New York Tribune*." *British Architect* 6 (14 July 1876): 19–21.
"The Philadelphia Exhibition." *Building News* 30 (12 May 1876): 461–62.
"The Philadelphia Exhibition." *Engineering* 21–22 (12 May, 9 June, 28 July 1876): 379, 497, 79.
Sweny, Hugh Willoughby. "Contributions to the International Exhibition, Philadelphia." *Art Journal* 38 (August, December 1876): 245–52, 361–70.

French

"L'exposition de Philadelphie." *Gazette des architectes et du bâtiment,* 2d ser., 5, no. 12 (1876): 95–98.
Molinari, M. G. de. *Lettres sur les États-Unis et le Canada.* Paris: Hachette, 1876.

German

"Die baulichen Anlagen zur Weltausstellung in Philadelphia." *Baugewerks-Zeitung* 8 (19, 26 March, 2 April 1876): 168–69, 184–86, 200–201.
Brachvogel, Udo. "Die philadelphier Weltausstellung." *Ueber Land und Meer* 36 (1876): 544–45, 554, 604, 614–15, 723–24, 963–65.
Dietrich, E. "Die Weltausstellung in Philadelphia im Jahre 1876." *Deutsche Bauzeitung* 10 (8, 29 July, 2 September, 21 October, 4 November 1876): 273–74, 303–5, 353–56, 426–29, 444–47.

1877

English

Archer, T. C. "On the Probable Influence Which the Centennial Exhibition Will Have on the Progress of Art in America." *Art Journal* 39 (January 1877): 7–8.
Bain, James. "American Locks." *Architect* 17 (30 June 1877): 413.

Leng, Sir John. *America in 1876*. Dundee: *Dundee Advertiser* Office, 1877.
"Observatory Tower [Fairmont Park Tower, 1876 Centennial]." *Engineering* 24 (28 December 1877): 490.
Turland, Ephraim. *Notes of a Visit to America*. Manchester: Johnson and Rawson, 1877.

French

Exposition internationale et universelle de Philadelphie 1876. Paris, 1877.
"Extraits et résumés [rebuilding in Chicago after the fire]." *La semaine des constructeurs* 1 (10 February 1877): 364–65.
"Maison en carton aux États-Unis." *La semaine des constructeurs* 2 (15 December 1877): 286.
Morton. "Les journaux étrangers: L'*American Architect and Building News*." *La semaine des constructeurs* 1 (6 October 1877): 165.
Pictou, M. C. [C. Piton]. "American Architecture from a French Standpoint." *American Architect* 2–3 (22 December 1877, 16 February 1878): 408–9, 57–58.
Piton, C. "Lettres de Philadelphie." *Revue générale de l'architecture et des travaux publics,* 4th ser., 4 (1877): 167–73, 231–38, 254–59.
Planat, P. "Chronique: La caisse des écoles." *La semaine des constructeurs* 1 (17 March 1877): 421–23.

German

Poschacher, Anton. "Architektur und öffentliche Bauten." In *Bericht über die Weltausstellung in Philadelphia 1876,* no. 14. Vienna, 1877.

1878

English

A.W.L. "Chicago and Its Architecture." *Building News* 34 (8 March 1878): 233–34.
"English Industries and American Competition." *Engineering* 26 (5, 26 July, 9, 30 August, 13 September, 27 December 1878): 1–2, 72–74, 114–16, 171, 211–14, 507–8; 27 (3, 17, 31 January, 28 February, 18 April 1879): 2–3, 47–48, 86–87, 170–71, 317–20.
Ferguson, Fergus. *From Glasgow to Missouri and Back*. Glasgow: Thomas D. Morison, 1878.
"Heating Towns from a Common Center." *Builder* 36 (1 June 1878): 573.
"'Imitated Architecture' in New York." *Builder* 36 (18 May 1878): 505.
"Marble, Iron, and Zinc Palaces in New York." *Builder* 36 (27 April 1878): 422–23.
"New York Household Taste." *Builder* 36 (11 May 1878): 477–78.
Vivian, H. Hussey. *Notes of a Tour in America*. London: Edward Stanford, 1878.
"The Women's Hotel, New York." *Builder* 36 (18 May 1878): 505.

German

Becker, Joh. H. "Ueber englische und amerikanische Hauseinrichtung." *Wissenschaftliche Beilage der Leipziger Zeitung,* 31 January, 3 February 1878, 49–51, 53–56.
Dietrich, Emil. "Reisebericht über die Philadelphia-Ausstellung 1876." *Baugewerks-Zeitung* 10 (27 October 1878): 621–22ff.
F. "Architekten-Verein zu Berlin [lecture by Herr Bartels on Chicago]." *Deutsche Bauzeitung* 12 (13 April 1878): 150–52.

Strohmayer. "Auszug aus dem Vortrage des Herrn dipl. Ingenieure Strohmayer: Über das amerikanische Wohnhaus." *Wochenschrift des oesterreichischen Ingenieur- und Architekten-Vereines* 33 (23 February 1878): 31–32.

1879

English

"American Building and General Ironmongery." *Irish Builder* 21 (1 January 1879): 4.
"Hospital Construction and Organization." *Builder* 37 (27 December 1879): 1417–19.
Loudon, J. B. *A Tour through Canada and the United States of America.* Coventry: Curtis and Beamish, 1879.
"Mechanical Genius in America." *British Architect* 12 (14 November 1879): 192–93.
Vizetelly, Henry. *Berlin under the New Empire.* 2 vols. London: Tinsley Brothers, 1879.

French

Turenne, Le Comte Louis de. *Quatorze mois dans l'Amérique du Nord.* 2 vols. Paris: A. Quantin, 1879.

German

Dietrich, Emil. *Reiseskizzen: Gesammelt auf einer im Sommer 1876 bei Gelegenheit der Philadelphia-Ausstellung im Auftrage des Handels Ministers ausgeführten Studienreise nach Nordamerika über England.* Berlin, 1879.

1880

English

"Architectural Education in New York." *Architect* 23 (10 April 1880): 256–57.
Berry, C. B. *The Other Side, How It Struck Us.* London: Griffith and Farron, 1880.
Day, Samuel Phillips. *Life and Society in America.* London: Neumann, 1880.
"Healthy Dwellings." *Builder* 39 (4 September 1880): 283–85.
"House Architecture." *Builder* 38 (6 March 1880): 269–71.
"Illustration: The Government Building, Chicago." *Irish Builder* 22 (1 March 1880): 67.
Stevenson, J. J. *House Architecture.* 2 vols. London: Macmillan, 1880.
[Trelat, M.]. "Contemporary Architecture from a French Point of View." *Builder* 38 (10 April 1880): 432.

French

"Maisons d'école." *La semaine des constructeurs* 4 (28 February 1880): 412–13.

German

"Central-Heizung für ganze Stadttheile in New-York." *Baugewerks-Zeitung* 11 (9 February 1880): 70–71.
Frohwein, Paul. "Das new-yorker Staatszeitung-Gebäude." *Zeitschrift für praktische Baukunst* 40, no. 22 (1880): 425–28.
Vogel, R. "Einiges über Villenbau in den Vereinigten Staaten von Nord-Amerika." *Zeitschrift für praktische Baukunst* 40, no. 17–18 (1880): 325–28, 346–49.

American

Hayes, A. "The Metropolis of the Prairies." *Harper's Magazine,* October 1880, 711–31.

1881

English

"The Godwin Bursary [purpose and stipulations]." *Royal Institute of British Architects, Proceedings* (27 October 1881): 46–48.
Hardy, Mary [Lady Duffus]. *Through Cities and Prairie Lands: Sketches of an American Tour.* New York: R. Worthington, 1881.

French

H.B. "Villa américaine." *Gazette des architectes et du bâtiment,* 2d ser., 10, no. 36 (1881): 213–14.

German

Br.St. [Bruno Stephany]. "Geschäftshaus in Cincinnati." *Wochenblatt für Architekten und Ingenieure* 3 (25 November 1881): 480–81.
F.W. "Verschiebung eines Hauses in Boston." *Deutsche Bauzeitung* 15 (28 December 1881): 585–86.
Stephany, Br. "Zwanglose Briefe aus Amerika." *Wochenblatt für Architekten und Ingenieure* 3 (6, 13, 20 May 1881): 184–85, 194–95, 204–5.

American

Beard, George M. *American Nervousness: Its Causes and Consequences.* New York: G. P. Putnam's Sons, 1881.
Blake, Anna Bowman. "Some Impressions of an Open-Air People." *Lippincott's Magazine,* December 1881, 571–79.

1882

English

"American Architecture in Its Constructive and Sanitary Aspects." *Builder* 43 (23 December 1882): 803–5.
"Architectural Frenzy in the New World." *Architect* 28 (16 September 1882): 167–68.
"The Architectural Treatment of Iron." *Builder* 42 (4 February 1882): 122–23.
"Architecture in America." *Architect* 28 (9 September 1882): 157–58.
"Continental Gatherings [backwardness of American architecture]." *Builder* 43 (19 August 1882): 233–34.
Freeman, Edward A. "Some Points in American Speech and Customs." *Longman's Magazine,* 1882, 80–98, 314–34.
Gale, Arthur John. "American Architecture from a Constructional Point of View." *Royal Institute of British Architects, Transactions* (1882–83): 45–56.
———. "The Godwin Bursary: Report of a Tour in the United States." *Royal Institute of British Architects, Transactions* (1882–83): 57–64.

———. "The Godwin Bursary 1882: Tour in the United States." *Royal Institute of British Architects, Proceedings* (21 December 1882): 42–45.

"Growth of the American Railway System." *Builder* 42 (11 March 1882): 298.

"Iron Architecture in the United States." *Architect* 28 (30 December 1882): 407–8.

Marshall, Walter. *Through America. Or Nine Months in the United States.* London: Sampson Low, Marston, Searle and Rivington, 1882.

"Some Publications on Decorative Design [concern in United States for comfort, not for art]." *Builder* 43 (18 November 1882): 641–42.

French

E.D.L. "Correspondance des États-Unis: Le génie civil et l'architecture." *Encyclopédie d'architecture,* 3d ser., 1 (1882): 62–65.

German

Bodenstedt, Friedrich M. *Vom Atlantischen zum Stillen Ocean.* Leipzig: F. A. Brockhaus, 1882.

Stephany, Br. "Bankhaus in New York." *Wochenblatt für Architekten und Ingenieure* 4 (17 March 1882): 113.

1883

English

"American Cottages." *Building News* 44 (1 June 1883): 747–48.

"Architectural Style and Criticism in the States." *Builder* 45 (15 September 1883): 344–45.

"Buildings and Fittings in the United States." *Builder* 45 (29 September 1883): 407–8.

Congdon, H. M. "An American Style of Architecture." *Architect* 29 (31 March 1883): 216–17.

"Dow's Stores, Brooklyn, New York." *Engineering* 36 (19 October, 2 November 1883): 362–63, 402–3.

Freeman, Edward A. "The Architecture of American Cities." *American Architect* 13 (24 February 1883): 91.

———. *Some Impressions of the United States.* New York: Henry Holt, 1883.

Greenwood, Thomas. *A Tour in the States and Canada: Out and Home in Six Weeks.* London: L. Upcott Gill, 1883.

"Labour and Wages in the Old World and the New." *Builder* 45 (29 September 1883): 408–9.

Sala, George Augustus. *America Revisited: From the Bay of New York to the Gulf of Mexico and from Lake Michigan to the Pacific.* 2 vols. London: Vizetelly, 1883.

"Sky Building in New York." *Building News* 45 (7 September 1883): 363–64.

"Very tall Building." *Architect* 30 (15 September 1883): 155–56.

French

C.H. [Ch. Haussoullier]. "Chalet à Evanston." *Gazette des architectes et du bâtiment,* 2d ser., 12, no. 39 (1883): 233.

Daly, César. "L'Amérique à la recherche d'un procédé de délassement." *Revue générale de l'architecture et des travaux publics,* 4th ser., 10 (1883): 82–83.

Haussonville, Gabriel de. *À travers les États-Unis.* Paris: Calmann Lévy, 1883.

"Hôtel privé à Chicago." *Gazette des architectes et du bâtiment,* 2d.ser., 12, no. 36 (1883): 215.

Léris, G. de. "L'habitation américaine." *Revue des arts décoratifs* 4 (1883): 116–23.

———. "La maison américaine." *Le moniteur des architectes,* n.s., 17 (1883): 5–10.

German

"Ausführung und Kosten öffentlicher Gebäude in den Vereinigten Staaten von Nordamerika." *Centralblatt der Bauverwaltung* 3 (29 September 1883): 357–58.
"Die Navarro Apartment-Häuser am Central-Park von New-York." *Deutsches Baugewerksblatt* 2 (1883): 742–43.
Z. "Vermischtes: Technische Schulen in Amerika." *Centralblatt der Bauverwaltung* 3 (3 November 1883): 402.

American

Land, John E. *Chicago: The Future Metropolis of the New World.* Chicago: By the author, 1883.
Stillman, W. J. "Characteristics of London." *Century Magazine,* October 1883, 821–28.

1884

English

"An American Exhibition in London." *Engineering* 37 (30 June 1884): 553–54.
"American Sanitation." *Engineering* 38 (14 November 1884): 455–56.
"American Technical Ability." *American Architect* 15 (24 May 1884): 249.
"An Architects' Convention in America [initial meeting of Western Association of Architects in Chicago]." *Architect* 32 (27 December 1884): 413–14.
"The Architectural Employment of Iron." *Architect* 31 (22 March 1884): 185–86.
"The Atmosphere of Art." *Architect* 32 (11 October 1884): 225–26.
"Berlin in 1884." *Blackwood's Edinburgh Magazine,* July, August 1884, 1–20, 230–49.
Blackall, C. H. "Some Features of American Construction." *British Architect* 22 (19 September 1884): 133–34.
Boult, Joseph. "Architectural Revivalism." *British Architect* 22 (11 July 1884): 17–18.
"Building in America." *Architect* 32 (1 November 1884): 285.
"Building in New York." *Architect* 31 (7 June 1884): 374–75.
Clark, T. M. "Fire-proof Building in New York." *British Architect* 22–23 (26 December, 2 January 1884): 314–15, 10–11.
"The Coming Renaissance." *Architect* 32 (23 August 1884): 111–12.
"English Architecture 1884." *Builder* 46 (5 January 1884): 1–11.
Griffin, Lepel Henry. *The Great Republic.* London: Chapman and Hall, 1884.
Hardman, William. *A Trip to America.* London: T. Vickers Wood, 1884.
"Illustrations [Pullman Building, Chicago]." *Building News* 46 (11 April 1884).
Kerr, Robert. "English Architecture Thirty Years Hence." *British Architect* 21 (16 May 1884): 242–44.
———. "On the Lofty Buildings of New York City." *Sanitary Engineer* 9 (January 1884): 113.
"The Magnitude of the Forest Products of the United States." *British Architect* 22 (10 October 1884): 170.
"The New York Produce Exchange." *Architect* 31 (22 March 1884): 191.
"Notes on Current Events: Architectural Criticism in the Daily Press." *British Architect* 23 (29 February 1884): 98–99.

"Notes on Current Events: On American Gas Jets." *British Architect* 21 (12 April 1884): 178–79.

Sedding, J. D. "The Modern Architect and His Art." *British Architect* 22 (14 November 1884): 232–36.

South, Colin. *Out West.* London: Wyman, 1884.

Spiers, R. Phené. "On the French Diplome d'Architecture and the German System of Architectural Education." *British Architect* 21 (23, 30 May 1884): 258–59, 271–72.

"The Steam-Users of Chicago and Smoke Consumption." *British Architect* 22 (5 September 1884): 118.

Thomas, W. Cave. "America's Stand-Point with Reference to the Fine Arts." *Builder* 46 (12 January 1884): 54–55.

French

Jaÿ, Aimé. *À travers les États-Unis d'Amérique.* Niort: L. Clouzot, 1884.

"Les maisons en Amérique." *Gazette des architectes et du bâtiment,* 2d ser., 13, no. 13 (1884): 78.

German

Lange, [Franz]. "Das Bauwesen in den Vereinigten Staaten von Nordamerika." *Centralblatt der Bauverwaltung* 4 (3, 6 September 1884): 355–58, 365–66. Also in: *Schweizerische Bauzeitung* 4 (13, 20, 27 September, 4 October 1884): 70–72, 78–79, 84–85, 87–89; *Deutsche Bauzeitung* 18 (15, 22, 29 November, 3 December 1884): 550–51, 560–62, 571–74, 577–79.

"Moderne Wohnhäuser in den grossen Städten Amerikas." *Schweizerische Bauzeitung* 3 (10 May 1884): 112.

"Personalien [K. Hinckeldeyn, first architect appointed to German Embassy in Washington]." *Schweizerische Bauzeitung* 3 (22 March 1884): 72.

"Personen-Aufzüge in öffentlichen und Privat-Gebäuden Nordamerikas." *Centralblatt der Bauverwaltung* 4 (16 August 1884): 333–35.

R. "Die Wohnungs-Karawanserien." *Deutsches Baugewerksblatt* 3 (1884): 741–43.

"Vermischtes: Die Statue der Freiheit." *Wochenblatt für Architekten und Ingenieure* 6 (7 October 1884): 407–8.

v.R. "Ein amerikanisches Familienhaus." *Deutsches Baugewerksblatt* 3 (1884): 38–41.

W.S. "Ein amerikanisches Mietshaus." *Deutsche Bauzeitung* 18 (27 September 1884): 461–62.

Ward, W. E. "Konstruktion in Eisen und Beton." *Baugewerks-Zeitung* 16 (26 April 1884): 306–7.

American

Butler, Anna Maynard. "The Berlin of To-Day." *Lippincott's Magazine,* March 1884, 217–24.

1885

English

"A Chat about Elevators." *British Architect* 24 (18 December 1885): 269–74.

Clark, T. M. "Building Construction in New York." *British Architect* 23 (27 February 1885): 103–4.

Gale, A. J. "English Impressions of American Architecture." *Builder* 49 (19 December 1885): 853–55.

Gass, John B. "The Godwin Bursary: Portions of Report of a Visit to the United States of America and to Canada." *Royal Institute of British Architects, Transactions*, n.s., 2 (1885–86): 145–52.

———. "Some American Methods." *Royal Institute of British Architects, Transactions*, n.s., 2 (1885–86): 129–44.

"House at Narragansett Pier." *British Architect* 24 (25 December 1885): 281.

Kerr, Robert. "Architecture Thirty Years Hence." *British Architect* 23 (13 February 1885): 82.

"The New Victoria Hotel, Manchester." *British Architect* 24 (25 September 1885): 134–37.

"Notes on Current Events: American Exhibition (London)." *British Architect* 23 (2 January 1885): 5.

"Retrospective—1884." *British Architect* 23 (2 January 1885): 1–2.

White, Arnold. "The Nomad Poor of London." *Contemporary Review* 47 (May 1885): 714–26.

French

"American 'Picturesque Architecture' as Seen from a French Standpoint." *American Architect* 18 (14 November 1885): 230.

"Les constructions à New York." *Gazette des architectes et du bâtiment*, 2d ser., 14, no. 10 (1885): 56–57, 62–63.

Mandat-Grancey, E. de. *En visite chez l'oncle Sam: New York et Chicago.* Paris: Plon, 1885.

Trasenster, Paul. *Aux États-Unis: Notes de voyage d'un ingénieur.* Paris: Auguste Ghis, and Liège: C. A. Desoer, 1885.

German

Hinckeldeyn, [Karl]. "Die Begründung eines Verbandes der 'Architekten des Westens' in Nordamerika." *Centralblatt der Bauverwaltung* 5 (24 January 1885): 38–40.

———. "Vermischtes: Das neue Börsengebäude der Handelskammer in Chicago." *Centralblatt der Bauverwaltung* 5 (29 August 1885): 368.

———. "Zeitschriften für Bau-und Eisenbahnwesen in Nordamerika." *Centralblatt der Bauverwaltung* 5 (19 September 1885): 391–92.

"Vermischtes: Ueber den Kunstwerth amerikanischer Bauwerke." *Centralblatt der Bauverwaltung* 5 (5 September 1885): 376.

American

"Adams Express Building, Chicago." *American Architect* 17 (14 February 1885): 477.

Editorial. "[Board of Trade Building]." *Inland Architect* 5 (April 1885): 46.

———. "[*Inland Architect* objects to 'Western Vernacular']." *Inland Architect* 6 (August 1885): 3.

Jenney, W. L. B. "The Construction of a Heavy, Fireproof Building on a Compressible Soil." *Inland Architect* 6 (December 1885): 100.

"A Mammoth Opera House [Adler and Sullivan's temporary opera house]." *Inland Architect* 5 (March 1885): 25.

Rauch, John H. "Chicago-River Pollution." *Science* 6 (10 July 1885): 27–30.

Sullivan, Louis H. "Characteristics and Tendencies of American Architecture." *Inland Architect* 6 (November 1885): 58–59.

"Synopsis of Building News: Chicago [concern about fireproofing]." *Inland Architect* 5 (March 1885): 27.

"Synopsis of Building News: Chicago, Ill. [advantages of tall buildings]." *Inland Architect* 5 (February 1885): 14.

1886

English

"American Architects in Congress [admission of women to WAA]." *Architect* 35 (29 January 1886): 56–57.

"American Architecture as Seen by English Architects." *American Architect* 19 (10 April 1886): 175–77.

"An American Convention of Architects." *British Architect* 26 (31 December 1886): 623–24.

"An American Gymnasium." *British Architect* 26 (24 December 1886): 619.

"American Villa Architecture." *Builder* 51 (25 December 1886): 907.

Brassey. "A Flying Visit to the United States." *Nineteenth Century* 20 (December 1886): 901–12.

Campbell, John Kerr. *Through the United States of America and Canada.* London: S. W. Partridge, 1886.

"The Chicago Convention." *Architect* 36 (24 December 1886): 360–61.

Editorial. "Studebaker Building by Beman Illustrated in *British Architect.*" *Inland Architect* 7 (March 1886): 19.

Gass, John B. "American Sanitation." *Architect* 36 (24 September, 1 October 1886): 187–88, 200–201.

———. "The Sanitary Institute at York: American Sanitation." *Engineering* 42 (1 October 1886): 352–53.

———. "Some American Methods." *Royal Institute of British Architects, Journal of Proceedings,* n.s., 2 (18 March 1886): 179–82. Also in *British Architect* 25 (26 March 1886): 323.

"The Home Insurance Building." *Irish Builder* 28 (15 May 1886): 143.

"A House at Nahant, America," *British Architect* 26 (17 September 1886): 264.

"The Late H. H. Richardson." *Architect* 35 (21 May 1886): 306–7.

"The Late H. H. Richardson, of Brookline, Mass." *Building News* 50 (21 May 1886): 817–18.

"A Modern American House." *British Architect* 25 (5 February 1886): 129.

Money, Edward. *The Truth about America.* London: Sampson Low, Marston, Searle, and Rivington, 1886.

"Our Illustrations: A Chicago Building [Studebaker Building]." *British Architect* 25 (29 January 1886): 102.

"Our Illustrations: New Business Premises for Mr. J. Liscombe, Newport." *British Architect* 26 (10 December 1886): 542.

"Public Works in Chicago in 1885." *British Architect* 26 (27 August 1886): 214.

Rickman, Thomas Miller. *Notes on a Short Visit to Canada and the United States in August and September 1885.* London: T. Bosworth, 1886.

"Royal Institute of British Architects: Some American Methods." *Architect* 35 (19 March 1886): 174–75.

"Royal Institute of British Architects: The Late Mr. Richardson." *Architect* 35 (21 May 1886): 306–7, 312.

"The Seventh Ordinary Meeting." *Royal Institute of British Architects, Journal of Proceedings* 2 (4 March 1886): 161–62.

"Superiority of American Goods." *Engineering* 41 (28 May 1886): 527.

Wight, P. B. "The Late Mr. Richardson." *Architect* 35 (28 May 1886): 322–24.

French

"American Architecture as Seen by the French." *American Architect* 19 (1 May 1886): 209–10.

L'architecture américaine. Vol. 1: Édifices publics et établissements privés; Vol. 2: Habitations urbaines; Vol. 3: Habitations suburbaines. Paris: André, Daly fils, 1886.

"Bibliothèque publique à Malden, Mass." *Le moniteur des architectes,* n.s., 20 (1886): 46–47.

Daly, César. "Maisons américaines." *Revue générale de l'architecture et des travaux publics* 4th ser., 13 (1886): 23–25.

Daly, Marcel. "Un coffre-fort monumental." *La semaine des constructeurs* 10 (9 January 1886): 330–32.

———. "Villas et maisons de campagne américaines." *La semaine des constructeurs* 10 (12 June 1886): 594–96.

Editorial. "[*La semaine des constructeurs* on American work]." *Inland Architect* 7 (July 1886): 95.

"The Mercantile Trust and Deposit Co., Baltimore, Maryland." *Le moniteur des architectes,* n.s., 20 (1886): 48.

Sédille, Paul. "American Architecture from a French Standpoint." *American Architect* 20 (11 September 1886): 122–24.

———. "Lettres sur l'Amérique: L'architecture américaine jugée par un critique français." *Encyclopédie d'architecture,* 3d ser., 5 (1886–87): 11–16.

Tissandier, Albert. *Six mois aux États-Unis.* Paris: G. A. Masson, 1886.

German

"Betrifft Geschäftsgebäude und Wohnhäuser in Chicago." *Centralblatt der Bauverwaltung* 6 (20 October 1886): 415.

"Das Geschäftshaus der 'Newyork' Gesellschaft in Berlin." *Baugewerks-Zeitung* 18 (20 November 1886): 925.

Hinckeldeyn, [Karl]. "Die Arbeiterstadt Pullman bei Chicago." *Centralblatt der Bauverwaltung* 6 (30 January 1886): 45–46.

———. "Die Entwicklung der Arbeiterstadt Pullman bei Chicago." *Centralblatt der Bauverwaltung* 6 (13 March 1886): 104.

———. "Grundsätze für Wettbewerbungen und Forderung von Staatsdiplomen für Architekten in Nord-America." *Centralblatt der Bauverwaltung* 6 (9 January 1886): 11–13.

———. "Henry H. Richardson." *Centralblatt der Bauverwaltung* 6 (5 June 1886): 221–22.

Lange, [Franz]. "Vergleichung amerikanischer und deutscher Bauweise." *Deutsche Bauzeitung* 20 (4, 11 December 1886): 583, 595–96.

"Wohngebäude aus Holz in den Vereinigten Staaten." *Baugewerks-Zeitung* 18 (11, 18 September 1886): 719–21, 742–43.

American

"American Architecture as Seen by Foreigners." *American Architect* 20 (17 July 1886): 26.

"Building Outlook [confidence about 1887]." *Inland Architect* 8 (December 1886): 87.

"Burying Wires in Chicago." *New York Times,* 16 April 1886, 5.

"The Chicago Shop Girls." *New York Times,* 30 July 1886, 5.

Editorial. "[Employer responsibility in worker injury]." *Inland Architect* 7 (June 1886): 78.

Glazier, Willard. *Peculiarities of American Cities.* Philadelphia: Hubbard Brothers, 1886.

Hawley, W. A. "Style in Architecture [fixed rules detrimental]." *Inland Architect* 7 (February 1886): 3.

"Members of the Western Asssociation of Architects [photo, St. Louis, 18 November 1885]." *Inland Architect* 6 (January 1886): 116.

"Rents in Chicago." *New York Times,* 18 February 1886, 5.

Root, John W. "Architectural Freedom." *Inland Architect* 8 (December 1886): 64–65.

"Structures on Compressible Foundations." *American Architect* 20 (10 July 1886): 23–24.

"Synopsis of Building News [nervousness over demand for eight-hour day]." *Inland Architect* 7 (May, June 1886): 68, 85.

"Underground Electric Wires in Chicago." *American Architect* 20 (10 July 1886): 13.

1887

English

"The American Exhibition." *Building News* 52 (10 June 1887): 863.

"The American Exhibition." *Engineering* 43 (18 March 1887): 258–59.

"The American Style of the Future." *Architect* 37 (7 January 1887): 3–5.

"Architects and Technical Education." *British Architect* 27 (7 April 1887): 263–64.

"Art in America, Lecture by Prof. Herkomer." *Architect* 37 (18 February 1887): 93.

Bates, C. Catherine. *A Year in the Great Republic.* 2 vols. London: Ward and Downey, 1887.

Beadle, Charles. *A Trip to the United States in 1887.* London: J. S. Virtue, 1887.

Champneys, Basil. "Victorian Architecture and Originality." *British Architect* 28 (2, 9 December 1887): 409–10 and 427–28, 437.

"Compulsory Sanitation in America." *Architect* 37 (4 March 1887): 132–34.

"The Conference on Architectural Education [praise for Columbia College training]." *British Architect* 27 (6 May 1887): 337–38.

[Cook, Joel]. "A Visit to the States." *Times* [London], 21, 24 October 1887, 4. Also in *Letters from the Special Correspondent of the Times,* 2 vols. London, 1887–88.

"The Elevator System." *British Architect* 27 (18 February 1887): 132–33.

"[English reservations about foundations in Chicago]." *Inland Architect* 10 (October 1887): 30.

Gass, John B. "Two New York Houses." *Building News* 52 (17 June 1887): 905–6.

"An Ideal American House." *Architect* 38 (30 December 1887): 403–5.

"Illustrations: American House Architecture." *Builder* 1887 (22 January 1887): 147–48.

"Notes and Comments: Prix de reconnaissance des architectes américains." *Architect* 37 (10 June 1887): 346.

"Notes on Current Events: On American Architectural Education." *British Architect* 27 (18 February 1887): 131.

Pond, Irving K. "An Ideal American Home." *Architect* 38 (30 December 1887): 403–5.

"A Remarkable Engineering Feat." *British Architect* 28 (26 August 1887): 168.

"Shingle House at the American Exhibition." *Building News* 53 (15 July 1887): 115.

Slater, J. "New Materials and Inventions." *Architect* 37 (6 May 1887): 268–70.

Smalley, G. W. "Notes on New York." *Nineteenth Century* 21 (February 1887): 206–26.

"Training of Architects in America." *Architect* 38 (25 November 1887): 334–36.

Verplanck, Gulian C. "Bygones: American Architecture in 1824." *Architect* 37 (28 January 1887): 54–56.

French

Boussard, J. "Cottage en Amérique." *Le moniteur des architectes,* n.s., 1 (1887): 95–96.

———. "Maisons de campagne au Massachusetts." *Le moniteur des architectes,* n.s., 1 (1887): 111.

Editorial. "[*La semaine* on American Architecture.]" *Inland Architect* 9 (April 1887): 32.

R. "Un intérieur américain." *La semaine des constructeurs,* 2d ser., 1 (22 January 1887): 356–57.

German

"American Houses as Considered by the Germans." *American Architect* 21 (12 March 1887): 122.

"Amerikanische Personen-Aufzüge in Berliner Häusern." *Deutsche Bauzeitung* 21 (5 February 1887): 61–64.

Deckert, Emil. "Das amerikanische Haus." *Gegenwart* 32 (30 July 1887): 67–69.

Hinckeldeyn, [Karl]. "Eingebaute Häuser und Miethswohnungen in den Großstädten Nordamerikas." *Centralblatt der Bauverwaltung* 7 (28 May, 4 June 1887): 211–13, 223–25.

———. "Feuershutz für Eisenconstructionen." *Centralblatt der Bauverwaltung* 7 (12, 19 November 1887): 435–36, 450–51.

———. "Hochbau-Constructionen und innerer Ausbau in den Vereinigten Staaten." *Centralblatt der Bauverwaltung* 7 (12, 19 March 1887): 102–3, 116–18.

———. "Mittheilungen über New-York." *Wochenblatt für Baukunde* 9 (4 November 1887): 442–43.

J.Z. "Eigenthümlichkeiten im amerikanischen Bauwesen." *Wiener Bauindustrie-Zeitung* 4 (17, 24, 31 March 1887): 293–94, 307–8, 323–24.

Lange, Franz. *Eigenthümlichkeiten im amerikanischen Bauwesen.* Cologne, 1887.

———. "Newyorker Miethshäuser." *Deutsche Bauzeitung* 21 (26 January 1887): 47–48.

Mühlke, [Karl]. "Das amerikanische Landhaus und die Preisbewerbung des 'American Architect.'" *Centralblatt der Bauverwaltung* 7 (8, 15 January 1887): 11–12, 18–19.

W.S. "Amerikanische Landhäuser." *Deutsche Bauzeitung* 21 (16 July, 3 August, 10 September 1887): 337–41, 369, 433–34.

American

Blackall, C. H. "Notes of Travel: Chicago, 1–2." *American Architect* 22 (24, 31 December 1887): 299–300, 313–15.

"Business Outlook [architects busy]." *Inland Architect* 9 (July 1887): 99.

"Building Outlook [prospects high]." *Inland Architect* 10 (October 1887): 38.

Editorial. "[Future of American architecture]." *Inland Architect* 10 (September 1887): 19.

"Elevators in England." *Inland Architect* 13 (January 1887): 110.

"Fourth Annual Convention of the Western Association of Architects." *Inland Architect* 10 (December 1887): 75–76.

"New Auditorium Building, Chicago." *Inland Architect* 9 (April 1887).

"Synopsis of Building News [increasing building statistics in Chicago]." *Inland Architect* 13 (January 1887): 111.

Maher, George W. "Originality in American Architecture." *Inland Architect* 9 (October 1887): 34–35.

1888

English

"American Architecture." *Building* 8 (28 April 1888): 133–34.

"American Architecture from an Engineering Point of View." *British Architect* 29 (8 June 1888): 410.

"American Faith in French Art." *British Architect* 29 (18 May 1888): 365.

"An American Ruling on Building Responsibility." *British Architect* 29 (13 April 1888): 259.

"The Architects of Western America." *Architect* 40 (28 December 1888): 358–59.

"Architectural Federation in the States." *British Architect* 30 (21 December 1888): 433.

Arnold, Matthew. *Civilization in the United States: First and Last Impressions of America.* Boston: Cupples and Hurd, 1888.

Aubertin, J. J. *A Fight with Distances.* London: Kegan Paul, 1888.

Bryce, James. *The American Commonwealth.* 3 vols. London and New York: Macmillan, 1888.

"[Canadian architect claims Chicago's commercial buildings are ugly]." *Inland Architect* 12 (December 1888): 75.

"The Characteristics of American Cities." *Westminster Review* 130 (July 1888): 32–47.

C.H.B. [Charles H. Brodie]. "Jottings about the United States." *American Architect* 23 (19 May 1888): 235–36.

Editorial. "[Yankee newspaper criticism]." *British Architect* 29 (20 January 1888): 42.

"Eighteen Hundred and Eighty-Seven." *British Architect* 29 (6 January 1888): 1–5.

"Electric Lighting in America." *Engineering* 46 (5 October 1888): 338–39.

"The Electric Light in the City of London." *British Architect* 29 (20 January 1888): 52.

"English and American Architecture." *Building* 8 (17 March 1888): 85–86.

Graham, Alex. "Architecture in the United States." *Royal Institute of British Architects, Journal of Proceedings,* n.s., 4 (8 March 1888): 193–96.

"The Late Mr. Richardson." *Royal Institute of British Architects, Journal of Proceedings,* n.s., 4 (9 February 1888): 141–42.

"Matthew Arnold on Art." *Architect* 39 (20 April 1888): 222–23.

"The Old 'Style' Question Again [reaction to paper by W. Simpson]." *Builder* 54 (24 March 1888): 204–5.

"Our Illustrations: An American Store [store in St. Paul by J. Walter Stevens]." *British Architect* 19 (13 April 1888): 264.

"The President's Address, Royal Institute of British Architects [Tribute to Richardson]." *Builder* 55 (10 November 1888): 336–40.

Simpson, W. "What Style of Architecture Should We Follow?" *British Architect* 29 (6 April 1888): 246, 255–56.

"Tall Building in Chicago." *British Architect* 30 (12 October 1888): 270.

"The Ventilation of the Chicago Auditorium." *British Architect* 30 (10 August 1888): 108.

Waterhouse, Alfred. "Presidential Address at the Institute [comments on M. G. van Rensselaer's book on Richardson]." *British Architect* 30 (9 November 1888): 339–42.

French

Biancour, F. de. *Quatre mille lieues aux États-Unis.* Paris: Paul Ollendorff, 1888.

Boussard, J. "Types de villas aux États-Unis d'Amérique." *Le moniteur des architectes,* n.s., 2 (1888): 63.

Brincourt, M. "États-Unis." *Encyclopédie de l'architecture et de la construction* 4, pt. 2 (1888–95): 422–38.

"Constructions américaines." *L'architecture* 1 (18 February 1888): 77–78.

Daly, Marcel. "Construction sur mauvais sol." *La semaine des constructeurs,* 2d ser., 2 (28 April 1888): 519–20.

———. "Les constructions en bois aux États-Unis." *La semaine des constructeurs,* 2d ser., 3 (1 September 1888): 112.

"Fabriques de maisons." *La semaine des constructeurs,* 2d ser., 2 (7 April 1888): 492.

Gout, Paul. "Maison à Boston." *Encyclopédie d'architecture,* 4th ser., 1 (1888–89): 132–33.

Hulot, Étienne G. *De l'Atlantique au Pacifique.* Paris: Plon, 1888.

"Maison à quinze étages." *La construction moderne* 4 (17 November 1888): 72.

"Maison de commerce à New York." *La semaine des constructeurs,* 2d ser., 2 (9 June 1888): 591.

Moreau, F. Frédéric. *Aux États-Unis: Notes de voyage.* Paris: Plon, 1888.

Osborne, C. Francis. "La construction moderne aux États-Unis." *La construction moderne* 3 (3 March, 15 September 1888): 241–43, 577–80.

German

"Ein amerikanisches Bahnhofs-Empfangs-Gebäude." *Deutsche Bauzeitung* 22 (22 December 1888): 613–14.

D.B. "Technische Mittheilungen: Feuersichere Eisenconstruction." *Wiener Bauindustrie-Zeitung* 5 (16 February 1888): 246.

Editorial. "[*Wiener Bauindustrie-Zeitung* on American houses]." *Inland Architect* 11 (May 1888): 58–59.

Gunesch, Rudolf von. "Mittheilungen über eine im vergangene Jahre unternommene Reise durch die Vereinigten Staaten Nordamerikas und Canada." *Wochenschrift des oesterreichischen Ingeneur- und Architekten-Vereines* 13 (27 April, 4 May 1888): 175–77, 181–83.

"Hochbauten in Chicago [receipt of seventy-eight photographs and list of illustrations from J. W. Turner, Chicago]." *Centralblatt der Bauverwaltung* 8 (28 March 1888): 141.

"Zu unseren Beilagen: Die amerikanische Holzarchitekturen." *Wiener Bauindustrie-Zeitung* 5 (9 February 1888): 234.

American

Adler, Dankmar. "Foundations of the Auditorium Building." *Inland Architect* 11 (March 1888): 31–32.

"American Architecture Winning Attention in Europe." *American Architect* 23 (17 March 1888): 122.

Blackall, C. H. "Notes of Travel: Chicago, 3–5." *American Architect* 23 (25 February, 24, 31 March 1888): 88–91, 140–42, 147–48.

Buffington, L. S. "[Letter explaining his structural system]." *American Architect* 24 (1 December 1888): 256.

"Building Outlook [lull before anticipated progress]." *Inland Architect* 11 (June 1888): 80.

"Chicago: The Effect on the Profession of the Commercial Atmosphere of the City." *American Architect* 23 (18 February 1888): 76.

"Chicago: Iron and Concrete Foundations." *American Architect* 24 (20 October 1888): 185–86.

"Chicago: Strengthening the Board of Trade Building." *American Architect* 24 (18 August 1888): 77.

"The Chicago Auditorium Building." *Inland Architect* 11 (July 1888): 89.

"Chicago Auditorium Building: Elevation of Tower, Showing Top Stories of Congress St. Elevation." *Inland Architect* 12 (October 1888): 3.

Editorial. "[America a country with no ruins]." *Inland Architect* 11 (February 1888): 1.

———. "[Building laws and accidents]." *Inland Architect* 11 (February 1888): 2.

———. "[*Chicago Tribune* and the smoke nuisance]." *Inland Architect* 12 (September 1888): 12.

James, Henry. "London." *Century Magazine,* December 1888, 219–39.

"[On proposed twenty-eight-story building in Minnesota]." *American Architect* 24 (17 November 1888): 226.

"Our Illustrations [Offices of Burnham and Root]." *Inland Architect* 12 (September 1888): 18.

"Our Illustrations: Design for Twenty-eight Story Office Building, Iron Construction, of L. S. Buffington, Architect, Minneapolis, Minn." *Inland Architect* 11 (July 1888): 89.

Platt, Walter B. "Injurious Influences of City Life." *Popular Science Monthly* 33 (August 1888): 484–89.

Root, John W. "Broad Art Criticism." *Inland Architect* 11 (February 1888): 3.

Van Rensselaer, M. G. "Open Letters [response to Matthew Arnold's architectural judgments]." *Century Magazine,* June 1888, 314–16.

Warner, Charles Dudley. "Studies of the Great West, 3 and 4: "Chicago." *Harper's Magazine,* May, June 1888, 869–79, 116–27.

1889

English

"American Architecture." *British Architect* 31 (18 January 1889): 47.

"An American Block of Offices [Drexel Buildings, Philadelphia]." *Engineering* 48 (15 November 1889): 564–66.

"The American Institute of Architects." *Architect* 42 (27 December 1889): 368–69.

Chiel. "Letter from London [influence of American sketching style]." *American Architect* 26 (27 July 1889): 40.

"English Praise of American Architectural Journals." *American Architect* 26 (26 October 1889): 200.

Graham, Alex. "Tall Buildings." *Royal Institute of British Architects, Journal of Proceedings,* n.s., 5 (29 August 1889): 354–56.

"The Height of London Buildings." *British Architect* 31 (31 May 1889): 387.

Kerr, Robert. "The Late H. H. Richardson." *Royal Institute of British Architects, Journal of Proceedings,* n.s., 5 (28 March 1889): 216–18.

"London Street Architecture." *British Architect* 31 (11 January 1889): 27.

"Mr. Stanford's New Premises, Cockspur Street." *Builder* 56 (12 January 1889): 31.

Mundie, W. B. "Sketch Clubs in America." *Architect* 41 (3 May 1889): 254–56.

"Notes on Current Events." *British Architect* 32 (4 October 1889): 232.

"Notes on Current Events: An American Hotel." *British Architect* 32 (20 September 1889): 197.

"Our Illustrations: Edinburgh Cafe Company New Building, Princes St., Edinburgh." *British Architect* 32 (27 September 1889): 217.

"Our Illustrations: Modern Architecture in Scotland: A Glasgow Warehouse, John Hutchison, I. A. Architect" *British Architect* 32 (22 November 1889): 362.

"Our Illustrations: The Tivoli." *British Architect* 32 (27 September 1889): 217.

Reade, F. T. "The Application of Iron and Steel to Building Purposes." *Royal Institute of British Architects, Transactions,* n.s., 6 (1889–90): 13–36.

"The Street Traffic of London." *British Architect* 31 (24 May 1889): vii.

Wills, Herbert W. "Our Illustrations: Types of American Architecture." *British Architect* 32 (6 December 1889): 402.

French

Boileau, L.-C., fils. "L'art et le fer." *L'architecture* 2 (9 March 1889): 110–15.

"Comments upon the Consolidation Movement [*La semaine* on the AIA and WAA merger]." *Inland Architect* 13 (February 1889): 2.

G.R. "Informations: Projet de tour colossale pour l'exposition de 1892, aux États-Unis [proposal of A. de Graf Hinsdale]." *Le génie civil* 16 (16 November 1889): 71–72.

"Informations: Les maisons géantes à New York." *Le génie civil* 15 (24 August 1889): 372.

J.C. [Combe, J.]. "Informations: Projet de tour de 500 mètres pour l'exposition de 1892, aux États-Unis [Judson tower proposal]." *Le génie civil* 16 (23 November 1889): 99.

"Les journaux d'architecture aux États-Unis." *L'architecture* 2 (2 November 1889): 527–28.

Moreau, G. "L'exposition de 1892 aux États-Unis [favors New York site]." *Le génie civil* 16 (9 November 1889): 35–37.

O'Rell, Max [Paul Blouët], and Jack Allyn. *Jonathan and His Continent.* Translated by Madame Paul Blouët. New York: Cassell, 1889.

"Revue de la Presse." *L'architecture* 2 (17, 24 August 1889): 396, 408.

Rossi, Auguste J. "Correspondance des États-Unis [preparation for the Columbian Exposition]." *Le génie civil* 16 (7 December 1889): 156–57.

———. "L'exposition universelle de 1892 aux États-Unis." *Le génie civil* 15 (26 October 1889): 629–30.

Roux, F. "Ingénieurs et architectes." *L'architecture* 2 (19, 26 October 1889): 502–3, 509–11.

Varigny, C. de. "L'Amérique à l'exposition universelle." *Revue des deux mondes* 95 (15 October 1889): 836–66.

Vogüé, Eugène-Melchoir de. "Impressions Made by the Paris Exposition." *Chatauquan* 10 (October 1889): 66–70.

German

Frühwirth, C. "Das Hotel der Vereinigten Staaten." *Ausland* 62 (8 April 1889): 274–76.

Hinckeldeyn, [Karl]. "Deutschlands Stellung in den baulichen Bestrebung der Gegenwart." *Centralblatt der Bauverwaltung* 9 (16, 20 March 1889): 102–3, 105–6.

————. "A Foreigner's View of American Architecture." *American Architect* 25 (25 May 1889): 243–44.

Hofmann, Albert. "Die kunstgeschichtliche Stellung der Bauten für die Weltausstellung von 1889 in Paris." *Deutsche Bauzeitung* 23 (9 November 1889): 543–45.

American

"Building Outlook [some commercial failures but labor quiet]." *Inland Architect* 13 (July 1889): 104.

"Building Outlook [availability of money reported]." *Inland Architect* 14 (October 1889): 43.

"Building Outlook [prospects for Chicago encouraging]." *Inland Architect* 13 (February 1889): 12.

"Chicago: Alteration of Old Buildings for Office Purposes. The Old Chamber of Commerce a Remarkable Instance." *American Architect* 26 (23 November 1889): 243–44.

"Chicago: Sixteen-Story Buildings. Proposed Ordinance to Restrict the Height of Buildings. The Tacoma Building." *American Architect* 25 (22 June 1889): 293–94.

"The Chicago Architectural Sketch Club." *Inland Architect* 14 (December 1889): 80–81.

Editorial. "As to High Towers for the World's Fair." *Inland Architect* 14 (September 1889): 16.

————. "[Chicago foolish to want exposition]." *New York Times,* 3 August 1889, 4.

————. "Chicago in Paris [Chicago tries to convince Parisian press it is best site for exposition]." *New York Times,* 19 November 1889, 4.

————. "The Design and Construction of the World's Fair Buildings." *Inland Architect* 14 (November 1889): 47.

————. "The Facts in Regard to the Owings Building." *Inland Architect* 13 (March 1889): 38.

————. "Foolish Rivalry [New Yorkers can not imagine exposition in another city]." *New York Times,* 14 August 1889, 4.

————. "[High buildings, New York and Chicago]." *Engineering News* 21 (19 January 1889): 50.

————. "The World's Fair and the Architectural Profession [calls for public project rather than exposition monument]." *Inland Architect* 14 (November 1889): 47.

————. "World's Fair, 1892, Site." *Engineering News* 22 (10 August 1889): 132.

"Fall of Ten Floors in the Owings Building, Chicago." *American Architect* 25 (23 February 1889): 85.

Harrison, Frederic. "The Transformation of Paris." *North American Review* 149 (September 1889): 326–38.

"High Price for a Lot." *New York Times,* 24 February 1889, 16.

Jenney, W. L. B. "A Few Practical Hints." *Inland Architect* 13 (February 1889): 7.

"Not for Crowded Streets [concern about cable car accidents]." *New York Times,* 18 May 1889, 1.

"A Proposed Ordinance to Limit Height of Buildings." *Inland Architect* 13 (June 1889): 81.

"Resignation of Health Commissioner in Chicago." *Inland Architect* 14 (August 1889): 2.

"Rules and Regulations Governing the Drainage and Plumbing of New Buildings." *Inland Architect* 14 (October 1889): 40–41.

Sullivan, Louis H. "The Artistic Use of the Imagination." *Inland Architect* 14 (October 1889): 38–39.

"World's Fair, 1892 Tower [proposed for New York City site]." *Engineering News* 22 (28 September 1889): 300.

1890

English

"American vs. European Architecture." *Architect* 43 (11 April 1890): 224–25.
"The Chicago Auditorium." *Architect* 43 (21 February 1890): 125–26.
"The Chicago Exhibition of 1893." *Engineering* 50 (19 December 1890): 731–33.
"The Chicago Fire Brigade [speed of system]." *Leisure Hour,* 1890, 142.
Child, Theodore. "Impressions of Berlin." *Harper's Magazine,* August 1890, 340–56.
"The Columbian Exposition." *Engineering* 50 (5 December 1890): 667–68.
Cox, A. Arthur. "A Tour in the United States." *Royal Institute of British Architects, Transactions,* n.s., 7 (1890–91): 351–88.
Darbyshire, Alfred. "Modern Secular Architecture." *British Architect* 33 (17 January 1890): 53–54.
Dredge, James. "The Chicago International Exhibition of 1893." *Engineering* 19 (5, 12 December 1890): 678–80, 709–10.
"An Englishman in Berlin." *Macmillan's Magazine,* April 1890, 439–44.
Gritton, C. E. "Lifts." *Architect* 43 (25 April 1890): 257–59. Also in *Society of Architects, Proceedings* 22 (17 April 1890).
"Illustrations: United States Trust Company's Premises, New York." *Builder* 58 (26 April 1890): 304.
"The Iron and Steel Institute in America: The Visit to Chicago." *Engineering* 50 (31 October 1890): 506–7, 509–10.
Jenney, W. L. B. "Economy in the Use of Steel in Building Construction." *British Architect* 33 (7 February 1890): 111.
"Modern Architecture under a Cloud." *British Architect* 33 (21 February 1890): 133.
"Office of the U. S. Trust Co., N.Y., Wall Street." *Architect* 43 (28 March 1890): 197.
"Our Illustrations: American Domestic Architecture." *British Architect* 33 (24 January 1890): 60.
"Our Illustrations: Studies of Street Architecture. No. 15. Premises on Ludgate Hill." *British Architect* 34 (7 November 1890): 341.
Raffles, W. Hargreaves. "The Darkness of London Air." *Nature* 43 (18 December 1890): 152–53.
"A 'Real' American Hotel for London." *British Architect* 33 (10 January 1890): 19.
Root, John. "City Architecture in Western America." *Builder* 59 (11 October 1890): 286–88.
"Too Bad [London *Times* calls Chicago unfinished compared to New York]." *New York Times,* 23 July 1890, 1.
"A Truly American Way [Jenison tower proposal]." *British Architect* 33 (4 April 1890): 237–38.
"The United States Exhibition." *Engineering* 49 (14 March 1890): 334–35.
"The United States Exhibition of 1892." *Engineering* 49 (7 March 1890): 305–6.
Van Brunt, Henry. "An American Architect on Architecture." *Architect* 43 (16 May 1890): 315–18.
———."Architecture in the West." *British Architect* 33 (6, 13 June 1890): 416ff, 431.
Wood, H. Trueman. "Chicago Exhibition, 1893." *Journal of the Society of Arts* 38 (26 September 1890): 927.
———. "M. Berger on the Chicago Exhibition." *American Architect* 28 (7 June 1890): 148–50.

French

A. "L'organisation des bureaux d'architectes aux États-Unis." *La semaine des constructeurs,* 2d ser., 4 (8, 15 March 1890): 436–38, 452.

Berger, Georges. "Suggestions for the Next World's Fair." *Century Magazine,* April 1890, 845–51.

Blitz, Albert. "Correspondance américaine: La construction aux États-Unis." *L'émulation* 15 (1890): 140–41.

———. "Lettre d'Amérique [ventilation and sanitation in American school buildings]." *L'émulation* 15 (1890): 42–44.

"Un cabinet d'architecte à Chicago." *Le moniteur des architectes,* n.s., 4 (1890): 11.

Combe, J. "La ville de Chicago: La nouvelle salle de l'Auditorium, à Chicago." *Le génie civil* 17 (3 May 1890): 10–13.

Francken, Daniel. "*The California Architect and Building News.*" *L'émulation* 15 (1890): 110–12.

"Les journaux d'architecture aux États-Unis: *The Inland Architect.*" *L'architecture* 3 (20 December 1890): 614–16.

Moreau, G. "L'exposition de Chicago en 1893." *Le génie civil* 18 (22 November 1890): 61–63.

R. "L'architecture américaine." *La construction moderne* 6 (13 December 1890): 109–11.

Reed, E. W. "L'Auditorium Building à Chicago." *La semaine des constructeurs,* 2d ser., 5 (4 October 1890): 170–72.

Sédille, Paul. *L'architecture moderne en Angleterre.* Paris: Librairie des Bibliophiles, 1890.

"*La semaine* aux États-Unis." *La semaine des constructeurs,* 2d ser., 4 (5 April 1890): 484–85.

Walker, C. Howard. "Essai: pour remmener le dessin d'architecture à une base logique." *L'architecture* 3 (6 September 1890): 438–40.

German

"Aus dem technischen Vereinsleben Amerikas [exchange between technical journals in Germany and U.S.]." *Deutsche Bauzeitung* 24 (15 January 1890): 25–30.

Fr.E. [Fritz von Emperger]. "Die geplante amerikanische Welt-Ausstellung 1893." *Deutsche Bauzeitung* 24 (14 May 1890): 234–35.

F.X.K. "Das Haus der Zukunft [hotel by Buffington]." *Innen-Dekoration* 1 (10 July 1890): 109.

———. "Das Haus der Zukunft [mistaken reference to Buffington's twenty-eight-story building]." *Wiener Bauindustrie-Zeitung* 7 (12 June 1890): 395–96.

Gunesch, Rudolf. "Chicago und seine Oper." *Wochenschrift des oesterreichischen Ingenieur-und Architekten-Vereines* 13 (28 March 1890): 123–26.

Hesse-Wartegg, Ernest. *Amerika als neueste Weltmacht der Industrie.* Stuttgart: Union Deutsche Verlagsgesellschaft, 1890.

Vogel, [Rudolf]. "Amerikanische Bauweise." *Zeitschrift des Architekten- und Ingenieur-Vereins zu Hannover* 36, no. 2 (1890): 146–54.

American

"A Great Office Building [Chamber of Commerce Building]." *Graphic* (Supplement) 3 (13 September 1890).

Barnum, P. T. "What the Fair Should Be." *North American Review* 150 (March 1890): 400–401.

Brownell, W. C. "The Paris Exposition: Notes and Impressions." *Scribner's Magazine,* January 1890, 18–35.

"Building Outlook [lively activity, strong prices, expanding trade]." *Inland Architect* 15 (July 1890): 91.

"Building Outlook [promises to be one of most prosperous years]." *Inland Architect* 15 (June 1890): 77.

"A Champion of Chicago [claims only Chicago could finish an exposition in two years]." *New York Times*, 2 March 1890, 12.

"Chicago [smoke, smells, and inconveniences are a serious problem]." *Building Budget* 6 (30 September 1890): 111–12.

"Chicago: Curtailing Railroad Speed within the City-Limits and Its Effect on Suburban Building." *American Architect* 27 (22 March 1890): 182.

"Chicago: The Great Tower [Columbian Tower Company proposal]." *American Architect* 28 (21 June 1890): 179–80.

"Chicago: The Proposed World's Fair Building [Jenison tower proposal]." *American Architect* 28 (19 April 1890): 38–39.

"Chicago: The Smoke Nuisance. Heightening Old Buildings. The Old and New Methods of Laying Foundations." *American Architect* 29 (20 September 1890): 185–86.

"The Chicago Exposition Buildings." *Engineering News* 23 (29 March 1890): 301–2.

"Chicago to Have a Tall Tower [New York and Chicago capitalists plan 1,500–foot private tower]." *New York Times*, 25 May 1890, 1.

"Completion of the Chicago Auditorium." *Inland Architect* 14 (January 1890): 87–88.

Editorial. "[Chicago cannot raise necessary money for the exposition]." *New York Times*, 6 March 1890, 4.

———. "The Lake-Front Site for the Columbian Exposition." *Inland Architect* 16 (September 1890): 15.

———. "Selection of Columbian Exposition Architects." *Inland Architecture* 16 (December 1890): 69–70.

———. "Shall We Have a World's Fair [exposition doomed now that Chicago has been chosen]?" *New York Times*, 21 August 1890, 4.

———. "A Threatened Strike among Carpenters in Chicago." *Inland Architect* 15 (March 1890): 30.

———. "What Will Chicago Do with It [Chicago cannot manage the exposition]?" *New York Times*, 27 February 1890, 4.

"Exposition, Chicago: Monument to Columbus." *Engineering News* 24 (18 October 1890): 348.

Ferree, Barr. "Utility in Architecture." *Popular Science Monthly* 37 (June 1890): 202–11.

"A Great Masonic Building." *New York Times*, 2 November 1890, 5.

Hamlin, A. D. F. "Modern French Architecture." *Architectural Record* 10 (October 1890): 150–77.

Jenney, W. L. B. "An Age of Steel and Clay." *Inland Architect* 16 (December 1890): 75–77.

———. "Economy in the Use of Steel in Building Construction." *Inland Architect* 14 (January 1890): 94.

Kennelly, A. E. "Electricity in the Household." *Scribner's Magazine*, January 1890, 102–15.

"A Novel Plan for the World's Fair Buildings [Jenison tower proposal]." *Engineering News* 23 (15 March 1890): 245.

"The Organization of an American's Architect's Office [offices of Burnham and Root]." *American Architect* 27 (25 January 1890): 50.

"Rich Men in Chicago." *New York Times,* 13 April 1890, 4.

Root, John W. "A Great Architectural Problem." *Inland Architect* 15 (June 1890): 67–71.

Smith, Mary Stuart. "Berlin, The City of the Kaiser." *Cosmopolitan,* March 1890, 515–28.

"The Strike Epidemic among the Carpenters." *Inland Architect* 15 (June 1890): 65–66.

"Strikes in the Building Trades in Chicago." *Inland Architect* 15 (April 1890): 42.

"Suggested High Tower for the Chicago World's Exhibition [1600 feet tall, ringed by spiral roadway]." *American Architect* 27 (22 March 1890): 177.

"Violating a City Ordinance [janitors throwing garbage in Chicago streets]." *New York Times,* 25 May 1890, 20.

"The World's Exposition and the Regulating of Railway Crossings." *Building Budget* 6 (31 March 1890): 28.

1891

English

Adler, Dankmar. "Some Technical Reflections on Tall Buildings." *British Architect* 36 (17 July 1891): 54.

"Architects and Their Critics." *British Architect* 35 (12 June 1891): 447–48.

"The Architectural Association: The Planning and Construction of American Frame (or Timber) Houses [talk by C. H. Brodie]." *Builder* 61 (21 November 1891): 384–88.

"The Auditorium Building, Chicago." *Engineering* 51 (3, 24 April 1891): 400, 490.

Brodie, C. H. "The Planning and Construction of American Frame Houses." *American Architect* 34 (12 December 1891): 168–70.

Bryce, James. *Social Institutions of the United States.* New York: Chautauqua Press, 1891.

"The Chicago Exhibition." *Engineering* 51 (17 April 1891): 461.

"Chicago Exhibition Buildings." *Builder* 41 (8 August 1891): 103.

"Chicago Exhibition, 1893." *Journal of the Society of Arts* 39 (16, 30 October 1891): 871–73, 903–5.

"The Chicago Exhibition of 1893." *Engineering* 51 (1 May 1891): 520–22.

"The Columbian Exposition." *Engineering* 52, 1891 (23 October): 469–72; (30 October): 499–503; (6 November): 523–25; (13 November): 562; (4 December): 649–50; 53, 1892 (1 January): 6–7; (8 January): 37; (15 January): 72; (22 January): 103–4; (29 January): 130–31; (5 February): 163–65; (12 February): 194; (19 February): 226; (4 March): 283–85; (11 March): 318; (18 March): 346; (25 March): 375–76; (8 April): 432; (15 April): 462; (22 April): 492; (29 April): 519; (13 May): 601; (20 May): 620; (27 May): 664; (10 June): 715–16; (24 June): 792.

"The Columbian Exposition: The Administration Building." *Engineering* 51 (5 June 1891): 667–70.

"The Columbian Exposition: The High Tower [Morison proposal]." *Engineering* 52 (18 December 1891): 711–13.

"The Columbian Exposition: The Transportation Building—The Horticulture Hall." *Engineering* 52 (31 July 1891): 123.

"The Columbian Exposition of 1893." *Engineering* 51 (29 May 1891): 635, 637.

"The Columbian Exposition of 1893: The Electricity Building." *Engineering* 51 (12 June 1891): 700.

"The Columbian Tower [Morison proposal regrettable]." *Engineering* 52 (20 November 1891): 596.

Cook, Joel. *World's Fair at Chicago.* Chicago: Rand, McNally, 1891.

Cox, A. A. "American Construction through English Eyes." *American Architect* 32–33 (13 June, 8, 29 August 1891): 167–70, 86–88, 131–32.

Davidson, T. Raffles. "Modern English Homes." *British Architect* 36 (8 December 1891): 451–56.

Dredge, James. "The Columbian Exposition of 1893." *Engineering* 52 (11, 18, 25 December 1891): 701–2, 734–36, 766–68; 53 (1, 8, 15 January 1892): 24–26, 58–59, 88–90.

Dredge, James, and Henry Trueman Wood. "The Grounds and Buildings for the World's Columbian Exhibition of 1893." *British Architect* 36 (30 October, 20 November 1891): 333–34, 389–90.

"Eighteen Hundred and Ninety." *British Architect* 35 (2 January 1891): 1.

"Electric Lighting in Chicago." *Engineering* 51 (19 June 1891): 721–22.

Fidler, T. Claxton. "Iron and Steel Considered as Building Materials." *British Architect* 35 (23 January, 6, 13 February 1891): 76–77, 113–14, 129–30.

Fox, John A. "American House Planning." *British Architect* 36 (31 July 1891): 77–78.

Jenney, W. L. B. "Tall Buildings on a Compressible Soil." *British Architect* 36 (4 December 1891): 416.

"The Masonic Temple." *Engineering* 52 (7 August 1891): 150–52.

"Our Illustrations: The Highest Building in New York: Bruce Price, Architect." *British Architect* 36 (9 October 1891): 265.

"Progress of the Electric Light during 1890." *British Architect* 35 (9 January 1891): 37.

"The Proposed Chicago Columbus Tower [Kinkel and Pohl proposal]." *British Architect* 35 (January 1891): 18.

"Roberts, Morley. "The Streets of London." *Littell's Living Age,* 1891, 159–63.

"Tall Buildings in Chicago [Dankmar Adler objects to height restrictions]." *Builder* 60 (30 May 1891): 426.

Townsend, Horace. "American Theatres." *Builder* 61 (19 December 1891): 464–65.

———. "The House that Jonathan Builds." *Builder* 60 (4 April 1891): 268–71. Also in *American Architect* 32 (23 May 1891): 121–23.

"The Tramways of the United States." *British Architect* 36 (3 July 1891): 18.

W.N.L. "American Houses." *Builder* 61 (19 September 1891): 221–22.

"The World's Columbian Exposition: The Machinery Hall." *Engineering* 51 (26 June 1891): 758.

"The World's Columbian Exposition of 1893: Fisheries Building." *Engineering* 52 (10 July 1891): 34–35.

French

B. "The Pulitzer Building." *La construction moderne* 6 (7, 21 March 1891): 257–59, 285–87.

Barre, A. "Chicago et son exposition en 1893." *Le génie civil* 20 (21 November 1891): 45–46.

"Bâtiment colossal à l'usage des bureaux, à Philadelphie." *Le génie civil* 19 (12 September 1891): 329.

B.Ch. "The Cleveland Arcade Roof: Ferme du passage Cleveland, à Cleveland (Ohio)." *La construction moderne* 6 (20 June 1891): 436–39.

Boileau, L.-C., fils. "L'architecture nationale moderne." *L'architecture* 4 (17 January, 14 March 1891): 26–29, 124–26.

Brincourt. "Architecture of the United States." *American Architect* 33 (18 July, 25 July, 1 August 1891): 35–37, 47–51, 63–65.

"Le clou de l'exposition de Chicago [iron mountain planned for exposition]." *La construction moderne* 6 (29 August 1891): 564.

"Constructions civiles: La tour de l'exposition de Chicago [Proctor tower proposal]." *Le génie civil* 19 (30 May 1891): 76–77.

E.R. "Les hautes maisons américaines." *La construction moderne* 7 (14, 21 November 1891): 69–72, 82–84.

"Exposition universelle de Chicago en 1893." *La construction moderne* 6 (3 October 1891): 613.

Germain, P. "Correspondance: Maisons colossales aux États-Unis." *Le génie civil* 19 (3 October 1891): 376–77.

Gout, Paul. "Maison américaine." *Encyclopédie d'architecture,* 4th ser., 1 (1891–92): 20–21.

H.M. "Les hautes maisons aux États-Unis." *Le génie civil* 18 (14 February 1891): 256–57.

Madison, R. "Correspondance: L'exposition de Chicago. Les hautes maisons américaines." *Le génie civil* 20 (19 December 1891): 107–9.

Moreau, Georges. "Exposition: L'exposition de Chicago." *Le génie civil* 19 (26 September 1891): 355–56.

O'Rell, Max [Paul Blouët]. *A Frenchman in America.* New York: Cassell, 1891.

———. "Reminiscences of American Hotels." *North American Review* 152 (January 1891): 85–90.

R.E. "Les grandes constructions américaines." *La construction moderne* 6 (5 September 1891): 568–69.

Sarcey, Francisque. "The Boulevards of Paris." *Scribner's Magazine,* June 1891, 663–84.

German

"Amerikanische Häuserbauten." *Schweizerische Bauzeitung* 17 (23 May 1891): 134.

B. "Die Weltausstellung in Chicago 1893." *Centralblatt der Bauverwaltung* 11 (31 October 1891): 431–34.

"Columbische Weltausstellung in Chicago." *Stahl und Eisen* 11 (August 1891): 646–48.

"Die Columbische Weltausstellung in Chicago." *Wochenschrift des oesterreichen Ingenieur- und Architekten- Vereines* 17 (10 July 1891): 248–49.

Droege, Ottokar A. *Chicago. Warum und Wie müssen wir dort ausstellen?* Berlin: M. Hoffschläger, 1891.

"Einiges über die Ausstellung in Chicago [Proctor tower proposal]." *Stahl und Eisen* 11 (May 1891): 437–38.

F.X.K. "Ein amerikanisches Haus in Wien [proposed Equitable Building for Vienna]." *Wiener Bauindustrie-Zeitung* 8 (9 July 1891): 435–37.

———. "Markante Beispiele amerikanischer Bauweise [criticism of skyscrapers; praise for domestic architecture]." *Wiener Bauindustrie-Zeitung* 9 (1, 8 October 1891): 1–2, 13–15.

Hesse-Wartegg, Ernst von. *Tausend und ein Tag im Occident.* 2 vols. Leipzig: Carl Reissner, 1891.

"Die neuesten Bau-Curiositäten in Chicago [Masonic Temple]." *Wiener Bauindustrie-Zeitung* 8 (15 January 1891): 172.

Schliepmann, Hans. *Betrachtungen über Baukunst: Zum Verständnis moderner Architekturfragen.* Berlin: Polytechnische Buchhandlung, 1891.

Strehl, J. "Das amerikanische Landhaus." *Zeitschrift für Bauhandwerker* (1891): 124–26.

Volkman, R. "Die Columbische Weltausstellung in Chicago." *Wochenschrift des oesterreichischen Ingenieur- und Architekten- Vereines* 14 (10 July, 25 September 1891): 248–49, 343–46.

"Die Weltausstellung in Chicago (Illinois)." *Baugewerks-Zeitung* 23 (10 October 1891): 1018–20.

W.G.R. "Das Riesenhaus am Broadway in New York." *Deutsche Bauzeitung* 25 (21 November 1891): 264–65.

American

Adler, Dankmar. "The Chicago Auditorium." *Architectural Record* 1 (October–December 1891): 415–34.

———. "Communications: The Auditorium Tower." *American Architect* 31 (4 April 1891): 15.

———. "Engineering Supervision of Building Operations." *American Architect* 33 (4 July 1891): 11–12.

———. "Tall Buildings [opposes restrictions on height]." *Inland Architect* 17 (June 1891): 58.

"Chicago." *American Architect* 32 (18 April 1891): 45.

"Chicago." *American Architect* 32 (23 May 1891): 120–21.

"Chicago: The High Building Question. The Masonic Temple. Other Buildings and Towers." *American Architect* 34 (21 November 1891): 117–19.

"Chicago: Projected High Buildings." *American Architect* 33 (25 July 1891): 51–52.

"Chicago: The Rise of Real Estate Values. Two Proposed Sixteen-Story Buildings. The Settling of the Auditorium Tower and Similar Structures." *American Architect* 29 (21 March 1891): 188–89.

"Chicago Carpenters' Working Agreement." *Inland Architect* 17 (April 1891): 36.

"Chicago's Growth." *New York Times,* 25 April 1891, 4.

"Chicago's Sky Scrapers." *New York Times,* 9 March 1891, 3.

"Columbian Exposition Success and Progress." *Inland Architect* 17 (June 1891): 53.

"The Columbian Memorial [Whyte and Vail tower proposal]." *Graphic* 4, no. 11 (14 March 1891): 169.

"A Complaint from Chicago [*Tribune* displeased with *NYT* criticism of Chicago's architecture]." *New York Times,* 8 December 1891, 4.

"Death of Architect John Wellborn Root." *Inland Architect* 16 (January 1891): 83.

Editorial. "Chicago Architects and the Chicago High Buildings." *American Architect* 34 (26 December 1891): 189.

———. "Chicago's Veneered Buildings." *New York Times,* 30 November 1891, 4.

———. "The Columbian Exposition [fears European countries will not participate]." *New York Times,* 1 February 1891, 4.

———. "Columbia Exposition Woman's Building; Progress in Columbian Exposition Work." *Inland Architect* 17 (February 1891): 1.

———. "The Crust at Chicago." *New York Times,* 18 October 1891, 4.

———. "[Doubts about veneered buildings in Chicago]." *American Architect* 34 (19 December. 1891): 174.

———. "[German attitude toward exposition becoming more positive]." *New York Times,* 23 August 1891, 8.

————. "New York and the World's Fair." *New York Times,* 6 November 1891, 4.

————. "Possible Prohibition of Lofty Buildings in Chicago." *American Architect* 34 (24 October 1891): 45.

————. "Progress in Work on World's Fair." *Inland Architect* 17 (March 1891): 18.

————. "Proposed High Building Ordinance for Chicago." *Inland Architect* 18 (October 1891): 26.

————. "[Skepticism about skeleton construction]." *New York Times,* 31 December 1891, 4.

————. "[The smoke problem and the exposition]." *New York Times,* 18 December 1891, 4.

————. "The Thin Crust at Chicago." *New York Times,* 17 November 1891, 4.

"The Floating Palace." *Graphic* 4, no. 14 (4 April 1891): 224.

Halpenny, J. B. "A Proposed Cantilever or Leaning Tower at the Columbian Exposition." *Engineering News* 25 (25 April 1891): 403.

Hamlin, A. D. F. "The Difficulties of Modern Architecture." *Architectural Record* 1 (October–December 1891): 137–50.

Hastings, Chas. W. "The Hastings Tower for the World's Fair." *Engineering News* 26 (1 August 1891): 103.

Industrial Chicago. Vols. 1, 2, 4. Chicago: Goodspeed, 1891–94.

Jenney, W. L. B. "The Chicago Construction or Tall Buildings on a Compressible Soil." *Inland Architect* 18 (November 1891): 41.

King, Charles. "The City of the World's Fair." *Cosmopolitan,* November 1891, 37–63.

"The Lake Shore Drive and Sheridan Road." *Graphic* 4, no. 25 (20 June 1891): 395–99.

Lang, Andrew. "Piccadilly." *Scribner's Magazine,* August 1891, 135–52.

"Model Newspaper Office [new quarters for the Chicago *Herald*]." *New York Times,* 22 November 1891, 17.

"The Movement to Limit the Height of Buildings in Chicago." *American Architect* 34 (5 December 1891): 141.

"The Plans to Be Changed [problems at exposition site]." *New York Times,* 29 August 1891, 5.

"The Proctor Steel Tower." *Engineering News* 25 (11 April 1891): 337.

"The Proctor Tower." *Graphic* 4, no. 10 (7 March 1891): 159.

Purdy, Corydon T. "The Steel Skeleton Type of High Buildings." *Engineering News* 26, 27 (5 December 1891, 2 January 1892): 534–36, 2–5.

Schick, L. *Chicago and Its Environs.* Chicago: L. Schick, 1891.

Schuyler, Montgomery. "Glimpses of Western Architecture: Chicago." *Harper's Magazine,* August, September 1891, 395–406, 540–70.

Shaw, Albert. "Paris: The Typical Modern City." *Century Magazine,* July 1891, 449–66.

"Smoke Nuisance in Chicago." *New York Times,* 18 December 1891, 4.

Sullivan, Louis H. "The High-Building Question." *Graphic* 5, no. 25 (19 December 1891): 404–5.

"To Arouse New-Yorkers [efforts to prove New York not opposed to the exposition in Chicago]." *New York Times,* 2 December 1891, 8.

"Underwriters Fix a Limit." *New York Times,* 18 December 1891, 1.

"Unity Building, Chicago." *American Architect* 34 (14 November 1891): 97.

"[Proctor Tower to be Built]." *New York Times,* 4 April 1891, 4.

"The Women's Building at the World's Fair." *Inland Architect* 18 (November 1891): 36.

1892

English

Adler, Dankmar. "Registration in America." *Architect* 48 (22 July 1892): 52–4.
"Architects in Chicago." *Architect* 47 (27 May 1892): 352.
"Architecture from an American Point of View." *Architect* 48 (14 October 1892): 249–51.
"Charles Brodie on American Frame Houses." *American Architect* 36 (30 April 1892): 62.
"The Chicago Exhibition." *Architect* 48 (7 October 1892): 239–40.
"Chicago's Higher Evolution [London *Times* claims Chicago lacks intellectual appeal]." *Dial*, 1892, 205–6.
"The Construction of Tall Buildings in Chicago." *British Architect* 37 (8 January 1892): 36.
Davidson, T. Raffles. "Studies of Street Architecture. No. 19: Metropolitan Life Assurance Society's Offices." *British Architect* 38 (15 July 1892): 38.
Dredge, James. *Chicago and Her Exposition of 1893*. Chicago: H. V. Holmes, 1892.
———. "The Chicago Exhibition of 1893 up to Date." *British Architect* 38 (16 December 1892): 484–86.
Elzner, A. O. "The Late Mr. Richardson." *Architect* 48 (7 October 1892): 238–39.
F. "English Architectural Drawings at Chicago." *Builder* 65 (9 September 1892): 184–87.
Gordon, H. Panmure. *The Land of the Almighty Dollar*. London: Frederick Warne, 1892.
The Iron and Steel Institute in America in 1890. London: E and F.N. Spon, 1892.
"New Business Buildings of Chicago." *Builder* 63 (9 July 1892): 23–25.
"Notes: [Depew thinks quality of art is determined by size]." *Builder* 63 (29 October 1892): 331.
"Notes: Glass-Aluminum Front in Chicago." *Builder* 63 (17 September 1892): 220.
"One of the Dangers of Lofty Buildings." *British Architect* 37 (29 January 1892): 95.
Patton, Normand S. "Basis for an American Style of Architecture." *Architect* 47 (29 April 1892): 289–91.
"Residence in Chicago." *Architect* 47 (27 May 1892): 349.
Sadler, Colonel [Hayes]. "The Trade of Chicago. Consular Report on Trade and Commerce of Chicago for 1891." *Journal of the Society of Arts* 40 (16 September 1892): 918–19.
———. "Interesting Chicago Statistics." *British Architect* 38 (26 August 1892): 159.
Smith, William. *A Yorkshireman's Trip to the United States and Canada*. London: Longmans, Green, 1892.
Stead, William Thomas. *From the Old World to the New; or, a Christmas Story of the World's Fair, 1893*. New York: Office of the *Review of Reviews*, 1892.
"Steel and Iron Frame Construction in the United States." *Builder* 63 (15 October 1892): 295–96.
Sullivan, Louis H. "The Chicago Building Question." *Architect* 47 (29 January 1892): 72.
Townsend, Horace. "English and American Architecture: A Comparison and a Prophecy." *Art Journal* 54 (October 1892): 294–300. Also in *American Architect* 38 (12 November 1892): 101–3.
White, William H. "The Massachusetts Curriculum." *Journal of the Royal Institute of British Architects, Transactions* 9 (8 December 1892): 81–84.
Wight, P. B. "Recent Fireproof Buildings in Chicago." *British Architect* 37 (29 April, 6 May 1892): 329–30, 347–48.

Wood, Henry Trueman. "Chicago and Its Exhibition." *Nineteenth Century* 31 (April 1892): 553–65.

———. "Chicago Exhibition Buildings." *British Architect* 38 (12 August 1892): 112–13.

French

Chevrillon, André. "La vie américaine." *Revue des deux mondes* 62 (1 April 1892): 554–85.

Croonenberchs, P. Charles. *Les États-Unis.* Paris: Delhomme and Briguet, 1892.

Daly, Marcel. "L'architecture américaine." *La semaine des constructeurs,* 2d ser., 6 (23, 30 April, 7 May 1892): 515–17, 532–33, 544.

"Exposition internationale de Chicago." *Le génie civil* 20 (23 April 1892): 406–8.

"A French Engineer's Approval of American Methods of Fireproofing [P. Germain]." *American Architect* 35 (5 March 1892): 146.

Gout, Paul. "Hôpital Wesley à Chicago." *Encyclopédie d'architcture,* 4th ser., 4 (1892): 99–102.

Madison, G. "Expositions: L'exposition de Chicago." *Le génie civil* 22 (16 July, 6 August, 15 October 1892): 182–83, 225–26, 400–402.

Mainard, Louis. *Livre d'or des voyages. L'Amérique.* Paris: Les grands magasins de la place Clichy, 1892.

Mainard, Louis, and Meyan, Paul. *Plus haut! Plus grand!! Le Chicago.* Paris: Lecène, Oudin, 1892.

"Les maisons monstres de Chicago." *La semaine des constructeurs,* 2d ser., 6 (2 April 1892): 481.

Nansouty, Max de. "Revue mensuelle: Expositions [Administration Building, Chicago]." *Le génie civil* 24 (5 November 1892): 1–2.

No Day. "À propos du dôme central de l'exposition de Chicago." *La construction moderne* 8 (31 December 1892): 145–46.

"Notes from Our French Exchanges [Marcel Daly, 'L'architecture américaine']." *Inland Architect* 20 (December 1892): 52–53.

"Notes from Our French Exchanges: American High Buildings as Conceived by the French." *Inland Architect* 19 (May 1892): 48–49.

"Nouvelles: Maison en aluminum." *La construction moderne* 8 (24 December 1892): 144.

Planat, P. "Modern Architecture." *American Architect* 37 (20 August 1892): 111–13.

Pontzen, Ernest. "Expositions: La grande tour de 315 mètres [Morison tower proposal]." *Le génie civil* 20 (7 January 1892): 159–61.

Rousiers, Paul de. *American Life.* Translated by A. J. Herbertson. Paris: Firmin-Didot, 1892. First published as *Le vie américaine, ranches, fermes, et usines* (Paris: Firmin-Didot, 1892).

"Le temple maçonnique à Chicago." *La construction moderne* 8 (5 November 1892): 50–52.

U.A. "École des Beaux-Arts." *La construction moderne* 7 (13 February 1892): 219–21.

Varigny, C. de. *Les États-Unis.* Paris: E. Kolb, 1892.

German

Barkhausen [Professor]. "Berichte über die Versammlungen des Vereins: Die Weltausstellung in Chicago geplanten Morison Thurm." *Zeitschrift des Architekten- und Ingenieur-Vereins zu Hannover* 38 (1892): 358–63.

Barth, Hans. "'Auch' eine Columbus Ausstellung." *Kunst für Alle* 8 (1 December 1892): 70–72.

"Eine Begrundung der höhen amerikanischen Thurmhäuser." *Schweizerische Bauzeitung* 19 (23 April 1892): 119.

Bk. "Die amerikanischen Weltausstellungsbauten." *Kunstchronik,* n.s., 3 (19 May 1892): 416–21.

"Die Columbus-Weltausstellung in Chicago." *Süddeutsche Bauzeitung* 1 (12 May 1892): 260–62.

"Die Columbus-Weltausstellung in Chicago 1893 [Machinery Hall]." *Baugewerks-Zeitung* 24 (28 May 1892): 516–17.

Deckert, Emil. *Die Neue Welt: Reiseskizzen aus dem Norden und Süden der Vereinigten Staaten, sowie aus Kanada und Mexiko.* Berlin: Gebrüder Paetel, 1892.

"Das Deutsche Haus in Chicago [Schiller Theater]." *Baugewerks-Zeitung* 24 (5 March 1892): 214.

Emperger, Fr. v. "Weltausstellung Chicago." *Zeitschrift des oesterreichischen Ingenieur- und Architekten-Vereines* 44 (7 October 1892): 527.

"Ein Gebäude, das echt amerikanisch ist [Elephant building in New York]." *Süddeutsche Bauzeitung* 1 (11 August 1892): 378.

"Gegen die höhen amerikanischer Wohnhäuser." *Wiener Bauindustrie-Zeitung* 9 (21 April 1892): 302.

Graff. "Dresdner Architekten-Verein: Die Weltausstellung in Chicago 1893." *Deutsche Bauzeitung* 26 (26 March 1892): 150–51.

"Eine Grenze in der höhen amerikanischer Thurmhäuser-Bauten." *Deutsche Bauzeitung* 26 (9 April 1892): 174–75.

Grossheim, C. *Das Sanitätswesen auf der Weltausstellung zu Chicago.* Vienna: W. Braumüller, 1892.

H. [Albert Hofmann]. "Die amerikanischen Thurmhäuser." *Deutsche Bauzeitung* 26 (16 January 1892): 29–30.

———. "Die columbische Weltausstellung in Chicago." *Deutsche Bauzeitung* 26 (7 May 1892): 217–18.

Lindau, Paul. "Unter den Linden." *Scribner's Magazine,* May 1892, 579–97.

M. "Der übertriebenen Höhe der amerikanischen Häuser." *Centralblatt der Bauverwaltung* 12 (5 March 1892): 108.

———. "Ueber die ausserordentlich rege Bautätigkeit und einige bauliche Sonderheiten in Chicago." *Centralblatt der Bauverwaltung* 12 (17 September 1892): 412.

"Ein neues Bauwunder in New York [proposed thirty-one-story building]." *Wiener Bauindustrie-Zeitung* 9 (11 February 1892): 195.

Pbg. "Henry Richardson und seine Bedeutung für die amerikanische Architektur." *Deutsche Bauzeitung* 26 (6 February 1892): 64–66.

Reusche, Friedrich. *Chicago und Berlin: Alte und Neue Bahnen im Ausstellungswesen.* Berlin: Carl Ulrich, 1892.

Seeger, Eugen. *Chicago: Die Geschichte einer Weltstadt.* Chicago: Max Stern, 1892. English ed.: *Chicago, The Wonder City* (1893).

Vogel. "Villa Heimchen: Eine amerikanische Cottage auf deutschem Boden." *Zeitschrift des Architekten- und Ingenieur-Vereins zu Hannover* 38, no. 8 (1892): 653–58.

Volkmann, R. "Die Columbische Weltausstellung in Chicago." *Zeitschrift des oesterreichischen Ingenieur- und Architekten-Vereines* 44 (1 January, 5 February, 18 March, 10 June 1892):

13–15, 90–92, 197–98, 218–30; 45 (13 January, 5 May, 22 September 1893): 28–30, 270–73, 508–9.

"Weltausstellung in Chicago." *Stahl und Eisen* 12 (January 1892): 51–52.

"Die Weltausstellung in Chicago 1893 [Morison tower proposal]." *Centralblatt der Bauverwaltung* 12 (22 June 1892): 269.

"Das Worldgebäude in New-York." *Baugewerks-Zeitung* 24 (12 March 1892): 238.

American

"The Action of the Underwriters on High-Buildings in Chicago." *American Architect* 35 (2 January 1892): 1.

Baumann, Frederick. "Thoughts on Style." *Inland Architect* 20 (November 1892): 34–37.

"Building Outlook [concern about market and strikes]." *Inland Architect* 19 (May 1892): 52–53.

"Building Outlook [good prospects ahead]." *Inland Architect* 20 (December 1892): 56–57.

Bunner, H. C. "The Making of the White City." *Scribner's Magazine,* October 1892, 398–417.

"Burning of the Chicago Athletic Club Building." *Inland Architect* 20 (November 1892): 32.

"The Chicago Foundation Question." *Engineering News* 28 (13 October 1892): 349–50.

"Chicago: The Brick and Steel-Frame System of Building Tested in the Athletic Club Fire." *American Architect* 38 (26 November 1892): 132–34.

"Chicago [discussion of office building interiors]." *American Architect* 36 (25 June 1892): 199–201.

"Chicago [drainage canal]." *American Architect* 37 (24 September 1892): 198.

"Chicago [insurance on high buildings]." *American Architect* 35 (30 January 1892): 69–71.

"Chicago [ordinance on building height]." *American Architect* 38 (24 December 1892): 201–3.

"Chicago [proposed high-building ordinance]." *American Architect* 35 (22 February 1892): 134–36.

"Chicago [Woman's Temple and Monadnock Block]." *American Architect* 36 (28 May 1892): 134.

"Chicago's Elevated Road." *New York Times,* 28 May 1892, 5.

"Chicago Supplement." *Real Estate Record and Builders Guide (New York)* 50 (8 October 1892).

Clarke, Thomas Curtis. "Rapid Transit in Cities." *Scribner's Magazine,* May, June 1892, 566–78, 743–58.

Cutler, H. G. *The World's Fair: Its Meaning and Its Scope.* Chicago: Star, 1892.

Davis, Richard Harding, et al. *The Great Streets of the World.* New York: Charles Scribner's Sons, 1892.

Editorial. "A National Error in Art [undemocratic style at exposition]." *New York Times,* 20 November 1892, 4.

Edwards, Tryon, ed. *The Story of Columbus and the World's Columbian Exposition.* Detroit: F. B. Dickerson, 1892.

"Engineering News of the Week [aluminum building in Chicago]." *Engineering News* 32 (29 September 1892): 289.

Ferree, Barr. "Chicago." *Architecture and Building* 16 (2, 9 January 1892): 10–11, 17.

Flinn, John. *Chicago, the Marvelous City of the West.* Chicago: Standard Guide, 1892.

Hamlin, A. D. F. "The Battle of the Styles." *Architectural Record* 1 (January–March, April–June 1892): 265–75, 405–13.

Haynes, Marion W. "The High Building Problem." *Graphic* 6, no. 1 (2 January 1892): 28.

Head, Franklin H. "The Heart of Chicago." *New England Magazine,* July 1892, 551–67.

Hotchkiss, William Horace. "Berlin, the City of the Kaiser." *Munsey's Magazine,* 1892, 507–19.

Jenney, W. L. B. "The Chicago Construction or Tall Buildings on a Compressible Soil." *American Architect* 36 (16 April 1892): 44–45.

———. "Chicago High Buildings." *Inland Architect* 20 (October 1892): 24–25.

Kirkland, Joseph. "Among the Poor of Chicago." *Scribner's Magazine,* July 1892, 3–27.

Kirkland, Joseph, and Carolyn Kirkland. *The Story of Chicago.* 2 vols. Chicago: Dibble, 1892–94.

MacVeagh, Franklin. "Chicago's Part in the World's Fair." *Scribner's Magazine,* November 1892, 551–57.

Mason, Edward G. "Chicago." *Atlantic Monthly,* July 1892, 33–41.

Monroe, Lucy. "Art in Chicago." *New England Magazine,* n.s., June 1892, 411–32.

Moran, George E., ed. *Moran's Dictionary of Chicago.* Chicago: George E. Moran, 1892.

Morgan, H. Horace. *The Historical World's Columbian Exposition.* St. Louis: James H. Mason, 1892.

"Notes and Clippings: An Aluminum and Glass Building." *American Architect* 38 (6 November 1892): 92.

Purdy, C. F. [T]. "Steel and Iron Construction in Buildings." *Inland Architect* 19 (June 1892): 59.

Ralph, Julian. "Chicago—The Main Exhibit." *Harper's Magazine,* February 1892, 425–36.

"Rapid Building in Chicago [Ashland Block]." *American Architect* 37 (10 September 1892): 172.

Smith, Gen. William Sooy. "Chicago Buildings and Foundations." *Engineering News* 28 (13 October 1892): 343–46.

Van Brunt, Henry. "Architecture at the World's Columbian Exposition." *Century Magazine,* May, October 1892, 81–99, 720–31.

Van Rensselaer, M. G. "The Artistic Triumph of the Fair-Builders." *Forum* 14 (December 1892): 527–40.

Views of Chicago: Photographs in Black from Recent Negatives by the Albertype Co. New York: A. Wittemann, 1892.

Wight, P. B. "Gen. William Sooy Smith's Paper on High Buildings Criticised." *Inland Architect* 19 (April 1892): 34–36.

———. "Recent Fireproof Building in Chicago, Pt. 2, 3, 5." *Inland Architect* 19 (March, April, June 1892): 21, 32–34, 57.

1893

English

"American Architecture [ridicules tall buildings, Auditorium, women architects]." *Saturday Review,* 21 January 1893, 71–72.

"American Architecture at the Chicago Exhibition." *British Architect* 40 (29 July 1893): 73.

"American Machines and Tools in Germany." *Engineer* 76 (6 October 1893): 322.

Anderson, J. Macvicar. "Session 1893–94: Opening Address [review of contemporary architecture]." *Royal Institute of British Architects, Journal,* 3d ser., 1 (6 November 1893): 1–15.

"Architectural Drawings at Chicago." *Builder* 65 (2 September 1893): 167–70.

"The Architecture of Chicago." *Architect* 50 (27 October 1893): 270–72.

Besant, Walter. "American Notes [Anglo-Saxons will dominate]." *Cosmopolitan*, November, December 1893, 64–72, 233–40.

———. "A First Impression [of the exposition]." *Cosmopolitan*, September 1893, 528–39.

"The Chicago Exhibition: A General View." *Builder* 65 (1 July 1893): 1–4.

Child, Theodore. *The Praise of Paris*. New York: Harper and Brothers, 1893.

"Colour Decoration at the Chicago Exhibition [Transportation Building Golden Door]." *Builder* 65 (26 August 1893): 151–52.

Cook, Thomas, and Son. *The World's Fair at Chicago, 1893*. London: Thos. Cook and Son, 1893.

Cravath, J. R. "Electricity at the World's Fair." *Review of Reviews* 8 (July 1893): 35–39.

Editorial. "[President opening the fair]." *Builder* 64 (6 May 1893): 338.

"An English Humorist on American Architecture." *American Architect* 39 (11 February 1893): 94.

"An Englishman on the Chicago Fair Buildings." *American Architect* 40 (24 June 1893): 204.

Fletcher, Banister F. "The Godwin Bursary Report, 1893." *Royal Institute of British Architects, Journal*, 3d ser., 1 (1893): 557–60.

"The Greater Buildings at the Chicago Exhibition [title differs in succeeding issues]." *Builder* 65 (15 July, 5, 19 August 1893): 39–42, 95–97, 131–32.

Hems, Harry. "Chicago and Its Exhibition." *Building News* 64 (26 May 1893): 699–700.

———. "The Chicago Exhibition." *Building News* 64 (5 May 1893): 621.

———. "The Wind-up of the World's Fair at Chicago." *Building News* 65 (1 December 1893): 738.

"High Building in Baltimore." *Architect* 49 (26 May 1893): 349–50.

Hill, George. "The Relation between the Engineer and the Architect in America." *Architect* 49 (24 March 1893): 191–93.

Hutton, W. R. "The Foundations of Some High Buildings in America." *British Architect* 40 (1 December 1893): 382, 391–92.

"The Influence of the Chicago Exhibition." *Engineer* 75 (3 March 1893): 190.

"In the Progress of the World: Electrical Progress and Our Character Sketches." *Review of Reviews* 8 (July 1893): 10.

"Is the Chicago Exhibition a Failure?" *British Architect* 40 (25 August 1893): 140.

Kerr, Robert. "The Problem of National American Architecture." *Architectural Record* 3 (October–December 1893): 121–32.

"London Street Architecture as at Present." *Architect* 50 (1, 8 September 1893): 131–32, 146–47.

Mansfield, G. Allen. "The Architect, the Engineer, and the Contractor." *Builder* 65 (16 September 1893): 205.

Naylor, Robert Anderton. *Across the Atlantic*. Westminster: Roxburghe Press, 1893.

Northcote, A. S. "American Life through English Spectacles." *Nineteenth Century* 34 (September 1893): 476–88.

"Opening of the Chicago Exhibition." *Builder* 64 (6 May 1893): 338.

"Points on the Construction of American Country Houses." *British Architect* 39 (9 June 1893): 397–98.

Robinson, John Beverley. "Modern American Country Houses." *Architect* 49 (30 June 1893): 428–29.

"Royal Institute of British Architects: Presentation of the Royal Gold Medal [to R. M. Hunt]." *Builder* 64 (24 June 1893): 484–87.

"The Royal Institute of British Architects Gold Medal, 1893." *Building News* 64 (16 June 1893): 795–97.

S.R.D. "Modern Architecture in England." *British Architect* 40 (17 November 1893): 343–45.

Stead, F. Herbert. "An Englishman's Impressions at the Fair." *Review of Reviews* 8 (July 1893): 30–34.

[Stephens, A. G.] "The Architecture of Chicago." *Architect* 50 (27 October 1893): 270–72.

Sturgis, Russell. "Lack of Originality in American Architecture." *Architect* 50 (20 October 1893): 253–54.

Villiers, Frederick. "An Artist's View of Chicago and the World's Fair." *Journal of the Society of Arts* 42 (8 December 1893): 49–54.

Wallace, Alfred R. "The Social Quagmire and the Way out of It [on capitalism and workers]." *Arena* 41 (March, April 1893): 395–410, 525–42.

"What Chicago People Read [from *London Daily Chronicle*]." *Critic*, 23 September 1893, 200–201.

"What Is It to Celebrate [reasons for exposition]." *All the Year Round,* 25 February 1893, 175–81.

Wight, P. B. "Fireproof Construction and Practice of American Architects." *British Architect* 40 (1, 8 September 1893): 148, 157, 175–76.

Windsor, Henry Haven. "Transit Facilities in Chicago and on the Fair Grounds." *Review of Reviews* 7 (June 1893): 548–50.

"The World's Columbian Exposition." *Engineering* 56 (3 November 1893): 534–44.

"The World's Columbian Exposition, 1893." *Engineering* 55 (21 April 1893): 503–96. Supplement devoted to exposition, including section on "The City of Chicago."

"The World's Show at Chicago." *Leisure Hour,* 1893, 283–85.

French

"L'architecture américaine." *La construction moderne* 8 (1, 28 July 1893): 459–60, 498.

Bailly, P. "L'exposition de 1900 à Paris d'après des remarques sur celle de Chicago." *La semaine des constructeurs,* 2d ser., 7 (29 July, 5 August 1893): 56, 68.

Barbier, Émile. *Voyage au pays des dollars.* Paris: E. Flammarion, 1893.

Barthélemy, A. *L'organisation des arts aux États-Unis.* London: RIBA Library, 1893.

Bentzon, Th. [Marie-Thérèse Blanc]. "Impressions of the World's Fair." *Critic,* 25 November 1893, 331–32.

Bocage, F. Adolphe. "Architecture in Apartment-Buildings." *Architect* 50 (3 November 1893): 277–78.

———. "Commission de l'exposition de Chicago." *L'architecture* 6 (25 March 1893): 121–22.

Bouilhet, André. "L'exposition de Chicago." *Revue des arts décoratifs* 14 (1893): 66–79.

Bourget, Paul. "A Farewell to the White City." *Cosmopolitan,* December 1893, 133–40.

Bruwaert, Edmund, and F. Régamey. *Chicago et l'exposition columbienne.* Paris: Hachette, 1893.

Bruwaert, François Edmond. "Chicago et l'exposition universelle columbienne." *Le tour du monde* 65 (1893): 291–304.

Chasseloup-Laubat, Marquis de. "A Frenchman on the World's Fair and America." *American Architect* 39 (28 January 1893): 58–60.

———. *Voyage en Amérique et principalement à Chicago.* Paris: Société des ingénieurs civils de France, 1893.

"Exposition de Chicago." *La construction moderne* 8 (25 February 1893): 252.

"L'exposition de Chicago [excerpts of Marcel Monnier's article in *Le Temps*]." *L'architecture* 6 (20 May 1893): 219–20.

"A Frenchman's Impressions of Chicago Itself [Octave Uzanne]." *American Architect* 41 (16 September 1893): 176.

G.M.J. "La grande escarpolette de Chicago." *La semaine des constructeurs,* 2d ser., 7 (21 October 1893): 197–98.

———. "Les grandes bâtisses aux États-Unis." *La semaine des constructeurs,* 2d ser., 8 (11, 18 November, 2, 9, 16, 23 December 1893): 232–33, 244–45, 269–70, 281, 291–92, 304–5; (6 January, 3, 10 February, 10 March, 7 April 1894): 327–29, 379–80, 387–88, 439–42, 487.

———. "Maisons américaines." *La semaine des constructeurs,* 2d ser., 8 (5 August 1893): 68.

Gausseron, B.-H. "Exposition de Chicago." *La revue encyclopédique* 3 (1 November 1893): 1084.

Hermant, Jacques. "L'art à l'exposition de Chicago." *Gazette des beaux-arts* 73 (September, November, December 1893): 237–53, 416–25, 441–61.

———. *Exposition internationale de Chicago en 1893. Rapport de M. Jacques Hermant, Comité 36: L'architecture et les industries qui en dépendent en Amérique et à l'exposition de Chicago.* Paris: Commissariat général à exposition internationale de Chicago, 1893.

———. "The *Gazette des beaux-arts* and the World's Fair." *American Architect* 42 (14 October 1893): 20–21.

Lourdelet, Ernest. *Exposition de Chicago.* Paris: Librairies impr. réunies, 1893.

Luberne, Henri La. "Chicago et l'exposition américaine." *La revue illustrée* 1 (1893): 338.

Lucas, Charles. "Les fondations des edifices aux États-Unis." *La construction moderne* 9 (21 October 1893): 28–30.

"Une maison de seize étages à Chicago." *L'architecture* 6 (28 January 1893): 44.

"Mission aux États-Unis [French delegation to study American architecture and training]." *L'architecture* 6 (25 February 1893): 84.

Monnier, Marcel. "*Le temps* à Chicago." *Le temps,* 16, 17, 18, 26, 27, 28, 30 May, 1, 4, 17, 23 June 1893.

Nansouty, Max de. "Revue mensuelle: Les maisons géantes aux États-Unis." *Le génie civil* 24 (4 November 1893): 5–6.

Rey, L., and A. de Dax. *Compte revue du voyage fait aux États-Unis d'Amérique et au Canada par une délégation de la Société des ingénieurs civils de France.* Paris: Société des ingénieurs civils de France, 1893.

Sauvin, G. *Autour de Chicago: Notes sur les États-Unis.* Paris: Plon, 1893.

"Les sociétés d'architectes à l'étranger: L'Institut américain des architectes." *La construction moderne* 8 (29 April, 17 June, 9 September 1893): 252–53, 437, 581.

"Timely Topics of Paris: Frenchmen Report New York City Gay, But Chicago Sad." *New York Times,* 2 July 1893, 10.

Uzanne, Octave. *Vingt jours dans le nouveau monde.* Paris: May and Motteroz, 1893.

Varigny, M. C. de. "The American Woman." *Popular Science Monthly* 43 (July 1893): 383–88.

W., Antony. "À Chicago: Une maison de verre." *La semaine des constructeurs,* 2d ser., 7 (27 May 1893): 565.

———. "À Chicago—dernières nouvelles." *La semaine des constructeurs,* 2d ser., 7 (29 April 1893): 517.

German

"Architektonische Aussichten aus der columbischen Weltausstellung in Chicago." *Deutsche Bauzeitung* 27 (9 September 1893): 437–38.

Baedeker, Karl, ed. *The United States with an Excursion into Mexico.* New York: Charles Scribner's Sons, 1893.

Blum, Emil. *Chicago und die columbische Weltausstellung 1893.* Hannover: Behrenberg's Druckerei, 1893.

Böttcher, Karl. *Chicago! Weltausstellungs-Briefe.* Leipzig: W. Friedrich, 1893.

Das Columbische Weltausstellung Album. Chicago: Rand McNally, 1893.

Cornely, Eugen. *Von deutschen Häfen nach New-York und Chicago.* Berlin: Albert Goldschmidt, 1893.

Dernburg, Friedrich. *Aus der weissen Stadt: Spaziergänge in der Chicagoer Weltausstellung und weitere Fahrten.* Berlin: Julius Springer, 1893.

Diercks, G. *Kulturbilder aus den Vereinigten Staaten.* Berlin: Allgemeiner Verein für Deutsche Litteratur, 1893.

Emperger, F. v. "Eiserne Gerippbauten in den Vereinigten Staaten." *Zeitschrift des oesterreichischen Ingenieur- und Architekten-Vereines* 45 (14, 21, 28 July, 15 September, 6 October 1893): 396–400, 410–12, 422–26, 497–504, 521–28.

"Ferris grosses Rad an der kolumbischen Weltausstellung zu Chicago." *Schweizerische Bauzeitung* 22 (29 July 1893): 28–29.

"German and French Complaints Touching the World's Fair." *American Architect* 41 (1 July 1893): 1.

"German Appreciation of Our Brick and Stone Masonry [Spies]." *American Architect* 42 (9 December 1893): 117.

Gottschalk, Louis. *20 Tage durch Chicago und die Weltaustelung 1893.* Stuttgart: Foerster, 1893.

Günzel, L. "Aus Amerika [letter home from emigrant architect]." *Baugewerks-Zeitung* 25, no. 49 (21 June 1893): 630.

———. "Privathäuser in Amerika." *Baugewerks-Zeitung* 25–26 (16 September, 28 October, 16 December 1893, 17 February 1894): 952–53, 1104–5, 1274–75, 156–57.

Gust. "Auf der Reise zur Weltausstellung." *Baugewerks-Zeitung* 25 (12 April 1893): 360–61.

———. "Aus Amerika [skyscraper foundations]." *Baugewerks-Zeitung* 25 (30 September 1893): 1006.

Hamster. "Chicagoer Ausstellungsbriefe." *Süddeutsche Bauzeitung* 3 (1893): 328–29, 338–40, 357–60.

"Haus aus Aluminum." *Baugewerks-Zeitung* 25 (4 January 1893): 5.

Hermann, Walther. *Chicago und die Kolumbian Weltausstellung.* Berlin: Walter and Apolants, 1893.

Herzberg, A. "Die Ausstellung deutscher Architektur- und Ingenieur- Werke auf der Columbischen Weltausstellung zu Chicago." *Deutsche Bauzeitung* 17 (16 December 1893): 613–15.

Hesse-Wartegg, Ernst von. *Chicago: Eine Weltstadt im amerikanischen Westen.* Stuttgart: Union Deutsche Verlagsgesellschaft, 1893.

———. *Curiosa aus der Neuen Welt.* Leipzig: Carl Reissner, 1893.

Hinckeldeyn, [Karl]. "Von der Weltausstellung in Chicago." *Centralblatt der Bauverwaltung* 13 (30 September, 14 October, 4 November, 2, 23, 30 December 1893): 405–8, 425–28, 457–58, 501–3, 536–38, 545–47.

Hoech, Th. "Die Haupt-Gewerbehalle der Weltaustellung in Chicago." *Centralblatt der Bauverwaltung* 13 (6, 13 May 1893): 189–91, 204–5.

———. "Die Maschinenhalle der Weltaustellung in Chicago." *Centralblatt der Bauverwaltung* 13 (8 July 1893): 282–84.

"Die höhen Häuser in Chicago." *Baugewerks-Zeitung* 25 (24 May 1893): 523.

J.S——r. "Amerikanische Schnellbauten." *Wiener Bauindustrie-Zeitung* 10 (10 August 1893): 531–32.

———. "Die 'höhen Häuser' in Amerika." *Wiener Bauindustrie-Zeitung* 10 (22 June 1893): 447–48.

J.W. "Winke für die Beschickung der Weltausstellung in Chicago." *Wiener Bauindustrie-Zeitung* 10 (2 February 1893): 191–93.

"Die kolumbische Weltausstellung in Chicago." *Schweizerische Bauzeitung* 21 (6, 13, 20, 27 May, 3, 17, 30 June 1893): 114–18, 125–26, 133–34, 138–40, 142–44, 159–60, 168–71; 22 (15 July 1893): 9–12.

Körber. "Architekten-Verein in Berlin: Reise-Eindrücke von der chicagoer Weltausstellung." *Deutsche Bauzeitung* 27 (8 March 1893): 118–19.

Lemcke, Heinrich. *Auf nach Chicago!* Hamburg: Verlagsanstalt und Druckerei, 1893.

Lessing, Julius. *Kunstgewerbe: Sonderblick aus dem amtlichen Bericht über die Weltaussstellung in Chicago 1893.* Berlin: Reichsdruckerei, 1893.

Lindau, Paul. *Altes und Neues aus der neuen Welt.* Berlin: Carl Duncker, 1893.

Luschka. "Das Ferris-Rad auf der Weltausstellung in Chicago." *Zeitschrift des oesterreichischen Ingenieur- und Architekten-Vereines* 45 (8 September 1893): 496.

M. "Vermischtes: Die Feuerbeständigkeit der neuerdings in Chicago üblichen Bauweise." *Centralblatt der Bauverwaltung* 13 (4 March 1893): 100.

Mikosch, Baron. *Auf der Ausstellung in Chicago: Eine Erlebnisse in Amerika und auf die Weltausstellung in Chicago.* Berlin: Neufeld and Henius, 1893.

"Das Modellhaus auf der Weltausstellung in Chicago." *Baugewerks-Zeitung* 25 (11 March 1893): 231.

"Modernes amerikanisches Schulgebäude." *Wiener Bauindustrie-Zeitung* 10 (23 March 1893): 275–77.

Mueller, Otto H. "Skizzen von der Weltausstellung in Chicago." *Zeitschrift des oesterreichischen Ingenieur- und Architekten-Vereines* 45 (1, 8 September 1893): 484–86, 493–95.

O. "Der 'Freimauer Tempel' in Chicago." *Wiener Bauindustrie-Zeitung* 11 (12 October 1893): 13–14.

R. "Skizzen von der chicagoer Ausstellung." *Schweizerische Bauzeitung* 22 (23 September, 7, 14 October 1893): 79–82, 92–96, 100–101.

Reisenotizen eines Chicagoreisenden. Lahr: Moritz Schauenberg, 1893.

Rs. "Vermischtes: Der Weltausstellungsthurm in Chicago [Lehmann tower proposal]." *Centralblatt der Bauverwaltung* 13 (21 January 1893): 32.

Spielhagen, Friedrich. "Berlin." *Cosmopolitan* 14 (March 1893): 515–31.

Spies. "Einiges über Ausführungsweisen im amerikanischen Hochbau." *Deutsche Bauzeitung* 27 (18 October 1893): 509–11.

Strande, Wilhelm von. *Chicago in Tears and Smiles.* Translated by Robert Edward Gutermann. Cleveland: Press of Lauer and Mattill, 1893.

"Ueber die Weltausstellung in Chicago [talk by Dr. Dürre of Aachen]." *Schweizerische Bauzeitung* 22 (19 August 1893): 48.

"Vereins-Angelegenheiten: Weltausstellung in Chicago 1893 [talk by Prof. Edlen von Radinger]." *Zeitschrift des oesterreichischen Ingenieur- und Architekten-Vereines* 45 (3 November 1893): 581.

Wattmann, J. "Briefe von der columbischen Weltausstellung." *Deutsche Bauzeitung* 27 (9, 19, 23 May, 15, 17, 29 June, 15 August 1893): 281–83, 293–95, 313–15, 349–50, 368–72, 404–8, 462–66.

Wedding, Herm. "Columbische Weltausstellung in Chicago." *Stahl und Eisen* 13 (September 1893): 726–29.

Werner, Emerik A. "Die Columbia-Welt-Ausstellung in Chicago 1893." *Allgemeine Bauzeitung* 58 (1893): 3–5, 9–14, 28–30.

American

[Adler, Dankmar]. "Piling for Isolated Foundations Adjacent to Walls." *Inland Architect* 20 (January 1893): 63–64.

"American Architecture." *Saturday Review,* 21 January 1893, 71–72.

"Annual Report of the Health Department of Chicago." *New York Times,* 4 January 1893, 4.

Bancroft, Hubert Howe. *The Book of the Fair.* 2 vols. Chicago: Bancroft, 1893.

Bigelow, Poultney. "How to Make a City Cholera Proof." *Cosmopolitan,* August 1893, 497–501.

Birkmire, William H. *Skeleton Construction in Building.* New York: John Wiley, 1893.

Blackall, C. H. "Live Loads in Office-Buildings." *American Architect* 41 (26 August 1893): 129–31.

Boyesen, Hjalmer Hjorth. "A New World Fable." *Cosmopolitan,* December 1893, 173–86.

Buel, C. C. "Preliminary Glimpses of the Fair." *Century Magazine,* February 1893, 615–25.

"Building Outlook [growing apprehension]." *Inland Architect* 21 (June 1893): 64.

"Building Outlook [financial depression unexpected]." *Inland Architect* 22 (September 1893): 24.

Burnham, Daniel H. "The Organization of the World's Columbian Exposition." *Inland Architect* 22 (August 1893): 5–8.

Cameron, William E., ed. *History of the Columbian Exposition.* Chicago: Columbian Historical Company, 1893.

———. *The World's Fair.* Chicago: Chicago Publication and Lithography, 1893.

"Chicago [elevator accident]." *American Architect* 40 (10 June 1893): 168–69.

"Chicago [litter in streets]." *American Architect* 39 (25 March 1893): 185.

"Chicago: The Cold Weather and Fires. Volume of the Year's Work. Important Buildings now in Hand." *American Architect* 39 (4 February 1893): 71–72.

"Chicago a Surprise." *Graphic* 9, no. 21 (18 November 1893): 423.

"Chicago in Good Health." *New York Times,* 23 April 1893, 8.

The Chicago Records History of the World's Fair. Chicago: *Chicago Daily News* Co., 1893.

"Chicago's Water All Right." *New York Times,* 7 April 1893, 2.

"A City of Vast Enterprise." *New York Times,* 24 December 1893, 20.

"A City of White Elephants." *New York Times,* 19 September 1893, 8.

Columbian Movable Sidewalk. Chicago: [Movable Sidewalk Company], 1893.

"Decadence of the Use of Gas as an Illuminant." *Inland Architect* 20 (January 1893): 60.

Deforth, J. "The Origination of the Skeleton Type of High Buildings." *Engineering News* 29 (5 January 1893): 15.

Editorial. "Architectural Superiority of the Columbian Exposition." *Inland Architect* 22 (August 1893): 2.

———. "[Height limit in Chicago]." *New York Times,* 11 March 1893, 4.

———. "The New Chicago." *Graphic* 9, no. 4 (July 1893): 60.

———. "[Typhoid deaths in Chicago]." *New York Times,* 4 January 1893, 4.

"Effect of a Fire on a Chicago Building of Fire-Proof Construction." *American Architect* 39 (14 January 1893): 27–28.

"The Effect of Cold on Iron and Steel Construction." *American Architect* 39 (18 March 1893): 162.

Fernald, Frederik A. "Household Arts at the World's Fair." *Popular Science Monthly* 43 (October 1893): 803–12.

Ferree, Barr. "Architecture in New York." *Architect* 50 (15 December 1893): 381–82.

———. "Chicago Architecture." *Lippincott's Monthly Magazine,* July 1893, 80–94.

"The Fire in the Chicago Athletic Club." *American Architect* 40 (1 April 1893): 2.

"A Foreigner's Impressions of the World's Fair Buildings [Cecilia Waern]." *American Architect* 40 (15 April 1893): 47.

Fuller, Henry B. *The Cliff-Dwellers,* 1893. Reprint. Ridgewood, N.J.: Gregg Press, 1968.

Halstead, Murat. "Electricity at the Fair." *Cosmopolitan,* September 1893, 577–83.

Hardy, Arthur Sherburne. "Last Impressions." *Cosmopolitan,* December 1893, 195–200.

Hawthorne, Julian. "A Description of the Inexpressible." *Lippincott's Monthly Magazine,* April 1893, 496–503.

Head, Franklin. "The Fair's Results to the City of Chicago." *Forum* 16 (December 1893): 524–26.

Holland, James P. "Chicago and the World's Fair." *Chautauquan,* May 1893, 136–39.

"Illustrations [New York Life Insurance Company's Building, Chicago]." *American Architect* 42 (11 November 1893): 78–79.

"Illustrations [Traveling Derrick and Construction, Iron Trusses, Manufactures and Liberal Arts Building, World's Columbian Exposition, Chicago]." *Inland Architect* 19 (June 1893).

"Impressions of the World's Fair." *Critic,* 25 November 1893, 331–34.

Ingalls, John J. "Lessons of the Fair." *Cosmopolitan,* December 1893, 141–49.

Ingals, E. Fletcher. "Chicago's Sanitary Condition." *Forum* 15 (July 1893): 585–93.

Ingleheart, William. "Electricity at the World's Fair." *Chautauquan,* June 1893, 264–67.

Kobbé, Gustav. "Sights at the Fair." *Century Magazine,* September 1893, 643–55.

Lungren, Charles M. "Electricity at the World's Fair." *Popular Science Monthly* 43, 44 (October, November 1893): 721–40, 39–54.

"The Mayor's View of Chicago." *New York Times,* 25 May 1893, 1.

Murphy, Richard J. *Authentic Visitor's Guide to the World's Columbian Exposition and Chicago.* Chicago: Union News Company, 1893.

"New Office Buildings in Chicago." *Engineering News* 29 (16 February 1893): 151–53.

"Official Praise of the World's Fair Buildings." *American Architect* 42 (28 October 1893): 51.

"Origin of the Chicago System of Skeleton Construction." *American Architect* 39 (21 January 1893): 33.

Palmer, Alice Freeman. "Some Lasting Results of the World's Fair." *Forum* 16 (December 1893): 517–23.

"[President opening Chicago Fair]." *New York Times,* 23 April 1893, 8.

Purdy, Corydon T. "Special Structural Details of the Old Colony Building, Chicago, Ill." *Engineering News* 30 (21 December 1893): 486+.

Ralph, Julian. *Harper's Chicago and the World's Fair.* New York: Harper and Brothers, 1893.

———. *Our Great West.* New York: Harper and Brothers, 1893.

Rand McNally and Co.'s Handbook of the Columbian Exposition. Chicago: Rand McNally, 1893.

Rand McNally and Co's Pictorial Chicago and Illustrated World's Columbian Exposition: Containing Views of Principal Buildings, Residences, Streets, Parks, Monuments, Etc. Chicago: Rand, McNally, 1893.

S.K. "The Columbian Exposition, 4." *Nation* 57 (24 August 1893): 132–33.

"The Slums of Chicago." *Graphic* 8, no. 8 (25 February 1893): 139.

"Street Railway Accident." *Graphic* 8, no. 11 (18 March 1893): 182.

"Synopsis of Building News [few architects busy]." *Inland Architect* 21 (May 1893): 53–54.

Tarbell, Ida M. "In the Streets of Paris." *New England Magazine,* November 1893, 259–72.

Truman, Benjamin C. *History of the World's Fair.* Philadelphia: W. H. Henry, 1893. Reprint. New York: Arno Press, 1976.

"Under the Electric Glare." *New York Times,* 9 May 1893, 2.

Van Brunt, Henry. "The Columbian Exposition and American Civilization." *Atlantic Monthly,* May 1893, 577–88.

Van Rensselaer, M. G. "At the Fair." *Century Magazine,* May 1893, 3–13.

[Warner, Charles Dudley]. "Editor's Study: The Fair." *Harper's Magazine,* October 1893, 798–801.

Wheeler, Candace. "A Dream City." *Harper's Magazine,* May 1893, 830–46.

White, Trumbull, and William Ingleheart. *The World's Columbian Exposition.* Boston: Standard Silverware Company, 1893.

Wight, P. B. "The Great Exhibition Reviewed." *American Architect* 42 (7, 14 October 1893): 7–8, 21–23.

"Why Owners Should Resume Building." *Inland Architect* 22 (September 1893): 14.

1894

English

"American Architects and Public Buildings." *Architect* 51 (13 April 1894): 246–47.

"American Methods of Working." *Engineer* 77 (11 May 1894): 400.

Bridgmen, George Soudon. "American Notes." *Building News* 66 (3 February, 9, 23 March 1894): 167–68, 321–22, 390.

"The British Commission's Report on the Chicago Exhibition: Conclusions." *British Architect* 41 (25 May 1894): 361–62.

"The Chicago Exhibition." *Architect* 51 (25 May 1894): 21–23.

Dewar, Thomas R. *A Ramble Round the Globe.* London: Chatto and Windus, 1894.

Dredge, James. *A Record of the Transportation Exhibits at the World's Columbian Exposition of 1893.* London: Office of *Engineering,* 1894.

Emerson, William. "The World's Fair Buildings, Chicago." *Royal Institute of British Architects, Journal,* 3d ser., 1 (1894): 65–74.

"An Englishmen on American Architecture [Theodore Stanton]." *American Architect* 43 (24 March 1894): 144.

Fletcher, Banister F. "American Architecture through English Spectacles." *Engineering Magazine* 7 (June 1894): 314–21.

"[Half-mile high building planned in New York]." *Building News* 67 (17 August 1894): 237.

"Illustrations: Building for the American Surety Company, New York." *Builder* 66 (14 April 1894): 289–90.

Kindl, F. H. "Fireproof Floors." *Engineering* 57 (23 February 1894): 273–74.

"The London *Architect* on the Architecture of the World's Fair." *American Architect* 43 (3 February 1894): 50.

"Metallic Construction in America." *Architect* 52 (30 November 1894): 340–41.

Mitchell, Edmund. "International Effects of the Fair." *Engineering Magazine* 6 (January 1894): 468.

"Proceedings of Allied Societies: Liverpool, Sessional Meeting [talk by James Cook]." *Royal Institute of British Architects, Journal,* 3d ser., 1 (1894): 362–63.

"Proceedings of Allied Societies: Sheffield, Monthly Meeting [talk by H. W. Lockwood on importance of speed in American practice]." *Royal Institute of British Architects, Journal,* 3d ser., 1 (1894): 90.

Stead, William T. *Chicago Today: or, the Labour War in America.* London: *Review of Reviews* Office, 1894.

———. *If Christ Came to Chicago! A Plea for the Union of All Who Love in the Service of All Who Suffer.* Chicago: Laird and Lee, 1894.

———. "My First Visit to America." *Review of Reviews* 9 (1894): 414–17.

———. "The Two Babylons: London and Chicago." *New Review* 10 (May 1894): 560–70.

Stephens, A. G. "A Queenslander's Travel Notes, 1894." In *A. G. Stephens: Selected Writings,* edited by Leon Cantrell. Sydney: Angus and Robertson, 1977.

Townsend, Horace. "H. H. Richardson." *Magazine of Art,* 1894, 133–38.

Van Brunt, Henry. "Architectural Education in America." *Architect* 52 (23 November 1894): 334–36.

French

Baudouin, Marcel. *Quelques remarques sur les hôpitaux des États-Unis.* Paris: Aux Bureaux des archives provinciales de chirurgie, 1894.

Bocage, Adolphe. "L'architecture aux États-Unis et à l'exposition universelle de Chicago: La maison moderne et la situation de l'architecte aux États-Unis." *L'architecture* 7 (13 October 1894): 333–39.

Boileau, L.-C., fils. "L'architecture aux États-Unis: et l'exposition universelle de Chicago." *L'architecture* 7 (19 May 1894): 150–51.

Bouilhet, André. "L'orfèvrerie américains à l'exposition de Chicago." *Revue des arts décoratifs* 15 (1894): 110–21, 136–48, 167–73.

Butin, A. "Constructions civiles: Les maisons géantes aux États-Unis." *Le génie civil* 25 (29 June 1894): 115.

Calonne, Alphonse de. "High Buildings in England and America." *Chautauquan,* July 1894, 427–31.

"Concours de maisons à Chicago." *L'émulation,* n.s., 4 (1894): 173.

"La dernière journée de l'exposition de Chicago." *Le génie civil* 25 (6 October 1894): 358.

"Exposition universelle de Chicago en 1893." *L'émulation,* n.s., 4 (1894): 22–27.

Fauconnet, Raoul. *L'employé aux États-Unis.* Rouen: Gagniard, 1894.

———. *Exposition internationale de Chicago.* Rouen: Gagniard, 1894.

Grandin, Madame Léon. *Impressions d'une Parisienne à Chicago.* Paris: Ernst Flammarion, 1894.

Grille, Antoine, and Henri Falconnet. *L'architecture et les constructions métalliques à l'exposition de Chicago.* Paris: E. Bernard, 1894.

———. *Revue technique de l'exposition universelle de Chicago en 1893.* Paris: E. Bernard, 1894.

Grille, Antoine, and Laborde. *Les travaux publics aux États-Unis.* Paris: E. Bernard, 1894.

Henry, J. A. *Quelques notes sur l'exposition columbienne de Chicago.* Lyon: Mougin-Rusand, 1894.

Hermant, Jacques. "L'architecture aux États-Unis et à l'exposition universelle de Chicago: L'architecture en Amérique et à la World's Fair." *L'architecture* 7 (20 October 1894): 341–46.

———. *Exposition universelle de Chicago en 1893, Comité 36, Génie civil. Travaux publics. Architecture. Rapport de M. Jacques Hermant, architecte de la ville de Paris.* Paris, 1894.

"The Industrial Arts of America Criticized by M. Victor Champier." *American Architect* 43 (31 March 1894): 146.

Lecomte, Gustave. "Les tendances de l'architecture fin-de-siècle." *L'architecture* 7 (20 January 1894): 19–20.

Lordereau, Gabriel. *Du Havre à Chicago.* Lyon: Alexandre Rey, 1894.

"Une maison à loyer à Paris." *L'architecture* 4 (28 March 1894): 150.

Monroe, Lucy. "Th. Bentzon [Marie T. Blanc] on Chicago." *Critic,* 18 August 1894, 109–10.

"Pabst Building, à Milwaukee." *L'émulation,* n.s., 4 (1894): 174.

"Rapport de M. Jules Macier, vice-président de la commission [medals awarded to Louis Sullivan]." *Revue des arts décoratifs* 14 (1894): 324.

Stanton, Theodore. "A Franco-American's Notes on the United States." *Westminster Review* 141 (1894): 194–204.

Varigny, Henry de. *En Amérique: souvenirs de voyage et notes scientifiques.* Paris: G. Masson, 1894.

Venre, Henri. *Exposition internationale de Chicago en 1893.* Paris: Imprimirie nationale, 1894.

Vyon, Maurice. "L'architecture aux États-Unis et à l'exposition universelle de Chicago: Naissance et développement de la ville de Chicago." *L'architecture* 7 (29 September, 6 October 1894): 317–21, 325–27.

German

Amtlicher Bericht über die Weltaussstellung in Chicago 1893. 2 vols. Berlin: Reichsdruckerei, 1894.

"Die Bauart der höhen Geschäftshäuser in Chicago." *Centralblatt der Bauverwaltung* 14 (14 February 1894): 61.

Bode, Wilhelm. "Moderne Kunst in den Vereinigten Staaten von Amerika." *Kunstgewerbeblatt,* n.s., 5 (1894): 113–21, 137–46.

CL. "Arch.- und Ing.-Verein zu Hamburg [talk by Wolbrandt]." *Deutsche Bauzeitung* 28 (24 January 1894): 42–43.

Emperger, Fr. von. "Live-Loads and Supports in Office-Buildings." *American Architect* 43 (10 March 1894): 118.

Fischer, H. "Das Heizungs- und Luftungswesen in den Vereinigten Staaten von Nord-Amerika." *Zeitschrift des Architekten- und Ingenieur-Vereins zu Hannover* 40, no. 4 (1894): 220–24.

Frahm. "Über eiserne Häuser in Nordamerika, besonders in Chicago." *Stahl und Eisen* 14 (15 March, 1 April 1894): 258–65, 303–10.

"A German Architect's Impressions in America [Leopold Gmelin]." *American Architect* 46 (13 October 1894): 10.

Gmelin, Leopold. "Architektonisches aus Nordamerika." *Deutsche Bauzeitung* 28 (15, 29 September, 3, 6, 20, 27 October, 17, 24 November 1894): 453–56, 481–83, 485–87, 495–98, 520–22, 532–34, 566–70, 582–83.

Götz, Hermann. *Meine Reise nach Chicago und die Kolumbische Weltausstellung.* Darmstadt: A. Koch, 1894.

Grzybowski, Paul. *Land und Leute in Amerika.* Berlin: H. Steinitz, 1894.

Hillger, Hermann. *Amerika und die Columbische Weltausstellung, Chicago 1893.* Leipzig: A. Twietmeyer, 1894.

Hofmann, Albert. "Das künstlerische Ergebniss der Weltausstellung in Chicago." *Deutsche Bauzeitung* 28 (28 April 1894): 209–10.

Jaffe, Franz. "Die Architekturausstellung fremder Länder." In *Amtlicher Bericht über die Weltaussstellung in Chicago 1893,* 1141–59. Berlin: Reichsdruckerei, 1894.

———. "Die Architektur der columbischen Weltausstellung zu Chicago, 1893." *Blätter für Architektur und Kunsthandwerk* 7 (April, May, June, August, September 1894).

Landsberg, Th. "Das Manhattan Lebens-Versicherungs-Gebäude in New York." *Centralblatt der Bauverwaltung* 14 (21 April 1894): 165–66.

Lessing, Julius. "Kunstgeschichte." In *Amtlicher Bericht über die Weltaussstellung in Chicago 1893,* 762–806. Berlin: Reichsdruckerei, 1894.

"Manhattan Life Insurance Company." *Architektonische Rundschau* 10, no. 4 (1894): plate 31.

Maier, Hermann. "Einige Wand- und Deckenconstruktionen in den amerikanischen unverbrennlichen 'Stahl-Rahmen-Gebäuden.'" *Deutsche Bauzeitung* 28 (16, 19, 23 May 1894): 241, 249, 253.

Meyer-Baeschlin, Joseph, and J. Lepori. *Architektur, Baukonstruktionen und Baueinrichtung in nordamerikanischen Städten.* Bern: Fritz Haller, 1894.

Ohrt, B. "Der Speicherbau in Amerika und die Massregeln gegen Feuersgefahr bei diesen Bauten." *Deutsche Bauzeitung* 28 (20 January 1894): 37–38.

"Das 'Pabst-building' in Milwaukee." *Blätter für Architektur und Kunsthandwerk* 7 (1 January 1894): 1.

Pbg. "Architekten-Verein zu Berlin [talk by Franz Jaffe on skyscrapers]." *Deutsche Bauzeitung* 28 (10 February 1894): 75.

Schliepmann, Hans. "Amerikanische Architektur." *Kunstwart* 7 (August 1894): 337–40.

———. "Zwei Hauptmotive amerikanischer Innen-Dekoration." *Innen-Dekoration* 5 (August 1894): 113–17.

Sievers, Wilhelm. *Amerika: Eine allgemeine Landeskunde.* Leipzig and Vienna: Bibliographisches Institut, 1894.

Stradal, Adalbert G. "Die Bauordnungen von New-York und Chicago." *Zeitschrift des oesterreichischen Ingenieur- und Architekten-Vereines* 46 (16, 23 March 1894): 155–61, 167–71.

———. "Ueber Hochbauten und Baumaterialen in den Vereinigten Staaten." *Zeitschrift des oesterreichischen Ingenieur- und Architekten-Vereines* 46 (11 May 1894): 278.

Thiergarten, Ferd. *Von Karlsruhe nach Chicago.* Karlsruhe: F. Thiergarten, 1894.

Wohltmann, Ferdinand. *Landwirtschaftliche Reisestudien über Chicago und Nord-Amerika.* Breslau: Schlett'sche Buchhandlung, 1894.

American

"Assaulted Workmen in Chicago Strike Back." *Inland Architect* 24 (December 1894): 41–42.

Barrett, John Patrick. *Electricity at the Columbian Exposition.* Chicago: R. R. Donnelley, 1894.

"Building Outlook [causes of unexpected depression]." *Inland Architect* 23 (July 1894): 65.

"Building Outlook [depression felt everywhere]." *Inland Architect* 23 (June 1894): 56.

"Building Outlook [prices, wages low]." *Inland Architect* 23 (February 1894): 9.

"Chicago [labor friction at Marquette Building]." *American Architect* 46 (29 December 1894): 135–37.

"Chicago [settling of Board of Trade Building]." *American Architect* 43 (24 February 1894): 91–92.

"Chicago [skyscrapers and lightning]." *American Architect* 45 (28 July 1894): 38–40.

"Chicago: New Office Buildings." *American Architect* 43 (20 January 1894): 30–32.

Clark, T. M. "Skeleton Construction and the Fire-Department." *American Architect* 46 (20 October 1894): 23.

"The Constructive Methods Used in the New York Life Building." *American Architect* 43 (10 February 1894): 71–72.

Editorial. "Do 'Skyscrapers' Pay?" *American Architect* 44 (12 May 1894): 58.

———. "The Effect of an External Fire on a Terracotta Protected Building." *American Architect* 44 (28 April 1894): 32.

———. "Gold Medal Awarded to *The Inland Architect.*" *Inland Architect* 24 (September 1894): 11.

———. "The Legality of the Corporate Ownership of the High Buildings in Chicago." *American Architect* 45 (8 September 1894): 89.

———. "The New York Superintendent of Buildings on Skeleton Construction." *American Architect* 43 (13 January 1894): 13–14.

"Effect of the Present Labor Disturbances." *Inland Architect* 23 (July 1894): 58.

"The Effect of Wind-Pressure on the High Buildings of Chicago." *American Architect* 44 (7 April 1894): 1.

Ferree, Barr. "An 'American Style' of Architecture." *Architectural Record* 1 (July–September 1894): 39–45.

———. "The High Building and Its Art." *Scribner's Magazine,* March 1894, 297–318.

Flagg, Ernest. "Influence of the French School on Architecture in the United States." *Architectural Record* 4 (October–December 1894): 210–28.

Gordon, F. C. "The 'Sky-Scraper.'" *American Architect* 46 (8 December 1894): 100–101.

Hastings, Thomas. "High Buildings and Good Architecture." *American Architect* 46 (17 November 1894): 67–68.

"High Buildings of Steel Skeleton Construction." *Engineering News* 32 (27 December 1894): 535–37.

Howells, William Dean. *A Traveler from Altruria.* New York: Harper and Brothers, 1894.

Jenney, W. L. B. "Live-Loads and Supports in Office-Buildings." *American Architect* 43 (10 February, 10 March 1894): 71–72, 118–19.

Preston, Thomas B. "Life on the Boulevards." *Chatauquan* 20 (1894): 58–64.

Schaefer, C. Bryant. "That New Style of Architecture." *Inland Architect* 24 (September 1894): 16–17.

Schuyler, Montgomery. "Last Words about the Fair." *Architectural Record* 3 (January–March 1894): 271–301.

"Smoke-Abatement in Chicago." *American Architect* 44 (21 April 1894): 36.

"Twenty-eighth Annual Convention of the American Institute of Architects, 2 [risk of enclosed steel frames]." *American Architect* 46 (27 October 1894): 35–36.

"The World's Fair in Retrospect." *Engineering Magazine* 6 (January 1894): 417–560.

1895

English

"American Decorative Art." *British Architect* 43 (17 May 1895): 356–57.

"Architectural Conservatism [avoid American mistakes]." *British Architect* 43 (25 January 1895): 57–58.

Bare, H. Bloomfield. "Philadelphia: An Architect's Notes in an American City." *Royal Institute of British Architects, Journal,* 3d ser., 2 (28 March 1895): 394–98.

Hole, S. Reynolds. *A Little Tour in America.* London: Edward Arnold, 1895.

"The Late Richard Morris Hunt." *Builder* 69 (17 August 1895): 111–12.

"Some Account of Concrete Construction in America [system of Ernest L. Ransome]." *Builder* 69 (14 September 1895): 181–83.

Ward, Martindale C. *A Trip to Chicago.* Glasgow: Alex. Malcolm, 1895.

French

Bernard, Hermann. "Architecture: Les maisons géantes aux États-Unis." *Le génie civil* 26 (23 February 1895): 262–66.

Blanc, Marie T. [Th. Bentzon]. *The Condition of Woman in the United States.* Boston: Roberts Brothers, 1895.

Bourget, Paul. *Outre-Mer: Impressions of America.* New York: Charles Scribner's Sons, 1895. Originally published as *Outre-Mer: Notes sur l'Amérique* (Paris: Alphonse Lemerre, 1895).

"Le confort dans l'habitation moderne." *La construction moderne* 10 (22 June 1895): 1–2.

"France Honors Louis H. Sullivan." *Inland Architect* 25 (March 1895): 20–21.

Gausseron, B.-H. "Maisons hautes aux États-Unis." *Le monde moderne* 1 (April 1895): 537–49.

"Influence de l'art français à l'étranger." *La construction moderne* 10 (7 September 1895): 579–80.

Krantz, Camille, ed. *Exposition internationale de Chicago en 1893: Rapports.* Paris: Imprimerie nationale, 1895.

"Nécrologie: M. Richard Morris Hunt." *La construction moderne* 10 (24 August 1895): 564.

"Notes from our French Exchanges: The Art Industries and Professional Schools of the United States." *Inland Architect* 25 (February 1895): 5–6.

"Notes from our French Exchanges: The High Buildings of the United States." *Inland Architect* 25 (February 1895): 6.

"La nouvelle architecture américaine [review of book by J. F. Kendall]." *L'architecture* 8 (19 October 1895): 360.

"Petite enquête sur l'architecture moderne." *L'architecture* 8 (5 October, 7 December 1895): 337–38, 409–10.

P.P. [Paul Planat]. "L'architecture américaine." *La construction moderne,* 2d ser., 1 (12 October 1895): 14–17.

R.D. [Raymond-Auguste Daly]. "Richard-Morris Hunt." *La semaine des constructeurs,* 3d ser., 1 (24 August 1895): 217–18.

Varigny, Charles Victor Crosnier de. *The Women of the United States.* New York: Dodd, Mead and Co., 1895.

German

Berg, Graf F. *1893 nach Chicago.* Jurjew: E. J. Karow, 1895.

"Die farbige Behandlung des Verkehrsgebäude auf der Weltausstellung in Chicago." *Centralblatt der Bauverwaltung* 15 (10 April 1895): 152.

"Einsturz eines Theater-Neubaues in Chicago [Colosseum]." *Schweizerische Bauzeitung* 24 (5 October 1895): 95.

"A German Appraisal of the United States." *Atlantic Monthly,* January 1895, 124–28.

H. [Albert Hofmann]. "Richard Morris Hunt." *Deutsche Bauzeitung* 29 (7 December 1895): 605–7.

Jaffe, Franz. "Amerikanische Innen-Dekorationen." *Innen-Dekoration* 6 (July 1895): 105–12, 120.

———. *Die Architektur der columbischen Welt-Ausstellung zu Chicago, 1893.* Berlin: Julius Becker, 1895.

Kraus, O. "Ueber englische und amerikanische Ein-Familienhäuser." *Wiener Bauindustrie-Zeitung* 12 (11 July 1895): 744–76.

Leitholf, O. *Die Construction höher Häuser in den Vereinigten Staaten von Amerika.* Berlin: W. Ernst and Sohn, 1895.

———. "Die Construction höher Häuser in den Vereinigten Staaten von Amerika." *Zeitschrift für Bauwesen* 45 (1895): 217–36.

Lessing, Julius. "Neue Wege." *Kunstgewerbeblatt,* n.s., 6 (1895): 1–5.

M. "Vermischtes: Einsturz eines achtstöckigen Haus." *Centralblatt der Bauverwaltung* 15 (28 September 1895): 416.

Maier, H. "Die Schiebefenster in Amerika." *Deutsche Bauzeitung* 29 (28 September 1895): 484–86.

Meyer, Julius. "Zwei new-yorker Geschäftstürme." *Ueber Land und Meer* 73, no. 11 (1895): 246–47.

Nordau, Max. *Degeneration,* 1895. Reprint. New York: Howard Fertig, 1968.

Pbg. "Architekten-Verein zu Berlin [talk by Hinckeldeyn on the Golden Door]." *Deutsche Bauzeitung* 29 (13 March 1895): 130.

"Vermischtes: R. M. Hunt." *Centralblatt der Bauverwaltung* 15 (17 August 1895): 356.

American

Adler, Dankmar. "An Important Letter [announces his retirement from private practice]." *Inland Architect* 25 (July 1895): 61.

Blackall, C. H. "The All-Around Architect." *Inland Architect* 26 (October 1895): 23–25.

"Building Outlook [expected upturn has not occurred]." *Inland Architect* 25 (February 1895): 10.

"Building Outlook [some signs of recovery]." *Inland Architect* 26 (September 1895): 18.

"The Burning of the Manhattan Bank Building in New York." *American Architect* 50 (23 November 1895): 85.

"Chicago [consequences of the height ordinance]." *American Architect* 49 (28 September 1895): 133–35.

"Chicago [two new office buildings]." *American Architect* 48 (22 June 1895): 118–19.

"Chicago: The Year '94 Better than the Previous One. The Last of the Very High Buildings." *American Architect* 47 (26 January 1895): 42–44.

Editorial. "Hunt's Influence on Modern Architecture." *Inland Architect* 26 (August 1895): 1.

Ellis, John, ed. *Chicago and the World's Columbian Exposition.* Chicago: Trans-Continental Art Company, 1895.

Freitag, Joseph K. *Architectural Engineering.* New York: John Wiley, 1895.

Fuller, Henry Blake. *With the Procession.* New York: Harper and Brothers, 1895. Reprint. University of Chicago Press, 1965.

"General Building Statistics for 1893 and 1894." *Inland Architect* 25 (February 1895): 7.

"The Justification for Using the Protected Steel Skeleton." *American Architect* 50 (23 November 1895): 85.

Moses, John, and Joseph Kirkland. *The History of Chicago.* Chicago: Munsell, 1895.

"Popular Miscellany: Steel Buildings." *Popular Science Monthly* 47 (August 1895): 567–68.

"Recent Chicago Tall Buildings." *Engineering News* 34 (17 October 1895): 250–52.

"San Francisco [Chicago—the representative city of commerce and labor]." *American Architect* 49 (10 August 1895): 62.

Schaefer, Conrad N. B. "Architectural Individuality." *Inland Architect* 26 (September 1895): 14.

Schuyler, Montgomery. "Architecture in Chicago." *Architectural Record* (December 1895): 3–110.

Stone, Melville E. "Chicago: Before the Fire, After the Fire, and To-Day." *Scribner's Magazine,* June 1895, 663–79.

Tolman, William Howe. *Municipal Reform Movements in the United States.* New York: Fleming H. Revell, 1895.

Willett, James B. "Skeleton Structures in Building." *Inland Architect* 26 (December 1895): 47–48.

1896

English

"Bricks and Mortar [tall buildings increase death rate]." *Builder's Journal* 4 (16 December 1896): 299.

Cleaver, A. W. "Johns Hopkins Hospital, Baltimore, U.S.A." Manuscript, RIBA Library, 1896.

"Concerning Things American [artistic weaknesses of skyscrapers]." *Builder* 70 (28 March 1896): 267–69.

Gass, John B. "American Architecture and Architects, with special Reference to the Works of the Late Richard Morris Hunt and Henry Hobson Richardson." *Royal Institute of British Architects, Journal,* 3d ser., 3 (6 February 1896): 229–32.

Kendall, John. *American Memories.* Nottingham: E. Burrows, 1896.

"Report of Manchester Society of Architects: American Architecture and Architects [talk by John B. Gass]." *Builder* 70 (8 February 1896): 117.

Shankland, Edward Clapp. *Steel Skeleton Construction in Chicago.* London: Institute of Civil Engineers, 1896.

"A Strong Opponent of High Buildings." *Review of Reviews* 13 (May 1896): 611–12.

French

Bentzon, Marie Thérèse [Marie T. Blanc]. *Notes de voyage, Les américaines chez elles.* 2 ed. Paris: Calmann Lévy, 1896.

Bing, Samuel. "L'architecture aux États-Unis." *Le moniteur des architectes,* n.s., 10–12 (1896): 9–14, 19–21; (1897): 27–28; (1898): 53.

———. *La culture artistique en Amérique.* Paris, 1896.

Boileau, L.-C. "L'enquête sur l'architecture moderne." *L'architecture* 9 (8, 15 February 1896): 45–47, 53–54.

Calonne, Alphonse de. "The French Universal Exposition of 1900." *Architectural Record* 5 (January–March 1896): 217–26.

Deschamps, Philippe. *À travers les États-Unis et le Canada.* 3d ed. Paris: Ernest Leroux, 1896.

Fabre, Auguste. *Les sky scratchers, ou les hautes maisons américaines.* Nîmes: Bureaux de l'émancipation, 1896.

Le Bon, Gustave. *The Crowd.* New York: Macmillan, 1896.

Soissons, S.-C. de. *A Parisian in America.* Boston: Estes and Lauriat, 1896.

Vaudoyer, A. "L'enquête sur l'architecture moderne: Le sentiment des architectes." *L'architecture* 9 (11 January 1896): 10–12.

German

"Amerikanischer Bau-Wahnsinn [proposed two-hundred-story building for New York]." *Süddeutsche Bauzeitung* 6 (21 May 1896): 173.

"Aus Amerika [houses in Chicago]." *Blätter für Architektur und Kunsthandwerk* 9 (May, June 1896): 27–28, 33.

"Aus Amerika [rise of European influence]." *Blätter für Architektur und Kunsthandwerk* 9 (1 December 1896): 69.

Benfey, Gustav. "Bau eines Chicagoer Sky-skraper [Fisher Building]." *Baugewerks-Zeitung* 28 (7 November 1896): 1195–98.

———. "Häuserbau in Nord-Amerika." *Baugewerks-Zeitung* 28 (13 June 1896): 615–17.

———. "Häuserheben und Bewegen in Chicago." *Baugewerks-Zeitung* 28 (23 September 1896): 1032.

F.G.L. "Richard Morris Hunt." *Zeitschrift des oesterreichischen Ingenieur- und Architekten-Vereines* 48 (24 January 1896): 39–42.

Grzybowski, Paul. *Amerikanische Skizzen.* Berlin: Schneider, 1896.

K. "Bücherschau: Chicago 1893, die Architektur der columbischen Weltausstellung." *Zeitschrift des oesterreichischen Ingenieur- und Architekten-Vereines* 48 (31 January 1896): 62.

Streiter, Richard. "Das deutsche Kunstgewerbe und die englisch-amerikanische Bewegung." *Innen-Dekoration* 7 (July 1896): 106–8, 114–15, 125–29.

American

"A Halt Called on the Skyscraper." *Scribner's Magazine,* March 1896, 395–96.

Adams, John Coleman. "What a Great City Might Be—A Lesson from the White City." *New England Magazine,* March 1896, 3–13.

Adler, Dankmar. "Slow-Burning and Fireproof Construction." *Inland Architect* 26 (January 1896): 60–62.

"Building Outlook [1895 better than expected]." *Inland Architect* 26 (January 1896): 66.

"The Field of Art [questioning whether the new tall buildings are architecture]." *Scribner's Magazine,* January 1896, 127–28.

Flagg, Ernest. "The Dangers of High Buildings." *Cosmopolitan,* May 1896, 70–79.

Himmelwright, A. L. A. "High Buildings." *North American Review,* November 1896, 580–86.

Sullivan, Louis H. "The Tall Office Building Artistically Considered." *Lippincott's Monthly Magazine,* March 1896, 403–9.

1897

English

Adler, Dankmar. "The Tall Business Building: Some of Its Engineering Problems." *Cassier's Magazine,* June 1897, 193–210.

"American Architects and Contemporary Architecture." *British Architect* 48 (9 July 1897): 33.

Capper, S. Henbest. "The American Tall Building from a European Point of View." *Engineering Magazine* 14 (November 1897): 239–52.

Creed, J. R. "Sky-Scrapers." *Pearson's Magazine,* August 1897, 184–89.

Fletcher, Banister. "The Influence of Material on Architecture." *Builder* 73 (4 September 1897): 181–83.

Statham, Henry Heathcote. *Modern Architecture.* London: Chapman and Hall, 1897.

Steevens, George Warrington. *The Land of the Dollar.* New York: Dodd, Mead, 1897.

French

America and the Americans from a French Point of View. New York: Charles Scribner's Sons, 1897.

Bing, S. "L'architecture et les arts décoratifs en Amérique." *Revue encyclopédique Larousse* 7 (December 1897): 1029–36.

Brunetière, Ferdinand. "A French Critic's Impressions of America." *McClure's Magazine,* November 1897, 67–74.

Coubertin, Pierre de. *Souvenirs d'Amérique et de Grèce.* Paris: Hachette, 1897.

"Une critique américaine: De l'architecture des villes en Amérique." *La construction moderne,* 2d ser., 3 (20 November 1897): 85–86.

Landry, Jean. *Hommes et choses d'Amérique.* Paris: J. Lefort, 1897.

Lutaud, Dr. A. *Aux États-Unis.* 2d ed. Paris: Ernest Flammarion, 1897.

Nodet, H. "The Modern Office Building." *La construction moderne,* 2d ser., 2 (20, 27 February, 13, 27 March, 3 April 1897): 242–44, 256–57, 283–4, 309, 319.

Wickes, Walter Herriman. "La construction métallique en Amérique." *L'architecture* 10 (4, 11 December 1897): 440–41, 447–50.

German

"Die amerikanische Cottage." *Deutsche Bauhütte* 1 (7, 14, 21, 28 October 1897): 1–2, 1–2, 1–2, 1–2.

Benfey, G. "Häuserbau in Nord Amerika." *Baugewerks-Zeitung* 29 (24 July 1897): 945.

Berlepsch, H. E. von. "Kunstleben in Amerika 1. Malerei, Plastik, Baukunst." *Kunst für Alle* 12 (15 April, 1 May 1897): 209–16, 229–39.

"Büchershau: *Neubauten in Nordamerika.*" *Centralblatt der Bauverwaltung* 17 (30 October 1897): 500.

Graef, Paul. *Neubauten in Nordamerika.* Introduction by Karl Hinckeldeyn. Berlin: J. Becker, 1897.

"Können uns die nordamerikanischen Riesenbauten etwas lehren?" *Deutsche Bauhütte* 1 (27 May 1897): 2–3.

"Mode in der Kunst in Bezug auf Einrichtung unserer Häuser." *Deutsche Bauhütte* 1 (22 July 1897): 1–2.

"Städtebau in Bezug auf Trennung von Wohn- und Geschäftsviertel." *Deutsche Bauhütte* 1 (10 June 1897): 1–2.

American

Brainard, Owen. "The Modern Tall Building." *Chautauquan,* November 1897, 131–39.

Fuller, Henry B. "The Upward Movement in Chicago." *Atlantic Monthly,* October 1897, 534–47.

Hamlin, A. D. F. "The Tall Building from an American Point of View." *Engineering Magazine* 14 (December 1897): 436–43.

Steffens, J. Lincoln. "The Modern Business Building." *Scribner's Magazine,* July 1897, 37–61.

1898

English

"An American Architecture School [rise of French influence]." *Builder* 75 (16 July 1898): 51.

Black, Frederick. "The 'Sky-scrapers' of New York." *Chamber's Journal,* 6th ser., 1 (9 July 1898): 507–12.

"Discussion of Mr. Paterson's Paper [Godwin Bursar's Report, 1896]." *Royal Institute of British Architects, Journal,* 3d ser., 5 (23 April 1898): 328–31.

Gibson, R. W. "Fireproof Construction of Buildings in the United States." *Royal Institute of British Architects, Journal,* 3d ser., 6 (10 December 1898): 49–64.

Jenney, W. L. B. "The Dangers of Tall Steel Structures." *Cassier's Magazine,* March 1898, 413–22.

Muirhead, James Fullarton. *The Land of Contrasts.* Boston: Lamson, Wolffe, 1898.

Paterson, A. N. "A Study of Domestic Architecture in the Eastern States of America in the Year 1896." *Royal Institute of British Architects, Journal,* 3d ser., 5 (23 April 1898): 309–28.

"Tall Buildings and Fireproof Construction." *British Architect* 50 (9 December 1898): 413.

French

Baudouin, Marcel. "Les maisons hautes et les maisons qui marchent aux États-Unis." *Revue scientifique,* 4th ser., 9 (22 January 1898): 109–113.

Blanc, Marie Thérèse [Th. Bentzon]. *Choses et gens d'Amérique.* Paris: C. Lévy, 1898.

"Les constructions élevées aux États-Unis." *La construction moderne,* 2d ser., 3 (17 September 1898): 612.

Planat, P. "Construction rapide." *La construction moderne,* 2d ser., 3 (20 August 1898): 564.

Wickes, Walter Herriman. "Comparaison entre la construction en Amérique et en France." *L'architecture* 11 (29 January 1898): 39–42.

German

"Die amerikanischen Riesenhäuser in kultureller und konstruktioneller Beziehung." *Deutsche Bauhütte* 2 (22, 29 September 1898): 341–43, 349–50.

Höfert, Victor. "Die alte und die neue Richtung in der Baukunst." *Der Architekt* 4 (1898): 33–36.

"Literatur: *Neubauten in Nordamerika.*" *Architektonische Rundschau* 14, no. 3 (1898).

"Nordamerikanische Architektur [critique of *Neubauten in Nordamerika].*" *Deutsche Bauhütte* 2 (30 June, 14 July 1898): 247–48, 264.

Schliepmann, Hans. "*Neubauten in Nord-Amerika* [review]." *Innen-Dekoration* 9 (January 1898): 1.

Streiter, Richard. *Architektonische Zeitfragen.* Berlin and Leipzig: Cosmos Verlag für Kunst und Wissenschaft, 1898.

———. "Nordamerikanische Architektur." *Allgemeine Zeitung,* 6 June 1898, 4–7.

V. [Rudolf Vogel]. "Zur neuen Richtung in der Architektur." *Deutsche Bauhütte* 2 (17, 24 February 1898): 53–54, 65.

American

Sturgis, Russell. "Good Things in Modern Architecture." *Architectural Record* 8 (July–September 1898): 92–110.

1899

English

Archer, William. *America To-Day.* New York: Charles Scribner's Sons, 1899.

"Architecture in America [artistic weaknesses]." *Builder's Journal* 10 (29 November 1899): 252.

Brydon, J. M. "Public Libraries: I. The Buildings." *Royal Institute of British Architects, Journal,* 3d ser., 6 (25 February 1899): 209–24.

"The Future of American Architecture." *British Architect* 51 (17 February 1899): 107–8.

H.B.P. "American Architecture [national style cannot be rushed]." *Builder's Journal* 9 (17 May 1899): 213–14.

Holmes, F. M. "The Tallest Dwellings in the World." *Cassell's Magazine,* August 1899, 269–75.

Kipling, Rudyard. *American Notes.* Philadelphia: Henry Altemus, c. 1899.

"Some American Architectural Designs [French influence]." *Builder* 76 (8 April 1899): 338–39.

German

"Amerikanische Architektur [more creative than European]." *Dekorative Kunst* 2, no. 9 (1899): 92.

Berehinak, Ferdinand. "Die Moderne in der Architektur und im Kunstgewerbe." *Zeitschrift des oesterreichischen Ingenieur- und Architekten-Vereines* 51 (24 March 1899): 183–89.

"Foreign Views of American Architecture [*Berliner Tageblatt* commends *Neubauten in Nordamerika*]." *Inland Architect* 34 (August 1899): 6.

Gmelin, Leopold. "American Architecture from a German Point of View." *Forum* 27 (August 1899): 690–704.

Huberti, Fritz. "Feuersichere Konstruktionen im amerikanischen Bauwesen." *Deutsche Bauzeitung* 33 (9 August 1899): 398–99.

———. "Grossfeuer in New-York am 4 Dezember 1898." *Deutsche Bauzeitung* 33 (8 February 1899): 67–69.

Lamb, Ch. "Der amerikanische Gesichtspunkt." *Dekorative Kunst* 1, no. 8 (1899): 49–53.

Linse, B. "Ueber die Feuersicherheit der Eisenkonstruktionen in amerikanischen Höchstbauten." *Deutsche Bauhütte* 3 (30 March 1899): 80–81.

"Vermischtes: Einschrankung der Gebäudenhöhen." *Centralblatt der Bauverwaltulng* 19 (11 March 1899): 116.

Vogel, F. Rud. "Feuersicher Eisenbau." *Deutsche Bauhütte* 3 (25 May, 1 June 1899): 129–30, 133–34.

———. "Ueber amerikanische Bauverhältnisse und Konstruktionen." *Deutsche Bauhütte* 3 (20, 27 April, 4, 18 May 1899): 97–98, 101–2, 110–11, 122–23.

American

Baker, Ray Stannard. "The Modern Skyscraper." *Munsey's Magazine,* October 1899, 48–58.

Peattie, Elia W. "The Artistic Side of Chicago." *Atlantic Monthly,* December 1899, 828–34.

Weber, Adna Ferrin. *The Growth of Cities in the Nineteenth Century.* New York: Macmillan, 1899. Reprint. Ithaca: Cornell University Press, 1969.

1900–1914

English

Budden, Harry. "An American Frame House." *Builder* 79 (22 December 1900): 585–87.

"English and American Practice Compared." *Builder* 78 (13 January 1900): 27–28.

Fraser, John Foster. *America at Work.* London: Cassell, 1903.

Heathcote, Chas. "Comparison of English and American Building Methods." *British Architect* 60 (4, 11 December 1903): 403–4, 413, and 422, 431–33.

"Outre Mer [unhealthy French influence]." *Builder* 79 (28 July 1900): 69–71.

Smith, William Sooy. "The Modern Tall Steel Building: Corrosion and Fire Dangers." *Cassier's Magazine,* May 1902, 56–60.

Stead, W. T. *The Americanization of the World.* New York: Horace Markley, 1901.

Swales, Francis S. "Architecture in the United States." *Architectural Review* 24 (August, September 1908): 61–68, 117–26; 25 (January, February 1909): 13–19, 82–91.

Voysey, C. F. A. "The English Home." *British Architect* 75 (27 January 1911): 68–70.

Wells, H. G. *The Future in America.* Leipzig: Bernhard Tauchnitz, 1907.

French

Champier, Victor. *The Arts of the Nineteenth Century: Painting, Sculpture, Architecture, and Decorative Arts of all Races.* Philadelphia: G. Barrie, 1901.

Escard, Paul. *Maisons pour ouvrières des grandes cités aux États-Unis d'Amérique*. Paris: R. Pièce, 1900.

Klein, Felix. *America of To-morrow*. Chicago: A. C. McClure, 1911.

Millet, Louis. "L'architecture aux États-Unis et l'influence française." *France-Amérique* 1912:240–44; 1913:288–91.

Schopfer, Jean. "American Architecture from a Foreign Point of View: New York City." *Architectural Review* 7 (1900): 25–30.

Vierendeel, Arthur. *La construction architecturale en fonte, fer et acier*. Brussels: Lyon-Claesen, 1902.

German

Deckert, Dr. Emil. *Nordamerika*. 2d ed. Leipzig: Bibliographisches Institut, 1904.

Dorn, Alexander. *Amerikanisches*. Vienna: Volkswirtschaft Verlag, 1900.

Hemberle, Eduard. "Erlebnisse und Beobachtungen eines deutschen Ingenieure in den Vereinigten Staaten 1867–1885." *Deutsch-Amerikanische Geschichtsblätter* 1 (July, October): 22–25, 1–12; 2 (January, April, July 1902): 15–24, 10–19, 21–31.

Holitischer, Arthur. *Amerika Heute und Morgen: Reiseerlebnisse*. Berlin: Fischer, 1912.

Münsterberg, Hugo. *American Traits from the Point of View of a German*. Boston: Houghton, Mifflin, 1902.

Muthesius, Hermann. *Architektonische Zeitbetrachtungen. Ein Umblick an der Jahrhundertwende*. Sonderausdruck *Centralblatt der Bauverwaltung*. Berlin: W. Ernst, 1900.

———. *Stilarchitektur und Baukunst. Wandlungen der Architektur im XIX Jahrhundert und ihr heutige Standpunkt*. Mülheim a/R.: K. Schimmelpfeng, 1902.

Vogel, Rudolph. *Das amerikanische Haus*. Berlin: Ernst Wasmuth, 1910.

———. "Die Architektur und das Kunstgewerbe in Nordamerika und ihr Einfluss auf die 'Moderne' in Deutschland." *Süddeutsche Bauzeitung* 10 (14 April 1900): 117–18.

American

Adshead, Stanley D. "A Comparison of Modern American Architecture with that of European Cities." *Architectural Record* 29 (February 1911): 113–25.

Bragdon, Claude. "'Made in France' Architecture." *Architectural Record* 16 (December 1904): 561–68.

Special Chicago Number, Harper's Weekly. New York: Harper, 1902.

Steffens, Lincoln. "Chicago: Half Free and Fighting On." *McClure's Magazine*, October 1903, 563–77.

Turner, George Kibbe. "The City of Chicago: A Study of the Great Immoralities." *McClure's Magazine*, April 1907, 575–92.

Chicago Tribune, 1885–93

A. Conditions, Environment, and Activities of Central Chicago and the Loop

1885

"Street-Railways and Public." 20 January 1885, 4.

"Chicago in Danger [filth and disease]." 1 March 1885, 19.

"Electric Lighting [city's electric light plant]." 26 June 1885, 6.

"The Sewage Problem." 12 August 1885, 3.

"The Latest Gas Ordinance [defrauding the public]." 15 August 1885, 4.

"The Sewage Problem [poor state of the river]." 16 August 1885, 4.

"Our Drinking Water." 16 August 1885, 8.

"Our Filthy River." 20 August 1885, 5.

"The Lake Front [position of Illinois Central Railroad]." 21 August 1885, 10.

"Drainage and Water." 28 August 1885, 3.

"Underground Conduits." 8 November 1885, 6.

"Chicago Drainage Problem." 30 November 1885, 4.

"Defective Drainage." 3 December 1885, 3.

"The Drainage Problem." 4 December 1885, 9.

"The Sewerage Problem." 9 December 1885, 3.

1886

"Railroad Accidents in Chicago [thirteen deaths in last six weeks]." 14 February 1886, 4.

"Rapid Transit [plans for underground railroad]." 7 March 1886, 4.

"Underground Railroads." 7 March 1886, 4.

"Cost of Street Lighting." 31 March 1886, 4.

"Redeem the City [through electrical cleaning]." 6 April 1886, 4.

"Chicago's Sewage Problem." 24 April 1886, 7.

"The City's Scavenger Work [new system needed]." 29 April 1886, 9.

"The Scavenger Service [recommendation to improve it]." 5 May 1886, 8.

"A Glimpse at the City [a day's disasters and accidents]." 22 June 1886, 2.

"Chicago Telephones." 25 June 1886, 3.

"Underground Wires." 27 June 1886, 12.

"Tearing up the Streets." 9 July 1886, 4.

"The Bridges of Chicago." 8 August 1886, 13.

"The New Crib Launched." 8 October 1886, 3.

"Chicago's Water Supply." 30 October 1886, 8.

"The City: Fast Driving in the Streets." 16 November 1886, 8.

"Our Sewerage System." 5 December 1886, 26.

"The Smoke Ordinance [city officials do nothing]." 12 December 1886, 3.

"Snow in the Streets [removal a problem]." 21 December 1886, 6.

"Hampered Pedestrians [sidewalk obstructions]." 23 December 1886, 3.

1887

"For the City's Health [water supply and drainage]." 15 January 1887, 4.

"We Drink It in Chicago." 17 January 1887, 9.

"Chicago Drainage Scheme." 25 January 1887, 4.

"Almost an Inundation [rains overwhelm sewers]." 9 February 1887, 5.

"A Drainage Outlet [need better flow through Des Plaines River to the Illinois]." 10 February 1887, 4.

"Drainage of Chicago." 17 February 1887, 1.

"Electric Lighting for Chicago." 14 April 1887, 4.

"Clean the Streets." 27 April 1887, 4.

"Chicago Water Supply." 22 May 1887, 13.

"Electric Lighting at the Crossings." 5 June 1887, 4.

"From Country to City [commuter railroad lines]." 12 June 1887, 25.

"The Mayor on Street-Railway Franchises." 10 July 1887, 4.

"The Street Railways [irresponsible franchises]." 17 July 1887, 9.

"Thousands of Rats." 17 July 1887, 18.

"Chicago's Suez Canal [activity on Chicago River]." 15 August 1887, 1.

"The Smoke Nuisance." 21 August 1887, 4.

"Chicago's Juggernaut [railroad accidents in city]." 4 September 1887, 15.

"How to Prevent Crossing Accidents." 9 September 1887, 4.

"The Perils of City Life." 9 September 1887, 2.

"Death at the Crossing." 13 September 1887, 2.

"How Streets Are Paved." 15 September 1887, 14.

"Safety at Crossings [draft ordinance in city council]." 23 September 1887, 8.

"The Smoky, Sooty Air." 27 November 1887, 17.

"Chicago's Misfortune [city is caged by tracks]." 17 December 1887, 15.

"The Crossings Protection Ordinance Passed." 18 December 1887, 4.

1888

"Complaints about Gas [customers complain about service]." 4 January 1888, 9.

"Chicago's Gehenna [need for garbage disposal plant]." 8 January 1888, 4.

"Sewer Gas and Its Remedy." 15 January 1888, 4.

"Crushed at a Crossing [collision of train and street car]." 18 January 1888, 1.

"They Say It Burns the Smoke [nonpolluting furnace]." 18 January 1888, 6.

"Crossing Protection." 20 January 1888, 8.

"A Street-Car Mass-Meeting [riders protest conditions]." 11 February 1888, 6.

"Crushed between Two Grip-Cars." 2 May 1888, 2.

"A Day on State Street [6:00 A.M. to 6:00 P.M. at corner of State and Madison]." 6 May 1888, 25.

"Tearing up Paved Streets." 19 May 1888, 4.

"Jackson Street Bridge." 19 July 1888, 5.

"Flush the Streets." 5 August 1888, 4.

"Cable Car Accidents." 12 August 1888, 2.

"Damage Done by Smoke." 17 August 1888, 1.

"A City's Smoke and Soot [impact on architecture]." 18 August 1888, 3.

"Chicago's Great Evil [soot-smoke]." 19 August 1888, 9.

"The Great Smoke Evil [discourages capitalists]." 22 August 1888, 8.

"A Deadly Atmosphere [doctors are concerned]." 23 August 1888, 8.

"Smoke-Ruined Pictures [artists complain]." 24 August 1888, 8.

"Shameful Car Service." 25 August 1888, 1.

"Crushed on the Rails [accidents in Chicago in July and August]." 26 August 1888, 2.

"Smoke Can Be Consumed." 8 September 1888, 9.

"The Smoke Nuisance Must Be Stopped." 9 September 1888, 4.

"The Tracks Obstructed." 11 October 1888, 1.

"Their Smoky Chimneys [*Tribune* identifies polluting buildings]." 20 October 1888, 9.

"Stokers are to Blame [blame for smoke pollution]." 22 October 1888, 3.

"Ugh! Those Awful Tugs [another source of smoke]." 29 October 1888, 9.

1889

"City Street Lighting." 4 January 1889, 2.

"Drainage of Chicago." 23 January 1889, 2.

"Incidents of Cable-Car Travel." 17 February 1889, 9.

"Wrecked at Crossing [train and grip car collide]." 23 February 1889, 8.

"How to Get Rid of It [smoke elimination through underground pipes]." 6 April 1889, 1.

"Smoke Nuisance Must be Abated." 19 May 1889, 4.

"Why the Drainage Bill Should Pass." 23 May 1889, 4.

"The Drainage Bill Passed." 25 May 1889, 4.

"Chicago's Deadly River." 7 July 1889, 9.

"It Is a Great Success [underground wires]." 20 August 1889, 9.

"The Smoke Nuisance Must Go." 8 September 1889, 4.

"To Beautify the City." 11 September 1889, 2.

"The Chief Cause of the Smoke Nuisance." 26 September 1889, 4.

"A Dangerous Practice [Chicago River now a fire hazard]." 18 October 1889, 3.

"Smoke or the Exposition—Which?" 20 October 1889, 12.

"Down-Town in a Smoker [a State Street smoking car]." 27 October 1889, 28.

1890

"The Drinking Water Polluted." 2 March 1890, 12.

"Steam for Every House [Chicago company proposes central steam plant]." 20 March 1890, 3.

"What Chicago Can Learn from Glasgow [example of well-run city]." 23 March 1890, 12.

"Deadly Mill Dust." 28 March 1890, 1.

"How to Abate the Smoke Nuisance." 19 April 1890, 4.

"How to End the Smoke Nuisance." 28 April 1890, 4.

"The Way to Clean Streets and Alleys." 28 April 1890, 4.

"This Is the Day of Big Things." 24 May 1890, 9.

"Catching the Smokers." 17 July 1890, 2.

"Crushed by Grip Car." 15 August 1890, 3.

"Responsibility of Cable Roads [must increase user safety]." 8 September 1890, 4.

"First Official Ride [opening of South Side elevated]." 22 October 1890, 1.

"Where are the Lights?" 24 November 1890, 13.

"Reeking with Filth." 12 December 1890, 1.

1891

"Death in the Streets [explosion below pavement]." 18 January 1891, 1.

"Pure Water in Sight." 4 February 1891, 6.

"Poisoning the Drinking Water." 6 April 1891, 4.

"Keep the Streets Clean." 29 April 1891, 4.

"Extinguishing Smoke." 4 May 1891, 4.

"The City Must Be Well Cleaned Up in 1893." 15 May 1891, 4.

"Cremate the Garbage." 22 May 1891, 4.

"Prinking for the Fair." 26 May 1891, 1.

"The Money Must Be Had to Clean up the City for the Fair." 26 May 1891, 4.

"Cheap Gas." 12 June 1891, 4.

"The Removal of Street Obstructions." 12 June 1891, 4.

"Our Choked-Up River." 18 June 1891, 4.

"Millions to be Spent [on city beautification]." 19 June 1891, 9.

"Peace and the New Loops [feuding cable companies]." 20 June 1891, 1.

"Ripping up Streets for New Gas Companies." 29 June 1891, 4.

"Keeping the Streets Free and Clean." 3 July 1891, 4.

"To Tear up the Streets." 26 July 1891, 1.

"How to Make the Streets Look Clean and Handsome." 26 July 1891, 12.

"The Chicago River Must Be Improved." 2 August 1891, 12.

"Asphalt Pavements." 15 August 1891, 4.

"Streets Torn Up Again." 20 August 1891, 1.

"Better Light Needed [pavements and lighting poor]." 24 August 1891, 5.

"To Find the Remedy [aldermen discuss crowded streets]." 4 December 1891, 8.

"Suppressing the Smoke Nuisance." 6 December 1891, 12.

"Go Ahead with Subway." 11 December 1891, 4.

"No Smoke Wanted [meeting at Union League Club]." 24 December 1891, 1.

"Smoke Prevention." 28 December 1891, 4.

1892

"Investigating the Street-Car Question." 3 January 1892, 12.

"Fighting the Smoke Ordinance [manufacturers resist fines]." 7 January 1892, 4.

"Death in a Wreck [streetcar-train collision]." 15 January 1892, 1.

"Let the City be Cleaned." 19 January 1892, 4.

"Deprived of Water [ice blocks crib]." 22 January 1892, 1.

"Growth of Typhoid [Chicago worst offender of major cities]." 22 January 1892, 2.

"In Mud and Slush [shocking condition of Chicago streets]." 25 January 1892, 1.

"Smoke Prevention." 28 January 1892, 4.

"Shrouded in Smoke [sun out but Chicago is dark]." 30 January 1892, 6.

"Talked of an Evil [smoke discussed at Commercial Club]." 31 January 1892, 1.

"Three Demonstrative Chimneys [smoke pollution of Masonic Temple]." 31 January 1892, 1.

"Many Asking Advice [owners of smoking chimneys]." 5 February 1892, 7.

"Crushed in Wreck." 11 February 1892, 1.

"City Water Impure." 12 February 1892, 1.

"For Better Streets." 13 February 1892, 14.

"Cable Cars Collide." 16 February 1892, 3.

"Smoke Is All Over." 16 February 1892, 10.

"No Haste to Assist [smoke records of some well-known tall buildings]." 19 February 1892, 7.

"Cleaning the City." 20 February 1892, 3.

"Report on a Plant [on smoke emissions]." 24 February 1892, 10.

"Seeking Pure Water." 1 March 1892, 10.

"Preventing Smoke [railroad tries to reduce pollution]." 2 March 1892, 4.

"How Smoke Is Made." 6 March 1892, 14.

"Is a Mighty Power [new age of electricity]." 6 March 1892, 26.

"To Purify Sewage." 7 March 1892, 10.

"The Women's Crusade against Filth." 13 March 1892, 12.

"To Clean the City." 13 March 1892, 28.

"The Anti-Smoke Society Preparing to Prosecute Incorrigible Offenders." 16 March 1892, 7.

"They Merit Censure [city streets a disgrace]." 16 March 1892, 12.

"For Clean Streets." 19 March 1892, 9.

"Clean the Streets [mass meeting at Central Music Hall]." 28 March 1892, 1.

"Our Sewage Problem." 28 March 1892, 4.

"The Smoke Nuisance [work of Society for the Prevention of Smoke]." 11 May 1892, 4.

"For a Cleaner City [how to dispose of garbage]." 15 May 1892, 29.

"Is after Offenders [Smoke Society brings thirty-two cases]." 22 May 1892, 8.

"Jumps the Track [grip car accident]." 25 June 1892, 7.

"Many of the Causes [poor condition of streets]." 3 July 1892, 19.

"To Clean the City [Mayor Washburne submits his plan]." 7 July 1892, 6.

"Preparing the City [city council passes 152 street paving ordinances]." 12 July 1892, 1.

"Hurries by a Part of the Street [construction holes on State Street]." 29 July 1892, 3.

"Smoke Is Needless [Masonic Temple a major offender]." 30 July 1892, 8.

"To End Its Smoking [Venetian Building to get new furnace]." 10 August 1892, 9.

"One Dozen Smokers [twelve of the most polluting buildings]." 11 August 1892, 9.

"For Better Streets [mayor's recommendation]." 13 September 1892, 9.

"Danger Lurks There [dangers for pedestrians on streets and sidewalks]." 14 October 1892, 1.

"Corners that Kill [most dangerous in city]." 16 October 1892, 33.

"Tearing up the Streets." 19 October 1892, 4.

"Block the Streets [construction barriers force people into streets]." 26 October 1892, 1.

"Clean up Chicago [streets have never been filthier]." 30 November 1892, 4.

"Dark as a Dungeon [smoke darkens skies during days]." 1 December 1892, 3.

"Freak of Cable [six collisions on Madison Street line]." 4 December 1892, 1.

"Told by Contrast [right and wrong ways to protect pedestrians near construction sites]." 11 December 1892, 1.

"Year's Smoke War [record of good work of Society for the Prevention of Smoke]." 17 December 1892, 1.

"Dangerous to Cross [intersection at State and Washington]." 18 December 1892, 46.

1893

"Crowded and Cold [West Side car line]." 15 January 1893, 1.

"To Clean the City [speeches at Union League Club]." 25 January 1893, 1.

"To Prevent Building Obstructions." 7 February 1893, 4.

"Opposing Smoke Prevention." 28 February 1893, 3.

"For Clean Thoroughfares." 8 March 1893, 4.

"Smoke Stopped by Injunction." 11 March 1893, 12.

"Boil the Drinking Water." 12 March 1893, 28.

"Our Filthy Thoroughfares [criticism by Jacob Riis]." 21 March 1893, 4.

"Street Cleaning in Paris [how it is done]." 2 April 1893, 28.
"Still Open Streets [never have streets been so poor]." 4 April 1893, 9.
"Street Cleaning in Berlin." 9 April 1893, 28.
"Electric Lighting for Chicago." 11 April 1893, 4.
"Like Corduroy Road [streets in terrible condition]." 12 April 1893, 11.
"Over Dirty Streets." 6 July 1893, 1.
"Defending Garbage Heaps." 23 July 1893, 12.
"Ever on the Swing [city's bridges]." 27 August 1893, 25.
"For Suppression of Smoke." 16 September 1893, 12.
"Down-Town Scenes [crowds on Chicago Day at fair]." 10 October 1893, 2.
"Crash on the Cable." 20 October 1893, 4.
"Killed by an Elevator [in Marshall Field wholesale store]." 2 November 1893, 13.
"Streets Obstructed by a Fence." 7 November 1893, 7.
"Now Sanitary Reform." 9 November 1893, 6.
"In Clouds of Smoke [sooty atmosphere]." 13 November 1893, 10.
"Sixteen are Hurt [grip-car accident]." 14 November 1893, 1.
"Bad Day for Cables." 14 November 1893, 5.
"Elevators Go Wild [in Home Insurance Building]." 15 November 1893, 8.

B. Commercial Buildings and Real Estate

1885

"The Fair [largest store in United States]." 1 January 1885, 13.
"A Grand Building [Field Building]." 20 March 1885, 8.
"A Unique Structure [temporary building of glass]." 29 March 1885, 3.
"Is the Business Quarter Becoming Crowded?" 29 March 1885, 3.
"A Booming Business [new and renovated buildings]." 2 April 1885, 8.
"The New Building [Board of Trade]." 29 April 1885, 4.
"Real Estate [new buildings]." 10 May 1885, 15.
"Real Estate [rents at State and Madison]." 7 June 1885, 2.
"Real Estate [buildings in Board of Trade area]." 14 June 1885, 17.
"Real Estate [State St. shortage, new buildings]." 21 June 1885, 8.
"Real Estate [Rialto Building]." 19 July 1885, 20.
"Real Estate [Studebaker Building]." 16 August 1885, 20.
"Real Estate [Marshall Field Wholesale Store]." 11 October 1885, 28.
"Real Estate [Phoenix Building]." 5 November 1885, 4.
"A Heavy Loss [fire destroys Farwell Block]." 7 November 1885, 6.
"Chicago Elevators [grain]." 21 November 1885, 13.
"A Great Building [Rookery]." 4 December 1885, 3.
"Real Estate [opposition to midwinter construction]." 27 December 1885, 19.

1886

"Chicago Architecture [impressive entranceways]." 10 January 1886, 20.
"A British Artist's Praises [Felix Moschel impressed by Chicago buildings]." 1 February 1886, 1.

"Chicago Real Estate: The Rookery Lot." 21 February 1886, 20.

"Our Fair Typewriters [women typists]." 17 October 1886, 27.

"Sanitary Architecture." 15 November 1886, 5.

"Chicago Real Estate: Office Buildings Near the Board of Trade." 21 November 1886, 7.

"Chicago Real Estate: The 'Grand Auditorium.'" 28 November 1886, 7.

"A Magnificent Enterprise [plans for the Auditorium]." 5 December 1886, 15.

"Chicago Real Estate [Auditorium and Lafayette Building]." 19 December 1886, 7.

1887

"Chicago Real Estate: As to Ninety-Nine Year Leases." 27 February 1887, 24.

"Chicago Real Estate: Office-Renting Goes on Apace]." 6 March 1887, 24.

"Chicago Real Estate: Will It Be Horizontal or Vertical?" 6 March 1887, 24.

"Chicago Real Estate [office space going quickly]." 25 March 1887, 3.

"The Studebaker Building." 26 March 1887, 7.

"The New Auditorium Building." 13 April 1887, 5.

"Yesterday's Big Fire [McGrath Building]." 14 April 1887, 3.

"Chicago Real Estate: As to Office Buildings [costs of operation]." 24 April 1887, 30.

"[Siegel-Cooper grand opening]." 28 May 1887, 8.

"Marshall Field and Co.'s New Store [wholesale store]." 12 June 1887, 16.

"No Collapse in Chicago: The Supervision of the 'Big Buildings.'" 15 September 1887, 6.

"Chicago Real Estate [office buildings in Loop]." 9 October 1887, 7.

"The Architects' Convention [praise for Chicago]." 19 October 1887, 4.

"Women as Architects." 24 December 1887, 16.

"Real Estate Records." 13 November 1887, 7.

"Chicago Real Estate." 17 November 1887, 10.

"The Real-Estate Field: Important Business Structures." 25 December 1887, 2.

1888

"Chicago Real Estate: A Building with Novel Features [early reference to iron and steel construction]." 15 January 1888, 6.

"Chicago Real Estate: The Growth of Cities Upward." 22 January 1888, 7.

"Telephone Facilities." 12 February 1888, 3.

"Chicago Real Estate: The Attractions of Central Property." 4 March 1888, 6.

"Chicago Real Estate: The Auditorium Building." 11 March 1888, 7.

"Chicago Real Estate: The Danger of Too Many Office Buildings." 25 March 1888, 31.

"The Great Auditorium [Republican Convention]." 10 June 1888, 13.

"The Decorator at Work [preparing interior of Auditorium]." 12 June 1888, 1.

"The Great Auditorium [importance to city]." 17 June 1888, 5.

"Thousands in the Hall [crowds in Auditorium]." 17 June 1888, 11.

"The Great Auditorium [history of construction]." 18 June 1888, 7.

"The Great Convention Hall [eight thousand in Auditorium]." 21 June 1888, 4.

"Chicago's Great Auditorium." 1 July 1888, 4.

"Chicago Real Estate: Characteristics of the Market." 8 July 1888, 18.

"A Twenty-eight Story Building [proposal of Leroy Buffington]." 2 September 1888, 27.

"Chicago Real Estate [Auditorium]." 16 September 1888, 28.

"Chicago Real Estate: Assessment of Market." 7 October 1888, 30.
"Chicago Real Estate: A Building of the Future [Chamber of Commerce Building]." 28 October 1888, 17.
"Chicago Real Estate: The Builder's Use of Iron." 11 November 1888, 28.
"Chicago Real Estate [market favorable]." 2 December 1888, 30.

1889

"Chicago Sky-Scrapers." 13 January 1889, 2.
"Woman's Headquarters [early design of Woman's Temple]." 24 January 1889, 1.
"Owings Building—For Rent." 10 February 1889, 16.
"More Than a Mere Sale [property value corner Madison-Dearborn]." 24 February 1889, 9.
"Chicago Real Estate [rents in the loop office buildings]." 3 March 1889, 5.
"More Cloud Supporters." 7 July 1889, 9.
"Chicago Real Estate: The Ninety-Nine Year Lease." 11 August 1889, 5.
"Chicago Real Estate [yields greater in Chicago]." 15 September 1889, 30.
"The Great Auditorium [complete description]." 21 September 1889, 9.
"Blessed by Masons [laying of capstone of the Auditorium]." 3 October 1889, 1.
"Chicago Real Estate [impact of skyscrapers on the market]." 13 October 1889, 11.
"Harmony in Decoration [Auditorium]." 16 November 1889, 12.
"The Auditorium and the Italian Opera Revival." 17 November 1889, 12.
"The Auditorium Stage." 7 December 1889, 12.
"The Dedication of the Auditorium." 8 December 1889, 12.
"Greatest in the World [Auditorium]." 8 December 1889, 30.
"Dedicated to Music and the People [Auditorium]." 10 December 1889, 1.
"Patti Sings Juliet [opera at Auditorium]." 11 December 1889, 1.
"King among Tenors [praise for the Auditorium]." 12 December 1889, 1.
"Patti on the Auditorium [perfect acoustics]." 12 December 1889, 1.
"The Auditorium Building." 15 December 1889, 4.

1890

"Chicago Real Estate [buildings for certain corners of Loop]." 5 January 1890, 10.
"A Mammoth Masonic Temple." 15 January 1890, 3.
G.S.W. "[Tall buildings will be profitable]." 26 January 1890, 10.
"New Era in Realty [changes in retail quarter]." 10 February 1890, 1.
"Chicago Real Estate [impact of the Fair Department Store on property value]." 2 March 1890, 10.
"Another Sky-Scraper [to be largest in city]." 3 April 1890, 1.
"A Grand Home for Masons." 6 April 1890, 26.
"More Huge Buildings." 25 April 1890, 3.
"Biggest Building Yet [Fair building]." 10 May 1890, 3.
"Chicago's Great Masonic Temple." 18 June 1890, 5.
"Largest in the World [new Fair building]." 8 October 1890, 3.
"Shrine of Temperance [Woman's Temple]." 2 November 1890, 1.
"Masonic Fraternity Temple." 2 November 1890, 3.
"Plumb, Level, Square [laying cornerstone of Masonic Temple]." 7 November 1890, 1.

1891

"New YMCA Building." 1 January 1891, 10.

"Buildings of 1891 [Chicago leads world in tall buildings]." 1 January 1891, 11.

"Real Estate in 1891 [new tall buildings]." 1 January 1891, 22.

"Architect Root Dead." 16 January 1891, 1.

"The Death of John Root." 17 January 1891, 4.

"New YMCA Building." 1 March 1891, 17.

"Two More Skyscrapers." 5 March 1891, 1.

"Home for the Germans [Schiller Theater Building]." 3 May 1891, 2.

"Another Dearborn Street Giant [Unity Building]." 10 May 1891, 9.

"Chicago Real Estate: Office Building Projects [compared to New York buildings]." 9 August 1891, 14.

"Higher than Others [proposed Odd-Fellows Building by Adler and Sullivan]." 5 September 1891, 1.

"Chicago's Big Buildings [history of 'Chicago construction.']" 13 September 1891, 25.

"Sixteen Stories High [Unity Building]." 1 November 1891, 29.

"Two New Big Buildings." 4 November 1891, 1.

"Five High Buildings [permits taken out before restrictions apply]." 24 November 1891, 1.

"Two Types of Office Buildings [spare and decorated]." 29 November 1891, 25.

"Building at Night [on Ashland Block]." 6 December 1891, 7.

"Prospects for Two Great Buildings Planned for the Wholesale District." 27 December 1891, 29.

1892

"Buildings of 1891." 1 January 1892, 11.

"Knows No Parallel [construction speed on Ashland block]." 17 January 1892, 27.

"It Is Now a Misfit [quick obsolescence of older commercial buildings]." 23 January 1892, 13.

"Chicago Real Estate: Among Architects and Builders [Hartford, Boyce, and Dexter Buildings]." 24 January 1892, 29.

"Chicago Real Estate: Among Architects and Builders [Columbus Memorial Building]." 31 January 1892, 28.

Roemheld, J. E. "Chicago Real Estate [tall buildings and pedestrian space]." 31 January 1892, 28.

"Real Estate Market: Among Architects and Builders." 5 February, 30; 21 August, 30; 18 December, 30.

"[Siegel, Cooper and Company, opening of new store]." 6 March 1892, 40.

"It Beats the World [elevator system of Masonic Temple]." 14 March 1892, 11.

"Work Soon to Begin on Another Dearborn Street Skyscraper [Boyce Building]." 27 March 1892, 18.

"Real Estate Market: Chicago's New Office Buildings [Woman's, Masonic, Unity, Ashland, Title and Trust, Venetian, Monadnock, Northern Hotel]." 8 May 1892, 39.

"Great Northern Fireproof Hotel." 15 June 1892, 7.

"Towering Skyward [premier city of tall buildings]." 17 July 1892, 14.

"Chicago Real Estate: Among Architects and Builders [sixteen-story aluminum building]." 21 August 1892, 30.

"Schiller Rings Up." 30 September 1892, 1.

"Its Big Buildings [necessity of tall buildings]." 16 October 1892, 35.

"Modern Buildings Necessary [little demand for old commercial buildings]." 30 October 1892, 30.

"His Sphere of Labor an Exalted One [worker on high steel skeleton]." 27 November 1892, 1.

"After Skyscraper [Buffington requests patent]." 4 December 1892, 26.

"Chicago Real Estate: First Steel Frame Building [Boston's first steel-frame building]." 18 December 1892, 30.

1893

"Sales of the Year [new commercial projects]." 1 January 1893, 27.

"Four Big Buildings [largest buildings in world]." 22 January 1893, 34.

"Real Estate Market: [Medina and Old Colony Buildings]." 5 February 1893, 30.

"New Stock Exchange." 25 February 1893, 4.

"Plan New Buildings [proposed Galena building]." 11 March 1893, 3.

"Rapid Building Operations [Boyce Building]." 12 March 1893, 30.

"Offices for Rent—Ellsworth Building [advertisement]." 30 April 1893, 30.

"Real Estate Market: Building Operations of Two Cities [New York and Chicago compared, 1886–93]." 20 August 1893, 14.

"Its New Home Ready [YMCA Building opens]." 2 November 1893, 13.

"Handsome Fifteen-Story Champlain Building under Construction." 11 November 1893, 6.

"Fourteen-Story Structure to be Known as the Marquette Building." 19 November 1893, 10.

"New Value of Land [high price of State Street property]." 23 November 1893, 1.

C. Concerns about Tall Buildings

1885

"A $250,000 Fire [Grannis Block]." 20 February 1885, 1.

"The Hotel Fire [Langham Hotel]." 23 March 1885, 4.

"A Heavy Loss [Farwell Block fire]." 7 November 1885, 6.

1887

"Fighting a Hot Blaze [five-story building]." 19 May 1887, 2.

"Enormously Increasing Fire Waste [rising costs of city fires]." 31 July 1887, 4.

1888

"Fighting a Fierce Fire." 8 January 1888, 9.

"Is the Tower Insecure [Board of Trade Building]?" 4 August 1888, 1.

"A Theatre Burned Out [Chicago Opera House]." 13 December 1888, 1.

1889

"Floor Crashes Down [floor collapse at Owings Building construction]." 18 February 1889, 3.

"It Was the Water Tank [Owings Building accident]." 19 February 1889, 8.

"The Owings Building [solid and strong]." 24 February 1889, 16.

"Chicago Real Estate: Is It a Skyscraper Trust [are owners pushing ordinance on height re-
    striction]?" 9 June 1889, 27.
"Legislating against Skyscrapers." 13 June 1889, 4.

1891

"More Exacting Regulations [countrywide sentiment to limit height]." 10 May 1891, 9.
"Burning up a Million [Siegel, Cooper and Company dry-goods store fire]." 4 August 1891, 1.
"Want No Sky-Scrapers [city council discusses height]." 7 October 1891, 12.
"Chicago's Building Foundations [reservations of General Fitz-Simons]." 11 October 1891, 12.
"It's a Serious Problem [General Fitz-Simons on settling of tall building]." 11 October 1891,
    13.
"It Will Be a Great Weight [proposed Odd-Fellows Building]." 11 October 1891, 13.
"After High Buildings [objections to them]." 13 October 1891, 1.
"Regulating the Height of Skyscrapers." 18 October 1891, 12.
"Limit for Skyscrapers [recommended by Chicago Real Estate Board]." 5 November 1891, 1.
"Sky Scraping Buildings [effect on health]." 6 November 1891, 4.
"Against High Buildings [Builders' and Traders' Exchange]." 15 November 1891, 10.
"The Fire Risk of Sky-Scraper Buildings." 19 November 1891, 4.
"Steel in Buildings [concern about safety]." 3 December 1891, 3.
"For High Pressure [water systems in high buildings]." 21 December 1891, 9.

1892

"High Block Rates [insurance rates pegged to height]." 4 February 1892,
"Frame Structure and High Buildings [height ordinance in committee]." 27 March 1892, 4.
"Safe High Buildings [Sooy Smith raises doubts]." 1 April 1892, 9.
"Death in the Wind [collapse of seven-story building]." 2 April 1892, 1.
"Chicago Foundations [*Tribune* seconds Sooy Smith's warnings]." 3 April 1892, 28.
"High Building Plans [Jenney refutes Sooy Smith]." 4 April 1892, 9.
"Reorganize the Building Department [concern about its effectiveness]." 15 April 1892, 4.

1893

"Deadly Work of Gas [gas fire in eight-story building]." 5 January 1893, 1.
"The New Building Ordinance." 26 January 1893, 1.
"Our High Buildings [Sooy Smith warns of dangers]." 2 March 1893, 12.
"Limit of Ten Stories [city council stipulates 130 feet or ten stories]." 9 March 1893, 3.
"The New Building Ordinance [*Tribune* endorses limits]." 10 March 1893, 4.
"Real Estate Market [reactions to height limit ordinance]." 12 March 1893, 30.
"Fire Insurance and Risk." 10 April 1893, 4.
"Fires in Big Cities." 18 June 1893, 31.
"Down Four Stories [freight elevator collapses in Stock Exchange Building]." 24 December
    1893, 5.

D. Residential and Suburban Chicago

1885

"Out Driving [Chicago's fine boulevards]." 10 May 1885, 17.
"Houses and Homes." 7 November 1885, 12.

1886

"Costly Dwelling House [new apartment building]." 5 June 1886, 1.
"Bits of Architecture [signs of a Chicago style]." 7 November 1886, 26.

1887

"On the Boulevards [private carriages in Chicago]." 10 April 1887, 8.
"Beautifying the Parks." 17 April 1887, 5.
"Chicago as a Summer Resort." 1 July 1887, 4.
"Edgewater [healthy suburban living]." 3 July 1887, 5.
"Four Striking Houses." 6 November 1887, 15.

1888

Hale, Edward E. "Relief for City Woes [a case for suburbs]." 8 January 1888, 3.
"Out Milwaukee Avenue [Chicago's most cosmopolitan thoroughfare]." 4 August 1888, 9.
"A Bride House Hunting." 30 September 1888, 25.
"Nora Goes A-Slumming [exposé of West Side flats]." 15 December 1888, 1.

1889

"Grandest in the World [drive from Evanston]." 15 February 1889, 1.
"A Great Thoroughfare [trip along fourteen miles of Halsted]." 24 February 1889, 15.
"Bits of Architecture [domestic details]." 31 March 1889, 26.
"Bits of Architecture [north side house details]." 14 April 1889, 34.
"Palaces on the Drive [houses on Lake Shore Drive]." 28 April 1889, 34.
"Are Women to Blame [causes of unhappiness in marriage]?" 4 May 1889, 12.
"[Advertisement for houses in Charlton Street]." 23 June 1889, 5.

1890

"Our Homes and Theirs [comparison of homes in New York and Chicago]." 23 November 1890, 34.

1891

"Typical Chicago Houses." 12 April 1891, 33.
"Chicago the Great Summer Resort." 16 June 1891, 4.
"Unhealthy Dwellings in Cities." 2 August 1891, 12.

1892

"Electric Light for Boulevards." 28 February 1892, 12.
"The Electric Force [electricity and transportation]." 8 May 1892, 28.
"West Side Drives [boulevards and private houses]." 28 August 1892, 33.
"It's an Ideal Home." 18 December 1892, 11.

E. Image, Reputation, and Aspirations of the City

1885

"Chicago's Dead [death rate for 1884]." 9 January 1885, 9.
"Where Will This End [election fraud]?" 16 January 1885, 4.
"Real Estate [Chicago's architecture grandest in world]." 22 February 1885, 8.
"Lies about Chicago." 12 May 1885, 4.
"Canvassing the City Vote [city council irresponsible]." 24 May 1885, 4.
"The City's Health." 17 June 1885, 3.
"Municipal Affairs [driving cattle through streets]." 15 September 1885, 10.
"A $2,000,000 Library [Newberry bequest]." 11 December 1885, 1.
"The Newberry Library." 11 December 1885, 4.

1886

"A Briton's View of Us [interview with James Anthony Froude]." 20 February 1886, 12.
"Infancy in the City [high infant mortality]." 13 March 1886, 13.
"The Perils of Infancy in Cities." 14 March 1886, 4.
"The Court-House [history of tolerated mismanagement]." 14 March 1886, 11.
"Clean the Council." 31 March 1886, 3.
"Chicago Gaming-Houses." 16 May 1886, 14.
"A New-Yorker on Chicago [shabby streets, efficient cable cars]." 17 June 1886, 10.
Griswold, Hattie Tyng. "A Critic Criticised [Theodore Child attacks American civilization]."
    29 June 1886, 10.
"Chicago's Great Need [an ambulance corps]." 12 September 1886, 14.
"Chicago People Lack Courage [insecure in buying art]." 14 November 1886, 7.
"State Street Dives Closed." 18 December 1886, 5.
"The Unlicensed Dives [rough saloons on State Street]." 19 December 1886, 13.

1887

"Wipe out the Pool Rooms." 5 February 1887, 4.
"Women in the Lock-Up." 6 February 1887, 15.
"Twin Gigantic Evils [bookmaking and pools]." 6 February 1887, 20.
"The Artistic Wants of Chicago." 15 May 1887, 4.
"The Public Library." 26 June 1887, 10.
"Chicago as a Thought Centre." 17 July 1887, 4.
"Orchestras in America." 31 July 1887, 18.
"The Art Exhibition." 7 September 1887, 1.
"Literature in Chicago [publishing center]." 6 November 1887, 28.
"The Convention City [both national parties likely to choose Chicago]." 24 November 1887,
    1.
"Chicago as a Financial Centre." 10 December 1887, 4.
"A Moribund City Council [inability to deal with problems of the streets]." 12 December 1887,
    4.
"Chicago's Misfortune [city imprisoned by railroad tracks]." 17 December 1887, 15.
"Regulation of Foreign Immigration." 23 December 1887, 4.

1888

"Chicago and Dante [Chicago attacked by *New York Sun*]." 29 January 1888, 4.
Clarke, John M. "To Beautify the City [urges hiding of lakefront tracks]." 18 March 1888, 31.
G.W.S. "Lampooning America [Matthew Arnold's critique of American civilization]." 3 April 1888, 9.
"Great, Modest Chicago [Charles Dudley Warner on Chicago]." 24 April 1888, 6.
"An Italian Tenement [atrocious conditions]." 2 June 1888, 9.
"The Wonders of Chicago [huge buildings, impressive feats]." 17 June 1888, 25.
"They Have Seen Chicago [reaction of visiting newspaper people]." 8 July 1888, 17.
"Compliments to Chicago [*Tribune* editor brags]." 9 July 1888, 4.
"As the English See Us." 14 October 1888, 29.
"Chicago's Ebb and Flow [number of daily commuter trains]." 30 December 1888, 15.

1889

"Max O'Rell on Americans." 3 January 1889, 9.
"Max O'Rell on Chicago." 20 January 1889, 26.
"Transients in Chicago [the new Rome of the modern world]." 24 February 1889, 15.
"Max O'Rell on America." 24 February 1889, 17.
"As It Should Be [growth by annexation]." 30 June 1889, 9.
"To Take in the Sights [Chicago's main attractions for visitors]." 19 October 1889, 2.
"An Opera Box for $2,000." 23 November 1889, 1.

1890

"Presenting Chicago's Claims [its case for the exposition]." 12 January 1890, 2.
"Some 'Previous' Chicagoans [confident city can meet exposition challenge]." 2 March 1890, 12.
"New-Yorkers Silenced." 7 March 1890, 1.
"Will Excel All Others [Chicago exposition will smash the record]." 9 March 1890, 2.
"Please, Mr. Depew, Don't!" 10 March 1890, 10.
"Wanted, An Orchestra." 23 March 1890, 12.
"The Weak Spot in American Social Life [insufficient respect for the elderly]." 5 October 1890, 12.
"Chicago in the World's Fair Year [optimism about city improvements]." 12 October 1890, 12.
"Chicago on Exhibition [visit of British and German engineers]." 14 October 1890, 2.
"The City's Statuary." 9 November 1890, 12.

1891

"Chicago Beat Them All [in increase in trade in 1890]." 1 January 1891, 10.
"Another Malignant New York Slanderer." 6 February 1891, 4.
"Trying to Kill the Fair [roadblocks in Congress]." 8 February 1891, 4.
"Lies Told about Chicago [by New York *Sun*]." 15 February 1891, 8.
"The Outcome of Cregier's One Term [Chicago's corruption and mismanagement]." 22 February 1891, 12.
"For an Art Institute [city council discussion]." 17 March 1891, 1.

"Chicago as an Educational Center." 29 March 1891, 12.

"No Gambling in Chicago." 29 April 1891, 1.

"A Prophet without Honor at Home [ex-mayor Cregier says Fair won't be ready]." 21 May 1891, 4.

"Seeking New Quarters [Art Institute Building may be sold]." 19 June 1891, 1.

Hatton, Joseph. "Three Cities Compared [English journals on New York, Boston, Chicago]." 28 June 1891, 34.

"View of the University [of Chicago]." 10 July 1891, 1.

"An English Tribute to the World's Fair City." 25 July 1891, 12.

"Means of Amusement in New York and Chicago [New Yorkers think Chicago boring]." 10 August 1891, 4.

"Chicago Is a Great City [statistical comparisons]." 15 August 1891, 9.

"Welcome to Chicago." 15 October 1891, 5.

"Mr. Villard's Estimate of Chicago." 23 November 1891, 4.

1892

"Facts about Chicago." 13 February 1892, 7.

"The Chicago Spirit." 7 March 1892, 4.

"Chicago a Fit Site [Trueman Wood commends city]." 14 April 1892, 9.

"A Boston Tribute to Chicago." 24 April 1892, 28.

"It Is Sour Grapes [attack on Chicago by New York *Sun*]." 30 May 1892, 1.

"Death Rate in Cities [Chicago relatively healthy]." 31 May 1892, 4.

Head, Franklin H. "Heart of Chicago." 3 July 1892, 6.

"As Others See Us [4 satirical drawings]." 3 July 1892, 14.

"In Bad Condition [city not ready for visitors]." 3 July 1892, 17.

Brisbane, Arthur. "Praise for Chicago." 12 July 1892, 9.

"Chicago as It Is [judged by *New York World*]." 18 July 1892, 1.

"She Took to Chicago [Mrs. Van Rensselaer on city]." 16 August 1892, 9.

"Chicago's Greatness." 21 August 1892, 16.

"Chicago the Future Metropolis." 21 August 1892, 16.

"None Can Approach Chicago [from the *London Times*]." 29 August 1892, 1.

"The London *Times* Criticism of Chicago." 4 September 1892, 28.

"Dollars and Cents [how rich and poor live in Chicago]." 4 December 1892, 33.

"Mayor Washburne's Christmas [major problems of city]." 26 December 1892, 4.

1893

"We're Not up to Date [Ward McAllister claims Chicago culturally backward]." 10 April 1893, 1.

"Real Estate Market: Skyscraper in New York [Manhattan Life Building]." 26 May 1893, 30.

"Libeling the Fair and Chicago [attack by *Liverpool Daily Post*]." 9 June 1893, 4.

"The Next World's Fair [Antwerp Fair will not compare with Chicago]." 22 July 1893, 12.

"Amende Honorable [New Yorker apologizes to Chicago]." 13 August 1893, 10.

"Progress of Chicago [reaction of British consul]." 23 August 1893, 4.

"As Bourget Sees It [Paul Bourget on Chicago]." 24 September 1893, 2.

"Chicago's Influence upon the Art of the Future." 3 October 1893, 4.

"From Canoe to Skyscraper [history of the city]." 9 October 1893, 18.

"Wealth of the City." 9 October 1893, 19.

"Reveals New World [fair represents shift from commerce to culture]." 6 November 1893, 4.

"Art Institute Open." 9 December 1893, 6.

"The New Art Institute [equal to New York and Boston]." 9 December 1893, 12.

"Malicious Assault upon Chicago." 21 December 1893, 12.

"Stead's Impertinence [meddles in workers' welfare]." 29 December 1893, 6.

"Bigger'n New York [prediction that city's population will top New York by 1897]." 31 December 1893, 3.

F. Business and Labor

1885

"American Enterprise [railroad development]." 4 August 1885, 4.

"The Eight-Hour Movement." 5 November 1885, 4.

"'Eight Hours a Day' [*Tribune* unsympathetic]." 19 November 1885, 4.

1886

"The Retail Store Eight-Hour Movement." 18 April 1886, 4.

"Chicago Realty: Effect of the Eight-Hour Movement on Building." 25 April 1886, 25.

"The Building Trades." 28 April 1886, 4.

"No Pronounced Boom." 15 August 1886, 3.

"Men at the Traps [operating the cable system]." 5 September 1886, 15.

"Chicago's Trade Boom [dry-goods trade]." 21 September 1886, 1.

"New Business Methods." 23 October 1886, 9.

"Socialism Would Destroy Progress." 21 November 1886, 4.

"A Night Car Conductor [routines he faces]." 12 December 1886, 25.

1887

"Railroad Building in 1887." 31 December 1887, 4.

1888

"Telephones a Nuisance." 1 January 1888, 9.

"English and American Wages." 2 January 1888, 4.

"Corporation-Wrecking [abuses of corporation management]." 14 January 1888, 12.

"Builders and Workmen." 5 February 1888, 12.

"The Business Situation." 20 February 1888, 4.

"The Foes of Competition [attack on trusts]." 22 February 1888, 9.

"The Steel-Beam Trust [growing importance of metal in construction]." 25 August 1888, 4.

"How Much Will You Earn [comparative wages in Chicago and England]?" 2 November 1888, 4.

1889

"Chicago Real Estate [the syndicate system of buying]." 17 November 1889, 10.

1890

"Cable Stock Booming." 19 August 1890, 1.

1891

"The Annual Review [trade and commerce]." 1 January 1891, 4.
"No Vacation in Chicago [schedules of businessmen]." 26 April 1891, 42.
"Less Hours, More Wages [call for eight-hour day]." 2 May 1891, 1.
"No Frills on Chicago [access to leading businessmen of city]." 14 December 1891, 10.

1892

"Prices Are Sagging [Wall Street sluggish]." 18 January 1892, 1.
"Millions of Bushels [capacity of grain elevators]." 3 July 1892, 15.
"Great Building Boom." 12 October 1892, 4.
"Chicago's Manufacturers [statistics]." 14 October 1892, 4.

1893

"Among Architects and Builders [economy not strong in Chicago]." 16 July 1893, 15.
"Real Estate Market [economy flat in 1893]." 23 July 1893, 14.
"Condition of the Chicago National Banks." 25 July 1893, 4.
"Real Estate Market [similar to 1873]." 30 July 1893, 13.
"Three Others Fail [three more failures at Board of Trade]." 3 August 1893, 1.
"Big Drop in Assets." 10 August 1893, 1.
"We Want Work." 22 August 1893, 1.
"Clash with a Mob [unemployment riot]." 27 August 1893, 1.
"Relief for the Needy." 3 September 1893, 12.
"Business Is Slow." 21 September 1893, 16.
"Our Commercial Progress [city's record since the 1871 fire]." 9 October 1893, 12.
"Real Estate Market [office buildings gradually filling]." 5 November 1893, 31.
"Strong Words Used [W. T. Stead and the plight of workers]." 13 November 1893, 1–2.
"Business Improves." 13 November 1893, 10.
"Hard Luck Stories [men sleeping in corridors of City Hall]." 10 December 1893, 25.
"Terrible Business Depression." 18 December 1893, 6.
"Business Is Dull." 18 December 1893, 10.

G. Columbian Exposition

1886

"Locality of the World's Exposition." 18 November 1886, 4.

1889

"The World's Fair of 1892 [first mention of fair]." 28 June 1889, 4.
"The World's Fair of 1892." 10 July 1889, 4.
"Chicago Makes Her Bid [for Columbian exposition]." 3 August 1889, 1.
"Big Fairs for All [review of international expositions]." 11 August 1889, 25.
"Tips on the World's Fair [support for Chicago's bid]." 3 September 1889, 8.

"An Army of Missionaries for the Fair in Chicago." 19 September 1889, 4.

"To Beat the Eiffel Tower [Ritchel tower proposal]." 12 October 1889, 12.

"To Overtop the Eiffel [Judson tower proposal]." 24 October 1889, 2.

"Towers to the Clouds [tower proposals]." 26 October 1889, 9.

"In Favor of New York." 2 November 1889, 9.

"World's Fair Projects [tower proposals]." 2 November 1889, 9.

"A Planetary World's Fair [Hosmer tower proposal]." 3 November 1889, 11.

"As Compared with Paris [Chicago's behavior as exposition city]." 3 November 1889, 30.

"In Memory of Columbus [tower proposals]." 9 November 1889, 9.

"World's Fair Features [exotic proposals]." 10 November 1889, 26.

"Towering to the Skies [exposition tower projects]." 16 November 1889, 9.

1890

"New York's Ten-Million Bribe for the Fair." 30 January 1890, 4.

"Chicago Wins the Prize [to be site for fair]." 25 February 1890, 4.

"All Exhibits under One Roof [Seaman tower proposal]." 7 March 1890, 1.

"A Plan to Put All the World's Fair Exposition Exhibits under One Roof [Jenison tower proposal]." 9 March 1890, 11.

"England and Chicago [*London Telegraph* and *Times* endorse Chicago's exposition]." 15 March 1890, 16.

"Plenty of Time Needed [suggestions for exposition]." 15 March 1890, 16.

"New York Playing the Dog in the Manger Act." 16 March 1890, 12.

"Benefits of the Fair [readers' hopes for fair]." 23 March 1890, 25.

"All under One Roof [Jenison tower proposal]." 3 April 1890, 1.

"The Circus Tent Plan [Jenison tower proposal]." 4 April 1890, 4.

"The World's Fair in a Tent [Jenison tower proposal]." 6 April 1890, 12.

"The Fair Must Be a Unit." 13 April 1890, 12.

"New York and the World's Fair." 27 April 1890, 12.

Beard, Charles H. "Ideas Anent the Fair [attack on single-building argument]." 10 May 1890, 12.

"Voice of the People [World's Fair tower on wheels]." 19 May 1890, 6.

"A Permanent Columbus Tower to Cost over $2,000,000 to Be Erected in Chicago [Kinkel and Pohl proposal]." 24 May 1890, 9.

"Broader Ideas about the World's Fair [discussion of location]." 28 May 1890, 4.

"Depew on the Fair." 6 June 1890, 1.

"The Columbian Exposition Cranks [*Tribune* dismisses wild schemes]." 15 June 1890, 12.

"The Ideal World's Fair Site Secured [three sites]." 23 September 1890, 4.

"World's Fair Jealousy [reactions from New York and London newspapers]." 24 September 1890, 4.

"World's Fair to Date." 4 October 1890, 9.

"Hotel at Jackson Park." 11 October 1890, 1.

"Towers for the Fair." 9 November 1890, 5.

"Where to Build the Art Palace." 11 November 1890, 4.

"View of the Columbus Dome [Hallock proposal]." 23 November 1890, 9.

"Now Ready for the Fair [first plans for Jackson Park]." 27 November 1890, 2.

"Ready with the Plans [Burnham's first report]." 27 December 1890, 8.

1891

"About Ready to Build [construction at Jackson Park]." 3 January 1891, 9.
"Five on the Lake-Front [plans of proposed buildings for second exposition site]." 20 January 1891, 1.
"They're in a Quandary [what exhibits to locate at Lake-Front site]." 23 January 1891, 8.
"In Lake-Front Park [proposed location for Woman's Building]." 24 January 1891, 7.
"England and the Fair." 24 January 1891, 9.
"It Will Be a Beauty [proposed design of Water Palace]." 24 January 1891, 9.
"Is Now Fairly Settled [temporary administration building staked at lakefront site]." 31 January 1891, 9.
"To Plan the Buildings [lakefront structures assigned to architects." 4 February 1891, 6.
"Would Use Electricity [transportation scheme at exposition]." 17 February 1891, 8.
"Hard Blow at the Fair." 21 February 1891, 1.
"Plans of Various Buildings [initial sketches are magnificent]." 24 February 1891, 1.
"Approved by the Board [designs of exposition halls]." 28 February 1891, 9.
"World's Fair Buildings [Proctor tower proposal]." 5 March 1891, 5.
"Standing on Two Lighthouses [Columbus monument proposed by L. Durand of Paris]." 7 March 1891, 2.
"Elevated Road for the Fair [four miles of track wind through grounds]." 10 March 1891, 2.
"What the Designs Are [Hayden's design for Woman's Building]." 28 March 1891, 9.
"Design for a Leaning Tower [Halpenny tower proposal]." 29 March 1891, 39.
"Modern Types Wanted [E. Atkinson objects to classical designs]." 30 March 1891, 6.
"Designs That Won Prizes [Woman's Building]." 31 March 1891, 7.
"What States Will Do [state buildings at Fair]." 4 April 1891, 7.
"Another World's Fair Scheme [De Dmidt proposed gateway]." 4 April 1891, 7.
"Description of the Plans [bird's-eye view of major buildings]." 4 April 1891, 7.
"Exhibit of Electricity [at the exposition]." 12 April 1891, 6.
"No Smoke at Fair [will use oil, not coal]." 8 May 1891, 2.
"Edison and the Big Fair." 13 May 1891, 2.
"The New York Papers and the Fair." 30 May 1891, 4.
"Viewing the Fair Site [foreign diplomats visit Chicago]." 14 June 1891, 1.
"Will Spread Fair News [delegation will go to Europe]." 19 June 1891, 8.
"To Be in Jackson Park [still debating location of exposition buildings]." 24 June 1891, 1.
"World's Fair Buildings [impact of Root's death on plans]." 30 June 1891, 9.
"Construction Is Begun [on Mines and Mining Building]." 4 July 1891, 9.
"Here's What the World Says [newspaper comments about the exposition]." 4 July 1891, 9.
"New York and the Fair." 4 July 1891, 9.
"Outsiders on the Fair." 4 July 1891, 9.
"To Build a Hotel and a Tower [near the exposition grounds]." 16 July 1891, 7.
"Eiffel Wants a Chance [to design tower for exposition]." 5 August 1891, 7.
"Engineers on the Tower Scheme [object to participation by Eiffel]." 16 August 1891, 8.
"M. Eiffel's Proposition [promises to make it higher than Eiffel Tower, Paris]." 25 August 1891, 8.
"Beautiful Night Scene [illumination at fair]." 12 September 1891, 12.
"Observatory Stations Planned [no tall tower planned]." 12 September 1891, 12.

"Talking about Our Fair [U.S. newspaper comments]." 18 September 1891, 9.
"Plan of a Fair Tower [Morison tower proposal]." 17 October 1891, 12.
"Plan for Observation Towers [proposed by Partelie and Company]." 24 October 1891, 12.
"Tripod Tower 1,500 Feet High [Hale tower proposal]." 24 October 1891, 12.
"Memorial of the Fair [new Art Institute for lakefront]." 13 November 1891, 1.
"Staff for the Fair [how the material is made]." 28 November 1891, 10.

1892

"The Fair up to Date [history and statistics]." 21 February 1892, 3.
"The World's Fair Buildings: As They Will Appear." 21 February 1892, 3–6.
"The World's Fair Buildings: Showing the Progress Made." 21 February 1892, 3.
"Largest on Earth [trusses for Manufactures Building at exposition]." 28 March 1892, 9.
"The Glory of the Fair [praise from New York paper]." 3 May 1892, 4.
"Towers at the Fair [three to be erected for observation]." 11 May 1892, 9.
"All for Fair [New York–Chicago friction dissipates]." 13 May 1892, 1.
"Novel Spiral Tower for the Fair [Atwood-Silsbee tower proposal]." 9 July 1892, 13.
"Will Whirl through the Air [Wachter wheel proposal for fair]." 23 July 1892, 13.
"Passes the House [Congress approves fair appropriations measure]." 28 July 1892, 1.
"Lofty as St. Paul's [Mrs. Schuyler Van Rensselaer on artistic quality of exposition]." 29 August 1892, 1.
"Great Art Building [at exposition]." 6 November 1892, 29.
"The World's Fair Tower [investment advertisement for Johnstone Tower]." 5 December 1892, 10.

1893

"Ferris Wheel to Be a Feature." 25 February 1893, 9.
"Will It Be Built [Johnstone tower proposal]?" 28 February 1893, 8.
"A 1,100–Room World's Fair Hotel Nearing Completion." 19 March 1893, 30.
"Require Pure Water." 15 April 1893, 1.
"History of the Fair." 30 April 1893, World's Fair Supplement, p. 3.
"Is Simply Massive [Manufactures Building at exposition]." 30 April 1893, 41.
"In Frame of Light [White City under lights]." 9 May 1893, 1.
"Fair Is Ready [all problems worked out]." 5 June 1893, 4.
"Great Ferris Wheel." 18 June 1893, 25.
"It Exceeds Itself ['None equal to it,' says Depew]." 19 June 1893, 1.
"What the Foreign Commissioners Say of the Columbian Exposition." 26 June 1893, 1.
"Eulogize the Fair [New York *Times* approves]." 26 June 1893, 5.
"The Ferris Wheel." 9 July 1893, 26.
"Electricity Exhibit." 6 August 1893, 29.
"Locating the Fair [history of selection of Jackson Park]." 23 August 1893, 10.
"The Ferris Wheel [crowning triumph of the age]." 27 August 1893, 37.
"Some Observations at the Fair [the greatest fair ever]." 16 September 1893, 12.
"New York Begins to Appreciate the Fair." 3 October 1893, 4.
"Electricity at the Fair." 8 October 1893, 25.
Harrison, J. B. "Review of the Fair." 8 October 1893, 32.

"The Woman's Exhibit." 9 October 1893, 12.

"Fair's Biggest Week." 15 October 1893, 5.

"Great Is New York [leads all states in number of exhibits]." 15 October 1893, 9.

"The Ferris Wheel." 22 October 1893, 15.

"The World's Fair Buildings [what to do with them]." 25 October 1893, 12.

"Lesson in Building [fair's impact on future architecture]." 29 October 1893, 31.

"The Close of the Fair [relief for Chicago]." 31 October 1893, 12.

"Caring for the Immense Crowds." 1 November 1893, 15.

"Closing of the Fair [newspapers call it the greatest]." 2 November 1893, 16.

"Keep the Buildings [at Jackson Park]." 10 November 1893, 2.

"Why This Excessive Haste [to dismantle exposition buildings]?" 11 November 1893, 12.

"Remove the Big Building to the Lake Front [Manufacturers Building]." 12 November 1893, 28.

"His Plan for a Wheel [proposal of H. W. Fowler]." 12 November 1893, 31.

"How Its Glory Fades [scenes of disintegration at Jackson Park]." 20 November 1893, 3.

"Germany's Success at the Fair." 7 December 1893, 12.

"Fate of the World's Fair Buildings." 10 December 1893, 36.

"The Manufacturers Building [plea to save it]." 15 December 1893, 4.

Selected Bibliography, Post-1914

Applebaum, Stanley. *The Chicago World's Fair of 1893*. New York: Dover, 1980.

Badger, Rodney Reid. *The Great American Fair: The World's Columbian Exposition and American Culture*. Chicago: Nelson Hall, 1979.

Benjamin, Walter. "Paris, Capital of the Nineteenth Century." In *Reflections: Essays, Aphorisms, Autobiographical Writings*. Translated by Edmund Jephcott. New York: Harcourt Brace Jovanovich, 1978.

Bing, Samuel. *Artistic America, Tiffany Glass, and Art Nouveau*. Introduction by Robert Koch. Translated by Benita Eisler. Cambridge, Mass.: MIT Press, 1970.

Bluestone, Daniel M. *Constructing Chicago*. New Haven: Yale University Press, 1991.

———. "Landscape and Culture in Nineteenth-Century Chicago." Ph.D. diss., University of Chicago, 1984.

Boorstin, Daniel J. "A Montgomery Ward's Mail-Order Business." *Chicago History* 5, no.2 (Spring-Summer, 1973): 142–52.

Bruegmann, Robert, Sarah Clark, Paul Florian, Douglas Stoher, and Cynthia Weese. *A Guide to 150 Years of Chicago Architecture*. Chicago: Chicago Review Press, 1985.

Burg, David F. *Chicago's White City of 1893*. Lexington: University Press of Kentucky, 1976.

Cain, Louis P. "The Creation of Chicago's Sanitary District and Construction of the Sanitary and Ship Canal." *Chicago History* 8 (Summer 1979): 98–110.

Cassell, Frank A., and Marguerite E. Cassell. "The White City in Peril: Leadership and the World's Columbian Exposition." *Chicago History* 12 (Fall 1983): 10–27.

Chandler, Alfred D., Jr. "Fin de siècle: Industrial Transformation." In *Fin-de-Siècle and Its Legacy*, edited by Mikulás Teich and Roy Porter, 28–41. Cambridge: Cambridge University Press, 1990.

Charernbhak, Wichit. *Chicago School Architects and Their Critics*. Ann Arbor: UMI Research Press, 1981.

Christison, Muriel B. "How Buffington Staked His Claim." *Art Bulletin* 26 (March 1944): 13–24.

Ciucci, Giorgio, Francesco Dal Co, Mario Manieri-Elia, and Manfredo Tafuri. *The American City*. London: Granada Publishing Limited, 1980.

Clayton, John. "How They Tinkered with a River." *Chicago History* 1 (Spring 1970): 32–46.

Commager, Henry Steele, ed. *America in Perspective: The United States through Foreign Eyes*. New York: Random House, New American Library, 1947.

———. *The American Mind: An Interpretation of American Thought and Character since the 1880s*. New Haven: Yale University Press, 1950.

Condit, Carl W. *The Chicago School of Architecture: A History of Commercial and Public Building in the Chicago Area, 1875–1925*. Chicago: University of Chicago Press, 1964.

———. *The Rise of the Skyscraper*. Chicago: University of Chicago Press, 1952.

Cotton, L., de. "A Frenchman's Visit to Chicago in 1886." Translated by George J. Joyaux. *Journal of the Illinois Historical Society* 47, no. 1 (Spring 1954): 45–56.

Cronon, William. *Nature's Metropolis: Chicago and the Great West*. New York: Norton, 1991.

Cronon, William J. "To Be the Central City: Chicago, 1848–1857." *Chicago History* 10 (Fall 1981): 130–40.

Crook, David H. "Louis Sullivan and the Golden Doorway." *Journal of the Society of Architectural History* 26 (December 1967): 250–58.

Cudahy, Brian J. "Chicago's Early Elevated Lines and the Construction of the Union Loop." *Chicago History* 8 (Winter 1979–80): 194–205.

Duhamel, Georges. *America the Menace: Scenes from the Life of the Future*. London: George Allen and Unwin, 1931.

Duis, Perry. *Chicago: Creating New Traditions*. Chicago: Chicago Historical Society, 1976.

———. "Whose City? Public and Private Places in Nineteenth-Century Chicago." *Chicago History* 12 (Spring, Summer 1983): 2–27, 2–23.

Duncan, Hugh Dalziel. *Culture and Democracy: The Struggle for Form in Society and Architecture in Chicago and the Middle West during the Life and Times of Louis H. Sullivan*. Totowa, N.J.: Bedminster Press, 1965.

Dyos, H. J., and Michael Wolff, eds. *The Victorian City: Images and Realities*. London: Routledge and Kegan Paul, 1978.

Eaton, Leonard K. *American Architecture Comes of Age: European Reaction to H. H. Richardson and Louis Sullivan*. Cambridge, Mass.: MIT Press, 1972.

Ericsson, Henry, and Lewis E. Myers. *Sixty Years a Builder: The Autobiography of Henry Ericsson*. Chicago: A. Kroch, 1942.

Evanson, Norma. "Paris, 1890–1940." In *Metropolis, 1890–1940*, edited by Anthony Sutcliffe. Chicago: University of Chicago Press, 1984.

"Father of Skyscraper." *Architect and Engineer* 105 (April 1931): 138.

Geraniotis, Roula Mouroudellis. "German Architectural Theory and Practice in Chicago, 1850–1900." *Winterthur Portfolio* 21 (Winter 1986): 293–306.

Gibbs, Kenneth Turney. *Business Architectural Imagery in America, 1870–1920*. Ann Arbor: UMI Research Press, 1984.

Giedion, Siegfried. *Mechanization Takes Command: A Contribution to Anonymous History*. New York: Norton, 1948.

———. *Space, Time and Architecture*. Cambridge, Mass.: Harvard University Press, 1941.

Gilbert, James. *Perfect Cities: Chicago's Utopias of 1893*. Chicago: University of Chicago Press, 1991.

Ginger, Ray. *Altgeld's America: The Lincoln Ideal Versus Changing Realities.* New York: Funk and Wagnalls, 1958.

Girouard, Mark. *Cities and People: A Social and Architectural History.* New Haven: Yale University Press, 1985.

Glaab, Charles N., and Theodore A. Brown. *A History of Urban America.* 2d ed., rev. New York: Macmillan, 1976.

Glauber, Robert H. "The Necessary Toy: The Telephone Comes to Chicago." *Chicago History* 7 (Summer 1978): 70–86.

"Godwin Bursars, 1882–1906." In *Catalogue: Royal Institute of British Architects,* Catalogue of the Royal Institute of British Architects Library, vol. 1. London: RIBA, 1937.

Grosz, Elizabeth. "Bodies-Cities." In *Sexuality and Space,* edited by Beatriz Colomina, 241–52. New York: Princeton Architectural Press, 1992.

Grube, Oswald W., Peter C. Pran, and Franz Schulze. *One Hundred Years of Architecture in Chicago: Continuity of Structure and Form.* Chicago: J. Philip O'Hara, 1976. Revision, with translations, of 1973 German edition.

Handlin, Oscar. *This Was America.* New York: Harper and Row, 1949.

Harris, Neil, ed. *The Land of Contrasts: 1880–1901.* New York: George Braziller, 1970.

———. "Shopping—Chicago Style." In *Chicago Architecture, 1872–1922: Birth of a Metropolis,* edited by John Zukowsky, 136–55. Munich: Prestel, 1987.

Hines, Thomas S. *Burnham of Chicago: Architect and Planner.* Chicago: University of Chicago Press, 1974.

Hitchcock, Henry-Russell. "American Influence Abroad." In *The Rise of an American Architecture,* edited by Edgar Kaufmann Jr., 3–48. New York: Praeger, 1970.

Hoffmann, Donald. *The Architecture of John Wellborn Root.* Baltimore: Johns Hopkins University Press, 1973.

Holt, Glen E. "Private Plans for Public Spaces: The Origins of Chicago's Park System, 1850–1875." *Chicago History* 8 (Fall 1979): 173–84.

Holt, Glen E., and Dominic A. Pacyga. *Chicago: A Historical Guide to the Neighborhoods. The Loop and South Side.* Chicago: Chicago Historical Society, 1979.

Horowitz, Helen Lefkowitz. *Culture and the City: Cultural Philanthropy in Chicago from the 1880s to 1917.* Lexington: University Press of Kentucky, 1976.

"How Chicago Happened." *Architectural Review* 162 (October 1977): 193–99.

Hoyt, Homer. *One Hundred Years of Land Values in Chicago: The Relationship of the Growth of Chicago to the Rise in Its Land Values, 1830–1933.* Chicago: University of Chicago Press, 1933. Reprint. New York: Arno Press, 1970.

Huizinga, Johan. *America: A Dutch Historian's Vision from Afar and Near.* New York: Harper and Row, 1972.

Jackson, Kenneth T. "A Nation of Suburbs." *Chicago History* 13, no. 2 (Summer 1984): 6–25.

Jay, Robert. "Taller than Eiffel's Tower: The London and Chicago Tower Projects, 1889–1894." *Journal of the Society of Architectural Historians* 46 (June 1987): 145–56.

Johnson, Geoffrey. "The World's Tallest Building, 1892." *Reader* 16, no. 50 (11 September 1987): 1–40.

Karlowicz, Titus Marion. "The Architecture of the World's Columbian Exposition." Ph.D. diss., Northwestern University, 1965.

Kern, Stephen. *The Culture of Time and Space 1880–1918.* Cambridge, Mass.: Harvard University Press, 1983.

Klein, Maury, and Harvey A. Kantor. *Prisoners of Progress: American Industrial Cities, 1850–1920.* New York: Macmillan, 1976.

Koch, Robert. "American Influence Abroad, 1886 and Later." *Journal of the Society of Architectural Historians* 18 (May 1959): 66–69.

Kogan, Herman. "'Grander and Statelier than Ever . . .'" *Chicago History* 1 (Fall 1971): 236–44.

Kouwenhoven, John A. *Made in America: The Arts in Modern Civilization.* Garden City, N.Y.: Doubleday, 1962.

Landes, David S. *The Unbound Prometheus.* Cambridge: Cambridge University Press, 1969.

Larson, Gerald R. "The Iron Skeleton Frame: Interactions between Europe and the United States." In *Chicago Architecture, 1872–1922: Birth of a Metropolis,* edited by John Zukowsky, 39–55. Munich: Prestel, 1987.

Larson, Gerald R., and Roula Mouroudellis Geraniotis. "Toward a Better Understanding of the Evolution of the Iron Skeleton in Chicago." *Journal of the Society of Architectural Historians* 46 (March 1987): 39–48.

Lees, Andrew. *Cities Perceived: Urban Society in European and American Thought, 1820–1940.* New York: Columbia University Press, 1985.

Lewis, Arnold. *American Victorian Architecture.* Notes by Keith Morgan. New York: Dover, 1975.

———. "Chicago 1893: Expectations and Reactions Abroad." *Journal of the Society of Architectural Historians* 30 (October 1971): 248.

———. "The Disquieting Progress of Chicago." In *American Public Architecture: European Roots and Native Expressions,* 114–37. State College: Pennsylvania State University, 1988. Papers in Art History from the Pennsylvania State University, vol. 5.

———. "A European Profile of American Architecture." *Journal of the Society of Architectural History* 37 (December 1978): 256–82.

———. "Hinckeldeyn, Vogel, and American Architecture." *Journal of the Society of Architectural Historians* 31 (December 1972): 276–90.

Lewis, Dudley Arnold. "Evaluations of American Architecture by European Critics, 1875–1900." Ph.D. diss., University of Wisconsin, 1962.

Lewis, Lloyd, and Henry Justin Smith. *Chicago: The History of Its Reputation.* New York: Harcourt, Brace, 1929.

———. *Oscar Wilde Discovers America (1882).* New York: Harcourt, Brace, 1936.

Lewis, Russell. "Everything under One Roof: World's Fairs and Department Stores in Paris and Chicago." *Chicago History* 12 (Fall 1983): 28–47.

Long, John F. "Matthew Arnold Visits Chicago." *Toronto Quarterly* 24, no. 1 (October 1954): 34–45.

Loyrette, Henri. "Chicago: A French View." In *Chicago Architecture, 1872–1922: Birth of a Metropolis,* edited by John Zukowsky, 121–35. Munich: Prestel, 1987.

MacFadyen, Dugald. *Sir Ebenezer Howard and the Town Planning Movement.* Manchester: Manchester University Press, 1933.

Mayer, Harold M., and Richard C. Wade. *Chicago: Growth of a Metropolis.* Chicago: University of Chicago Press, 1969.

McCarthy, Kathleen D. *Noblesse Oblige: Clarity and Cultural Philanthropy in Chicago, 1849–1929*. Chicago: University of Chicago Press, 1982.

Mendelsohn, Erich. *Amerika: Bilderbuch eines Architekten*. Berlin: Rudolf Mosse, 1926.

Miller, Ross. *American Apocalypse: The Great Fire and the Myth of Chicago*. Chicago: University of Chicago Press, 1990.

Monaghan, Frank. *French Travelers in the United States, 1765–1932*. New York: New York Public Library, 1933.

Morley, Charles, ed. and trans. *Portrait of America: Letters of Henryk Sienkiewicz*. New York: Columbia University Press, 1959.

Morrison, Hugh. "Buffington and the Invention of the Skyscraper." *Art Bulletin* 26 (March 1944): 1–2.

Musil, Robert. *The Man without Qualities*. 2 vols. London: Secker and Warburg, 1953.

Neutra, Richard J. *Amerika*. Vienna: Anton Schroll, 1930.

———. *Wie baut Amerika?* Stuttgart: Hoffmann, 1927.

Nevins, Allan, ed. *America through British Eyes*. New York: Oxford University Press, 1948.

Olsen, Donald J. *The City as a Work of Art: London, Paris, Vienna*. New Haven: Yale University Press, 1986.

Phipps, Linda S. "European Reaction to the World's Columbian Exposition: Its Contribution to the History of American Architecture." Paper presented at Harvard University, seminar, 16 January 1987.

Piehl, Frank J. "Chicago's Early Fight to 'Save Our Lake.'" *Chicago History* 5 (Winter 1976–77): 223–32.

Pierce, Bessie Louise. *As Others See Chicago: Impressions of Visitors, 1673–1933*. Chicago: University of Chicago Press, 1933.

———. *A History of Chicago*. Vol. 3, *The Rise of a Modern City, 1871–1893*. New York: Knopf, 1957.

Prestiano, Robert. *The Inland Architect: Chicago's Major Architectural Journal, 1883–1908*. Ann Arbor: UMI Research Press, 1985.

Randall, Frank A. *History of the Development of Building Construction in Chicago*. Urbana: University of Illinois Press, 1949.

Rapson, Richard L. *Britons View America*. Seattle: University of Washington Press, 1971.

Reinink, A. W. "American Influences on Late Nineteenth-Century Architecture in the Netherlands." *Journal of the Society of Architectural Historians* 29 (May 1970): 163–74.

Rodrigues, Gustave. *The People of Action*. New York: Charles Scribner's Sons, 1918.

Rosenberg, Nathan. *Perspectives on Technology*. Cambridge: Cambridge University Press, 1976.

———, ed. *The American System of Manufactures*. Edinburgh: Edinburgh University Press, 1969.

Rydell, Robert W. *All the World's a Fair: Visions of Empire at American International Expositions, 1876–1916*. Chicago: University of Chicago Press, 1984.

Schlereth, Thomas J. "Solon Spencer Beman, 1853–1914: The Social History of a Midwest Architect." *Chicago Architectural Journal* 5 (1985): 8–31.

Service, Alastair. *London 1900*. New York: Rizzoli, 1979.

Sheppard, Francis. *London, 1808–1870: The Infernal Wen*. Berkeley: University of California Press, 1971.

Sprague, Paul. "The Origin of Balloon Framing." *Journal of the Society of Architectural Historians* 40 (December 1981): 311–19.

Steinberg, Leo. "Contemporary Art and the Plight of Its Public." *Harper's Magazine,* March 1962, 31–39.

Strohmeyer, Klaus. "Rhythmus der Großstadt." In *Die Metropole: Industriekultur in Berlin im 20. Jahrhundert,* edited by Jochen Boberg, Tilman Fichter, and Eckhart Gillen, 32–51. Munich: C. H. Beck, 1986.

Tocqueville, Alexis de. *Democracy in America.* Translated by Henry Reeve. Revised by Francis Bowen. New York: Random House, 1945.

Tolzmann, Rainer Hanns. "Objective Architecture: American Influences in the Development of Modern German Architecture." Ph.D. diss., University of Michigan, 1975.

Trachtenberg, Alan. *Democratic Vistas.* New York: Braziller, 1970.

———. *The Incorporation of America.* New York: Hill and Wang, 1982.

Trautmann, Frederic. "Arthur Holitischer's Chicago: A German Traveler's View of an American City." *Chicago History* 12 (Summer 1983): 36–50.

Tselos, Dimitri. "The Chicago Fair and the Myth of the 'Lost Cause.'" *Journal of the Society of Architectural Historians* 26 (December 1967): 259–68.

———. "Richardson's Influence on European Architecture." *Journal of the Society of Architectural Historians* 29 (May 1970): 156–62.

Tselos, Dimitris. "The Enigma of Buffington's Skyscraper." *Art Bulletin* 26 (March 1944): 3–12.

Turak, Theodore. "Remembrances of the Home Insurance Building." *Journal of the Society of Architectural Historians* 44 (March 1985): 60–65.

———. *William Le Baron Jenney: A Pioneer of Modern Architecture.* Ann Arbor: UMI Research Press, 1986.

Twombly, Robert. *Louis Sullivan: His Life and Work.* Chicago: University of Chicago Press, 1986.

Upjohn, E. M. "Buffington and the Skyscraper." *Art Bulletin* 17 (March 1935): 48–70.

Van Zanten, Ann Lorenz. "Form and Society: César Daly and the *Revue Générale de l'Architecture.*" *Oppositions* 8 (Spring 1977): 136–45.

Van Zanten, David. "The Nineteenth Century: The Projecting of Chicago as a Commercial City and the Rationalization of Design and Construction." In *Chicago and New York: Architectural Interactions,* 30–49. Chicago: Art Institute of Chicago, 1984.

Ven, Cornelis van de. "Ideas of Space in German Architectural Theory, 1850–1930." *AAQ* 9 (2–3 1977): 30–39.

Vernes, Michel. "Le gratte-ciel toujours recommencé." *Archi-Créé* 211 (April–May 1986): 49–59, 74–93.

Viskochil, Larry A., and Grant Talbot Dean. *Chicago at the Turn of the Century in Photographs.* New York: Dover, 1984.

Wallis, George, and Joseph Whitworth. *The American System of Manufactures.* 1854. Edited with an introduction by Nathan Rosenberg. Edinburgh: University of Edinburgh Press, 1969.

Weisman, Winston. "A New View of Skyscraper History." In *The Rise of an American Architecture,* edited by Edgar Kaufmann Jr., 115–60. New York: Praeger, 1970.

Williams, Kenny J. *In the City of Men: Another Story of Chicago.* Nashville: Townsend Press, 1974.

Wilson, Richard Guy. "Architecture and the Reinterpretation of the Past in the American Renaissance." *Winterthur Portfolio* 18, no. 1 (Spring 1983): 69–87.

Wit, Wim de, ed. *Louis Sullivan: The Function of Ornament.* New York: Chicago Historical Society and Saint Louis Art Museum in association with W.. Norton, 1986.

Woodward, C. Vann. *The Old World's New World.* New York: Oxford University Press, 1991.

Woud, Auke van der. "De Nieuwe Wereld." In *Nederlandse Architectuur 1880–1930: Americana,* 8–27. Amsterdam: Rijksmuseum Kroeller-Müller, 1975.

Wright, Gwendolyn. *Moralism and the Model Home: Domestic Architecture and Cultural Conflict in Chicago, 1873–1913.* Chicago: University of Chicago Press, 1980.

Wurm, Heinrich. "Deutsch-amerikanische Architektur Beziehungen in drei Jahrhunderten." In *Festschrift Viktor Wurm.* Göttingen, 1968.

Zabel, Craig. "Capturing Time: Muybridge and the Nineteenth Century." In *The Art and Science of Eadweard Muybridge,* edited by David Robertson, 9–13. Carlisle, Pa.: The Trout Gallery, Emil R. Weiss Center for the Arts, Dickinson College, 1985.

Zukowsky, John, ed. *Chicago Architecture, 1872–1922: Birth of a Metropolis.* Munich: Prestel, 1987.

Index

ARNOLD LEWIS is professor emeritus of art history at the College of Wooster. He is the author of *American Country Houses of the Gilded Age;* coauthor of *American Victorian Architecture,* with Keith Morgan; and coauthor of *The Opulent Interiors of the Gilded Age,* with James Turner and Steven McQuillin.

UNIVERSITY OF ILLINOIS PRESS
1325 SOUTH OAK STREET
CHAMPAIGN, ILLINOIS 61820-6903
WWW.PRESS.UILLINOIS.EDU